The Rise of Over-the-Top (OTT) Media and Implications for Media Consumption and Production

Nithin Kalorth
Mahindra University, India

IGI Global
PUBLISHER of TIMELY KNOWLEDGE

A volume in the Advances in Multimedia and Interactive Technologies (AMIT) Book Series

Published in the United States of America by
IGI Global
Information Science Reference (an imprint of IGI Global)
701 E. Chocolate Avenue
Hershey PA, USA 17033
Tel: 717-533-8845
Fax: 717-533-8661
E-mail: cust@igi-global.com
Web site: http://www.igi-global.com

Library of Congress Cataloging-in-Publication Data

Names: Kalorth, Nithin, 1988- editor.
Title: The rise of over-the-top (OTT) media and implications for media consumption and production / edited by Nithin Kalorth.
Description: Hershey, PA : Information Science Reference, [2024] | Includes bibliographical references and index. | Summary: "This book provides a comprehensive overview of the impact of digital media on the way we consume and produce content, including the business models, revenue streams, and market trends of the OTT industry. The book will also explore the competitive dynamics of the OTT market, including the emergence of new players and the impact on traditional media companies"-- Provided by publisher.
Identifiers: LCCN 2023034645 (print) | LCCN 2023034646 (ebook) | ISBN 9798369301166 (hardcover) | ISBN 9798369301173 (paperback) | ISBN 9798369301180 (ebook)
Subjects: LCSH: Mass media--Social aspects. | Streaming technology (Telecommunications)--Social aspects. | Mass media--Economic aspects. | Streaming technology (Telecommunications)--Economic aspects.
Classification: LCC HM1206 .R56 2024 (print) | LCC HM1206 (ebook) | DDC 302.23/4--dc23/eng/20231220
LC record available at https://lccn.loc.gov/2023034645
LC ebook record available at https://lccn.loc.gov/2023034646

This book is published in the IGI Global book series Advances in Multimedia and Interactive Technologies (AMIT) (ISSN: 2327-929X; eISSN: 2327-9303)

British Cataloguing in Publication Data
A Cataloguing in Publication record for this book is available from the British Library.

Advances in Multimedia and Interactive Technologies (AMIT) Book Series

Joel J.P.C. Rodrigues
Senac Faculty of Ceará, Fortaleza-CE, Brazil; Instituto de Telecomunicações, Portugal

ISSN:2327-929X
EISSN:2327-9303

Mission

Traditional forms of media communications are continuously being challenged. The emergence of user-friendly web-based applications such as social media and Web 2.0 has expanded into everyday society, providing an interactive structure to media content such as images, audio, video, and text.

The **Advances in Multimedia and Interactive Technologies (AMIT) Book Series** investigates the relationship between multimedia technology and the usability of web applications. This series aims to highlight evolving research on interactive communication systems, tools, applications, and techniques to provide researchers, practitioners, and students of information technology, communication science, media studies, and many more with a comprehensive examination of these multimedia technology trends.

Coverage

- Digital Communications
- Internet Technologies
- Digital technology
- Digital Images
- Multimedia Services
- Mobile Learning
- Audio Signals
- Social Networking
- Gaming Media
- Multimedia Technology

IGI Global is currently accepting manuscripts for publication within this series. To submit a proposal for a volume in this series, please contact our Acquisition Editors at Acquisitions@igi-global.com or visit: http://www.igi-global.com/publish/.

The Advances in Multimedia and Interactive Technologies (AMIT) Book Series (ISSN 2327-929X) is published by IGI Global, 701 E. Chocolate Avenue, Hershey, PA 17033-1240, USA, www.igi-global.com. This series is composed of titles available for purchase individually; each title is edited to be contextually exclusive from any other title within the series. For pricing and ordering information please visit http://www.igi-global.com/book-series/advances-multimedia-interactive-technologies/73683. Postmaster: Send all address changes to above address.

Titles in this Series

For a list of additional titles in this series, please visit:
http://www.igi-global.com/book-series/advances-multimedia-interactive-technologies/73683

Transformed Communication Codes in the Mediated World A Contemporary Perspective
Hasan Gürkan (Girona University, Spain) and Aybike Serttaş (Istinye University, Turkey)
Information Science Reference • © 2024 • 407pp • H/C (ISBN: 9798369308967) • US $240.00

Examining Multimedia Forensics and Content Integrity
Sumit Kumar Mahana (National Institute of Technology, Kurukshetra, India) Rajesh Kumar Aggarwal (National Institute of Technology, Kurukshetra, India) and Surjit Singh (Thapar Institute of Engineering and Technology, India)
Information Science Reference • © 2023 • 301pp • H/C (ISBN: 9781668468647) • US $225.00

Handbook of Research on Advanced Practical Approaches to Deepfake Detection and Applications
Ahmed J. Obaid (University of Kufa, Iraq) Ghassan H. Abdul-Majeed (University of Baghdad, Iraq) Adriana Burlea-Schiopoiu (University of Craiova, Romania) and Parul Aggarwal (Jamia Hamdard, India)
Information Science Reference • © 2023 • 379pp • H/C (ISBN: 9781668460603) • US $295.00

Dynamics of Dialogue, Cultural Development, and Peace in the Metaverse
Swati Chakraborty (GLA University, India)
Information Science Reference • © 2023 • 236pp • H/C (ISBN: 9781668459072) • US $240.00

Handbook of Research on New Media, Training, and Skill Development for the Modern Workforce
Dominic Mentor (Teachers College, Columbia University, USA)
Business Science Reference • © 2022 • 439pp • H/C (ISBN: 9781668439968) • US $295.00

Handbook of Research on New Media Applications in Public Relations and Advertising
Elif Esiyok (Atilim University, Turkey)
Information Science Reference • © 2021 • 572pp • H/C (ISBN: 9781799832010) • US $295.00

Multidisciplinary Perspectives on Narrative Aesthetics in Video Games
Deniz Denizel (Bahcesehir University, Turkey) and Deniz Eyüce Şansal (Bahcesehir University, Turkey)
Information Science Reference • © 2021 • 300pp • H/C (ISBN: 9781799851103) • US $195.00

Recent Advances in 3D Imaging, Modeling, and Reconstruction
Athanasios Voulodimos (University of West Attica, Athens, Greece) and Anastasios Doulamis (National Technical University of Athens, Athens, Greece)
Information Science Reference • © 2020 • 396pp • H/C (ISBN: 9781522552949) • US $215.00

IGI Global
PUBLISHER of TIMELY KNOWLEDGE

701 East Chocolate Avenue, Hershey, PA 17033, USA
Tel: 717-533-8845 x100 • Fax: 717-533-8661
E-Mail: cust@igi-global.com • www.igi-global.com

Table of Contents

Section 2
User Experience

Section 3
Psychological and Social Implications

Detailed Table of Contents

Foreword

It is my pleasure to write the forward and introduce the book, *The Rise of Over-the-Top (OTT) Media and Implications for Media Consumption and Production*, edited by Dr. Nithin Kalorth. I am sure that this collection will serve as a good starting point for much more research work in OTT media studies for future. The chapters included in this collection informs the academic world the importance of the need of thinking and placing OTT media as an exclusive field of study, not only in terms of technology and distribution, but also focusing content production and consumption.

The chapters shows testament to the excellent curation and thoughtful editing done by Nithin Kalorth, which ensures the topics discussed are equally unique yet connecting the dots to provide a panoramic view of the central theme of the book. There is a clear evidence of interconnection between chapters which help readers to corelate the production and consumption patterns in OTT media. The interdisciplinary approach used in this book in terms of chapter themes and academic background of contributing authors are particularly noteworthy. These include work from traditional media studies, psychology, law, sociology, literature, and critical studies. This in fact, the true multifaceted nature of OTT media revolution. The chapters such as *OTT platforms from the perspective of critical algorithm studies* and *Advancing personalization and recommendation algorithms in the OTT industry*, attempt to bring a innovative approach in understanding user-oriented consumption. Such studies are resulted because of the rise in OTT media. They shed light on the mechanisms that drive our content consumption, opening up avenues for future research and discussion. Similarity, chapters on FOMOphobi and OTT Syndrom helps readers to rethink critical psychological questions of media studies from an OTT media approach. These chapters brings a critical layer of in-depth understanding of the societal implications of binge-watching and on-demand entertainment. The inclusion of a chapter focusing on the Indian perspective in the chapter *Effect of OTT Platforms on Juvenile Behavior* demonstrates a commitment to global inclusivity, recognizing the diverse impact of OTT platforms on different cultural contexts.

The edited volume, *The Rise of Over-the-Top (OTT) Media and Implications for Media Consumption and Production* by Nithin can be considered as an importance contribution to the field of media studies. It not only captures the current trends in digital age but also paves the way for future scholarship. Nithin Kalorth's attempts in curation and the diverse insights offered by the contributing authors make this volume a must-read for scholars, industry professionals, and enthusiasts alike. As we stand on the face of a new era in media production and consumption, this collection provides an area which will guide us through the complex landscapes of OTT media with clarity and understanding.

Sumit Narula
Amity School of Communication, Amity University, Gurgoan, India

Foreword

Sumit Narula is working as the Director at Amity School of Communication, Amity University Gurgoan, India. He is the Founding Editor in Chief of the bi-annual SCOPUS indexed Journal named Journal of Content Community and Communication which has a Cite Score of 2.6. One of his books Environmental Awareness and Role of Social Media with IGI Global has recently been indexed by Clarivate's Book Citation Analysis (Web of Science). He has taken 500 plus workshops on the topic 'How to catch Fake/Predatory/Cloned journals in Academics'. He has recently released an App named 'Amity Quality Journal Checker' on both Google Play Store and the IOS Platform. It has a list of all the fraud/cloned and predatory journals. He also got two major Copyright named 'Eight Novel ways to identify Fake/Misleading Impact Factor' and 'Eight Novel ways to catch a Cloned Journal'.

Preface

The increase in popularity of major streaming services is having a massive impact on more traditional media outlets. Over-the-Top (OTT) media is the term given to these types of services, which bypass the traditional media sources through an internet connection. The concerns around this flourishing media industry are coming from multiple directions, including more traditional media providers, publishers and producers, as well as experts attempting to predict how this trend will impact the future of entertainment media industries. The present volume, *The Rise of Over-the-Top (OTT) Media and Implications for Media Consumption and Production* is an effort edited volume that delves into the transformative emergence of Over-the-Top (OTT) media, which is reshaping the landscape of media consumption and production.

OTT content can be in different forms such as OTT television (e.g. Netflix for viewing films, documentaries, tv shows and webs series), OTT messaging (e.g. WhatsApp for online chatting) and OTT video call (e.g. Facetime, Skype). The current book focuses on the OTT television or video services which are subscription-based video on demand (SVoD) services by studying, evaluating, understanding and developing the field of OTT media's production and consumption practices and patterns. The chapters of this volume are dealing with different dimensions of OTT media, providing valuable insights into its evolution, technological infrastructure, content production, distribution strategies, and social and cultural implications.

The current book discusses the impact of OTT on media production, distribution and consumption. Beyond the media studies importance, impact of OTT media in our everyday life is also notable. OTT enables the content to be individual user wherever they go and whenever they want. This has changed the meaning of user experience. This makes the scope of this book beyond the media and communication studies. The chapters of this book provides dedicated and inclusive insights into the evolution of OTT platforms, examining their influence on various aspects of media ecosystems. From production to distribution and consumption, the book explores into how OTT media have reshaped the landscape of entertainment and information dissemination.

The volume is aimed at media professionals, media managers, policymakers, and scholars in the field of media and communication studies. The reader is guided through an exploration of the technological advancements that facilitate seamless content delivery, empowering users to personalize their viewing experiences. The edited volume is divided into three sections such as "Evolution and Industry Landscape, User Engagement and Psychological and Social Implication." The chapters are logically distributed in these three sections to provide readers an improved reading experience. Each chapter is a result of careful method of research with is supported with theories. The chapters focusing different aspects of OTT media is aimed at noting current trends in production and consumption and also to define research agenda for future.

There are five chapters in the section "Evolution and Industry Landscape" in which the first introductory chapter "Content Production and Consumption in the Digital Age" by Nithin Kalorth and Vidya Deshpande is an overview of content production and consumption trends in the digital age through OTT. The chapter is developed with production and consumption practices from India (which is an emerging market which is much more elaborated in few of other chapters) and from global. The chapter points out the role of Covid 19 pandemic and lockdowns as catalysts in increasing demands for OTT media. The chapter uses some important quotes from OTT media industry leaders to understand the industry vision on rise of OTT. The chapter advocates for the need of an independent area of OTT media studies which is separated from film and television studies. The OTT media production has emerged to attain its own visual language and grammar which makes the field interesting.

The chapter "Streaming Revolution: Tracing the Evolution of OTT Media from its Origins to the Present" Nitesh Behare and others is an in-depth and detail note on evolution of OTT media which provides a better understanding of where the medium stands currently. The chapter traces the history of OTT in the line with development of technologies. The chapter successfully maps the important technological events in internet and communication which led the revolution in OTT media industry. The strength of this chapter lies in identifying and classifying OTT media from traditional methods of media (such as Cable TV) and also direct towards the future (such as AI and VR) in way that readers can navigate through each development. The chapter credits the industry pioneers, market force and technological advancement in the evolution and growth of OTT media.

The chapter "Users Adoption of Over-the-Top (OTT) Streaming Platforms" by Sujith T.S. is an extension from the above chapter with concentration on users. The shift from media audience to media user (technological user) is a significant change in content consumption understanding in OTT media. The users here are more powerful in terms of selection of content, navigation of content such as skipping the scene, changing language and subtitles. pause etc. which is impossible in the traditional media ecology. The quantitative research methods used by Sujith suggested a positive relationship between the adoption of OTT streaming platforms and user satisfaction. The chapter tries to present OTT media platforms as a technological product and provides connection between user adoption of technology and performance expectancy, effort expectancy, social influence, facilitating conditions of user.

As discusses earlier, it is impossible to think the rise OTT after 2020 without mentioning the Covid 19 pandemic. The pandemic not only provided a reinvention of content distribution for producers but also challenged the traditional production practices. The chapter "Shifting Discourse of Digital Entertainment in Covid-19" by Vijaykumar compared the audience experience from traditional cinema hall and that of OTT. The chapter has identified and explained different variables such as cost, content customizing, multi-device Connection, screen sharing, time and language flexibility for the shift in digital entertainment. The chapter stresses that OTT platforms offer alternative ways of entertaining, hence the OTT platforms and the cinema industry coexist in the entertainment industry by offering different content to audiences. This coexistence model of entertainment provides an ample space to conduct future studies in the area of platform and user/audience experience.

The last of chapter of first section titled "Instagram's Role in the Rise and Success of Over-the-Top (OTT) Media" by Harry and Vijaykumar explains the role of social media platforms such as Instagram in promoting the OTT media content and platforms. The chapter is built on the visual storytelling and promotion campaigns of some notable films and web series on OTT media platforms indicates towards different marketing and promotional methods of content dissemination. The practice of collaboration between content creators and social media influencers are studied in this chapter to develop a new understanding of content promotion. As we understood, entertainment industry can't neglect the rise of OTT, the content marketing methods needs to be integrated for online and offline releases of films in future. The idea of user centric content and shift from audience to user is renounced in this chapter too – which signifies the unity the ideas presented in the different chapters in this volume.

The second session of the book, "User Engagement" starts with the chapter "Impact of OTT Media on Advertising and Marketing" by Munise Hayrun Sağlam and İbrahim KIRÇOVA examines the impact of OTT media on marketing and advertising activities as logical development of television. The chapter provides importance of recognizing local culture and content, pricing flexibility, mobile access in the growth of OTT media. By examining user habits, the suggest that that OTT platforms have significantly changed traditional media content consumption patterns among consumers. As quoted in the chapter "*There is a complex relationship between data collection, quality of OTT service, and customer interest. A possible inconsistency in the minds of consumers between data protection statements and targeting options offered by OTT media services to their advertised customers will undermine trust in the platform*".

The significant chapter by Elif Karakoç Keskin titled "Platforms from the Perspective of Critical Algorithm Studies: The Algorithmic Paradox of the Audience" *opens* up importance discussion on crucial role of data in OTT media suggest that *"Behavioral data is at the heart of the digital world"*. The chapter decodes complicated algorithmic paradox where the audience has far more control over what they watch, how they watch it, and how long they watch it than in the traditional watching process. However, it is also paradoxically controlled by the algorithmic structure of the platform through its behavioral data within the framework of recommender systems adopted as one of the business models of the platform ecosystem.

The similar idea is taken forward in the chapter "Advancing Personalization and Recommendation Algorithms in the OTT Industry" by Ruth Neyah and Vijayakumar in their attempt to investigate the mechanisms, benefits, challenges, and future prospects of enhancing user experiences and driving engagement through advanced personalization techniques. The chapter discuses that algorithms are able to accurately predict and suggest content that is in line with individual preferences when they consider user interactions, viewing history, and contextual data. The chapter also raises concerns of ethical considerations and user privacy in algorithmic world, but also hopes that transparent communication fosters trust among users and gives them more agency. This shows that the OTT media's future research and concerns has to be interdisciplinary with help from areas of phycology, computer science and data management.

The second section concludes with the chapter "The Art and Science of User Engagement: Personalization and Recommendations in the OTT Era" by Nitesh Behare and Daman Jeet, pointing out that consumer engagement, in terms of personalization and recommendations, has shed light on the profound impact of OTT on media consumption and production, both globally and domestically. Personalization and recommendation algorithms are at the core of OTT platforms, tailoring content to individual preferences and interests. Through personalized experiences, these algorithms successfully elevate consumer engagement and satisfaction by employing various techniques, like collaborative filtering and content-based filtering, combined with artificial intelligence and machine learning. The chapter directs future research on the role of recommendation algorithms in content discovery, binge-watching, influencing user behavior, and cross-platform consumption.

The third and final thematic section of this volume "Psychological and Social Implications" deals with interplay between psychological factors and social dynamics in the context of OTT consumption by asking how the availability and accessibility of content through OTT platforms influence individuals' cognitive processes, emotional responses, and social behaviors. The section starts with chapter on

FOMOphobia titled "FOMOphobia: The Psychological Drivers of OTT Media Consumption through Social Comparison, Self-Esteem, and Anxiety" by Sridevi Gopakumar and Madhava Priya Dananjayan. This chapter explores the relationship between individuals' media consumption habits and their psychological well-being, focusing on perceived social comparison, self-esteem, anxiety, and the emerging concept of FOMOphobia. The findings reveal the profound impact of social media and OTT platforms on individuals' perceptions of social comparison, where the constant exposure to others' media consumption patterns triggers various emotional responses. The participants in the study expressed feelings of excitement, curiosity, envy, and dissatisfaction when encountering others' OTT experiences on social media. This dynamic suggests that social media platforms play a pivotal role in shaping individuals' viewing preferences and fostering a fear of missing out on culturally relevant content.

The chapter "The OTT Syndrome: Psycho-Social Impact of Binge-Watching" by Aditi Singh Sharma brings out identifiable aspects of OTT syndrome. As per the chapter, the primary dimensions is the physical and psycho-social impact experienced by netizens engaging in binge-watching. Notably, the psychological ramifications are more pronounced among the youth, manifesting as behavioral issues such as heightened anxiety, stress, and feelings of loneliness. The decline in the need for physical socialization is highlighted across all age groups, with a notable effect on the socialization skills of millennial kids. Concerns are raised about the potential hindrance to the development of well-rounded personalities in individuals. A significant concern addressed in the chapter is the strain on family relationships as each member increasingly seeks personal time on digital platforms, contributing to a collective phenomenon termed as "my time."

A collaborated effort by Pritesh Pradeep Somani and others with an interdisciplinary nature resulted in the chapter titled "The Rise of OTT: A Dynamic Shift Towards Binge Watching an Increase for On-Demand Entertainment" tries to understand the dynamic landscape of entertainment consumption, emphasizing that binge-watching is not just a passing trend but is composed to intensify over time. The chapter identifies the accessibility of data packs and the widespread availability of OTT platforms with diverse content genres contribute to the reasons of binge-watching. The chapter provides the health concerns of binge-watching such as severe headaches, back pain, and a sense of social isolation are prevalent, affecting individuals of all ages, from teenagers to senior citizens. The chapter announces a careful blend of linear and on-demand models, incorporating technological advancements for a personalized and immersive viewing experience. These suggestions can be taken into consideration not only for future researchers but also for content producers and policy makers for a responsible and sustainable OTT media.

The chapter "Effect of OTT Platforms on Juvenile Behavior: Indian Perspective" by Sheeba Khalid and others debates around regulation of OTT platforms and pertinent backdrop. The chapter develop the necessity and challenges of governing these platforms by highlighting the concerns such as increased screen time leading to health issues, psychological impacts, and potential addiction among viewers of all age groups. The clash between the government's regulations and the platforms' self-regulation is illuminated, with a focus on the proposed content classification, a soft-touch self-regulatory architecture, and grievance redressal mechanisms. The chapter probes into the conflicting perspectives on third-party monitoring, highlighting concerns over independence and potential conflicts of interest. The chapter calls for the need for further research to understand the effects of OTT content and media on mental health and behavior.

The final chapter of this section, as well as the entire volume, titled 'The Impact of OTT Services on Television Talk Shows: Navigating New Horizons' by Elisa Paz, comprehensively assesses the evolution of television talk shows in the context of Over-The-Top (OTT) services. The chapter explains how the talk show format has adapted and thrived, navigating through various eras of media technologies and disruptions. Addressing audience engagement, the chapter underlines the critical role of social media in on-demand consumption through OTT platforms. Social television practices and direct interaction with audiences via official program handles enhance viewer engagement and potential loyalty. The global reach of OTT platforms is seen as an opportunity for producers to address an expanded audience base with diverse cultural backgrounds. The chapter concludes with recommendations for OTT talk shows, including enhancing interactive viewer engagement through social media, fostering second-screen practices, and integrating multiple channels for a cohesive experience.

Overall, the current volume accommodates to media professionals, policymakers, general interest readers and scholars, offering valuable insights into the dynamic intersection of technology, content creation, and audience engagement.

Nithin Kalorth
Mahindra University, India

Section 1
Evolution and Industry Landscape

Chapter 1
Content Production and Consumption in the Digital Age

Nithin Kalorth
Mahindra University, India

Vidya Deshpande
Bennett University, India

ABSTRACT

This comprehensive chapter helps to provide an insight into the transformative era of content production and consumption ushered in by over-the-top (OTT) platforms. The chapter focuses on India's pivotal role in the global OTT landscape, and navigates the post-pandemic surge, revealing shifts in consumer behaviour and the profound impact on storytelling. With an analysis of the unique production practices within the OTT domain, the chapter calls for independent OTT media studies, recognizing the need for academia to explore the evolving nature of this distinct storytelling form. The narrative balances positive aspects, acknowledging OTT's data-driven strategies, while also addressing concerns about potential regulations impacting creative freedom. The chapter not only highlights the global success of OTT platforms but also contributes to the discourse on their transformative potential in shaping the future of entertainment.

INTRODUCTION

Over-The-Top (OTT) platforms have emerged as a production, distribution and consumption capital capital. These platforms along with transforming the way content is produced and consumed globally, it also demand for new methods of studying this digital content independently. One might argue that, the content delivered is similar to already prevailing film, television and other broadcasting structures, however, this chapter and the chapters following this argues and urges for an OTT media theory.

This chapter tries to establish an insightful overview of the content production and consumption trends in the digital age, with a particular focus on India, an emerging market that has seen a remarkable surge in OTT consumption. The rapid increase in popularity of major streaming services is having a massive

DOI: 10.4018/979-8-3693-0116-6.ch001

impact on more traditional media outlets. OTT Media is the term given to these types of services, which bypass the traditional media sources through an internet connection. The concerns around this booming media industry are coming from multiple directions, including more traditional media providers, publishers and producers, as well as experts attempting to predict how this trend will impact the future of entertainment media industries.

THE RISE OF OTT IN INDIA POST PANDEMIC

India, a diverse and rapidly growing market, has witnessed a paradigm shift in the entertainment industry with the advent of OTT platforms. The availability of affordable high-speed internet, coupled with the widespread adoption of smartphones, has fuelled the surge in OTT consumption. The convenience of anytime, anywhere access to a vast array of content has resonated well with the Indian audience.

OTT platforms such as Netflix, Amazon Prime Video, Jio Cinema, and Disney+ Hotstar have not only capitalized on the diverse cultural and linguistic preferences of the Indian audience but have also played a pivotal role in promoting homegrown content. Indian filmmakers and content creators are now leveraging OTT platforms to showcase their work to a global audience, breaking geographical barriers and reaching unparalleled heights.

The first OTT platform in India, BigFlix by Reliance was launched in 2008 (Dangwal, 2017), it wasn't until Netflix launched in 2016 that the hunger for fresh content grew (Kumar et. al, 2020). The research on content on OTTs is relatively new and there is a need to provide a fresh angle to in this area. Films and TV serials have been studied continuously since they launched in the early 1900s with focus on its evolution, technological advancement, impact on society, cultural values and political economy.

The content produced and distributed in OTT platforms, which are a mix of films, series, documentaries, and all other formats served to the audience on a view-what-you-want, when-you-want kind of menu. This concept is not new (Fairchild, 1996) but still it needs a deeper understanding on a critical reality of platforms, algorithm, technology, production practices, distribution strategies, partnership models and consumption trends. While these seems to be vast and complicated area, a careful study of each will itself help in establishing a new academic area of OTT studies which as mentioned above independent from film and television studies. There are some practical problem with OTT media content as few may see the key differentiator as the lack of governmental control over this medium (Henten and Tadayoni, 2020). While films go through a rigorous censorship through state-controlled body and TV content regulated by an industry body, video platforms are still unregulated. This can be the also reason for why OTT media content is difficult to streamline. When it is not practically defined, it will be more complex to see from a theoretical view.

The mobile market and internet penetration are on the rise in India. TRAI says Indian has the second highest penetration after China with 687 million subscribers (TRAI, 2020). 5G telecom services entering the market, it has been a major disruptor in the way content is consumed. With faster and cheaper Internet services available, Indian smartphone users have potentially become the largest consumers of content in the world (FICCI, 2019).

Uday Shankar, former President The Walt Disney Company, Asia Pacific said:

"The M&E sector is poised to kickstart a new era of growth. Technological disruptions are creating new opportunities for the sector. New age digital media with direct-to-customer (D2C) capabilities are on

an upward trajectory making Indian M&E ever more vibrant, against the backdrop of already popular broadcast TV and films. The sector's incumbents need to innovate, transform and increase their relevance to mass and individual consumers" (FICCI, 2019).

Netflix entered the Indian market in 2016 followed by rival *Amazon Prime*. Star Sports introduced *Hotstar* as a mobile app just before 2015 IPL season. In 2017, a outbreak of OTT platforms like *Voot* (Viacom 18), *Jio Cinemas* (Reliance), *Alt Balaji* (Balaji Telefilms) *Zee5* (Zee TV) *SonyLiv* (Sony Entertainment) followed in quick succession. Regional players like *Hoichoi* in Bengali (Sree Venkatesh Films), *SunNxt* in Tamil (Sun TV), *Manorama Max* in Malayalam (Manorama Newspapers) have since begun streaming in this relatively fledgling market.

The Indian market is growing and how internet users are slowly replacing traditional forms of entertainment like TV and films with OTT platforms. The number of people opting for OTT in 2018 were mainly consumers in the age group 18-35 play a role in shaping content on OTT services as binge watching, content quality were paramount factors in OTT services (Moochhala, 2018). The growth has been tremendous in the OTT sector. EY reports subscription growth was driven by OTT video consumption (111%), film (10%) and television (7.5%). The TRAI New Tariff Order also had an impact on OTT platforms with the increased parity in content choice and costs. With so many OTT platforms in the market subscribers are already feeling the fatigue.

The pandemic year (2020) had a huge effect on the way we consume video content. Being locked indoors, whetted the appetite of consumers to view more and more video content. Business Magazine, *Forbes (USA)* says: "The average U.S. consumer now pays for four different streaming video subscriptions. Nearly one-quarter of U.S. consumers (23%) have added at least one new paid streaming video service since the pandemic began" (Fatemi, 2021). In India, pre-pandemic Disney+ Hotstar had a subscription base of 8 million, which more than tripled to 25 million by the end of 2020 (Farooqui, 2021). While Disney+ Hotstar has 41% market share, the leading platform Eros has 24% of the market. It is important to note here that the Eros platform has only Hindi content with serials and movies.

This has pushed Netflix to number 4 slot with just 7% of the market, while it is the number 1 platform worldwide. Amazon Prime is at number 3 with 9% of the market. While Netflix is losing out on number of subscribers, it has higher revenues generated through its partnership and subscription.

The 2020 lockdown played a major role in the increase in viewership of OTT platforms, with the work from home cultural increasing OTT usage (Mandani et. al, 2020). The authors have noted that the average hours spent on OTT have increased from 0–2 to 2–5 hours and average spending that users are willing to make on OTT platforms is Rs 100–300 (USD 1.3 to 4 per month). The satisfaction level of customers is directly related to space to watch with family, time to use OTT platforms, the quality of content on OTT platforms.

The Covid-19 pandemic and subsequent lockdowns around the world have acted as catalysts, accelerating the already growing trend of OTT consumption. With cinemas shuttered and traditional production methods disrupted, audiences turned to OTT platforms for their entertainment needs. The surge in subscriptions during the lockdown period was not merely a temporary phenomenon but marked a fundamental shift in consumer behaviour. The pandemic has demonstrated that streaming is mainstream, and that subscribers around the world want access to the best stories from anywhere

CONTENT PRODUCTION AND CONSUMPTION ON OTT

Chatterjee (2012) illuminates the historical dominance of Hindi in India's television content during the era of state-controlled television. However, with the advent of liberalization, a proliferation of television channels ensued, notably from the southern regions of the country. This shift enabled Dravidian language communities in the south, historically excluded from the national communication space, to leverage global resources effectively (Chatterjee, 2012).

The observable transformation is apparent in the substantial increase in the viewership of both Hindi and southern languages between 2016 and 2019. This surge aligns with a noteworthy expansion in the number of television channels. A key driver of this evolution is the inclusion of regional languages in sports channel commentaries, a departure from the previous exclusive use of English. Despite the predominant influence of political families in southern Indian television channels, OTT platforms maintain an apolitical stance, appealing to diverse political and social identities. This is also an opportunity look into representation and political mapping of narratives in OTT. While this seems to a matter of concern for Indian productions, it can be seen worldwide. As discussed above, the control of content and distribution on OTT platforms are often outside state's censorship as compared to traditional television and films, the content producers can bring a new method of storytelling which can studies by analysing visual language and grammar of OTT content.

The influence of quality content on OTT platforms is underscored by global acclaim, exemplified by the International TV Emmy awarded to the Indian series "Delhi Crime," which loosely recounts the Nirbhaya case. Other Indian series, such as Amazon Prime's "Four Shots More" and "Made In Heaven," have garnered international nominations, showcasing India's talent on a global stage. The theme of these films can be compared with international coming of age or crime thrillers, the visual language and grammar used in these films are divergent wile comparing to that with Indian television and film traditions. Netflix's data-driven narrowcasting strategy, originally successful in the global market, has set a precedent for subsequent streaming platforms. However, regional language players like HoiChoi and SunMax have disrupted the landscape, prompting major streaming services like Netflix and Amazon Prime to recalibrate their strategies by investing in regional content.

The Covid-19 pandemic-induced lockdowns further elevated the significance of OTT platforms in the cinematic landscape. Many film producers opted to release their movies on these platforms, with notable success stories such as the multilingual film "Soorarai Pottru" on Amazon Prime. Fitzgerald (2019) raises concerns about the extent to which Indian content providers should be protected by telecom policies from global platforms adopting subscription-based business models.

Contrary to Fitzgerald's (2019) concerns, local OTT platforms have proven resilient. Disney's strategic acquisition of Hotstar and the entry of new players like AltBalaji into content-sharing arrangements demonstrate the dynamism of the Indian OTT market. As the government seeks to regulate OTT platforms under the Ministry of Information and Broadcasting, concerns regarding potential impacts on content quality and censorship compliance arise. Filmmakers and content producer's express dissatisfaction, anticipating changes in content dynamics, akin to the conventional regulations governing satellite channels.

The potential convergence of OTT platforms with traditional television and films models, observed through the integration of cable, satellite TV, and streaming app offerings, raises questions about the future of content production consumption. While some argue for a re-evaluation of streaming entertainment business practices, others express concerns about reverting to outdated models reminiscent of cable TV. The imminent shake-up in India and the global entertainment landscape suggests an evolving paradigm with transformative potential.

There is no doubt that OTT platforms have emerged as influential players, challenging traditional models of television and film consumption. As the current book studies the potential convergence of OTT platforms with conventional television and film models, scrutinizing the integration of cable, satellite TV, and streaming app offerings. Furthermore, we have to explore the future trajectory of content production and consumption, examining how unique production practices within the OTT realm contribute to a transformative paradigm shift.The integration of cable, satellite TV, and streaming app offerings signifies a dynamic shift in how audiences access and engage with content. This transformation prompts critical reflections on the evolving nature of production practices and the potential impact on the global entertainment landscape.

OTT platforms, such as Netflix and Amazon Prime, have revolutionized the entertainment industry with their data-driven, narrowcasting strategies. The success of these platforms in catering to individual viewer preferences has set a precedent for the industry. The potential convergence with traditional television and film models suggests an era where personalized content consumption takes center stage.

The unique production practices within the OTT domain contribute significantly to its transformative potential. Unlike traditional models, which often adhere to mainstream norms, OTT platforms embrace diversity and experimentation. Original series and films on platforms like Netflix and Amazon Prime often push boundaries, exploring unconventional themes and narratives that resonate with niche audiences.

OTT platforms have become champions of diverse narratives, featuring stories that were traditionally marginalized or overlooked. The inclusivity in casting and storytelling fosters a global understanding of cultures and perspectives. For instance, the Indian series "Delhi Crime" on Netflix not only received international acclaim but also shed light on a critical social issue, demonstrating the power of OTT platforms to drive meaningful conversations.

Traditional television and film models often adhere to established genres to cater to a broad audience. OTT platforms, however, thrive on breaking genre barriers. Series like "Four Shots More" and "Made In Heaven" showcase the flexibility of the OTT format, combining elements of comedy, drama, and social commentary. This approach caters to diverse viewer preferences and challenges the conventional norms of storytelling.

The use of data analytics in content creation is a hallmark of OTT platforms. By analyzing user behavior and preferences, these platforms make informed decisions about content creation and distribution. This data-driven approach not only enhances user experience but also enables content creators to tailor their productions for specific target audiences, contributing to the platforms' global success.

However, filmmakers and content producers fear that if stringent regulations are imposed, creative freedom may be compromised, leading to a potential decline in the quality of productions. OTT platforms have played a pivotal role in globalization, transcending geographical boundaries and introducing audiences to a diverse array of content.

As the government in India considers regulating OTT platforms under the Ministry of Information and Broadcasting, challenges and opportunities emerge. While regulatory measures may ensure content quality, they also risk stifling creativity. The integration of Disney into the OTT market and the strategic acquisition of Hotstar exemplify the adaptability of OTT platforms in response to evolving market dynamics. As thc industry navigates concerns surrounding regulation and creative freedom, OTT platforms remain at the forefront of shaping the future of content production and consumption on a global scale.

The imminent shake-up signals not just a shift in how we consume media but a redefinition of the very nature of storytelling and entertainment in the digital age.

THE NEED FOR INDEPENDENT OTT MEDIA STUDIES

As OTT platforms continue to redefine the entertainment landscape, there is a growing need for an independent area of OTT media studies. Traditional film and television studies, while relevant, may not fully encapsulate the unique characteristics of OTT content production and consumption. OTT platforms operate on a different model, often releasing entire seasons at once, catering to binge-watching habits, and experimenting with narrative structures. OTT platforms are not just an extension of television or film; they are a unique form of storytelling that requires its own academic exploration. This signals a call for academia to research deeper into the nuances of OTT, exploring production practices, its impact on storytelling, audience engagement, and the broader media landscape. OTT media production has evolved to attain its own visual language and grammar. The absence of traditional constraints allows content creators to experiment with storytelling techniques, cinematography, and narrative structures. The binge-worthy nature of OTT content has led to the development of narrative arcs that span entire seasons, providing a rich and immersive experience for viewers. The visual language of OTT often transcends traditional boundaries, blending cinematic and episodic storytelling seamlessly. This evolution presents an exciting prospect for content creators to push artistic boundaries and explore new avenues of storytelling.

OTT platforms experiment with narrative structures, unconstrained by the conventional constraints of television scheduling or feature film duration. Story arcs are not confined to specific time slots, and creators have the freedom to explore more complex and unconventional storytelling techniques. This shift not only impacts the creative process but also raises questions about audience expectations and the ways in which narratives are constructed and consumed. In recognizing the unique characteristics of OTT platforms, it becomes evident that they are not mere extensions of traditional television or film. Instead, they represent a distinctive form of storytelling with its own set of rules, challenges, and opportunities. Therefore, there is an imperative for academia to embark on a comprehensive exploration of OTT media studies. This academic endeavour should encompass a range of topics, including in-depth analyses of production practices specific to OTT, the impact of this new medium on storytelling conventions, and the dynamics of audience engagement within this on-demand landscape. an independent OTT media studies discipline should aim to bridge the gap between theory and industry practice. Collaborations with industry professionals could provide valuable insights into the rapidly changing dynamics of OTT content creation, distribution, and consumption.

CONCLUSION

The digital age has ushered in a transformative era in content production and consumption, with OTT platforms at the forefront of this revolution. India, with its burgeoning market, has become a key player in the global OTT landscape. The Covid-19 pandemic has acted as a catalyst, accelerating the shift towards OTT consumption, making it a mainstream form of entertainment.

As OTT platforms continue to redefine storytelling and audience engagement, there is a pressing need for independent OTT media studies. The unique characteristics of OTT content production and consumption demand dedicated academic exploration. The emergence of a distinct visual language and grammar in OTT content adds an extra layer of intrigue to this dynamic and rapidly evolving field. The future of entertainment lies in the hands of OTT, and understanding its intricacies is essential for both industry professionals and academics alike.

REFERENCES

Chatterjee, A. N. (2012). Inequalities in the public sphere: Emergence of community television in India. *Asian Ethnicity*, *13*(3), 229–250. doi:10.1080/14631369.2012.638803

Dangwal, S. (2017, April 27). Reliance Entertainment launches BIGFLIX, India's first global multi-language HD movie platform. *India.com*. https://www.india.com/business/reliance-entertainment-launches-bigflix-indias-first-global-multi-language-hd-movie-platform-2074662/

Farooqui, J. (2021, May 7). Disney+ Hotstar has 41% share of Indian online video subscription market: Omdia. *Exchange4Media*. https://www.exchange4media.com/digital-news/disney-hotstar-has-41-share-of-indian-online-video-subscription-market-omdia-112817.html

Fatemi, F. (2021, February 1). How The Pandemic Has Changed Video Content And Consumption. *Forbes*. https://www.forbes.com/sites/falonfatemi/2021/02/01/how-the-pandemic-has-changed-video-content-and-consumption/?sh=3ea570f36ec0

Federation of Indian Chambers of Commerce and Industry. (2019, March 12). *Press Release*. FICCI. https://www.ficci.in/pressrelease-page.asp?nid=3374

FICCI. (2019). *Indian Media and Entertainment industry clocks 13% growth to reach INR 1.67 trillion in 2018: FICCI-EY report*. FICCI. https://beta.ficci.in/pressrelease-page.asp?nid=3374

Fitzgerald, S. (2019). Over-the-Top Video Services in India: Media Imperialism after Globalization. *Media Industries*, *6*(2).

Henten, A., & Tadayoni, R. (2020). *Fading public control of audiovisual media. International Telecommunications Society*. ITS.

Kumar, J., Gupta, A., & Dixit, S. (2020). Netflix: SVoD entertainment of next gen. *Emerald Emerging Markets Case Studies*, *10*(3), 1–36. doi:10.1108/EEMCS-04-2020-0108

Madnani, D., Fernandes, S., & Madnani, N. (2020). Analysing the impact of COVID-19 on over-the-top media platforms in India. *International Journal of Pervasive Computing and Communications*, *16*(5), 457–475. doi:10.1108/IJPCC-07-2020-0083

Moochhala, Q. (2018). *The Future of Online OTT Entertainment Services in India*. Lexipedia.

Telecom Regulatory Authority of India. (2020, January 8). Indian Telecom Services Performance Indicator Report. *TRAI*. https://trai.gov.in/sites/default/files/PR_No.04of2020.pdf

Chapter 2
Streaming Revolution:
Tracing the Evolution of OTT Media From Its Origins to the Present

Nitesh Behare
https://orcid.org/0000-0002-9338-8563
Balaji Institute of International Business, India

Vinayak Chandrakant Shitole
https://orcid.org/0000-0002-5488-6543
RIIM - The Academy School of Business Management, India

Shubhada Nitesh Behare
Independent Author, India

Shrikant Ganpatrao Waghulkar
https://orcid.org/0000-0002-3767-3765
Independent Author, India

Tabrej Mulla
Arihant Institute of Business Management, India

Suraj Ashok Sonawane
Sinhgad Institute of Management, India

ABSTRACT

This chapter embarks on an engrossing journey, unravelling the transformational landscape of OTT media. It traces its humble beginnings to its disruptive force in the entertainment industry, exploring the impact on traditional media models. With on-demand content and cord-cutting on the rise, traditional broadcasters face challenges. Global expansion brings localized content and fierce competition between players, while technological innovations enhance user experiences with AI-driven personalization, VR, and AR. As the future of OTT unfolds, emerging business models and cutting-edge tech promise boundless possibilities. Understanding its historical context is vital, paving the way for an ever-evolving world of captivating entertainment.

DOI: 10.4018/979-8-3693-0116-6.ch002

1. INTRODUCTION

OTT is a term used to describe the content delivery over the internet, bypassing satellite television providers or traditional cable. OTT services offer extensive range of content, comprising TV shows, movies, live sports, concerts and many more. Typically, OTT Content can be accessed through a subscription model, but some services also offer a freemium option with limited content (Adjust, 2020). The historical development of OTT media can be traced back to the early days of the internet where few independent websites were offering streaming video content. But, these services were limited by the slow speeds of dial-up internet. As broadband internet became more widespread in early 2000s, OTT industry began to take off. Netflix is considered to be the pioneer of OTT industry, which launched in 1997 as a DVD-by-mail rental service. Netflix began to offer streaming video content in 2007 and quickly became the company's primary business model. Other important OTT services have emulated Netflix's approach, with names like Disney+, Hulu, Amazon Prime Video and many other joining the fray. Over the past years, these platforms have experienced rapid development and emerged as significant players within the media industry (Matt, 2023).

The increase of OTT media has intense influence on media production and consumption. For consumers, OTT platform provide many advantages over satellite television or traditional cable. OTT services provide more option and are more budget-friendly where they allow audience to watch their desired contents on demand. For content producers, OTT platforms establish novel avenues for distribution, enabling large audience outreach and offering room for experimentation with fresh formats and genres (Swarnima, 2023). Grasping the history of OTT is fundamental to fully grasp its present status and the direction it headed in the future. OTT media is relatively a new phenomenon, but it has already had a major impact on the media and entertainment industry (Gupta D. S., 2019). As the popularity of OTT industry continue to grow, it is expected to have even greater impact on the way people consume media in the future. Here are major milestones in the development of OTT media (Sabharwal, 2018) (Hayes, 2018):

- 1993: RealNetworks launches the RealPlayer, one of the first streaming media players.
- 1995: DirectTV launches the DirectTV satellite television service, which offers a limited amount of streaming content.
- 1997: Netflix launches as a DVD-by-mail rental service.
- 2000: Apple releases the iPod, which helps to popularize digital video downloads.
- 2005: YouTube launches, becoming one of the first major online video platforms.
- 2007: Netflix begins offering streaming video content.
- 2008: Hulu launches, offering a streaming service that combines content from major television networks.
- 2010: Amazon Prime Video launches, offering a streaming service that is included with Amazon Prime memberships.
- 2015: Disney+ launches, offering a streaming service that focuses on content from Disney and its subsidiaries.

The historical development of OTT industry has been defined by prompt but continuous evolution in the media and entertainment industry. Though comparatively new, it has already made a considerable effect on the media industry. As OTT industry gain even more acceptance, their impression on media production and consumption is expected to grow further in the future (Frank Arthofer, 2016). OTT media has revolutionized the way producers and consumers both interact with content. For consumers, OTT platform offer several benefits over conventional cable or satellite TV, such as affordability, wide varieties of content and on-demand viewing options. However, for producers, OTT platforms present a fresh distribution channel to reach broader audiences and experiment with innovative formats and genres (Bohra, 2021) (Shalparni P Y, 2022). Following are some of the precise implications of OTT media for media consumption and production:

1.1. Consumers

- *More choice*: OTT platform offer diverse contents comprising movies, TV shows, live sports and more. This offers varieties to the consumers and allow them to discover new content which consumers might not have found otherwise.
- *More control*: OTT platform allow their consumers to watch streaming content on demand and allow viewers to skip commercials. This allows consumers to control over their viewing experience and it also makes it easier for them to find the content that they want to watch.
- *More convenience*: OTT platforms are easily available on variety of devices such as computers, laptops, tablets, smartphones and smart TVs, offering appropriate access for consumers to watch content at their convenience, regardless of location or time.

1.2. Producers

- *New distribution channels:* OTT services have offered new method of content distribution which can benefit producers to stretch an extensive audience and to make more revenue.
- *More creative freedom:* OTT services are less restrictive than conventional television networks. This allows producers to experiment with innovative formats and genres, and to produce tailored content to their target audience.
- *More data insights:* OTT services accumulate users' data which can be used to track viewership patterns and to target ads more efficiently. This can help producers to make better decisions about the content that they create.

2. EARLY BEGINNINGS OF OTT MEDIA

The early beginnings of OTT services can be traced back to the advent of streaming technologies and the emergence of the internet. Revolutionary efforts by OTT business such as Netflix, Amazon Prime Video and Hulu laid the foundation for this transformative industry, offering unprecedented control to the consumers over their content consumption. Furthermore, changing consumer preferences and advancements in technology accelerated the growth of OTT platforms, forever altering the entertainment landscape. As we endure to witness the evolution of OTT media, it is obvious that revolution in streaming entertainment has only just initiated, encouraging future filled with creativity, innovation and immeasurable possibilities (Mystory, 2023). Over the past few decades, the way people consume media, has experienced an extraordinary transformation. The rise of OTT has revolutionized the whole entertainment industry, offering viewers unparalleled convenience, choice and control over their content consumption (Park & Kwon, 2019).

2.1. The Emergence of the Internet and Streaming Technologies

In the emerging phase of OTT services, the proliferation of internet and developments in streaming technologies paved the way for a transformative shift in media consumption. The era of 1990s witnessed the innovative way of delivering digital content directly to users, bypassing conventional broadcasting and cable TV as internet speeds improved. Netflix, a trailblazing company founded in 1997, played a pivotal role in reshaping the OTT landscape. Evolving from a DVD rental-by-mail service, Netflix introduced its streaming platform in 2007, marking a significant turning point in media consumption (McFadden, 2020). Hulu, in 2008, launched its services, further established the potential of OTT platforms by streaming recent episodes of popular TV shows online through an ad-supported model (Sanson, 2019).

Subsequently, Amazon Prime Video arisen as a key player, expanding rapidly from its incorporation into the Amazon Prime subscription in 2011 (Winston, 2018). YouTube, transforming user-generated content since 2005, became a leader in online video sharing (Leskin, 2020), while Apple TV+ and Disney+ entered the scene in 2019 with original content and extensive libraries from renowned franchises (Apple, 2019). HBO Max, established in the United States, emphasized exclusive content and premium offerings, contributing to the diverse and competitive OTT landscape. The rise of smart TVs and connected devices, coupled with media conglomerates building their streaming platforms like Amazon Prime Video and Disney+, underscored the industry's potential (Disney, 2019) (Imschloss, 2019). Simultaneously, the cord-cutting trend, where consumers abandoned traditional cable or satellite TV subscriptions in favour of streaming services, marked a significant shift in consumer behaviour that aligned with the flourishing growth of OTT platforms (Plunkett, 2021) (Bhaisare, 2022).

2.2. Technological Advancements and Market Forces

Beyond the appearance of platforms such as Amazon Prime Video, Netflix, and Hulu, the growth of the OTT business has been shaped by technology breakthroughs. The accessibility and affordability of high-speed internet connections have offered customers with seamless streaming experiences, allowing them to watch contents without interruption. With the growth of smart devices customers now have more alternatives for engaging with OTT content on their preferred screens. The speedy development of cloud infrastructure has enabled OTT companies to easily store large content libraries and deliver them to the global audience. Additionally, the strategy of acquiring licensing rights for popular TV shows and movies, coupled with ventures into original content production, has enabled OTT platforms to offer exclusive and diverse content, proving instrumental in attracting and retaining subscribers

3. DISRUPTIVE IMPACT ON TRADITIONAL MEDIA

The rapid advent of OTT media has significantly disrupted traditional media consumption and production models. The leading OTT platforms have revolutionized the way audiences access and consume content which is leading to challenges for conventional broadcasters and cable providers. The disruptive impact of OTT on conventional media, analyzing the challenges faced by traditional broadcasters, the shift from linear television to on-demand streaming, the rise of cord-cutting, and the changing dynamics of advertising revenue.

3.1. Challenges Faced by Traditional Broadcasters and Cable Providers

Traditional broadcasters and cable providers have long held a leading position in the media industry. Though, the advent of OTT platforms has posed several challenges to their traditional business models. OTT platforms offer to the audience the freedom of access content at their convenience, effectively breaking the fixed schedule of linear television. This paradigm shift in consumer behaviour has reflected in decreasing viewership for conventional broadcasters as audiences increasingly turn to on-demand streaming services for a personalized and flexible viewing experience. In favour of OTT platforms cable providers have faced challenges due to cord-cutting – a trend where viewers cancel their cable or satellite TV subscriptions (Shiana Aggarwal, 2022). The increasing costs of cable subscriptions, coupled with the abundance of diverse and affordable content on OTT platforms which have led many consumers to switch towards streaming services as a cost-effective alternative. Consequently, conventional cable providers have experienced a decline in subscribers as of impacting their revenue and profitability (Banik, 2023).

3.2. The Shift from Linear Television to On-Demand Streaming

The changeover from conventional linear television to on-demand streaming, fuelled by OTT media, stands as one of the most profound disruptions in the media landscape. Modern viewers, no longer tethered to scheduled programming, pursue control over their content consumption, leading to the ascendance of on-demand streaming platforms (Tiger, 2023). This paradigm shift has considerably eroded viewership for traditional television networks, resulting in a loss of advertising revenue and a challenge to justify huge advertising costs. Distinguishing this change, advertisers are progressively allocating considerable portions of their budgets to digital advertising on OTT platforms, attracted by the platforms' capability to target demographics with precision and measure campaign impact accurately (Bidyarthy, 2023) (Masand, 2023).

Personalization in viewing habits is crucial to this transformation. OTT services have interchanged scheduled programming with on-demand content, allowing users to watch what they want, when they want, fuelling the growth of streaming and diminishing live TV viewership (BMS, 2023). Cord-cutting, the suspension of traditional cable or satellite TV subscriptions in favour of OTT alternatives, has become commonplace, contributing to the financial woes of conventional media companies while bolstering the revenue of OTT platforms. The phenomenon of disintermediation, facilitated by OTT media, eliminates the need for middlemen in content dissemination (Manifold, 2023). Content producers can now communicate directly with their audiences, bypassing conventional distribution channels. This has led to a dispersal of audiences across multiple OTT platforms, in stark contrast to the centralized model of traditional media, resulting in a fragmented viewing landscape (Masand, 2023).

The competition for content rights has intensified, with OTT platforms like Amazon Prime Video, Netflix, and Disney+ substantially investing in original programming, often outbidding traditional networks for exclusive content. OTT's impact on advertising revenue dynamics is noteworthy. The rise of ad-free models on OTT platforms has disrupted traditional advertising ecosystems (Bidyarthy, 2023). Some platforms have adopted a hybrid approach, offering both ad-free and ad-supported tiers, challenging the efficiency of traditional advertising. While ad-supported models can still deliver value by reaching targeted audiences, they are often less advantageous compared to traditional television ads (Ruether, 2023) (Felicia, 2023).

In this evolving landscape, the relationship between OTT platforms and traditional media is both symbiotic and competitive. Traditional media corporations are adapting by developing their own streaming services or partnering with existing OTT platforms to remain relevant. The key to success for traditional media lies in embracing digital innovation and finding novel ways to engage viewers in the era of OTT dominance, necessitating adaptability and relevance in the ever-changing media landscape.

4. GLOBAL EXPANSION OF OTT PLATFORMS

OTT services are still in their infancy at the moment, but they are quickly becoming a popular platform on a global scale. According to estimates, the global OTT market would be worth $121.61 billion in 2019 (AMR, 2020). From the pre-COVID-19 $171.36 billion share in 2020, it is anticipated to expand quickly to $1039.03 billion by 2027 (Statista, 2021). From 2020 to 2027, this corresponds to a CAGR growth rate of almost 29.4%. The industry is expanding swiftly and steadily, with the availability of its products in many other languages playing a significant role (MI, 2023).

4.1. Market Overview

In 2021, the size of the worldwide over-the-top market was estimated at USD 276.02 billion (VMR, 2020). By 2030, it is anticipated to reach USD 2,838 billion, expanding at a CAGR of 29.55% from 2022 to 2030 (PR, 2023). In contrast to traditional cable or satellite pay-tv services like Time Warner Cable or Comcast, over-the-top (OTT) applications or services allow users to stream movies and television shows over the internet. Traditional delivery methods are more expensive than over-the-top (OTT) platforms, which provide media and communication services but do so at a lower cost overall. The widespread usage of smartphones and their compatibility with OTT applications are expected to cause the demand for OTT services to increase significantly over the next several years. Additionally, the availability of low-cost high-speed mobile internet encourages the adoption of OTT services.

It is possible to virtually broadcast OTT services or content across devices like smart TVs, smartphones, and gaming consoles; however, this is not subject to the administrative regulations of the OTT service or content provider. The scope of OTT services has been broadened by technical developments to now encompass any service or content that is accessible online. Online video and audio contents was once linked to OTT services. The development of the global over-the-top sector is facilitated by the emergence of subscription video-on-demand (SVoD) services, the accessibility of a wide range of content, and the increased demand for live streaming channels (MI, 2023).

The Indian OTT market is experiencing robust growth, with a projected CAGR of 14.32% from 2023 to 2027, set to reach US$5,586 million by 2028 (Pandit & Parmar, 2021). Currently, it boasts over 45 million subscribers (Pandit & Parmar, 2021), a number expected to be triple by 2030. This surge is fueled by increased internet accessibility, affordable data plans, and diverse content. In the mature U.S. market, platforms like Netflix and Hulu continue to shape the landscape, while China's colossal OTT market is dominated by iQiyi and Tencent Video. Latin America, Europe, Southeast Asia, and MENA are witnessing increased OTT adoption, with diverse platforms gaining traction. The nascent African OTT market, driven by growing interest and improved infrastructure, holds promise for the future (Omdia, 2020) (Mishra, 2023). The expansion of OTT platforms has modify revolutionizing the way audiences across the world access, the global media landscape, and consume content. OTT platforms such as Netflix, Amazon Prime Video, and Disney+ have effectively expanded into international markets, breaking geographical barriers and providing diverse audiences with an extensive range of content options.

Following are some key pointers which delves into the worldwide expansion of OTT platforms, emphasizing their influence on media consumption trends on a global scale.

4.1.1 Global Localization Efforts by OTT Providers

OTT providers have incorporated localization strategies to serve to diverse cultural and linguistic preferences for gaining success in different regions. One of the substantial characteristics of localization is offering content in many languages so that users can enjoy movies and TV shows in their native tongues. This effort has been predominantly essential in regions with multiple language demographics, such as India and Southeast Asia. For instance, Netflix, has offered their content in several Indian languages, including Hindi, Bengali, Tamil and Telugu to appeal to a broader audience. They have established partnerships with local production houses and studios to produce original content tailored to specific markets. Additionally, payment methods for OTT subscription have been localized to cater to regional preferences.

4.1.2 Competition between Regional and International OTT Players

The global expansion of OTT platforms has boost the competition between regional and international players with each seeking to establish dominance in diverse markets. International players like, Amazon Prime Video and Netflix acquired a significant advantage in respect of their extensive content libraries and established brand recognition. OTT Platforms introduced in new markets with a broad range of content engaging to viewers' attraction with international shows and movies (NAFDE, 2023).

Though, regional players have an advantage in comprehending local preferences, cultural nuances, and content demands. These players frequently grant access to popular regional content for securing a loyal user base. In Southeast Asia, such as, iFlix has gained traction by providing a rich catalog of local movies and TV shows, successfully competing with global giants in the region.

4.1.3 Key Success Stories and Challenges in Different Regions

a. India: India has emerged as one of the most significant growth markets for OTT platforms. Netflix and Amazon Prime Video have invested heavily in producing original Indian content across various languages and genres. Conversely, they face tough competition from local players which gained popularity by offering a mix of regional content, popular movies and live sports (Srivastava, 2022).
b. China: With strict content regulations and government control, the Chinese OTT market is dominated by local players like iQiyi and Tencent Video. Global players face many challenges in this highly competitive and regulated market and making it difficult to establish a significant presence (Perez, 2017).
c. Europe: The European OTT market offers a combination of regional and international OTT platforms in which Amazon Prime Video and Netflix have gained considerable market share, local players like Germany's Joyn and France's Canal+ have also established themselves by catering to local tastes and preferences (Businesswire, 2023).

d. Latin America: Latin America has witnessed substantial expansion by international players like Disney+ and Netflix. They succeeded by offering a blend of international and regional content, along with localized subtitles and dubbing options (Businesswire, 2023).

4.1.4 Challenges in Global Expansion

Global expansion for OTT platforms comes with different set of challenges. One important obstacle is adhering to changing content regulations and censorship laws in different countries. Content providers must navigate complex legal landscapes to ensure compliance with local regulations while offering diverse content to users. Another challenge lies in managing licensing agreements for content distribution in different regions. Negotiating with various content owners and adhering to exclusive distribution rights can be intricate and time-consuming. Furthermore, different economic conditions and disposable income levels in various regions can impact subscription pricing and revenue models. OTT providers must find the right balance between affordability and profitability to attract and retain users (Nagoriastha, 2020).

5. TECHNOLOGICAL INNOVATIONS AND OTT MEDIA

Our consumption of information and entertainment has been changed by OTT (Over the top) services. Online streaming services have proliferated in recent years, including Netflix, Amazon Prime, Hulu, and Disney+. Watching TV shows, live events and movies from anywhere, at any time and on any device is now simpler than ever thanks to these services. The OTT sector is, however, continually changing, and new technical developments are influencing how we consume and produce content. Industry experts and amateurs alike should keep up with the newest trends and advancements to stay ahead of the curve (Banik, 2023).

5.1. The Origin, Technical Evolution and Growth of the OTT Landscape

The development of peer-to-peer (P2P) file-sharing networks in the early 2000s is credited with giving rise to the OTT business. Without relying on centralized servers, these networks allowed users to share digital contents, such as music and video files. P2P networks were largely employed for piracy, but also opened the door for the creation of authorized OTT services. The introduction of Netflix's streaming service in 2007 marked the true OTT industry breakthrough. Netflix began as a DVD rental (Banik, 2023) service but quickly realized the advantages of online video streaming. Early on, Netflix mostly obtained its content through the licensing of works from studios and networks, but it later began creating its own contents, which has since distinguished the service from competitors.

Technology breakthroughs in the OTT sector have been fuelled by improvements in broadband accessibility, video compression, and device compatibility. Tt low bitrates, the H.264 (Banik, 2023) codec can produce high-quality video, which is one of the main video compression standards utilized by OTT services. Due to this, OTT providers may now stream content across slow connections and reach viewers in distant places. The expansion of the OTT ecosystem has been significantly influenced by the availability of bandwidth. OTT companies have been able to give better-quality video and more engrossing experiences as internet speeds have risen. By lowering potential and empowering new technologies like

Virtual Reality (VR) and Augmented Reality (AR), the development of 5G networks is anticipated to substantially improve the user experience on OTT platforms (Banik, 2023).

The OTT industry's expansion has been significantly influenced by device compatibility as well. Smartphones, tablets, smart TVs, and gaming consoles are just a few of the devices that can access OTT platforms today. Viewers may now stream their favorite TV series and films on their preferred devices with greater ease than ever before. The OTT industry has grown in nothing short of fantastic fashion and will likely continue to have a bright future. According to a research, the worldwide OTT market is anticipated to surpass $434 billion in revenue by 2027 and expand at a CAGR of 16.5% from 2022 to 2027 (Banik, 2023).

The market has become more fragmented as a result of the expansion of existing providers' offerings and the entry of new players due to the growth of the OTT industry. More options and choices for viewers have resulted from this, but it has also made it more difficult for providers to stand out in a competitive market. Following are the major technological developments in the OTT sector in 2023 -

5.2. Advancements in Streaming Technologies

The foundation of OTT media is built on the advancements in streaming technologies. In the early days of OTT platforms, buffering issues and inconsistent video quality were common problems due to limited internet speeds. Conversely, streaming technologies have significantly improved with the growth of broadband and mobile internet. Adaptive bitrate streaming, for example, dynamically the video quality based on the viewer's internet connection, securing a smooth and uninterrupted viewing experience. In addition, the advancement of HTML5 and HTTP Live Streaming (HLS) protocols has simplified the delivery of content for OTT platforms, enabling seamless access across different devices without the requirement of specific plug ins or applications. As a result, multi-platform compatibility has increased, allowing viewers to access their favorite content on smartphones, tablets, smart TVs, and computers with easily (IAS, 2022).

5.3. Content Delivery Networks (CDNs)

CDNs have emerged as integral components in optimizing the delivery of OTT content. Comprising strategically positioned servers globally, CDNs facilitate the caching of content in proximity to end-users, leading to decreased latency and faster load times for viewers accessing OTT platforms (Altomare, 2023). Particularly beneficial for OTT providers with a global user base, CDNs efficiently manage high demand and mitigate traffic spikes during peak events or content releases. The advantages of utilizing CDNs include enhanced performance through minimized latency, resulting in quicker page loads; scalability to manage heavy traffic and unexpected surges in demand; global reach by distributing servers worldwide, enabling organizations to connect with audiences in diverse locations; heightened reliability with increased redundancy and failover capabilities across multiple servers, reducing the risk of service interruptions; and cost savings for website owners by outsourcing content distribution to edge servers, thereby alleviating the bandwidth burden on origin servers (Altomare, 2023). This strategic integration of CDNs not only optimizes the viewing experience for end-users but also ensures the operational efficiency and global accessibility of OTT platforms in the dynamic landscape of online content delivery.

5.4. Video Compression Techniques

Video compression technologies have been instrumental in enabling the efficient delivery of high-quality content over the internet. Advanced video codecs, such as H.265 (HEVC) and VP9, have significantly reduced file sizes while maintaining video quality. This not only optimizes bandwidth usage but also ensures smooth streaming even on lower internet speeds. Moreover, the emergence of AV1 and a royalty-free video codec holds the potential to further improve video compression capabilities. This progress empowers OTT platforms to offer viewers with enhanced resolutions and immersive experiences, all without imposing a substantial increase in bandwidth demands (Kaustubh, 2023).

5.5. Device Compatibility

The variety of devices utilized by consumers for content consumption has played essential role in influencing the progression of OTT media. Recognizing its importance, OTT providers have prioritized ensuring compatibility across a various array of devices to extend their influence. Multi OTT platforms now provides dedicated applications for smartphones, tablets, gaming consoles and smart TVs. Additionally, they have undertaken to optimize their websites for diverse screen sizes, offering a consistent and easy to use experience across devices.

5.6. Top Technical Advancements in the OTT Platforms: in 2023 and Beyond

5.6.1 AI-Powered Personalization

Artificial Intelligence (AI) has significantly reshaped the Over-The-Top (OTT) media landscape, particularly in personalization techniques. OTT platforms leverage AI to analyse user data, including viewing history and preferences, crafting tailored content recommendations that enhance viewer engagement and retention (Banik, 2023). This not only introduces viewers to fresh content aligned with their tastes but also aids OTT providers in making data-driven decisions about content generation and licensing, contributing to financial success (L&T, 2022). Beyond entertainment, AI-powered personalization extends to healthcare, streamlining content recommendation processes and optimizing resource allocation (Banik, 2023). In essence, AI's integration in OTT platforms not only enriches the viewer experience but also fosters data-informed decision-making across diverse sectors.

5.6.2 Adaptive Bitrate Streaming

The cornerstone of the OTT market lies in Adaptive Bitrate Streaming (ABS) technology, ensuring a seamless viewing experience by adjusting video quality based on viewers' network conditions (Cloudflare, 2021). ABS dynamically selects the optimal bitrate, encoding videos at different qualities to accommodate varying network speeds. This adaptability is crucial for slow networks, preventing buffering by playing videos at lower quality, while on fast networks, ABS ensures a higher quality for an enhanced viewing experience (Banik, 2023). ABS offers flexibility in delivering high-quality content despite network challenges, making it vital for users with limited bandwidth. Moreover, ABS contributes to cost reduction by lowering data transmission, cutting bandwidth expenses, and optimizing streaming efficiency. Notably, ABS minimizes buffering and playback issues, enhancing viewer satisfaction and retention by automatically adjusting to diverse network conditions (Banik, 2023).

5.6.3 Cloud-Based Infrastructure

Cloud-based infrastructure serves as the backbone for OTT platforms, facilitating efficient and widespread content distribution to a global audience (Mujumdar, 2022). With the ability to scale operations swiftly in response to rising service demands, OTT platforms leverage cloud services to dynamically adjust server capacity, reducing expenses by only utilizing resources as needed (Banik, 2023). This scalability is crucial for addressing unexpected traffic spikes and subsequently scaling down when traffic levels stabilize. Moreover, cloud-based infrastructure enables OTT platforms to distribute content seamlessly across diverse geographic regions, reducing latency and enhancing user experience, particularly in live streaming scenarios requiring real-time content delivery. Leveraging cloud-based Content Delivery Networks (CDNs), OTT platforms can strategically cache frequently accessed content closer to users, optimizing content delivery times and ensuring a smooth user experience (Banik, 2023).

Beyond performance enhancement and cost reduction, cloud-based infrastructure allows OTT platforms to focus on their core strengths—creating and delivering high-quality video content—while outsourcing the maintenance of underlying IT infrastructure to cloud service providers. This strategic utilization of cloud technology not only streamlines operations but also positions OTT platforms for sustained growth and innovation in the dynamic landscape of digital content delivery (Banik, 2023).

5.6.4 Virtual and Augmented Reality

Virtual and Augmented Reality (VR/AR) technology stands at the forefront of potentially revolutionizing the way audiences interact with video content, prompting OTT platforms to explore its integration for enhanced user experiences (Banik, 2023). In the realm of virtual reality, users can immerse themselves fully in a 360-degree experience, offering unique perspectives for live events such as sports or concerts. OTT platforms are considering virtual movie theatres, allowing users to watch films as if in a cinema, selecting preferred camera angles for personalized experiences (Radianti, Majchrzak, Fromm, & Wohlgenannt, 2020). Augmented reality overlays digital content onto the physical world, presenting an engaging layer to video consumption. OTT services could utilize AR to furnish users with additional information about the content they're watching, offering an interactive element. Users might, for instance, point their smartphones at objects on the screen to access detailed information. While early implementations include Netflix's VR app for a cinematic experience and an interactive AR experience for "Stranger Things," widespread use of VR/AR in OTT platforms faces challenges, notably in production costs and content complexity. As technology advances and production costs decrease, the integration of VR/AR is expected to grow, fundamentally altering and enriching the user experience across various OTT platforms.

5.6.5 Multi-Platform Compatibility

The ability to access content on a number of devices, such as smartphones, tablets, smart TVs, and game consoles, has become a crucial element of OTT platforms. With the help of this function, customers may watch contents on numerous devices without interruption whenever and wherever they choose (Banik, 2023). Content on OTT platforms with multi-platform compatibility must be accessible on a variety of hardware, software, and browsers. Regardless of the device being used, they must also make sure that the user experience is constant across all platforms. Reaching a larger audience is one of the main advantages of multi-platform compatibility for OTT services. OTT systems may accommodate various viewing habits and reach consumers who might not have access to a specific device or platform by offering content across a variety of devices.

5.6.6 Blockchain-Based Content Distribution

OTT platforms can revolutionize data control and fair compensation for content providers by leveraging the security and transparency inherent in blockchain technology (Banik, 2023). Through blockchain's decentralized network, data is distributed across multiple nodes, enhancing security by preventing easy hacking or alterations to content. Each transaction is recorded on the blockchain, establishing a verifiable record of content ownership and distribution, fostering transparency. Platforms implementing blockchain for content distribution empower users with greater control over their data. Instead of having their data harvested without consent, users can choose to share data with content producers in exchange for premium content access (Banik, 2023). Blockchain also facilitates transparent and efficient monetization. Whether through modest access fees or micropayments, content creators can be fairly compensated, with blockchain ensuring swift and open execution of these transactions. The challenge lies in achieving widespread blockchain adoption for content delivery. A robust ecosystem necessitates the participation of both consumers and content producers to realize the potential of secure, transparent, and fairly compensated content distribution (Banik, 2023).

5.6.7 Dynamic Ad-Insertion

OTT platforms can offer targeted advertisements to consumers based on their viewing tastes and behaviours with the help of effective mechanism i.e. dynamic ad-insertion. OTT platforms can deliver interesting and relevant advertisements by analysing user data in real-time, giving viewers a better viewing experience and generating more revenues for advertisers. Critical analysis of the users' data is important in dynamic ad-insertion process to discover viewing preferences and patterns. To increase the probability of viewer engagement, this data is then used to provide targeted advertisements to viewers.

5.6.8 Advanced Analytics

Rising OTT service popularity has unleashed a data boom, with platforms collecting user preferences and viewing behaviour. Advanced analytics harness this wealth of data, allowing platforms to make data-driven decisions for an enhanced user experience (Banik, 2023). By evaluating viewer behaviour, OTT platforms can recommend content aligned with user interests, incorporating social media activity, search queries, and viewing history. This data-driven approach extends to content optimization, where user engagement statistics guide personalized content adjustments based on audience preferences. Additionally, advanced analytics, by tracking user interactions, provide valuable insights into effective user interface designs, preferred features, and navigation patterns, further refining the overall user experience (Banik, 2023).

5.6.9 Collaborations with AI Assistants

The integration of AI assistants has elevated the OTT experience, allowing users to access and manage content through voice commands. Collaborations with AI assistants like Siri, Google Assistant, and Alexa enhance convenience, enabling users to effortlessly find shows, adjust volume, or navigate episodes with simple voice prompts (Banik, 2023). Beyond convenience, AI assistants contribute to a more personalized viewing experience by analysing user data to understand preferences, viewing patterns, and even mood, tailoring content recommendations accordingly (Brown, 2021) (Anderson & Rainie, 2018). Additionally, partnerships with AI assistants can enhance content accessibility, providing audio explanations for users with visual impairments and closed captions for those who are hard of hearing, enriching the overall viewing experience.

6. REGULATORY CHALLENGES AND POLICY IMPLICATIONS

The speedy rise of OTT media has reformed the entertainment sector, granting audience unmatched access to a broad array of content and reshaping the way content is consumed. on the other hand, this transformative expansion has presented many regulatory complexities and policy considerations neither for governments nor regulatory bodies across the globe. Following are regulatory hurdles and policy implication linked to the surge of OTT media. Furthermore, it inspects the different strategies employed by various nations and regulatory entities in tackling these issues, along with their potential effects on the future trajectory of OTT media (Srivastava U. K., 2016) (Akhila, 2023).

For instance, India has taken an active role in addressing regulatory issues in the OTT sector. Concerns were expressed about content filtering, data privacy, and consumer protection in the lack of defined rules. Recognizing the need for self-regulation in the sector, the Internet and Mobile Association of India (IAMAI) issued a detailed code of conduct for OTT platforms in 2018 (IAMAI, 2018). However, driven by escalating concerns and public grievances, the Indian government took a more assertive stance. It proposed the Information Technology (Intermediary Guidelines and Digital Media Ethics Code) Rules in 2021 (GoI, 2021), with the goal of particularly regulating digital media, including OTT platforms. The rules include critical provisions such as the mandatory classification of content into age-based categories, the formation of robust grievance redressal mechanisms to address user complaints, disclosure requirements for content information, including ratings and descriptors, and encouragement for OTT platforms to develop and implement self-regulation mechanisms. In the changing world of digital content distribution, this regulatory framework represents the government's efforts to find a balance between regulation and business autonomy.

Following are some regulatory challenges and policy implications associated with the rise of OTT media

6.1. Net Neutrality

Net neutrality has been a subject of discussion in relation to OTT media. The concept of net neutrality supports an open internet where all internet traffic is treated evenly by internet service providers (ISPs). This implicit that no content or service should receive exceptional treatment or reduced speed based on its source, destination, and data type. For OTT providers, net neutrality is vital to make sure fair access to their content and to prevent ISPs from potentially favouring their own content or charging OTT platforms for faster delivery to end-users. Equally, Internet Service Providers (ISPs) contend that The OTT services require substantial bandwidth and enforce a burden on their networks making it difficult to uphold consistent quality for all users. Countries assume varying regulatory approaches to net neutrality. Several nations have imposed diligent rules to protect an open and unrestricted internet, whereas others have acquired a more compassionate standpoint, permitting internet service providers (ISPs) to employ specific traffic management measures. The consequences of net neutrality regulations can substantially influence the fairness between OTT providers; shape the trajectory of content delivery and consumption in the future (Jog, Joshi, Thenuan, & Dixit, 2016) (Apoorva, 2016).

6.2. Content Regulation

The global scope of OTT media presents hurdles for content regulation. National regulatory bodies established traditional broadcasting and cable television which are subject to content regulations. OTT platforms regularly work across international boundaries rendering the application of conventional content regulations to their services a complex task. The range of content available on OTT platforms prompts inquiries to decide what is suitable for viewers. Countries own distinct cultural, social, and political norms; content that is deemed suitable in one nation may be regarded as inappropriate or unpleasant in another. Striking a balance among freedom of expression and cultural sensitivities presents an intricate challenge for regulators. To deal with content regulation concerns several countries have executed regional content rating systems, empowering audience to make informed decisions about the content they engage with. on the contrary, other nations have mandated that the OTT platforms hold to the content regulations of their home countries often resulting in conflicts between regulatory domains (Nisal, 2020) (Kudeshia & Jain, 2021).

6.3. Taxation

The global reach of OTT media more complicates taxation matters. Conventional media enterprises typically pay taxes in accordance with their physical presence within a country. on the contrary, OTT platforms often operate within digital frameworks, creating challenges in identifying the origins of revenue and establishing appropriate taxation protocols. These circumstances have activated discussions regarding the taxation of OTT platforms across various nations. Several countries have established digital services taxes or started global tax arrangements to make certain equitable taxation of these platforms. Though, these strategies have encountered backlash due to concerns about potential double taxation and the potential to impede innovation within the digital economy (Kashyapnath, 2020) (TRAI, 2015).

6.4. Copyright Issues

OTT platforms provide a wide library of content like licensed content as well as original productions. OTT providers ensuring a significant challenge with copyright laws and licensing agreements. Copyright holders aim to protect their intellectual property and secure equitable compensation for the utilization of their content on OTT platforms. Newly emerging technologies, like digital rights management based on block chain, have the ability to deal with copyright concerns by offering transparent and secure mechanisms for content licensing and distribution. on the other hand, the process of standardizing these technologies and forging international agreements for copyright protection remains a challenging attempt (Akhila, 2023) (Arora, 2022) (Shinde & Dalvi, 2022).

6.5. Regulatory Approaches in Different Countries

Countries have accepted different strategies to tackle the regulatory complexities brought about by OTT media. Certain countries have adopted a laissez-faire stance enabling the market to autonomously regulate itself and encourage innovation. This strategy underscores the importance of competition and consumer autonomy, relying on market dynamics to resolve any probable concerns. In contrast, some countries have implemented targeted regulations, and directives to oversee OTT platforms. For e.g., some countries mandate that OTT platforms conform to content regulations, enclosed censorship and content rating frameworks. Furthermore, certain countries implement data localization stipulations to safeguard user data and uphold adherence to local statutes (Nisal, 2020) (Kudeshia & Jain, 2021).

6.6. Market Competition and Monopoly Concerns

Concerns regarding monopolistic behaviour and possible market competition can arise from the dominance of some OTT media firms. Promoting fair competition, stopping anti-competitive behaviour, and defending consumer interests are difficult tasks for regulators. A significant regulatory difficulty is finding the correct balance between encouraging innovation and minimizing market consolidation (Preta, 2019).

6.7. International Jurisdiction and Cooperation

Due to the international nature of OTT media services, issues with jurisdiction can arise. It becomes difficult to determine which laws apply and how to enforce them across borders. Cross-border problems like copyright infringement, content distribution rights, and jurisdictional conflicts are addressed in regulatory challenges. To properly address these issues, international cooperation and harmonization initiatives are required (Kashyapnath, 2020) (TRAI, 2015) (Akhila, 2023) (Arora, 2022) (Shinde & Dalvi, 2022).

6.8. Technological Advances and Regulatory Adjustment

Regulators face difficulties keeping up with the rate of innovation due to the quick development of OTT media technology and business models. To meet new technology, content formats, and distribution strategies, regulators must continuously evaluate and change their policies. OTT media services face a variety of regulatory obstacles that need for a complex strategy that strikes a balance between innovation, consumer protection, competition, and cultural considerations. To create frameworks that guarantee an equitable and sustainable environment for both consumers and industry players, regulatory agencies must traverse these difficulties (Nisal, 2020) (Kudeshia & Jain, 2021).

6.9. Potential Impact on the Future of OTT Media

The regulatory challenges and policy implications facing OTT media will continue to shape the future of the industry. Striking an optimal equilibrium between innovation and regulation will play a fundamental role in cultivating a dynamic and competitive OTT market. Rigorous and excessively stringent regulations could potentially suppress innovation and curtail the array of content accessible to audience. on the contrary, an absence of well-suited regulations might give rise to apprehensions related to content standards, data privacy, and equitable competition. The conclusions drawn from discussions on net neutrality, taxation, content regulation and copyright matters will determine the extent of access, choice, and autonomy viewers possess within the OTT media sphere. However, the resolution of these challenges will affect the operational models and profitability of OTT platforms as well as their capacity to expand their reach and thrive in the international market (Park & Kwon, 2019).

7. FUTURE TRENDS AND OUTLOOK

The realm of OTT media is in a perpetual state of transformation, directed by technological progressions, shifting consumer dynamics, and the industry's implicit competitiveness. This concluding part delves into the subsequent trends and prospects for OTT media, content tactics, exploring emergent business models, and technological strides that will mould the sector in the coming years. It also scrutinizes the plausible repercussions of variables like, smart TVs, 5G networks and novel market participants on the competitive panorama of OTT media.

7.1. Emerging Business Models

New business models are liable to emerge, catering to diverse consumer needs and preferences of the consumers as the OTT market matures. One such model is ad-supported tier, wherein consumers can access content of the OTT for free which are supported by commercials. This model allows OTT platforms to reach a broader audience and attract users who may be unwilling to pay for subscriptions of OTT. This approach of the OTT platforms offers greater choice and flexibility to the consumers as they can choose best suitable model which aligns with their viewing habits and budget. Furthermore, pay-as-you-go models, where users pay for specific events or specific pieces of content, may gain traction, especially for live sports and special events. These models can be attractive to casual viewers who do not wish to commit to long-term subscriptions (E. & N., 2020) (Naushad, 2023) (Zemoga, 2022).

7.2. Content Strategies

Behind the success of OTT platforms, content will continue to be the driving force. OTT providers will focus on original content production and exclusive licensing agreements to remain competitive in the streaming industry. Original content helps OTT platforms to differentiate themselves from competitors and build a loyal user base. Additionally, international co-productions and content collaborations are expected to increase, as OTT platforms search to increase their global content libraries and cater to diverse audiences worldwide. These collaborations can also help to diminish the content acquisition costs and offer fresh perspectives to their viewers. Content diversification will be a significant business strategy for OTT platforms, offering an extensive range of genres and formats to cater to different viewer segments (E. & N., 2020) (Naushad, 2023) (Zemoga, 2022). Furthermore, investing in localized content will be important for OTT platforms to gain a foothold in precise markets with unique cultural preferences.

7.3. Technological Advancements

Technological innovations will continue to redesign the landscape of future of OTT media. Infrastructural development in offering high speed bandwidth will transform content delivery by empowering faster streaming and reduced latency. This will lead to higher quality video experiences and better support for VR and AR applications. Additionally, smart TVs and connected devices will play critical role in augmenting OTT viewing experience. Integration with smart home ecosystems and voice assistants will provide seamless control and accessibility for viewers, making content consumption even more convenient. Moreover, advancements in adaptive bitrate streaming and video compression technologies will continue to enhance bandwidth usage and improve video quality, ensuring smooth playback even on lower internet speeds (E. & N., 2020) (Naushad, 2023) (Zemoga, 2022).

7.4. Impact of New Market Entrants

The OTT media landscape is expected to see an invasion of new market entrants comprising traditional media companies, tech giants as well as niche players. To cater to their existing customers and compete with established players, traditional media companies are gradually launching their own OTT platforms. These companies will deliver wide content libraries and well-established brand recognition, possibly disrupting the competitive dynamics. Tech giants like, Apple and Google, are also entering the OTT market, leveraging their existing user bases and technological expertise. Their entry to the OTT industry can strengthen competition and lead to more innovations in content delivery and user experience. Niche players with dedicated content offerings may also emerge, targeting specific demographics or genres. These players can carve out a niche audience and compete with larger platforms by offering unique and tailored content experiences (E. & N., 2020) (Naushad, 2023) (Zemoga, 2022).

7.5. Advertising and Marketing

OTT platforms will keep providing tailored advertising options, using user information and cutting-edge analytics to deliver relevant and individualized adverts. The use of programmatic advertising, which automates ad placements and improves campaign success, will spread more widely. Viewer engagement and brand awareness will increase with the use of interactive ad formats and branded content integrations (E. & N., 2020) (Naushad, 2023) (Zemoga, 2022).

7.6. E-commerce and Retail

E-commerce features will be incorporated into OTT platforms, allowing customers to make purchases right from the streaming environment. Shoppable content will let companies display the goods seen in TV shows or movies, enabling a smooth purchase experience and generating extra income (E. & N., 2020) (Naushad, 2023) (Zemoga, 2022).

7.7. Sports and Live Events

With live streaming, on-demand contents, and interactive experiences, the OTT sector will upend the landscape of sports and live events. Businesses will be able to reach a worldwide audience and monetise their content thanks to viewers' access to multi-angle watching, real-time analytics, and interactive fan involvement (E. & N., 2020) (Naushad, 2023) (Zemoga, 2022).

7.8. Education and Training

By providing online courses, virtual classrooms, and interactive learning opportunities, OTT platforms will play a big role in the education and training sector. The way people learn will change as a result of personalized learning routes, collaboration tools, and access to educational content (E. & N., 2020) (Naushad, 2023) (Zemoga, 2022).

7.9. Telehealth and Healthcare

The development of telehealth and remote healthcare services will be fuelled by OTT platforms, which will make it easier to provide health education, remote patient monitoring, and virtual medical consultations. Personalized healthcare experiences will be made possible by integration with wearables and AI-driven diagnostics, increasing accessibility and effectiveness (E. & N., 2020) (Naushad, 2023) (Zemoga, 2022).

7.10. Financial Services

OTT platforms which offer digital banking, payment and investing solutions will increase their market share in the financial services industry. Businesses of financial industry will use OTT to reach their target markets, improve consumer experiences, and propel their respective sectors forward (E. & N., 2020) (Naushad, 2023) (Zemoga, 2022).

8. CONCLUSION

The evolution of Over-the-Top (OTT) media has been revolutionary, redesigning content consumption and production. Understanding historical context of OTT industry is crucial in comprehending its impact on media industry and its probable future trajectory. Pioneering companies have already laid down the groundwork for OTT media, assisted by technological advancements and market forces. This disruption has led to a shift in the dynamics of consumer behaviour, favouring flexible and personalized content experiences, challenging conventional broadcasters and cable service providers to adapt. The universal development of OTT platforms has broken geographical barriers, catering to diverse markets and preferences through localization efforts and fierce competition. Technological innovations in streaming, video compression, content delivery and compatibility of the devices have augmented user experiences. Emerging technologies like AI, VR, and AR hold promise for the future, offering interactive and personalized content. Regulatory challenges on content regulation, net neutrality, taxation and copyright entail careful balancing between innovation and consumer protection. Looking forward, the future of OTT media appears promising with emerging business models like ad-supported tiers and hybrid subscriptions, enhancing viewer flexibility. Original content production, international collaborations, and content diversification remain key strategies for OTT platforms to stay competitive. Advancements in 5G networks and smart TVs will elevate the viewing experience, while new market entrants, including traditional media companies and tech giants, intensify competition and innovation. Embracing further research and adaptation in this rapidly evolving environment will be essential to unlock the full potential of OTT media for the media industry's future.

REFERENCES

Adjust. (2020). What is over-the-top (OTT)? *Adjust.* https://www.adjust.com: https://www.adjust.com/glossary/ott-over-the-top/

Akhila, A. (2023). Legal Framework of Over the Top (OTT) Platforms. [IJSR]. *International Journal of Scientific Research, 12*(05), 420–426. doi:10.21275/SR23503195932

Altomare, F. (2023). *What is a Content Delivery Network? CDN Explained.* Global Dots. https://www.globaldots.com: https://www.globaldots.com/resources/blog/content-delivery-network-explained/

AMR. (2020). *Over-the-top Market.* Allied Market research. https://www.alliedmarketresearch.com/over-the-top-services-market

Anderson, J., & Rainie, L. (2018). *Improvements ahead: How humans and AI might evolve together in the next decade.* Pew Research. https://www.pewresearch.org: https://www.pewresearch.org/internet/2018/12/10/improvements-ahead-how-humans-and-ai-might-evolve-together-in-the-next-decade/

Apoorva. (2016). *The Net Neutrality Debate in India.* Apoorva. https://prsindia.org: https://prsindia.org/theprsblog/the-net-neutrality-debate-in-india?page=153&per-page=1

Apple. (2019). *Apple unveils Apple TV+, the new home for the world's most creative storytellers.* Apple. https://www.apple.com: https://www.apple.com/in/newsroom/2019/03/apple-unveils-apple-tv-plus-the-new-home-for-the-worlds-most-creative-storytellers/

Arora, G. C. (2022). Copyright Commercialisation in the Entertainment Industry: Changing paradigms in the era of OTT Platforms. In IPRs in Knowledge Era: Changing Contours (pp. 161-174). Springer. doi:10.1057/9781137378477.0008

Banik, I. (2023). *The Technological Advancements in OTT Platforms: Things You Must Know to Stay Ahead of the Curve.* MUVI. https://www.muvi.com/blogs/the-technological-advancements-in-ott-platforms

Bhaisare, D. S. (2022). A study on User Perspective on OTT platform in India. *Journal of Positive School Psychology, 6*(3), 7351–7364. https://www.journalppw.com/index.php/jpsp/article/download/4604/3038/5226

Bidyarthy, A. (2023). *The rise of the OTT platform and its impact on the entertainment industry by 2040.* Insights. https://insights.blackcoffer.com: https://insights.blackcoffer.com/the-rise-of-the-ott-platform-and-its-impact-on-the-entertainment-industry-by-2040/

Bohra, R. (2021). Impact of OTT on traditional mode of entertainment. *Times of India.* https://timesofindia.indiatimes.com/readersblog/raghavi/impact-of-ott-on-traditional-mode-of-entertainment-39292/

Brown, S. (2021). *Machine learning, explained.* MIT. https://mitsloan.mit.edu: https://mitsloan.mit.edu/ideas-made-to-matter/machine-learning-explained

Businesswire. (2023). *Europe Over The Top (OTT) Market Report 2023: Several Regional Players Look to Cut Into Netflix's Dominance.* DUBLIN: ResearchAndMarkets.com. https://www.businesswire.com/news/home/20230221005506/en/Europe-Over-The-Top-OTT-Market-Report-2023-Several-Regional-Players-Look-to-Cut-Into-Netflixs-Dominance---ResearchAndMarkets.com

Chulkov, D., & Nizovtsev, D. (2015, July). Bundling, cord-cutting and the death of TV as we know it. *Journal of the International Academy for Case Studies, 21*(5), 27-34. https://www.researchgate.net/publication/301557055_Bundling_cord-cutting_and_the_death_of_TV_as_we_know_it

Cloudflare. (2021). *What is adaptive bitrate streaming?* Cloudflare. https://www.cloudflare.com: https://www.cloudflare.com/learning/video/what-is-adaptive-bitrate-streaming/#:~:text=Adaptive%20bitrate%20streaming%20adjusts%20video,%2C%20location%2C%20or%20Internet%20speed

Disney. (2019). *Disney+ Launches Today—and a New Era of Disney Entertainment Begins.* Disney. https://thewaltdisneycompany.com: https://thewaltdisneycompany.com/disney-launches-today-and-a-new-era-of-disney-entertainment-begins/

Dixon, A. (2022). *BETWEEN CTV AND LINEAR TV, WHICH ONE IS BETTER?* Strategus. https://www.strategus.com: https://www.strategus.com/blog/between-ctv-and-linear-tv-which-one-is-better

E., S., & N., E. (2020). Emergence and future of Over-the-top (OTT) video services in India: an analytical research. *International Journal of Business, Management and Social Research*, 489-498. doi:10.18801/ijbmsr.080220.50

Felicia. (2023). *STUDY CASE: From Ad-Free Haven to Ad-Inclusive: Netflix's Transition Towards a Not-So Ad-Free Entertainment Experience**. Linkedin. https://www.linkedin.com/pulse/: https://www.linkedin.com/pulse/study-case-from-ad-free-haven-ad-inclusive-netflixs-not-so-theodorus/?trk=article-ssr-frontend-pulse_more-articles_related-content-card

Frank Arthofer, M. K. (2016). *The Future of Television: The Impact of OTT on Video Production Around the World.* BCG. https://www.bcg.com/publications: https://www.bcg.com/publications/2016/media-entertainment-technology-digital-future-television-impact-ott-video-production

GoI. (2021). *IT(Intermediary Guidelines and Digital Media Ethics Code).* GoI. https://mib.gov.in: https://mib.gov.in/sites/default/files/IT%28Intermediary%20Guidelines%20and%20Digital%20Media%20Ethics%20Code%29%20Rules%2C%202021%20English.pdf

Gupta, A. (2022). *Antitrust Laws In The OTT Regime – Old Wine In A New Bottle.* Khurana and Khurana. https://www.khuranaandkhurana.com: https://www.khuranaandkhurana.com/2022/08/04/antitrust-laws-in-the-ott-regime-old-wine-in-a-new-bottle/

Gupta, D. S. (2019). Understanding Adoption Factors Of Over-The-Top Video Services Among Millennial Consumers. *International Journal of Computer Engineering & Technology (IJCET, 10*(1), 61-71. https://pure.jgu.edu.in/id/eprint/1970/1/S.Dasgupta2019.pdf

Hayes, D. (2018, May 16). *Advanced Copyright Issues on the Internet.* JD Supra. https://www.jdsupra.com/legalnews/advanced-copyright-issues-on-the-75571/

Hossain, M. M. (2016). *A Literature Review of OTT- related Policy and Regulatory Issues.* Research Gate. https://www.researchgate.net/publication/306323748_A_Literature_Review_of_OTT-_related_Policy_and_Regulatory_Issues

IAMAI. (2018). *Public Policy and Advocacy.* IMAI. https://www.iamai.in/our-initiatives/public-policy-and-advocacy

Ias, D. (2022). *Rise of the Streaming Industry in India: Daily Current Affairs.* IAS. https://dhyeyaias.com/current-affairs/daily-current-affairs/rise-of-the-streaming-industry-in-india

Imschloss, W. R. (2019, September). The impact of digital transformation on the retailing value chain. *International Journal of Research in Marketing, 36*(3), 350–366. doi:10.1016/j.ijresmar.2018.12.002

Jog, P. Y., Joshi, P. S., Thenuan, P., & Dixit, M. (2016, Jun). Net Neutrality and Impact of Regulation on Over the Top (OTT) Services and Study of responses of Public and Telecom Service Provider. *International Journal of Management, IT and Engineering (IJMIE), 6*(6). https://www.researchgate.net/publication/303785031_Net_Neutrality_and_Impact_of_Regulation_on_Over_the_Top_OTT_Services_and_Study_of_responses_of_Public_and_Telecom_Service_Provider

Kashyapnath, D. (2020). *Regulatory Framework for Over-The-Top (OTT) communication Services.* Sabarkantha, Gujarat: Consumer Protection Association Himmatnagar. https://trai.gov.in/sites/default/files/ConsumerProtectionAssociationHimmatnagar08012019.pdf

Kaustubh. (2023). *VP9 vs. H.265 - Comparison Between Video Codecs.* Gumlet. https://www.gumlet.com/learn/vp9-vs-h265/

KPMG. (2017). *The 'Digital First Journy' - How OTT Platform can remain 'on demand ready?'.* KPMG. https://assets.kpmg.com/content/dam/kpmg/in/pdf/2017/10/The-Digital-First-journey.pdf

Ksiazek, T. B. (2019). The International Encyclopedia of Journalism Studies. *The International Encyclopedia of Journalism Studies.* doi:10.1002/9781118841570.iejs0049

Kudeshia, A., & Jain, S. (2021). Regulation of OTT Platforms: Need for a Separate Legislation. *International Journal of Law Management and Humanities, 5*(6), 1841-1861. doi:https://doij.org/10.10000/IJLMH.113985

Leskin, P. (2020). *YouTube is 15 years old. Here's a timeline of how YouTube was founded, its rise to video behemoth, and its biggest controversies along way.* Business Insider. https://www.businessinsider.in/tech/news/youtube-is-15-years-old-hereaposs-a-timeline-of-how-youtube-was-founded-its-rise-to-video-behemoth-and-its-biggest-controversies-along-way/slidelist/76111673.cms

L&T. (2022). *AI AND OTT MEDIA: HOW ARTIFICIAL INTELLIGENCE IS SHAPING THE FUTURE OF OTT MARKETS.* LTTS. https://www.ltts.com/blog/AI-shaping-future-of-OTT-markets

Manifold, K. (2023). *What is an OTT Platform? A Complete Guide to OTT Business!* Vodlix. https://vodlix.com/blog/what-is-an-ott-platform-a-complete-guide-to-ott-business

Masand, J. (2023). The impact of streaming services on traditional TV and the future of the industry. *Times of India.* https://timesofindia.indiatimes.com: https://timesofindia.indiatimes.com/blogs/voices/the-impact-of-streaming-services-on-traditional-tv-and-the-future-of-the-industry/?source=app&frmapp=yes

Masand, J. (2023). The impact of streaming services on traditional TV and the future of the industry. *Times of India.* https://timesofindia.indiatimes.com/blogs/voices/the-impact-of-streaming-services-on-traditional-tv-and-the-future-of-the-industry/

McFadden, C. (2020). *From DVDs to streaming, here's the incredible history of Netflix.* Interesting Engineering. https://interestingengineering.com: https://interestingengineering.com/culture/the-fascinating-history-of-netflix

MI. (2023). *OTT MARKET SIZE & SHARE ANALYSIS - GROWTH TRENDS & FORECASTS (2023 - 2028).* Mordor Intelligence. https://www.mordorintelligence.com/industry-reports/over-the-top-market

Mishra, S. (2023). *OTT Platforms: The Next Big Industry in Cinema with Prominent Players Across the World.* LinkedIn. https://www.linkedin.com/pulse/ott-platforms-next-big-industry-cinema-prominent-players-mishra/

Mujumdar, P. (2022). *Cloud Computing For The Media Industry & OTT Platforms: How Does It Work?* LinkedIn. https://www.linkedin.com/pulse/cloud-computing-media-industry-ott-platforms-how-does-priti-mujumdar/

Mukerjee, S. (2022, January 19). Rethinking Audience Fragmentation Using a Theory of News Reading Publics: Online India as a Case Study. *The International Journal of Press/Politics.* doi:10.1177/19401612211072700

Mystory. (2023). *EVERYTHING YOU NEED TO KNOW ABOUT OTT TECHNOLOGY.* Your Story. https://yourstory.com/mystory/everything-you-need-to-know-about-ott-technology

NAFDE. (2023). *Global Over the Top (OTT) Market is projected to be worth USD 490.13 Billion by 2028, growing at a CAGR of 15.72%: Bonafide Research.* Clifton, New Jersey: Global News wire. https://www.globenewswire.com/en/news-release/2023/05/31/2679028/0/en/Global-Over-the-Top-OTT-Market-is-projected-to-be-worth-USD-490-13-Billion-by-2028-growing-at-a-CAGR-of-15-72-Bonafide-Research.html

Nagoriastha. (2020). *Censorship Of OTT Platforms: A Boon Or Bane.* Legal Services in India. https://www.legalserviceindia.com/legal/article-3418-censorship-of-ott-platforms-a-boon-or-bane.html

Naushad, S. (2023, Feb 06). *OTT & It's Trends.* To the New. https://www.tothenew.com/blog/ott-its-trends/#:~:text=OTT%20streaming%20has%20become%20increasingly,size%20by%20the%20year%20 2023!

Nisal, K. S. (2020). The Convergence Model And Content Regulation Of Ott Platforms In India: An Analytical Study. *SANSHODHAN, 10*, 36-41. https://jattjournal.net/index.php/Sanshodhan/article/viewFile/160456/110195

Nordin, F., Brozovic, D., & Holmlund, M. (2013, October 11). Disintermediation in Business-to-Business ServiceChannels: Mechanisms and Challenges. *Journal of Business-To-Business Marketing, 20*(4), 179–192. doi:10.1080/1051712X.2013.813717

Omdia. (2020, Jul 31). *Media & Technology Digest - April 2020*. Omdia. https://omdia.tech.informa.com/OM000323/Media--Technology-Digest--April-2020

Pandit, M., & Parmar, K. (2021, March). *The Evolution of Mediated Youth Culture: OTT as "New Television" in India*. Research Gate.

Park, S., & Kwon, Y. (2019). Research on the Relationship between the Growth of OTT Service Market and the Change in the Structure of the Pay-TV Market. Towards a Connected and Automated Society. Helsinki, Finland: International Telecommunications Society (ITS).

Perez, B. (2017, Oct 17). *Tencent Video, iQiyi in race to lead China's online video market*. SCMP. https://www.scmp.com/tech/china-tech/article/2113720/tencent-video-iqiyi-race-lead-chinas-online-video-market

Plunkett, J. K. (2021). Standing on the shoulders of tech giants: Media delivery, streaming television and the rise of global suppliers. *new media & society, 23*(11), 3206-3228. doi:10.1177/1461444820946681

PR. (2023). *Over the Top (OTT) Market Size Expanding to USD 1,241.6 BN by 2030*. Ottawa: Precedence Research. https://www.globenewswire.com/en/news-release/2023/06/28/2696331/0/en/Over-the-Top-OTT-Market-Size-Expanding-to-USD-1-241-6-BN-by-2030.html

PretaA. (2019, Feb 13). Platform Competition in Online Digital Market. SSRN. doi:10.2139/ssrn.3272839

Radianti, J., Majchrzak, T. A., Fromm, J., & Wohlgenannt, I. (2020, April). A systematic review of immersive virtual reality applications for higher education: Design elements, lessons learned, and research agenda. *Computers & Education, 147*, 103778. doi:10.1016/j.compedu.2019.103778

Rubenking, B., & Bracken, C. C. (2021, December). Binge watching and serial viewing: Comparing new media viewing habits in 2015 and 2020. *Addictive Behaviors Reports, 14*, 100356. Advance online publication. doi:10.1016/j.abrep.2021.100356 PMID:34124334

Ruether, T. (2023). *Free Ad-Supported Tv (Fast): Ultimate Guide For Advertisers*. Strategus. https://www.strategus.com/blog/free-ad-supported-tv-fast-advertising

Sabharwal, K. (2018, Jan 140-142). Amazon Vs Netflix: Who will win Indian battleground? *International Journal of Multidisciplinary Research and Development*. https://www.coursehero.com/file/58563852/5-2-20-726pdf/

Sanson, K. (2019, Jan 17). *Hulu, streaming, and the contemporary television ecosystem*. Sage. doi:10.1177/0163443718823144

Shalparni P Y, P. B. (2022). Impact of OTT on Entertainment Industry in India. *IJERT, 10*(11). doi:10.17577/IJERTCONV10IS11023

Sharma, K., & Mishra, D. P. (2023). An Empirical Study: Unveiling the Influence of Over-the-Top (OTT) Platforms on the Indian Film Industry. *Europian Chemical Bullitin, 12*(8), 7358–7380. doi:10.48047/ecb/2023.12.Si8.625

Shiana Aggarwal. (2022, July). *RISKS FACED BY OTT PLATFORMS.* GRM Institute. https://grm.institute/blog/research-study-on-risks-faced-by-ott-platforms

Shinde, R., & Dalvi, K. (2022, May). An Overview of Copyright Infringement in India And OTT Platform. *Multi-Disciplinary Journal, 1*(2), 1-4. http://210.212.169.38/xmlui/bitstream/handle/123456789/10183/An%20Overview%20of%20Copyright%20Infringement%20in%20India%20And%20OTT%20Platform-%20Rucha%20Shinde%2C%20Ketki%20Dalvi.pdf?sequence=1&isAllowed=y

Shon, M., Lee, D., & Kim, J. H. (2021, July). Are global over-the-top platforms the destroyers of ecosystems or the catalysts of innovation? *Telematics and Informatics, 60*, 101581. doi:10.1016/j.tele.2021.101581

Srivastava, K. (2022, Apr 29). *How Amazon is intensifying the OTT game in India.* E4M. https://www.exchange4media.com/digital-news/how-amazon-is-intensifying-the-ott-game-in-india-119975.html

Srivastava, U. K. (2016). *OTT SERVICES IN INDIA.* Delhi: TRAI. https://www.itu.int/en/ITU-T/Workshops-and-Seminars/bsg/201609/Documents/OTT%20in%20India.pdf

Statista. (2021). *OTT Video - Worldwide.* Statista. https://www.statista.com/outlook/amo/media/tv-video/ott-video/worldwide#revenue

Swarnima. (2023). *How OTT is changing streraming landscape?* SkyQuest. https://www.skyquestt.com/insights/how-ott-is-changing-the-streaming-landscape

Tiger, C. (2023, Oct 25). *Linear TV vs CTV vs OTT, Difference Explained in Detail.* LinkedIn. https://www.linkedin.com/pulse/linear-tv-vs-ctv-ott-difference-explained-detail-calm-tiger-b1d3f/?trk=organization_guest_main-feed-card_feed-article-content

TRAI. (2015). *Regulatory Framework for Over-the-top (OTT) services.* Mahanagar Doorsanchar Bhawan. New Delhi: TRAI, GOI. https://www.trai.gov.in/sites/default/files/OTT-CP-27032015.pdf

VMR. (2020). *Global Over-The-Top Market Size By Content Type (Voice over IP, Texts and Images, Videos, Music Streaming), By Deployment (On Cloud, On Premise), By Platform (Gaming Consoles, OTT Streaming Devices), By Geographic Scope And Forecast.* Verified Market Research. https://www.verifiedmarketresearch.com/product/over-the-top-market/?gclid=Cj0KCQjw3JanBhCPARIsAJpXTx5dSj8hoHFESrhj3zJaHTXqGLzPLGMxudLKx3LD5rBxb4kSRLAKTNYaAj3ZEALw_wcB

Winston, B. (2018). *Amazon Prime Video Uses AWS to Deliver Solid Streaming Experience to More Than 18 Million Football Fans.* AWS. https://aws.amazon.com: https://aws.amazon.com/solutions/case-studies/amazon-prime-video/

Zemoga. (2022). *OTT trends & future.* Zemoga. https://magnetglobal.org/getattachment/463ee095-e71c-4dc4-8415-4fa0f394dffd/ott_trends_and_future_predictions_zemoga.pdf?lang=en-US&ext=.pdf

Chapter 3
Users' Adoption of Over-the-Top (OTT) Streaming Platforms:
A Study With Special Reference to Kerala

T.S. Sujith
https://orcid.org/0000-0002-6089-1285
Amrita Vishwa Vidyapeetham, Kochi, India

ABSTRACT

The proliferation of smartphones, increasing internet penetration, and affordable data plans have played a crucial role in driving the growth of OTT platforms in India. The aims this study is to understand the users' adoption of OTT streaming platforms in Kerala using the UTAUT model as a theoretical framework. To achieve the research objectives the researcher used a descriptive and exploratory research design. The researcher developed a well-structured questionnaire and administered 180 OTT users in Kerala, collecting quantitative data on their usage patterns, preferences, and adoption factors. The researcher validate the UTAUT model along with impact of COVID-19 for measuring the users' adoption behaviour. The study concluded that the factors such as Performance expectancy, Effort expectancy, Social influence, Facilitating conditions, and COVID-19 influence the adoption of OTT video streaming platforms.

INTRODUCTION

The availability of high-speed internet connections, coupled with affordable data plans, has made OTT platforms accessible to a large segment of the Indian population. The advent of Over-the-Top (OTT) streaming platforms has revolutionized the entertainment industry, providing users with on-demand access to a vast array of media content. The expansion of 4G networks and the impending rollout of 5G technology expected to boost OTT adoption. Internet Penetration and Smartphone Usage, Variety of OTT Platforms, Content Diversity, Original Content and Exclusive Releases, Affordability and Flexible Pricing Models, Regional and Localized Content, Convenience and Flexibility, Integration with Smart TVs and Streaming Devices has contributed to the widespread adoption of OTT platforms in India, making them a dominant player in the entertainment landscape. This trend expected to continue as more users embrace digital platforms for their entertainment needs.

DOI: 10.4018/979-8-3693-0116-6.ch003

In recent years, these platforms have witnessed widespread adoption globally, including in the state of Kerala, known for its tech-savvy population and high literacy rates. Over-the-Top (OTT) streaming platforms refer to digital services that provide video content directly to users over the internet, bypassing traditional broadcast and cable television networks. Platforms like Netflix, Amazon Prime Video, Hot star, and others, provide on-demand access to a wide range of movies, TV shows, documentaries, and original content through internet-connected devices. These platforms enable users to consume content anytime, anywhere, on various devices such as smartphones, tablets, smart TVs, and gaming consoles. OTT platforms refer to digital content distribution services that deliver media content, such as movies, TV shows, and web series, directly to viewers via the internet, bypassing traditional cable or satellite providers. These platforms have gained immense popularity in Kerala due to their convenience, diverse content offerings, and accessibility on various devices, such as smartphones, tablets, and smart TVs.

Several Factors Contribute to The Increasing Popularity and Widespread Adoption of OTT Streaming Platforms by Users in Kerala

1. **Diverse Content Offerings:** One of the key drivers of OTT adoption in Kerala is the diverse range of content available on these platforms. With an extensive library of movies, TV shows, web series, documentaries, and regional content, OTT platforms cater to the varied preferences and interests of Kerala consumers. Local language content, especially Malayalam-language content, holds a special appeal, allowing viewers to connect with familiar stories and cultural nuances.
2. **Convenience and Flexibility:** OTT platforms offer unmatched convenience and flexibility to viewers in Kerala. Users can access their favourite content at any time and from any location, as long as they have an internet connection. The availability of these platforms on various devices, including smartphones, tablets, and smart TVs, further enhances accessibility and enables users to watch content on their terms.
3. **Cost-Effectiveness:** For many consumers in Kerala, OTT platforms offer a cost-effective alternative to traditional cable or satellite TV subscriptions. With affordable subscription plans and the option to choose from various pricing tiers, users can tailor their viewing experience to suit their budget and preferences. Additionally, the absence of advertisements in premium subscriptions is a significant draw for viewers seeking an uninterrupted and immersive viewing experience.
4. **Original Content and Exclusive Releases:** OTT platforms have become a hub for original content production, including web series and movies. The presence of exclusive releases and highly acclaimed originals attracts viewers to subscribe to these platforms, fostering customer loyalty and retention.
5. **High Internet Penetration:** Kerala boasts a high rate of internet penetration, making it an ideal market for OTT platforms. With a significant portion of the population having access to high-speed internet, streaming content seamlessly has become a reality for many consumers in the region.
6. **Time Flexibility:** Kerala, like any other state, has a diverse population with different schedules and lifestyles. OTT platforms allow users to watch content at their preferred time, enabling them to balance their work and personal commitments without missing their favourite shows and movies.
7. **Multi-Device Usage:** The prevalence of multiple internet-enabled devices in households further contributes to the adoption of OTT platforms. Users can seamlessly switch between devices, making it convenient to continue watching their favourite content from where they left off.

REVIEW OF LITERATURE

Kwon et al., (2020) examined the recommendation agent values influencing the search experience of OTT users and find the effects of decision satisfaction and continuous subscription of the users in Korea. Mainly study focused on agent variables such as match score accuracy, recommended content variety and thumbnail image appeal affect search experience variables such as perceived diagnosticity and perceived serendipity. The research model identified the specific value of recommendation agents enhancing subscribers' search experience, which in turn increases their decision satisfaction and subscription continuance. The study concluded that decision satisfaction increases intention to continue to subscribe to OTT services. **Bhullar & Chandigarh, (2020)** studied the perception of users' adoption towards online media platforms. The study identified seven factors that affect the user adoption of OTT media platform services. The study revealed that Customization, Content quality, perceived enjoyment, and user interface were the essential factors that affect the user adoption towards the Over The Top (OTT) media platform. The other factors such as perceived ease of use, perceived usefulness, and compatibility have no significant association with the adoption among the users towards OTT media platform in Chandigarh. **Ripal Madhani & Vidya Nakhate, (2020)** explored the factors affecting viewers to shift from Traditional Television channels to OTT video platforms in Maharashtra. The study identified that the factors such as convenience, availability of affordable data connectivity, penetration of smartphones, availability of affordable and even free access to OTT video platforms, the sheer breadth of content, and quality of content are the key factors affecting audience to shift towards the OTT Video Platforms. Nevertheless, traditional television channels will not be entirely replaced by OTT Video platforms. Traditional Television channels unmoving have a chink of viewers loyal to it, with some adjustment in the quality of content and strategies they can still attract consumers and survive. **Tran et al., (2020)** investigated the factors influence on continuance using intention OTT apps among the young generation. The study revealed that satisfaction, habit, emotional trust, perceived usefulness directly influence using intention. The factors such as perceived usefulness and perceived enjoyment indirectly affected the using intention of OTT apps among the generation. The study also points out that the mediation effects of satisfaction were found between perceived usefulness, perceived enjoyment, socialites, and intention to use.

Lee et al., (2018) examined the factors, which consumers consider for choosing cable TV and online streaming options. The researcher explored the seven factors ease of use, additional purchases, media options, social trends, available options, cost, and customer service. The study pointed that additional purchase, social trend (negative), cost, and customer service factors were statistically significant in the case of cable TV and two factors such as social trend and available options were significant in the case of online streaming. **Ota et al., (2020)** analysed the preference of customers about OTT video platform with special reference to Jamshedpur market during COVID pandemic. The researchers selected NETFLIX and 'HOTSTAR' two major players in the Indian market for measuring customer preference. The study observed that hot star is the highly preferred OTT service compared to Netflix. Live streaming of cricket and IPL garnered a massive range of connectivity with its contents and local touch. Netflix had great support from the student community because of original content and foreign language web series, along with movies, but in terms of overall performance and preference, Hot star has advanced marginally. **Udoakpan & Tengeh, (2020)** attempted to study the impact of OTT television service on Pay-Television subscription service in South African customers. The finding of the study pointed that OTT TV services are complementary services to Pay-TV services. Low-income group customers are using Free/paid mobile applications to consume TV content. The researchers suggested that the pay-tv operators should focus on new and continuous innovations for attracting and retaining customers. The study also pointed out that the same service providers implement an option for those who prefer to consume content online, to sign in without buying a setup box and paying for the installation. Such options would result in a reduction in subscription fees, which would benefit consumers in terms of costs and benefits for pay-tv operators in terms of acquiring and retaining customers.

Madnani et al., (2020) investigated the impact of COVID-19 on increasing the viewership of Over-The-Top media platforms in India and change in behaviour of People before and during lockdown using visual representation. The study revealed that lockdown has diverted the people from the traditional way of watching to OTT platforms. People who like work from home are using OTT platforms more. In addition, the satisfaction level of the customers is very high compared to television. The average hours spent on OTT have increased from 0-2 to 2-5 hours and the customers are willing to spend Rs.100-300 per month for OTT platforms. The study suggested that the OTT platform should reduce its subscription rate and also provide fresh content and restore HD quality for retaining the customers.

Sundaravel & Elangovan, (2020) explored the future of OTT service in India. The study identified major OTT players in the Indian market. Researchers concluded that there was an increasing trend for adopting OTT video platforms in India. At the same time as Indian streaming services like Hot star and Jio Cinema have gained a stronger foothold, global players like Netflix and Amazon Prime have progressively full-fledged their market share in India. **Jose, (2020)** identified the factors affecting the changing behaviour of customers from traditional TV to OTT platforms. The user-friendliness and content richness are the main study concluded that the majority of them depends on television, but most parts of the younger generation in the middle class and upper class society are moving to OTT platforms. **Koo, (2018)** analysed the factors affecting streamers' loyalty to live streaming platforms. The researcher identified mainly two factors such as satisfaction and trust leads to streamers loyalty. Satisfaction was found the most vital variable in explaining loyalty. The trust factor is ineffective to explain loyalty directly, it affects loyalty through satisfaction. **Chang & Chang, (2020)** studied the factors influencing continuance usage of OTT service in Taiwan. The study developed through four variables such as perceived interactivity, perceived value, satisfaction, and continuance usage. The study confirmed that the perceived platform interactivity is the most critical indicator of OTT use. The study also revealed that the perceived interactivity and perceived value lead to satisfaction and continuance usage of OTT services.

Singh et al., (2020) founded the antecedents influencing the continued use of live streaming services in India. The study found six factors as Convenience Value, Monetary Value, Social Value, Emotional Value, Performance Expectancy, and Effort Expectancy are leads to continued intention, and continued intention leads to perceived enjoyment, perceived risk, and addition to heavy viewing. The study revealed that convenience has the highest influence on the viewer's continued intention followed by perceived enjoyment. The study also suggested that the managers of live-streaming apps should promote their apps among consumers by highlighting various consumption values, attractiveness, and user personal experience. **Dasgupta & Grover, (2019)** attempted to study the adoption factors of OTT video service among millennial consumers. The researcher defined the Millennial consumers are those having the age group of 18-30 and dynamic, post-graduate individuals. The study found that Convenience, mobility, content, and cost are the major adopting factors of OTT video service and convenience is the most influencing factor. **Kumari, (2020)** studied the consumption and behavioural pattern of OTT consumers in India and identified the factors affecting the success of the OTT platforms in India. The study revealed that the majority of the respondents are switching their viewing habits from TV to OTT. The introduction of smartphones is one of the important devices that affect the respondent's viewing behaviour. The affordable rate of the internet is one of the technological reasons for the growth of OTT. Content and quality of service, cost, and ease of use, convenience, and user customization are the important factors that lead to the success of the OTT platform in India. The study concluded that the two factors like lack of technological awareness and content openness are stopping the viewers from shifting to OTT platforms. **Sujata et al., (2015)** studied the impact of the Over the Top (OTT) service on telecom service providers in India and identified factors driving the consumer preference towards OTT services like WhatsApp skype and Netflix etc. There are eight factors such as cost, convenience, features, social propensity, content availability, smartphone and mobile internet penetration, user experience, net neutrality are affecting the adoption of OTT service. The study concluded that there is an influence on these eight factors on operators' voice, messaging, and data services.

Nijhawan & Surbhi Dahiya, (2020) examined the effect of the COVID-19 pandemic on the adoption of the OTT video platform in India. The researcher observed that the content availability in OTT platforms, ad-free, user-friendly, trendy, and convenience are the main reason for increasing the adoption of OTT. The study concluded that the majority of the respondents (75%) are preferred the OTT platform and 20% of the respondents like both the traditional way of streaming and OTT media platforms. **Patel et al., (2020)** analysed the impact of COVID-19 national lockdown and increase in the viewership of OTT platform in India and examined the attitude of people towards the cinema halls in watching experience. The researcher found that increasing the usage of smartphones, the cost of the internet, an international collaboration between media moguls and the digital quality of media, and anytime access are the reasons behind the progression of OTT video platforms in India. The study also showed that viewers have the same mind-set about the future of the movie theatre. The study suggested that movie theatre owners should think of more amenities and offerings to the customers and that should be must be cost-effective to the people. **Chen, (2019)** examined the competition between the traditional television and OTT platforms in Taiwan. The study follows niche analysis through primary data from 620 respondents. The research found that dimensions such as information, relaxation, amusement, social, finance, ease of use and convenience are highly influenced people over traditional TV. The researcher concluded that OTT TV and traditional TV share are amusement and easy to use with a high level of similarity and OTT TV's competitive dominance surpasses traditional TV at all the seven dimensions. **Reshma & Chaithra, (2020)** examined the impact of OTT video streaming apps. On college students academic and personal life. The study found that there is a significant of OTT on student's personal as well as academic life. Moreover, the majority of the teenagers and students are aware of the OTT platform and amazon prime is the most preferred OTT platform among the students because the app. provides a variety of facilities compared to other similar application. The study concluded that the students prefer more international shows compared to national shows.

Objectives of the study:

- To understand the users' adoption of OTT streaming platforms in Kerala using the Unified Theory of Acceptance and Use of Technology (UTAUT) model.
- To measure the impact of OTT streaming platforms adoption on User Satisfaction.

RESEARCH METHODOLOGY

The researcher adopted a descriptive research design to measure the users' adoption and satisfaction of OTT streaming platforms in Kerala. A structured questionnaire was developed based on the Unified Theory of Acceptance and Use of Technology (UTAUT) model to assess the factors influencing users' adoption of OTT platforms. The questionnaire included items related to performance expectancy, effort expectancy, social influence, facilitating conditions, COVID-19 and behavioural intention to use (Adoption) OTT platforms. The questionnaire also included a user satisfaction scale to measure the impact of OTT platform adoption on user satisfaction. This scale encompassed aspects such as content quality, platform reliability, ease of navigation, and overall user experience. The researcher selected the 180 sample respondents through a purposive sampling technique, targeting respondents from Thrissur district, Kerala. Descriptive analysis were performed to summarize the demographic characteristics of the respondents from Thrissur District. The data related to the UTAUT model constructs (performance expectancy, effort expectancy, social influence, facilitating conditions) with COVID-19 were subjected to regression analysis to understand the factors influencing users' adoption of OTT platforms in Kerala.

RESEARCH MODEL

Figure 1. Research model

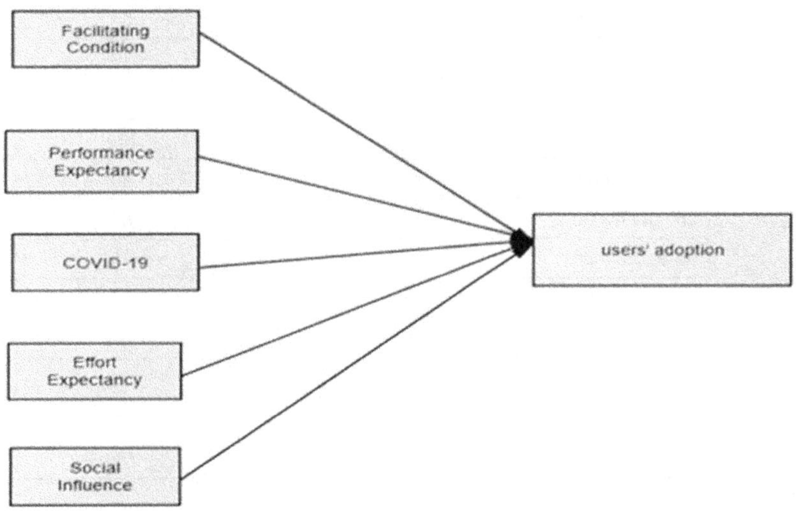

ANALYSIS AND DISCUSSION

This socio-demographic profile provides an overview of the characteristics of the respondents in terms of age, marital status, gender, education, occupation, income, and area of residence. Analysing the socio-demographic profile can help researchers understand the sample composition and potential variations in responses based on these demographic factors. The majority of respondents (47.2%) fall within the age group of 20 to 35 years age group. Younger respondents below the age

Table 1. Socio-demographic profile of the respondent

Variable	Description	Frequency	Percentage
Age	Less than 20	17	9.4%
	20-35	85	47.2%
	36-50	38	21.1%
	Above 50	40	22.2%
Total		***180***	***100%***
Marital Status	Single	64	35.6%
	Married	116	64.4%
Total		***180***	***100%***
Gender	Male	117	65.0%
	Female	63	35.0%
Total		***180***	***100%***
Educational qualification	SSLC	63	35.0%
	+2	17	9.4%
	Graduation	62	34.4%
	Post-graduation	38	21.1%
Total		***180***	***100%***
Occupation	Govt. Sector	32	17.8%
	Private Sector	85	47.2%
	Business	40	22.2%
	Others	23	12.8%
Total		***180***	***100%***
Income	Below 20,000	40	22.2%
	20,001-30,000	60	33.3%
	30,001-40,000	48	26.7%
	Above 40000	32	17.8%
Total		***180***	***100%***
Area of Residence	Rural	77	42.8
	Urban	103	57.2
Total		***180***	***100***

(Source: primary data)

of 20 and those in the age group of 36 to 50 represent 9.4% and 21.1% of the sample respondents, respectively. The majority (64.4%) of the respondents are Married. 35.0% have completed SSLC, Graduates and post-graduates account for 34.4% and 21.1% of the sample respondents, respectively. 47.2% of the respondents employed in private field, Government sector employees represent only 17.8%. 33.3% of the respondents falls in the income range of 20,001 to 30,000. The majority of respondents (57.2%) reside in urban areas.

Confirmatory Factor Analysis (CFA)

Confirmatory Factor Analysis (CFA) is a statistical technique used to verify the factor structure of a set of observed variables. The objective of CFA is to assess how well the observed variables align with the proposed latent factors and to evaluate the overall fit of the model.

The above figure represent the confirmatory factor analysis of research model of the study. The confirmatory factor analysis of performance expectancy consist of three items or observed variables. Each of the items symbolized is labelled as PE1 to PE3. The result showed that all the three items of performance expectancy have been retained because the factor loadings are above 0.40. The other factor COVID-19 consist of three items. Each of the items symbolized is labelled as COVID1 to COVID 3. The result showed that all the three items of COVID -19 have been retained because the factor loadings are above 0.40. The factor social influence consist of three observed variables and all the three items of social influence have been retained because the factor loadings are above 0.40. The other factor facilitating condition consist of three items and all the three items of facilitating condition have been retained because the factor loadings are above 0.40. The three items of effort expectancy have been retained because the factor loadings are above 0.40. Hence, all the items of measurement model are positive and significant and it ensure the unidimensionality of the items.

From the above table, it is clear that the Goodness of Fit Index (GFI) value (0.94) and Adjusted Goodness of Fit Index (AGFI) value (0.93) is greater than 0.9 which represents it is a good fit. The calculated Normed Fit Index (NFI) value (0.98) and Comparative Fit Index (CFI) value (0.96) indicates that it is a

Figure 2. C FA for research model

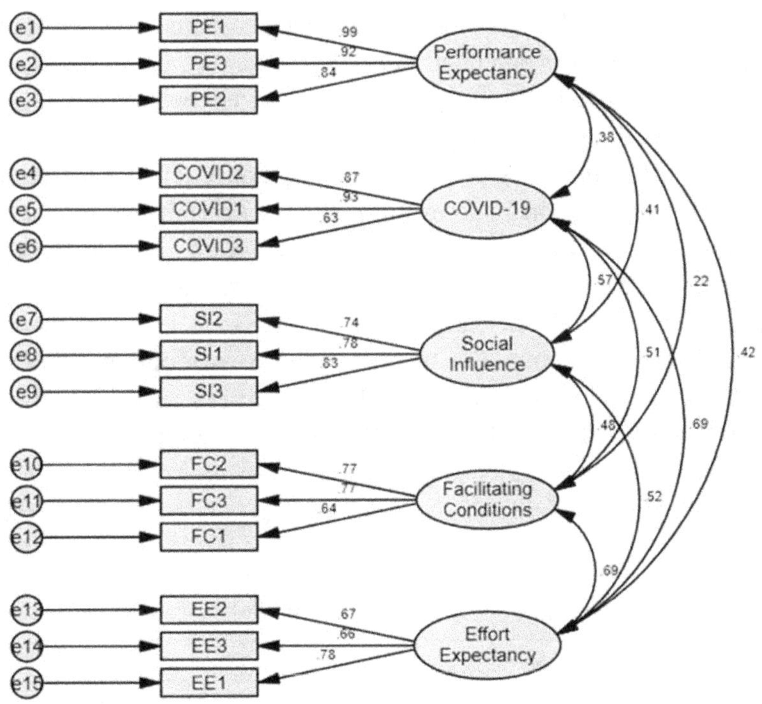

Table 2. Results of goodness of fit

Fit Indices	CMIN/DF	GFI	AGFI	NFI	CFI	RMR	RMSEA	TLI
Model Value	2.076	0.94	0.93	0.98	0.96	0.06	0.02	0.99
Acceptable Value	≤ 3	> 0.9	> 0.9	> 0.9	>0.95	≤0.10	< 0.06	>0.95

(Source: Computed from Primary Data)

perfect fit, the Root Mean square Residuals (RMR) is 0.06, and Root Mean Square Error of Approximation (RMSEA) value is 0.02 which is less than 0.06 which indicated it is perfectly fit.

Regression Analysis

To understand users' adoption of OTT (Over-The-Top) streaming platforms in Kerala using the UTAUT (Unified Theory of Acceptance and Use of Technology) model along with one variable COVID-19, the researcher conducted multiple regression analysis. In this analysis, the researcher used performance expectancy, effort expectancy, social influence, facilitating conditions, and COVID-19 as independent variables and users' adoption as the dependent variable in the first regression model.

R represents the correlation between the predicted values and the actual values of the dependent variable (users' adoption). In this case, the R value is 0.981, which indicates a strong positive relationship between the predictors and the dependent variable. R-square value indicates the proportion of variance in the dependent variable explained by the predictors included in the model. Here, the R-square value is 0.963, which means that approximately 96.3% of the variance in the dependent variable is explained by the predictors (Performance expectancy, Effort expectancy, Social influence, Facilitating conditions, and COVID-19) included in the model. The regression model explains a significant amount of variance in the dependent variable. The regression equation is

Y= .0689+ 0.154 Performance expectancy+ 0.199 Effort expectancy+ 0.243 Social influence+ 0.257 Facilitating conditions+ 0.203 COVID-19

To study the impact of OTT streaming platforms adoption on User Satisfaction the researcher used simple regression. Simple regression helps to examine the relationship between two variables: one independent variable (in this case, OTT streaming platforms adoption) and one dependent variable (user satisfaction). The regression analysis help to understand the direction and strength of the relationship between these variables. Therefore, the research hypothesis is

H_0: There is no significant impact of OTT streaming platforms adoption on user satisfaction.

The results suggest that there is a strong positive relationship between the adoption of OTT streaming platforms and user satisfaction. The correlation coefficient (R) is a measure of the strength and direc-

Table 3. Model summary

Model	R	R Square	Adjusted R Square	Std. Error of the Estimate
1	.981[a]	0.963	0.962	0.076
a. Predictors: (Constant), Performance expectancy, Effort expectancy, Social influence, Facilitating conditions, COVID-19				

(Source: Computed from Primary Data)

Table 4. Model summary

Model	R	R Square	Adjusted R Square	Std. Error of the Estimate
1	.825[a]	.681	.679	.219
a. Predictors: (Constant), OTT streaming platforms adoption				

(Source: Computed from Primary Data)

tion of the linear relationship between the independent variable (OTT streaming platforms adoption) and the dependent variable (User Satisfaction). In this case, the value of R is 0.825, which indicates a strong positive correlation between OTT streaming platforms adoption and user satisfaction. The coefficient of determination (R Square) represents the proportion of variance in the dependent variable (User Satisfaction) that explained by the independent variable (OTT streaming platforms adoption). The R Square value of 0.681 means that approximately 68.1% of the variance in user satisfaction explained by the adoption of OTT streaming platforms.

CONCLUSION

The majority of respondents fall within the age group of 20 to 35 years, which suggests that this age group might be more familiar with and open to adopting OTT streaming platforms. They are likely to be more tech-savvy and comfortable using digital entertainment platforms. Higher educational attainment might correlate with higher digital literacy and more openness to adopting new technologies, including OTT streaming platforms. The majority of respondents work in the private sector, which may imply that they have access to better internet connectivity and are more likely to use OTT platforms for entertainment during their leisure time. The income distribution shows that a significant portion of respondents falls in the mid-range income category (20,001 to 40,000). This suggests that OTT streaming platforms are popular among middle-income individuals in Kerala. The regression analysis conducted to understand users' adoption of OTT streaming platforms the result indicate that Performance expectancy, Effort expectancy, Social influence, Facilitating conditions, and COVID-19 are all positively associated with users' adoption, signifying that as these factors increase, the likelihood of adoption also increases. The study also revealed a strong positive relationship between the adoption of OTT streaming platforms and user satisfaction. 68.1% of the variance in user satisfaction attributed to the adoption of OTT streaming platforms. This means that the adoption of these platforms explains a significant portion of the variability in user satisfaction levels.

LIMITATIONS AND SCOPE FOR FURTHER RESEARCH

The sample used for studying users' adoption of OTT streaming platforms in Kerala may not fully represent the diversity of the population that might affect the generalizability of the findings. To enhance the generalizability of the findings, future research can aim to use larger and more diverse samples that had better represent the entire population of OTT users in Kerala. Here the researcher used UTAUT model by adding one new variable COVID-19, other factors not included in the UTAUT model, such as internet connectivity, content availability, pricing, and competing media platforms, could influence users' adoption of OTT streaming platforms. Researchers can explore potential mediating and moderating effects of variables like internet connectivity, content availability, pricing, and competing media platforms on the relationships between UTAUT constructs and OTT adoption.

REFERENCES

Bhullar, A., & Chandigarh, R. (2020). Key Factors Influencing Users ' Adoption Towards OTT Media Platform : An Empirical Analysis. *International Journal of Advanced Science and Technology*, *29*(11), 942–956.

Chang, P.-C., & Chang, H.-Y. (2020). Exploring the Factors Influencing Continuance Usage of Over- the-Top Services : The Interactivity, Consumption Value. *International Journal of Technology and Human Interaction*, *16*(4), 118–138. doi:10.4018/IJTHI.2020100108

Chen, Y. K. (2019). Competitions between OTT TV platforms and traditional television in Taiwan : A Niche analysis. *Telecommunications Policy*, *43*(9), 101793. doi:10.1016/j.telpol.2018.10.006

Choi, C. H., & You, Y. Y. (2017). The study on the comparative analysis of EFA and CFA. *Journal of Digital Convergence*, *15*(10), 103–111.

Dasgupta, S., & Grover, P.DASGUPTA. (2019). Understanding Adoption Factors of Over-the-Top Video Services Among Millennial Consumers. *International Journal of Computer Engineering & Technology*, *10*(1), 61–71. doi:10.34218/IJCET.10.1.2019.008

Hamilton, A. J. S. (1988). Evidence for biasing in the CfA survey. *Astrophysical Journal*, *331*.

Jose, R. J. (2020). Factors influencing the shift from traditional TV to OTT platforms in India. *International Journal of Advanced Science and Technology*, *29*(7), 4044–4051.

Kim, J., Kim, S., & Nam, C. (2015). Telematics and Informatics Competitive dynamics in the Korean video platform market : Traditional pay TV platforms vs. OTT platforms. *Telematics and Informatics*. Advance online publication. doi:10.1016/j.tele.2015.06.014

Koo, H. (2018). Factors affecting streamers' loyalty to live streaming platforms. *22nd Biennial Conference of the International Telecommunications Society (ITS): "Beyond the Boundaries: Challenges for Business, Policy and Society*.

Kumari, T. (2020). A Study on Growth of Over the Top (OTT) Video Services in India. *International Journal of Latest Research in Humanities and Social Science*, *03*(09), 68–73.

Kwon, Y., Park, J., & Son, J. (2020). *Accurately or accidentally ? Recommendation agent and search experience in over-the-top (OTT) services*. Emerald. doi:10.1108/INTR-03-2020-0127

Lee, C. C., Nagpal, P., Ruane, S. G., & Lim Hyoun Sook. (2018). Communications of the IIMA Factors Affecting Online Streaming Subscriptions SUBSCRIPTIONS. *Communications of the IIMA*, *16*(1).

Madhani, R., & Nakhate, V. (2020). Comparative Study Of Viewers ' Behaviour Over Traditional Television Channels And Over Ott Video Platforms In Maharashtra. *International Journal of Advanced Science and Technology*, *29*(12), 1046–1057.

Madnani, D., Fernandes, S. F., & Madnani, N. (2020). Analysing the impact of COVID-19 on over-the-top media platforms in India. *International Journal of Pervasive Computing and Communications*, *16*(5), 457–475. doi:10.1108/IJPCC-07-2020-0083

Marsh, H. W., Muthén, B., Asparouhov, T., Lüdtke, O., Robitzsch, A., Morin, A. J., & Trautwein, U. (2009). Exploratory structural equation modeling, integrating CFA and EFA: Application to students' evaluations of university teaching. *Structural Equation Modeling*, *16*(3), 439–476. doi:10.1080/10705510903008220

Nijhawan, G. S., & Dahiya, S. (2020). ROLE OF COVID AS A CATALYST IN INCREASING ADOPTION OF OTTS IN INDIA : A STUDY OF EVOLVING CONSUMER CONSUMPTION PATTERNS. *Journal of Content. Community & Communication*, *12*, 298–311. doi:10.31620/JCCC.12.20/28

Ota, R., Ray, S. S., & Chandra, A. (2020). *An analysis of customer preference towards OTT Platform during a pandemic : A special reference to Jamshedpur Market. IX*(Viii), 192–202.

Patel, M. K., Khadia, R., & Awasya, G. (2020). A Study : OTT Viewership in " Lockdown " and Viewer ' s Dynamic Watching Experience. *International Journal on Transformations of Media. Journalism & Mass Communication*, *5*(2), 10–22.

Reshma, & Chaithra. (2020). Proliferation of OTT apps in India: an empirical study of OTT apps and its impact on college students. *International Journal of Research and Analytical Reviews (IJRAR), 7*(1), 427–435.

Singh, S., Singh, N., Kalinić, Z., & Liébana-cabanillas, F. J. (2020). Assessing determinants influencing continued use of live streaming services: An extended perceived value theory of streaming addiction. *Expert Systems with Applications*, *114241*. doi:10.1016/j.eswa.2020.114241

Sujata, J., Sohag, S., Tanu, D., Chintan, D., Shubham, P., & Sumit, G. (2015). Impact of Over the Top (OTT) Services on Telecom Service Providers. *Indian Journal of Science and Technology*, *8*(February), 145–160. doi:10.17485/ijst/2015/v8iS4/62238

Sujith, T. S., & Jisha, M. K. (2017). Tourism in India: Opportunities and Challenges. *Imperial Journal of Interdisciplinary Research*, *3*(10), 201–204.

Sujith, T. S., & Julie, C. D. (2018). Environmental accounting: A conceptual study. *IJAR*, *4*(12), 147–149.

Sujith, T. S., & Sumathy, M. (2021). Anticidence of Buying Behaviour of Parents Towards Educational Mobile Applications. *SJCC Management Research Review*, 1-12.

Sumathy, M., & TS, S. (2018). A Comparative Study on Perception of Customers towards Service Quality of Canara and ICICI Bank. *RESEARCH REVIEW International Journal of Multidisciplinary, Special Issue*, 187-190.

Sumathy, M., & Sujith, T. S. (2018). Effect of Brand on Customer Loyalty among SBI Banking Customers. *International Journal of Scientific and Engineering Research*, *6*(9), 2015–2018.

Sundaravel, E., & Elangovan, N. (2020). *Emergence and future of Over-the-top (OTT) video services in India : an analytical research. 08*(02), 489–499.

Tran, T., Tran, Q., & Le, H. (2020). An Empirical Study on Continuance Using Intention of OTT Apps with Young Generation. *Springer Nature Singapore Pte Ltd., 3*, 219–229. doi:10.1007/978-981-32-9244-4_31

TS, S., & Sumathy, M. (2021). User Perception Towards OTT Video Streaming Platforms in Kerala (With Special Reference to Thrissur). *Analytical Commerce and Economics, 2*(4), 27–32.

TS, S., & Sumathy, M. (2021). Millennial Satisfaction on Amazon Prime Video Platform with Special Reference to Thrissur District. *Vidyabharati International Interdisciplinary Research Journal*, 3153-3157.

TS, S., & Sumathy, M. (2021). User Perception Towards OTT Video Streaming Platforms in Kerala (With Special Reference to Thrissur). *Analytical Commerce and Economics, 2*(4), 27–32.

TS, S., & Sumathy, M. (2022). Application of Technology Acceptance Model (TAM) on Adoption of Food Delivering Applications (Apps.) among University students in Tamil Nadu. *RVIM Journal of Management Research, 22*.

TS, S., & Sumathy, M. P, S., & K, MN. (2022). Sustainability of over the top (OTT) video platforms in india: Examining the TAM model on the adoption of OTT video streaming platform among millennial consumers. *International Journal of Biology, Pharmacy and Allied Sciences, 11*(1), 628–640.

Udoakpan, N., & Tengeh, R. K. (2020). The Impact of Over-the-Top Television Services on Pay-Television Subscription Services in South Africa. *Journal of Open Innovation, 6*(4), 139. doi:10.3390/joitmc6040139

Chapter 4
Shifting Discourse of Digital Entertainment in COVID-19:
Investigating Revolutionary Consumeristic Strategies of OTT Platforms

C. Suganya
Vellore Institute of Technology, India

M. Vijayakumar
https://orcid.org/0000-0002-1079-5383
Vellore Institute of Technology, India

ABSTRACT

The advancement in Internet technology tremendously improves the quality of human lives, especially during and post Covid-19. Covid-19 has challenged all aspects of lives around the globe, and people avail everything by being at home, as the way consume media and entertainment has changed. The adversity of the pandemic impedes people in the four walls settings, propelling the OTT medium to reach rocket profit for its original and dynamic content, unlimited access and round-the-clock (24/7) service. The demand for quality content compels OTT platforms to devise novel strategies to attract consumers' demands in the competitive entertainment industry. This chapter investigates the revolution of OTT in the media and entertainment industry, its diverse contents, viewers' consumption patterns, freemium plans and revenue, the growth of OTT with the effect of Covid-19, and its comparison with conventional cinema to understand whether the OTT platforms supersede the most popular conventional medium of entertainment i.e., cinema theatre.

INTRODUCTION

Our globe is digitally transforming from domestic to business at a rapid pace and has transformed the life of everyone and everything more convenient and comfortable. The internet has shifted communication to the digital realm by adopting technical breakthroughs like smartphones, laptops, and smart TVs. The medium of entertainment has entirely changed with the digital advancements and Covid-19 has impacted

DOI: 10.4018/979-8-3693-0116-6.ch004

the conventional medium of entertainment such as televisions and cinema theatres. Though televisions are streaming diverse content, over-the-top (OTT) competes with television, at a much faster pace during and post covid globally. The advent of many private channels, HD channels and the internet results in 1.6 billion OTT subscribers in the world in 2023 which is expected to reach 1.8 billion by the end of 2023 (Pennington, 2023). People who were hesitant for subscriptions are attracted or forced to subscribe to Netflix, Disney+ and Amazon Prime Video in surplus numbers during the Covid-19 lockdown. The global pandemic and work from home (WFH) resulted in loneliness and depression and people started binge-watching to get rid of it. Warner Bros. Discovery reported, 1.6 million users in Q1, 2022 surged to 94.9 million active sign-ups in Q3, 2022, to reach more than 130 million by 2025 (Forristal, 2023). The number of Disney+ subscribers also increased to 164.2 million, and the number of Apple TV+ paid members also increased (Pennington, 2023). The content across genres and needs is the ultimate key for lifetime subscribers, and "content services who want to acquire and keep subscribers every month, with low churn, must provide more than one kind of content, and/or offer more than one type of service" (Pennington, 2023).

Digital media offers ample opportunities for individuals to choose, customize and comprehend media, and India holds the second-highest population of internet users around the globe. Covid-19 has accelerated the digital transformation globally, and forced business, education, healthcare, news, sports, entertainment, etc., into digital platforms (Hassani, et.al., 2021). The unprecedented lockdown forces people to share their screen time together, thus relying on one home device (TV) minimizes the choice of individuals. OTT comes as a redeemer in the media and entertainment industry for consumers (against conventional media without cables and satellites) with innovative and engaging content, easy access to multiple devices, unrestricted location streaming and round-the-clock service (Patnaik et.al, 2021). Though OTT platforms emerged in 1997 with Netflix in America, it focuses on the most populated country like India for its success, and 80% of the subscriptions have surged during the Covid-19 lockdown. According to the Statista report 2023, the OTT revenue is expected to reach $294 billion in 2023 and exceed $397 billion with 4.22 billion users by 2027 (Statista, 2023). Netflix and Amazon Prime Video are the giants in the OTT market among the other OTT platforms like Disney+, Hulu, ESPN+, Zee5, HBO, YouTube, Aha and others (Singh & Singh, 2022). Providing all categories including education, professional, business, sports, health, spiritual and entertainment drives phenomenal growth, thus people adopt OTT media for its convenience, 24*7 services, cost-effectiveness, content quality, easy access to internet, content recommendation based on customers and AI's personalization based on individuals' choice. Though humans are social organisms, OTT strategizes to retain customers by streaming original content, and in recent days many movies of big stars are lined up for OTT release to reach the audience straight. Thus, it is a great challenge for the film industry to go for theatrical release. With this background, the introduction chapter traces the drastic changes in the media and entertainment industry with the effect of Covid-19 and the emergence and rise of OTT platforms globally. A few most popular OTT platforms in India and their content diversity is traced in the next chapter. The third chapter comprehends the strategies of OTT platforms 'survival of the fittest' to retain their position in the media and entertainment industry. The following chapter analyses whether OTT replaces the conventional medium of media such as TV and cinema theatre. The concluding remarks comprehend the consumers' choice of platforms in the media and entertainment industry with technological advancements.

LITERATURE REVIEW

To assess the consumers' choice of OTT platforms in India, a study by Bihade and Kumar (2023) found that YouTube is leading among Netflix and Amazon Prime Video, yet the OTT platforms are struggling to replace traditional TV consumers due to internet access. Young adults spend more than 5 hours a day during the pandemic on OTT platforms and they are extremely satisfied with the OTT content. OTT platforms offer high-quality video and audio at flexible timings for all ages, by serving educational content for kids, adults by offering entertainment and for the elderly by offering spiritual content (Parihar & Kant, 2021). Gender and age have a significant influence on OTT platforms' success and it is measured by Gupta (2021) that young adults between 10-29 ages prefer to watch web series on OTT platforms, while elders above 40 years prefer to watch TV series, and subscribers from urban prefer more web series as they have high-speed internet and the preference relies on the internet significantly. The respondents accepted that OTT platforms influence the habit of watching TV and cinema significantly and access through smartphones increases the subscribers for OTT platforms. The freshness in OTT content is appealing to youngsters whereas TV content has been same for the two decades (Kumar, 2020). Customization in content is analyzed by Pajkovic, the recommendation system is the key feature for influencing content choosing, thus the consumption pattern is tracked by algorithms for sustainability in the competitive OTT market (Pajkovic, 2022). The covid-19 escalated the use of digital platforms and the consumption of media changed drastically; thus, the digital platforms changed their subscription plans and content according to the demand of the customers and market (Gupta & Singharia, 2021). A study by Haritha and Joesph (2021) among 100 respondents to find the factors that attract consumers to OTT platforms found that the quality of content and the affordable price of accessing the content at their convenience at any time are a major part of the success of the digital platforms.

Covid-19 has changed the pattern of consuming media and entertainment, and people adopted the new pattern of OTT and found one subscription for all family members on multiple devices with different types of content (Bhattachharyya et.al, 2020). Kala's study on the impact of popular OTT platforms on Indian adults scrutinized that youngsters choose to remain indoors and experience different cultures across countries through binge-watching which is overtaking the conventional cinema experience. Though youngsters are aware of different cultures, OTT platforms inflict their minds with uncensored adult content, which becomes great for Indian culture (Kala, 2022). Due to cost-effectiveness, people prefer to watch movies on OTT platforms, money spent for a single movie with family is equal to the monthly or annual plan subscriptions, where all the family members can get access and watch at their convenience (Robert et.al, 2022). Dutta (2021) claimed that virtual reality is our reality now and people are hooked on their screens more than ever during the pandemic. The cultural warfare in the content is cultural policing in a country like India which has diverse faiths, languages and cultures. OTT platforms are successful in the market by offering a variety of content and attractive subscription plans to satisfy the customers, thus the customers frequently switch to different platforms and multiple subscriptions (Mohan & Jadhav, 2022). OTT platforms are struggling to establish in the entertainment industry initially, as conventional TV medium has 70-80 million Indian audiences. However, OTT platforms have grown intensely within the first three months of the lockdown. Covid-19 has changed lifestyles and the new normal offers flexible schedules through work from home. The tea time break in the office is replaced with an episode of a web series (Sontakke, 2021).

OTT: A New Cinema for Young Adults

Though the living room TV concept is predominant in India, it is superseded by mobile phones, in which 85% of India's internet is driven. OTT has emerged as the 'new television' in India and consumption through mobile phones swift the subscribers expeditiously (Parmar & Pandit, 2021). The Digital India Mission plays a significant role in digitalization and provides high-speed internet to rural areas of India which accelerates the use of smartphones. The introduction of 5G is a game changer in the Indian OTT industry, as India is the third largest 5G smartphone market globally with 30 million users from just 3 million in 2020. Indians spend an average of 5 hours on smartphones and streaming is an integral part of millions of users, including urban and rural India. The affordability and availability of smartphones resulted in the adoption of OTT platforms and the consumption of online video reached 6.1 trillion minutes from Jan 2022 to March 2023. The rise in OTT platforms has revolutionized the entertainment industry globally, and it has emerged as a transformative force in the Indian entertainment industry. The proliferation of smartphones, affordable subscription plans, high-speed internet connectivity, individual gadgets (laptops, tablets and smartphones), diverse content, privatization and personalization lead the OTT platforms to experience exponential growth in the entertainment industry. The OTT platforms available based on content through digital platforms such as, Netflix, Hotstar, SonyLIV, Amazon Prime, Voot, Zee5, Jio Cinema etc., are running a race in the Indian OTT market. The personalization and privatization of content and the medium (mobile phones, smart TV, Laptops) have led to this revolution in OTT platforms, which is lacking in television. The traditional method of going to cinemas is fading immensely after Covid-19 and people are enjoying comfortably sitting at their cozy places (home) with families and friends. Thus, the entertainment industry shifted from theatres to OTT to get audiences from smaller cities and towns. Even after the new normal, the top stars prefer direct OTT releases specifically in Bollywood, Shahrukh Khan and Deepika Padukone's Pathaan (2023) and Shahid Kapoor's Farzi (2023) were released on Amazon Prime. The future entertainment sector relies on OTT platforms as the world becomes individual-centric and personalized.

Effects of OTT Content in India: Changing Perspective of Thoughts

Modern technologies with the internet are mostly consumed by the young adults of today's world and India ranks the highest in the most populated country with 808 million young adults (66% of the overall population) (Chukwuemeka, 2023). Youngsters are found social media addicts and the first Netflix-addicted person found in Bangalore. Thus, the media and entertainment industry targets India as its best marketplace by providing content that attracts young adults, whereas the conventional medium of TV and cinema has censorship issues. Youngsters are easily attracted to the culture that is shown in web series and social media which has a great impact in shaping and molding the behaviors and characters. Web series are the most watched content by youths on OTT platforms, and an Indian youth spends 6-8 hours in a day watching web series which exceeds the time in their classrooms (Koravi, 2019). Though web series is the replication of TV serials, superiority in content, availability of all episodes and people's belief that the TV content is inferior trigger people to shift to web series. In order to create curiosity and attract consumers, trailers of the web series are promoted on YouTube and other social media sites through a marketing strategy. As most of youngsters are social media addicts, web series easily attract young adults with its original and Western content (Kumar, 2020). Covid-19 pandemic makes the situation worse as everyone in the home shares the same screen and binge-watch forces youngsters for subscriptions to access original and exclusive content from Netflix, APV and Disney+ Hotstar witnessing excessive growth in income. Though India is known for its heritage and culture, OTT content has a huge impact on spreading the Westernization concept in young minds. Every Indian house has Wi-Fi connections and separate bedrooms for children and parents which lacks parental control in watching internet videos leads porn watch and abusive content. The wide variety of content in English and regional languages attracts young adults and Bollywood shares a major part in shaping culture, and it changes the behavior and languages among young adults' results.

Indian market is diverse and one of the key factors in the success of OTT platforms is the extensive diversity in the content. Along with Hindi and English, OTT has provided more regional content to Indian audiences which gained immense popularity. The regional language content is doubled from 27% in 2020 to 54% in 2024, according to the FICCI EY report. This shift drives content creators to create more original programs in regional languages with over 46 providers, and Netflix, Amazon Prime Video and Disney Plus rank at the top. Hindi, one of India's official languages is widely spoken in India, and Hindi cinema (Bollywood) has a deep root in reflecting Indian culture and society to the world. It preserves Indian culture by presenting historical monuments and places such as the Taj Mahal and the Redfort in movies like *Jodhaa Akbar, Padmaavat, Jab Tak Hai Jaan, Dil Chahta Hai* and *Bajirao Mastani* which have increased the tourism industry and also it never fails to address the social issues and different aspects of human emotions, such as Indian culture and tradition, women empowerment, LGBTQ+ rights, caste system, mental health, environmental and educational issues, corruption, disability rights, religious harmony and substance abuse (Ghosh, 2023). It has the greatest influence on language learning by adopting more English words and phrases into films. Non-native speakers of any language learn the different languages by watching movies and movies like *Lagaan* and *Rang De Basanti* help non-native speakers to learn Hindi easily. Bollywood also presents the colorful and lively life of people around India through music, songs and dance. It also promotes the cross-cultural exchange between India and other countries, through movies like Slumdog Millionaire which deals with the life of a slum dweller in India produced by a British production company. My name is Khan movie helps to understand the cross culture between India and the United States.

In spite of all the significant impacts on Indian culture and society, it has negative impacts on young adults. It reinforces gender stereotypes intentionally or unintentionally by presenting the harsh realities of men as superior and women as passive and inferior to men and the primary goal of a girl is getting married and bearing children through movies like *Thappad, Bulbbul, Pink* and *Chhapak,* which is contributing to rampant sexism in India. Bollywood has become the prime reason for Indians' obsession with fair skin and slim bodies, which endorse billion-dollar business for beauty products. Brown-skinned women are ridiculed mercilessly by representing they are unworthy to love and marry in many movies such as *Doosri Sita, Pyaas, Brahmachaari* and *Apne Rang Hazar.* The aggressive, malice, alcoholic and violent youth characters are promoted through the movies like *Kabir Singh* and the acceptance of caste discrimination is promoted in *Ram Leela.* The LGBTQ+ is underrepresented through comedy though they tried to normalize in movies such as *Dostana, Shubh Mangal Zyada Saavdhan* and *Badaai Do.* The impact of Bollywood remains an integral part of Indian culture, still, the negative impact is significant on young adults (Thought Chakra, 2023). Anurag Thakur, Union Minister of Information and Broadcasting condemns the OTT platform for projecting the nation's culture and heritage in a bad light. And also, insists the providers strike a balance between creativity and responsibility while creating content, that does not demean the nation's pride to review the scripts and promote family-oriented entertainment, success stories and nationalistic narratives to promote nationalism (E times, 2023).

Comparing Cinema Theatre and OTT

During covid-19 theatres were closed for almost two years and the television channels streamed without original content and entertaining people by retelecasting great Indian epics Mahabharata and Ramayana. OTT grasped the opportunity and the movies from renowned stars are also getting released in OTT, as the theatrical release was highly impossible. Celebrated Indian actors like Vidya Balan, Amitabh Bachchan, Pankaj Tripathi, Kajol and Vicky Kaushal understand that OTT is a new dynamic in the cinema industry that can reach huge audiences across countries. Vidya Balan admits that the realm of entertainment has changed with the pandemic and accepting the new change and adopting digital platforms is wise for career options. Also, she agrees that she will do content for direct OTT releases and her film *Sherni* has a worldwide (240 countries) audience which is not possible in theatrical release. Further, she adds, it is surprising to know that only 3% of the population prefers to watch cinema in theatres, whereas OTT offers content to access through mobile phones, laptops and multiple devices, in which mobile phone is the most preferable device among young adults. Thus, OTT is a game changer in the entertainment industry. Amitabh Bachchan's *Gulabo Sitabo* was released worldwide in OTT in June 2020 and was nominated into 13 categories. Bachchan mentioned in his tweet that he is honored to face a new challenge in his career for his digital release. Sidharth's *Shersaah* on Amazon Prime Video, *Dil Bechara*, a tributary film for the late Sushant Singh released on Disney+ Hotstar, Vicky Kaushal's *Sardar Udham*, the most controversial history of India's Jallianwala Bagh Massacre premiered on Amazon Prime Video and 83 based on India's 1983 Cricket World Cup was released on Netflix hits a huge success in OTT release. Though Vicky's *Sardar Udham* had made for theatrical release, it was released in OTT and the film gets recognition as an Indian film more than a Bollywood film. Vicky adds theatrical release always has such limits on finding screens and release on Friday to target audiences on the weekend, content should pass the censor board for all types of audiences and sometimes the big stars' movies are prioritized and clashed with other small budget movies, whereas OTT does not have such pressures, the film is timeless and the subscribers can watch at their convenience on whenever and wherever through mobile phones. Small-budget films which have good contemporary content are recognized after the OTT release. Though movies like *Brahmastra, Good Night and Maamannan* were released in theatres it is well-recognized and popularized among all kinds of audiences and the critics' favorites after its OTT release. The OTT platforms have attracted consumers particularly young adults with many benefits while it has its own negative impact on young minds.

Cost Effectiveness

After benefiting from the rocket boom in the OTT platforms for the past two years, the entertainment industry, now struggling to sustain in the Indian market as Indians are always concerned about the money they spend on entertainment. Indians are hesitant to pay for multiple platforms and they are using the applications free of cost with advertisements that resemble the conventional TV medium. The majority of people are not ready to pay for OTT platforms, and an average they pay 50-200 rupees per month for the OTT applications. A very few people pay more than 200 rupees for an OTT subscription and password sharing among friends hinders individual subscriptions, compared to the subscriptions the consumers are in large numbers (Singh, 2019). The main source for the profit of OTT platforms is ads and for the ads-free content consumers are demanded to pay more which is two times higher than the free content. Thus, Indians prefer to watch free content with advertisements. Manish Kalra, chief executive of ZEE5 says that most Indians prefer advertising-based videos at free of cost, and it is challenging to convert them to paid users. Thus the OTT platforms offer different subscription plans for different consumers on their demand and some OTT platforms offer free content to watch at any time like Hotstar and Amazon Prime Video whereas Netflix does not offer any content for trial and watch free. Hence Hotstar and Amazon Prime Video become popular platforms among Indians. An Indian home pays an average of 300 rupees for cable or direct-to-home (DTH) connections. Compared to conventional TV medium prices, OTT platforms offer the same and low prices for subscriptions from 99 rupees per month in Hotstar and 149 rupees in Netflix for mobile plans. A movie in the theatre costs triple times of a monthly subscription to any OTT platform and the new normal makes people to watch the cinema at home environment. The big stars' movies are also released in direct OTT which demands the OTT subscription among Indians.

Content Customizing on OTT

Personalization and customization permeate the business in all aspects of the entertainment industry. The OTT platforms strategize carefully about the personalization and customization of content for their customers in the competitive markets by accessing various scales such as an individual's searches, likes, watch lists, shares, downloads, and watch laters. Gone are the days when people ran behind the cable operators and DTH services for new connections, nowadays with the help of the internet and smartphones everything is available on hand. OTT platforms capture the customers' demand and provide content based on their previous watch and AI chatbots play a significant role in suggesting the content through their Google searches and social media surfing. Netflix is mastering this customization of content and it personalizes the homepage for individuals with the data of what you search and watch. The traditional TV medium fails to customize and suggest content. Personalization increases viewing and subscriptions and decreases deviations among consumers. The various strategies, such as personalized emails, suggestions, recommendations, thumbnails and playlists which are lacking in the traditional TV medium help the OTT platforms to be dominant in the entertainment industry. Personalization benefits both the platforms and the customers, and it enables the customer to get the content that they like very quickly without manual search which deviates the customer to switch to different platforms. 80% of the Netflix content is viewed by personalization and recommendations. This helps the content providers to produce the content based on the likes of the consumers which boosts the revenues in the market.

Multi-Device Connection and Screen Sharing

The best strategy for the OTT platforms' huge success is the multiple device connection and screen sharing for single subscriptions which is highly impossible in TV and theatre. This feature motivates millions of users to pay for their desired content economically which increases the revenue of the platforms. Netflix allows the primary account holder to share their passwords to a maximum of five devices with limitless access, ZEE5 extends the connection to 2 devices, up to five devices are allowed in Amazon Prime Video, Sun NXT allows four devices at a time, Disney+ Hotstar allows to watch at two devices simultaneously and some other platforms also offer different subscription plans for screen sharing which is less than the single home cable TV price and a single movie watch in theatres. More than 60 OTT platforms are available in India, which creates confusion among consumers to which platforms they can subscribe to, Splitsub, goDutch and Tools Zap come with a solution for sharing subscriptions, a startup launched in August 2020 to find partners for sharing subscription plans and is available in iOS and Android. The information shared in the app is encrypted and the transactions are refundable. The incorporation of AI chatbots and machine learning supports these apps vehemently.

Language Acquisition

India is a country known for its diverse culture, tradition and languages, and India has the second highest number of spoken languages (780) in the world and Hindi is widely spoken in India. Bollywood (Hindi) cinema is known as Indian cinema dominant among the other language industries in India. Mass media plays an undeniable role in language preservation and learning, and audio-visual methods have been widely adopted in foreign language learning. Language is the essence of any culture which reflects the culture, heritage and tradition of a nation. The global platforms and the regional OTT platforms preserve the linguistic diversity of a nation by creating and offering opportunities for local content creators. The regional platforms support to a great extent in promoting and preserving local languages and cultures and fostering a multi-cultural environment in India. Global platforms like Netflix, Amazon Prime Video and Disney offer content in 20 languages and regional platforms such as Hoichoi in Bengali, Aha in Telugu, and Sun NXT in Tamil, Telugu, Malayalam, Kannada and Bengali support significantly local languages.

Hindi is the most preferred language in India among other regional languages and a study by Singh (2019) found that 80 percent of people prefer Hindi to watch OTT content, 15 percent watch in English and 3 percent find Punjabi as their choice of language (Singh, 2019). 'Netflix and Chill' is the common phrase pronounced among youngsters for binge-watching. *Breaking Bad* on Netflix, *The Office UK* on Hulu and *Suits* and *The Big Bang Theory* on Amazon Prime Video improve the English vocabulary, British accent, business English and scientific language. Dubbing and inter and intra-linguist subtitles facilitate language learning, and pausing, forwarding, replaying and audio tracking are possible in OTT platforms while traditional TV and cinema theatres lack it (Caruana, 2021).

Marketing Strategies

OTT industry finds challenges in their strategies after the new normal. During Covid-19, the OTT industry boomed in rocket growth and the platforms struggled with strategies to retain subscribers. Freemium is the best strategy used by OTT platforms by providing free movies and series for 30-day trials to attract audiences to sign into their platforms. Some platforms offer the first few episodes of the series to attract a large pool of audience for subscription. The trailers and teasers promote curiosity among audiences to watch movies. Promotion through social hands by the producers and actors makes a huge impact on promoting movies. In addition to that, interactive videos, chats, rapid fires and coffee talks with the cast and crew have been done to promote movies. Notifications and reminders play a major role in subscriptions. If a customer is subscribed to a basic plan, the apps offer some discounts to customers for premium plans through notifications and reminders which upsell the subscription plans. Influencers also share a major part in promoting the platforms, for instance, big stars' partnership with the platforms. Creators and influencers use the new release content for reels and posts which generate views and promotions by acknowledging the actors of the movies.

The Negative Impact of OTT among Young Adults

Bollywood has been influenced by Western culture and the success of Bollywood in India relies on the integration of Western culture into Indian movies. Though Westernization enables Indian audiences to explore more cultures, young adults from India perceive it in a destructive way. The integration of Western elements, such as location, culture and language into Indian films deeply motivated to get wider audiences. Binge-watching negatively impacts young adults' physical and mental health and results in multiple failures: scholastic and career failure, low self-esteem, high blood pressure, junk food habits, obesity, negligence of social life, anxiety, depression and others. Binge-watching needs a maximum number of hours in a day to complete the episodes of a series, which promotes loneliness among adults which solely results in depression and anxiety. As they consume the content more, the mood of the series is reflected in the rest of the day which has hostility, abusive language and sexual content resulting in psychological repercussions. Social life is greatly neglected by youngsters as they prefer virtual reality to reality, and their daily schedule is slumped due to lack of sleep. The promotion of tobacco, drugs and alcohol have a huge impact of disrupting the existing culture of the system, and youngsters replicate what they have seen on media. Anurag Thakur, a Union Minister also resented for increasing vulgarity, abusive language and negative portrayal of Indian culture and traditions in OTT platforms which have more freedom in content creation. The use of abusive language in OTT platforms become a controversial topic in recent years, as it has freedom in content creation and no censor restrictions, whereas the traditional TV network has regulations and restrictions as it targets family audiences. Traditional TV has strict broadcasting rules and regulations for offensive language and scenes, while OTT platforms are not bound to these restrictions in content creation as they target young adults. The government should impose strict restrictions on content creation to ensure the content is applicable for all audiences. Though adults enjoy explicit languages and scenes, it is deeply deteriorating our culture and habits, thus OTT platforms sensibly utilize the freedom and responsibility in content creation and distribution (Dhiman, 2023).

The Regrowth of Cinema in Theatres

Generally, it seems that the changes in consuming the media and entertainment have a huge impact on television and cinema theatres. Yet, the studies show that young adults depend on OTT platforms for entertainment while adults rely on the traditional medium of television. 92 percent of people agree that OTT platforms have a great influence on changing the pattern of consuming entertainment, and OTT is more convenient and comfortable (Singh, 2019). Despite the great downfall in the cinema industry, 2023 is witnessing a surge in cinema-goers after the pandemic, recording the highest ticket booking with the release of Pathaan, PS 2 and others. The audience is back in theatres but not the same as before covid, with a 16 percent drop in cinema-goers before the covid pandemic (Magan, 2023). Still, the numbers are trying to reach the highest, as social life is still celebrated among youngsters. The cinema theatres get its box office full when the big stars' movies are released in theatres, whereas the aspiring actors' movies are still struggling to reach the box office revenue but those movies are getting its appreciation after the OTT release. The recent release of south Indian actor Rajinikanth's Jailer steadily running in theatres since the fourth week of the release and it collected 375 crores in the first week, 150 crores in the second week, 77 crores in the third week and total of collection is grossed around 602 crores (E Times, 2023) The trailer of the Pathan was specially screened on Burj Khalifa and it was released on more than 4,000 screens and recorded great success in theatres after covid-19. Ponniyin Selvan 2 was promoted across India and the cast and crew played a great part in the success of the movie.

CONCLUSION

India has roughly 46 OTT platforms and the OTT boom with the pandemic and the love for OTT remain even after the new normal. Netflix, Amazon Prime Video and Disney+ Hotstar are the major platforms ruling the Indian OTT industry. Though OTT platforms offer content in English, Hindi and other regional languages, Hindi is the most preferred language in OTT platforms. India is sharing significantly in the revenue of OTT platforms; still, Indian audiences love to watch content at free of cost. Web series is the most preferred content and then movies in OTT platforms. The success of OTT hugely depends on smartphones and high-speed internet. The perception towards TV and cinema theatres is changing predominantly with the OTT medium's quality, originality and freshness in content. Theatrical release films and television content are produced for commercial purposes and target all types of audiences including children and adults. People do not want the same commercial family dramas, thus the OTT emerges with different content targeting young adults. Young adults are addicted to binge-watching, which is available on OTT platforms in different languages and Korean drama is mostly watched by Indian female adults, whereas male prefers web series on Netflix. OTT platforms undoubtedly change the perspective of the way people consume the media but the craze for cinema remains in India, and the cinema experience is never replaced. It is concluded that OTT platforms offer alternative ways of entertaining, hence the OTT platforms and the cinema industry coexist in the entertainment industry by offering different content to audiences.

REFERENCES

Bhattacharyya, R., Kohli, S., & Rupali, M. (2020). Change In Consumption Habits Of Entertainment During Lockdown And The Role Of OTT Platforms. *Ilkogr. Online-Elem. Educ. Online*, *19*(4), 4686–4695.

Bihade, V., & Kumar, M. (2023). Customer Preference towards OTT Platform in India. *Global Media Journal*, *21*(61), 355.

Caruana, S. (2021). An overview of audiovisual input as a means for foreign language acquisition in different contexts. *Language and Speech*, *64*(4), 1018–1036. doi:10.1177/0023830920985897 PMID:33435785

Chukwuemeka, E. S. (2023, April 7). Countries with the highest young/youth population 2023. *Top (Madrid)*, *11*. https://bscholarly.com/countries-with-the-highest-youth-young-population-2022-top-9/

DhimanD. B. (2023). A Critical Analysis of Vulgar Language on OTT Platforms: A Systematic Review. *Available at* SSRN 4404547. doi:10.2139/ssrn.4404547

Ghosh, A. (16 Aug 2023). Preserving Films means Preserving History, Culture and Memories. *Times of India*. https://timesofindia.indiatimes.com/india/preserving-films-means-preserving-history-culture-and-memories/articleshow/102755505.cms?from=mdr. Accessed on 31/08/23

Gupta, G., & Singharia, K. (2021). Consumption of OTT media streaming in COVID-19 lockdown: Insights from PLS analysis. *Vision (Basel)*, *25*(1), 36–46. doi:10.1177/0972262921989118

Gupta, P. (2021). The factors effecting shift of Indian customers from TV series to web series-the future of OTT services in India. [IJMR]. *EPRA International Journal of Multidisciplinary Research*, *7*(2), 143–150.

Kala, G. (2022). The Growing Popularity of OTT platform and its impact on the younger generation. *Mahratta*, *1*(2), 1–7.

Koravi, V. S. (2019). Analysis of various effects of web series streaming online on Internet on Indian youth. *IJRULA*, *2*(1), 28–42.

Magan, S. (25 Jan 2023). Percentage of citizens likely to visit cinemas increased by 150%: Local Circles Survey. *Business Insider.* https://www.businessinsider.in/entertainment/news/percentage-of-citizens-likely-to-visit-cinemas-increased-by-150-as-perreport/articleshow/97281514.cms. .

Mohan, M., & Jadhav, A. (2022). Predicting Customer Churn on OTT Platforms: Customers with Subscription of Multiple Service Providers. *Journal of Information and Organizational Sciences*, *46*(2), 433–451.

Pajkovic, N. (2022). Algorithms and taste-making: Exposing the Netflix Recommender System's operational logics. *Convergence (London)*, *28*(1), 214–235. doi:10.1177/13548565211014464

Parihar, S., & Kant, D. K. (2021). Impact of Marketing Mix on Consumers Satisfaction-A Study of Consumers of OTT Platforms in India. *IJRAR*, *8*(3), 260–272.

Robert, M. P. W., & Raj, J. J., & JOSEPH, D. T. (2022). THE FUTURE OF MOVIES: WILL OTT TAKE OVER THEATRES? *Journal of Positive School Psychology*, *6*(3), 7614–7620.

Singh, P. (2019). New Media as a Change Agent of Indian Television and Cinema: A study of over the top Platforms. *Journal of Content. Community and Communication*, *9*(1), 131–137.

Sontakke, K. S. (2021). Trends in OTT Platforms Usage During COVID-19 Lockdown in India. *Journal of Scientific Research*, *65*(8), 23. doi:10.37398/JSR.2021.650823

Times, E. (18 July 2023). Don't demean Indian society, culture in the name of creative freedom. *Times of India.* https://timesofindia.indiatimes.com/articleshow/101881313.cms?from=mdr&utm_source=contentofinterest&utm_medium=text&utm_campaign=cppst. Accessed on 31/08/23.

Chapter 5
Instagram's Role in the Rise and Success of Over-the-Top (OTT) Media

B. Harry
Vellore Institute of Technology, India

Vijayakumar Muthusamy
https://orcid.org/0000-0002-1079-5383
Vellore Institute of Technology, India

ABSTRACT

This comprehensive chapter delves into the pivotal role of Instagram's role in shaping over-the-top (OTT) media, highlighting its visual storytelling, marketing potential, and strategic influencer collaborations. It also explores user-generated content and fan networks, fostering kinship and audience loyalty. by investigating the Instagram's dynamic discovery features, including hashtags, trends, and algorithmic recommendations, amplify OTT content's reach and resonance. Real-time interaction between creators and audiences also shapes content production, marketing campaigns, and informed decision-making. The chapter also explores Instagram's revenue-generating potential for both OTT platforms and content creators, with influencer endorsements, sponsored posts, and product integrations emerging as avenues for supplementary revenue streams. Overall, this comprehensive exploration of Instagram's impact on OTT media provides a comprehensive understanding of their symbiotic relationship, fueling the contemporary media landscape.

1. INTRODUCTION

The media landscape is undergoing a notable shift, primarily driven by the rise of Over-the-Top (OTT) platforms. These online channels have disrupted traditional broadcasting methods and revolutionised how audiences interact with media content. Simultaneously, social media platforms have transformed the way people consume and engage with content. Among them, Instagram has emerged as an immer-

DOI: 10.4018/979-8-3693-0116-6.ch005

sive visual platform that wields significant influence over the trajectory and triumph of OTT media. The confluence of OTT platforms and Instagram generates a synergy surpassing conventional media paradigms, ushering in a new media production and consumption era.

The emergence of OTT platforms has brought about a transformative change in the media landscape, paving the way for innovative content delivery mechanisms and challenging the conventional industry norms. OTT platforms have revolutionised media consumption from offering many binge-worthy shows to providing an ad-free viewing experience. OTT platforms like Netflix, Amazon Prime Video, Hulu, and Disney+ have shattered the constraints of scheduled programming, granting users the liberty to consume content at their convenience and across devices (Hill, 2020). The popularity of over-the-top (OTT) platforms can be attributed to their ability to provide viewers with more freedom by breaking geographical and temporal barriers. This allows for a personalised viewing experience that caters to the changing preferences of modern-day consumers. This potential for transformation has led to the dominance of OTT platforms, which have redefined the media industry and consumer expectations.

Concomitantly, social media platforms have redefined how audiences engage with content, precipitating a paradigm shift from passive consumption to active participation (Kaplan & Haenlein, 2010). Instagram, an embodiment of this social media evolution, has garnered over a billion active users globally (Statista, 2021). Renowned for its visually captivating format, Instagram transcends textual boundaries, allowing users to communicate, connect, and express themselves through images and videos (Dijck, 2013). This shift towards visual communication aligns seamlessly with the ethos of OTT platforms, where visually-driven narratives reign supreme. Instagram's impact extends beyond mere engagement, encompassing content discovery, brand promotion, and the creation of digital communities (Krieger & Systrom, 2012).

The intersection of transformative forces is where Instagram's strategic placement enables it to catalyse and amplify the reach and resonance of over-the-top (OTT) media. The intertwined evolution of Instagram and OTT platforms reflects a deep-seated symbiosis that reshapes media consumption patterns and redefines audience engagement. Its visual exuberance and interactive ecosystem have characterised Instagram's meteoric rise, engendered a paradigm where viewers are no longer passive consumers but active participants in the media landscape. This participatory framework aligns with the ethos of OTT platforms, which prioritise audience agency and empowerment in content selection and engagement.

Instagram has proven to be a powerful influencer in the trajectory of OTT media. The symbiotic relationship between the two has given rise to a new media ecosystem characterised by visual immersion and dynamic interaction. This chapter provides a confident and thorough exploration of Instagram's significant role in shaping the success of OTT media. It navigates through various dimensions, each intricately woven into the fabric of contemporary media dynamics, highlighting the essential role of Instagram in this new landscape.

1.1 Overview of the Rise of OTT Media and the Popularity of Instagram

The media consumption landscape is amid a profound and unprecedented transformation driven by the meteoric ascent of Over-the-Top (OTT) platforms. Platforms like Netflix, Amazon Prime Video, Hulu, and Disney+ have redefined the way audiences engage with content, marking a seismic shift from traditional broadcasting models (Jones, 2020). These OTT platforms offer viewers a liberation from the constraints of scheduled programming, providing the flexibility to consume media at their convenience and across various devices. Within the contours of this media revolution lies Instagram, an integral platform that has not only redefined user engagement but has also emerged as a pivotal force shaping the trajectory and success of OTT media. The convergence of the proliferation of OTT platforms and the popularity of Instagram epitomises a symbiotic relationship redefining the essence of media consumption and production.

The proliferation of OTT platforms represents a watershed moment in the evolution of media consumption. The advent of platforms like Netflix has marked a definitive departure from the traditional media delivery models, where present schedules no longer bind viewers. This new paradigm empowers audiences to curate their viewing experience, transcending the confines of time and space (Jones, 2020). Such platforms cater to modern consumers' preferences, who seek content tailored to their schedules and tastes. This democratisation of content consumption has led to the unprecedented growth and dominance of OTT platforms, challenging the traditional hierarchies of media distribution and reshaping the industry landscape.

Instagram is central to this transformative landscape, a platform that has emerged as a cultural and technological phenomenon. With over a billion active users globally (Instagram, 2021), Instagram's impact extends far beyond its role as a social media platform. This visual-centric platform has redefined the way users interact with content, emphasising imagery and videos as primary forms of communication. This shift towards visual communication aligns organically with the ethos of OTT platforms, where captivating visuals are pivotal in driving viewer engagement (Dijck, 2013). Instagram's user-friendly interface, diverse content formats, and innovative features have positioned it as a virtual gallery, enabling users to showcase trailers, behind-the-scenes glimpses, and creative renditions of their favourite OTT shows and movies.

The synergy between the burgeoning popularity of Instagram and the ascent of OTT platforms is emblematic of a transformative era in media. Instagram's staggering growth underscores its status as a cultural phenomenon that has redefined the digital landscape. Its platform encapsulates the contemporary ethos of visual communication, aligning seamlessly with the essence of OTT media, which thrives on captivating visuals to enthral audiences in immersive narratives (Dijck, 2013). This coalescence has ushered in a paradigm where Instagram serves as a medium for engagement and a dynamic catalyst in propelling the success of OTT media.

In the nexus of these transformative dynamics emerges the central focus of this chapter: the profound role of Instagram in shaping the rise and triumph of OTT media. This exploration traverses an intricate web of interrelated themes, each instrumental in sculpting the symbiotic relationship between Instagram and OTT platforms. The subsequent sections embark on an insightful journey, dissecting the multifaceted ways Instagram has shaped the narrative and reception of OTT content.

1.2 Significance of Investigating the Role of Instagram in the Success of OTT Media

The alignment between Instagram and OTT media is no coincidence; it is a strategic convergence that significantly contributes to the latter's accomplishments. The captivating visuals intrinsic to OTT content resonate harmoniously with Instagram's visual language, creating a seamless blend (Smith, 2018). This harmony between their graphic dimensions forms the foundation for an enriched viewer experience, underscoring the significance of their mutual interplay.

OTT platforms' distinct on-demand nature necessitates innovative promotional approaches that deviate from traditional broadcasting models (Brown, 2019). In this context, Instagram emerges as a pivotal platform for such endeavours. Its emphasis on visual aesthetics and dynamic content formats provides an optimal stage for crafting promotional campaigns that captivate and engage viewers, amplifying their curiosity about forthcoming OTT content.

However, the collaboration between Instagram and OTT media transcends mere promotional activities. Instagram's interactive capabilities, such as real-time commenting, direct messaging, and polling, establish a direct conduit for audience engagement and insights (Roberts, 2017). This real-time bridge between creators and consumers is a testament to the platform's role in facilitating instant communication, enabling creators to garner audience feedback, refine content, and respond swiftly to preferences.

Moreover, Instagram's distinctive features, including hashtags, trends, and discoverability mechanisms, assume a pivotal role in propelling the virality of content – a paramount factor in elevating the visibility of OTT offerings (Johnson, 2019). The platform's algorithms operate as dynamic curators, directing users toward content that aligns with their preferences, effectively extending the reach of OTT media beyond conventional boundaries.

As the quest for monetisation gains prominence, Instagram's influencer-driven economy presents a distinct advantage for OTT platforms and content creators (Williams, 2022). The platform's vast user base has spawned a new breed of influencers who wield considerable influence over consumer choices. OTT entities can leverage this influencer phenomenon to establish an alternative revenue stream through avenues like sponsored posts, endorsements, and product placements, effectively capitalising on the platform's formidable user engagement.

Given the intricacies of these multifaceted interactions, it becomes imperative to comprehensively explore Instagram's role in the ascendancy and prosperity of OTT media. This chapter embarks on an analytical journey, meticulously dissecting the intricate interplay between Instagram and OTT media. This chapter offers an insightful perspective into the contemporary media landscape's transformation by illuminating the multifaceted dimensions of their collaborative potential.

2. INSTAGRAM AS A PLATFORM FOR VISUAL STORYTELLING AND PROMOTION

OTT (Over-the-Top) is a revolution in the entertainment industry. With the advent of live-streaming video and audio, the distribution of movies and television shows over the internet has become a reality. This means you can enjoy your favourite shows and movies without needing a typical pay TV subscription like Comcast or Time Warner Cable. The internet era has transformed how we consume media, and mobile phones have become a primary source of entertainment. Instagram's interactive features allow for the seamless integration of promotional content within users' feeds, creating a more organic and immersive viewing experience. This integration captures the audience's attention and enhances the narrative journey of over-the-top (OTT) content, drawing viewers deeper into the story and generating a sense of anticipation for the next episode or season. For example, Disney+ has a visually appealing grid layout on its Instagram page, which entices users to scroll through the content, revealing enticing snippets and behind-the-scenes glimpses that further pique their interest.

Similarly, Netflix's "Stranger Things" campaign utilises Instagram's interactive features, including quizzes, polls, and interactive stories, to engage viewers, creating a sense of active participation and community around the show. These strategies foster a stronger connection between the audience and the content and tap into cognitive psychology by triggering a sense of belonging and investment in the narrative. Overall, the success of these campaigns demonstrates the efficacy of using Instagram's interactive features to promote OTT content and engage with audiences in a more immersive and meaningful way.

2.1 The Visual-Centric Nature of Instagram and its Alignment with OTT Media

In the ever-evolving digital landscape, storytelling has transcended traditional mediums, evolving into a dynamic art that hinges on captivating visual narratives. This transformation is particularly evident in social media, where platforms have become fertile grounds for weaving stories that resonate deeply with audiences. Among these platforms, Instagram emerges as an epitome of the potency of visual content in conveying messages and evoking emotions. Its colossal user base, which surpassed a billion active users as of 2021 (Instagram, 2021), underscores its status as a cultural phenomenon and a formidable instrument for shaping narratives and propelling content into the spotlight.

Within this backdrop, the visual-centric nature of Instagram resonates with remarkable synergy with the landscape of Over-the-Top (OTT) media. OTT platforms, characterised by their distinctive approach to media consumption, rely heavily on the immersive power of compelling visuals to draw viewers into multifaceted storytelling journeys. Instagram's alignment with OTT media is profound, grounded in their shared visual language that provides a captivating arena for OTT creators and platforms to unfurl the essence of their content.

The symbiotic relationship between Instagram and OTT media, as articulated by Smith (2018), serves as a testament to the convergence of these two influential domains. Instagram's captivating visual framework dovetails harmoniously with OTT media's core emphasis on immersive storytelling, creating an organic partnership that enhances user engagement, anticipation, and content exploration. This partnership thrives on the shared understanding that the modern digital audience craves narratives that not only captivate but also resonate on a visceral level. By harmonising visual elements, these platforms craft an environment where users are passive observers and active participants in the storytelling process.

To comprehend this dynamic synergy, one must delve into the psychology of visual engagement. Neuroscientific research has demonstrated that the human brain processes visual information remarkably. According to Johnson et al. (2017), the brain processes images nearly 60,000 times faster than text, allowing viewers to absorb and internalise complex narratives within seconds. This cognitive advantage has catapulted visual storytelling to the forefront of content creation strategies. Instagram's foundation is built upon this neurological predisposition, utilising its visually immersive design to captivate users and foster engagement. By aligning seamlessly with the visual appetite of the human brain, Instagram establishes an environment ripe for promoting captivating narratives that echo the ethos of OTT media.

The alignment between Instagram and OTT media is not confined to their inherent visual appeal. It extends into the realm of experiential engagement. OTT platforms redefine how users engage with media, offering on-demand content accessible across devices. Instagram seamlessly complements this experiential shift by providing an avenue for content previews, behind-the-scenes glimpses, and interactive elements that heighten viewer anticipation. This phenomenon is similar to "previews" in traditional movie theatres, where glimpses of upcoming attractions build tension and foster community among cinephiles.

Furthermore, the very fabric of Instagram's content presentation aligns with the principles of OTT media. For instance, the platform's Stories feature mirrors the episodic structure prevalent in the OTT series, where content is broken down into consumable segments. Instagram's dynamic content formats, such as IGTV and Reels, encapsulate the snackable nature of OTT content – content designed to fit seamlessly into the viewer's busy lifestyle. This intuitive alignment fosters an immersive and accommodating user experience, mirroring the viewer-centric ethos of OTT platforms.

The relationship between Instagram and OTT media is based on their shared visual language and commitment to storytelling.This alignment transcends the realms of mere content promotion; it underscores a profound understanding of the contemporary audience's penchant for visual engagement. In an age where stories unfold across screens of all sizes, Instagram emerges as a potent canvas for crafting narratives that resonate deeply. At the same time, OTT media offers an immersive journey through captivating visuals. The importance of social networking sites in our lives and the content we are getting is far better than traditional forms of media. This intersection of digital realms epitomises the art of storytelling in the modern era, where images and videos are not just tools of communication but avenues of emotional connection and shared experiences (Verma & Kalorth, 2017)

2.2 Strategies Employed by Content Creators and OTT Platforms for Visual Storytelling and Promotion on Instagram

The relationship between Instagram and OTT media transcends surface-level visual aesthetics; it delves into a realm of strategic ingenuity that content creators and OTT platforms wield to optimise the platform's potential for narrative weaving and content promotion. Beyond the captivating images and videos, a deeper layer of calculated strategies comes into play, where the art of storytelling is interwoven with the platform's interactive features. This strategic dance between Instagram's dynamic tools and the ambitions of OTT content promotion encapsulates a profound understanding of modern digital dynamics, ultimately shaping the trajectory of content engagement.

For content creators, Instagram is a versatile canvas that accommodates a rich array of visual storytelling techniques. The platform's toolbox of features, ranging from the immersive swipeable photo carousels to the ephemeral storytelling space of Stories to the more extended formats like IGTV and Reels, presents a palette for crafting multifaceted narratives (Roberts, 2020). This diversity of content formats reflects an acknowledgement of the contemporary audience's fragmented attention span. By presenting stories in compact and consumable formats, content creators tap into cognitive processes optimised for quick information absorption. Neurologically, the brain is predisposed to process visual content more efficiently than textual information (Johnson et al., 2017). As such, Instagram becomes a conduit for content creators to narrate and curate memorable moments that resonate in a fraction of a second.

Moreover, Instagram's interactive and snackable nature aligns seamlessly with OTT content's core tenets. The micro-narratives within Stories, for instance, mirror the episodic structure that characterises the OTT series. Each Story segment becomes an encapsulated chapter, fostering anticipation and inviting viewers to follow the narrative arc. This strategy resonates with the psychological concept of the "Zeigarnik effect," where incomplete narratives trigger a state of cognitive tension, compelling audiences to return to resolve it (Zeigarnik, 1927). This psychological principle becomes a strategic ally for content creators, propelling user engagement and enhancing the memorability of their narratives.

On the other side of the spectrum, OTT platforms have recognised Instagram's formidable influence and carved sophisticated promotional campaigns that leverage the platform's inherent strengths. Instagram's expansive user base and engagement tools allow OTT platforms to bring their content's essence to life. Teaser videos tantalise audiences, stoking curiosity and building a sense of anticipation reminiscent of classic cliffhangers (Brown, 2019). Behind-the-scenes glimpses transform the content into a living experience, inviting users to become a part of the creative journey. Challenges and interactive elements foster a participatory culture, deepening the viewer's connection with the content and cultivating community.

In content discovery, hashtags and location tags emerge as strategic signposts guiding audiences toward OTT content gems. The power of these tools lies in their capacity to transcend linguistic barriers and categorise content into thematic clusters. Research by De Cicco et al. (2019) delves into the cognitive mechanisms behind hashtags, revealing their role as mental shortcuts that streamline content discovery. By integrating relevant hashtags, OTT platforms amplify the visibility of their content across user searches and trending topics, positioning their offerings for viral propagation.

Influencer collaborations constitute another dimension of Instagram's strategic allure for OTT platforms. As the social currency becomes increasingly linked to the endorsements of influencers and celebrities, OTT platforms leverage this phenomenon to tap into existing fan bases (Brown, 2019). This extends the content's reach and infuses it with the credibility and aura of influencers, thus fostering a heightened level of engagement. The science of social influence, explored by Cialdini (2001), underscores the impact of authority figures on decision-making processes. By enlisting influencers as advocates, OTT platforms capitalise on this psychological phenomenon to sway user choices in favour of their content.

The intricate interplay between Instagram and OTT media is a subject that warrants closer examination. The astute utilisation of Instagram's dynamic features plays a critical role in crafting narratives that resonate, captivate, and linger in users' minds. The versatility of Instagram enables content creators to tailor their stories to an audience with fragmented attention spans and a penchant for interactivity. On the other hand, OTT platforms choreograph meticulously designed campaigns that leverage Instagram's expansive user base, engagement tools, and the power of influencer culture. The resulting symphony of strategies propels content into the digital stratosphere, shaping engagement metrics and the evolving nature of content consumption in the digital era.

2.3 Case Studies and Examples Showcasing Successful Visual Storytelling and Promotion Campaigns on Instagram

The marriage of Instagram's visually immersive environment with the captivating narratives of OTT media is not just a fortunate coincidence; it is a strategic rendezvous engineered to captivate and engage modern audiences in unprecedented ways. This dynamic synergy between the platforms is not merely theoretical; it has been brought to life through a series of ingenious case studies and real-world examples that illustrate the true potential of their collaboration.

One striking example of this collaboration is the strategic partnership between Netflix and the wildly popular series "Stranger Things." Netflix, known for its innovative approach to content promotion, capitalised on Instagram's interactive Story feature to create a pre-release buzz for the show's upcoming seasons. Teaser trailers, enigmatic puzzles, and interactive challenges were strategically rolled out, each piece of content weaving a thread of intrigue and anticipation. This strategic use of Instagram Stories offered a dynamic canvas for Netflix to showcase the eerie, suspenseful essence of "Stranger Things," effectively engaging audiences visually and cognitively. This approach ignited enthusiastic discussions among fans and catapulted the show's visibility and anticipation to new heights (Jackson, 2020).

Disney+, a powerhouse in the OTT media, harnessed Instagram's unique features to craft a tantalising preview of its offerings. With a vast library of classic animations and fresh originals, Disney+ orchestrated a visually rich narrative using the platform's grid layout. Each tile became a brushstroke on a larger canvas, telling the story of Disney+'s diverse content spectrum. This approach catered to a spectrum of audiences - from those driven by nostalgia to the younger generation unfamiliar with Disney's legacy. By tapping into Instagram's visually engaging format, Disney+ managed to evoke a sense of familiarity and novelty, making their OTT media content alluring to a wide range of viewers (Smith, 2020).

These instances underscore the symbiotic relationship between Instagram's visual storytelling potential and the narrative ambitions of OTT media. The dynamic capabilities of Instagram, such as Stories and Grids, are not just digital tools; they are portals to create immersive experiences. They offer a space where narratives are constructed not only through words but also through evocative visuals, leveraging the cognitive mechanisms of visual processing and storytelling comprehension.

Cognitive psychology sheds light on why such strategic visual storytelling works. According to Paivio's (1986) dual coding theory, the brain processes information using verbal and visual codes. When presented through both channels, communication is more likely to be encoded into memory and retrieved later. In the case of Netflix's "Stranger Things" teasers, the blend of enigmatic visuals and tantalising textual cues forms a dual-code approach, enhancing memorability and emotional engagement. Disney+'s grid strategy, too, capitalises on this dual coding by allowing viewers to connect with content through both linguistic and visual channels.

Moreover, the engagement metrics from these campaigns resonate with psychological theories like the mere exposure effect (Zajonc, 1968). This principle suggests that repeated exposure to a stimulus enhances people's attitudes and preferences toward it. Instagram's interface facilitates repeated exposure as users navigate through Stories and grids seamlessly. Netflix's teasing strategy, fuelled by Instagram's interactive nature, harnesses this psychological effect, reinforcing the show's presence in the viewer's consciousness.

In conclusion, the strategic pairing of Instagram and OTT media exemplifies a realm where visual storytelling transcends conventional boundaries. Real-world success stories, such as Netflix's "Stranger Things" campaign and Disney+'s visually alluring grid, vividly showcase the power of Instagram's interactive features in promoting OTT content. These campaigns are successful marketing endeavours and examples of how Instagram's immersive environment enriches the narrative journey, captures audience attention, and fuels anticipation. By tapping into cognitive psychology and the principles of storytelling, these case studies illuminate the transformative potential of the Instagram-OTT nexus in shaping the landscape of digital media consumption.

3. INSTAGRAM INFLUENCER MARKETING AND PARTNERSHIPS

In the ever-evolving digital media landscape, a compelling symbiosis has emerged between social media platforms and the influential power of marketing. This intricate relationship has redefined content promotion and has become a dominant force shaping consumer behaviours and preferences. At the forefront of this revolution stands Instagram, an undisputed social media titan, which has harnessed this phenomenon to reshape the fabric of content promotion. This segment of exploration plunges into the realm of influencer marketing and strategic partnerships on Instagram, unearthing the pivotal role of influencers as catalysts in propelling the reach and impact of Over-the-Top (OTT) media content.

In the expansive digital arena, the ascendancy of influencer marketing is akin to the fusion of traditional word-of-mouth endorsement with the boundless outreach of the digital age. However, within this fusion, Instagram's distinct influence shines through, transforming it into a cradle of modern content promotion. Central to this transformation are influencers, individuals who wield considerable sway over their substantial follower counts, making them a formidable conduit for disseminating content messages.

The fusion of psychology and digital media dynamics plays a vital role in the effectiveness of influencer marketing, with Instagram acting as the perfect canvas for this phenomenon. Influencers capitalise on a psychological phenomenon known as "social proof," where individuals tend to mimic the actions and choices of others, particularly those they deem credible and informed (Cialdini, 2001). In this regard, influencers wield authority and rapport with their followers to tap into this tendency. When influencers endorse OTT content, they present an imprimatur that resonates profoundly with their audience.

This relationship between influencers and OTT content is not haphazard but a meticulously crafted collaboration. Influencers, in the age of digital role models, bridge the gap between content creators and consumers. Their endorsement is not just a promotion but a conduit that enriches their followers' feeds with high-quality content while opening new vistas for content creators to engage with a dedicated fan base.

Observational learning, a concept laid bare by Bandura's social cognitive theory, finds a striking reflection in this partnership (Bandura, 1986). In this context, influencers serve as tangible role models whose opinions carry significant weight. This dynamic provides the foundation for influencer marketing, where a trusted influencer's endorsement translates into a virtual peer's blessing. The principles of observational learning are amplified through Instagram, where visual content creates a compelling narrative that resonates deeply with viewers.

The potency of influencer marketing is more comprehensive than its initial engagement metrics. Its true prowess lies in transforming engagement into lasting subscriptions and consistent viewership. Research by Lin and Lu (2011) emphasises the role of social influence in shaping consumers' adoption of new media. Their findings underline that individuals are more likely to adopt new technologies and services when they perceive them as famous within their social circles. In influencer marketing, the influencer's endorsement becomes a virtual seal of approval, nudging their followers to engage with and actively subscribe to the content.

Instagram's seamless integration of links and content within posts and Stories further amplifies this process. This integration aligns with the technology acceptance model's concept of compatibility, where ease of use and familiarity contribute to users' adoption of new technology (Davis, 1989). The influencer's endorsement, presented within a familiar and trusted platform, bridges the gap between engagement and actionable steps, enhancing the transition from interest to sustained viewership.

In summation, Instagram's role in catalysing influencer marketing within the realm of OTT media promotion is a testament to the platform's profound influence on modern content consumption. Influencer marketing is not merely an advertising strategy but a psychological journey guided by conformity and observational learning principles. In this context, Instagram has seamlessly transformed into a platform where influencers bridge the gap between creators and consumers, turning engagement into enduring loyalty. This partnership exemplifies the intricate dance between psychology, technology, and media dynamics that underscores the digital era.

3.1 The Role of Influencers in Promoting OTT Content on Instagram

Influencer marketing is a dynamic fusion of traditional word-of-mouth advertising with the digital age's reach and impact. With its expansive user base and diverse content creators, Instagram has become the hub for this marketing revolution. Influencers who command substantial follower counts and wield niche expertise can drive purchasing decisions and shape consumer preferences. In OTT media, influencers leverage authoritative positions to endorse content and create immersive narratives.

The science behind the effectiveness of influencer marketing can be linked to the concept of social proof. Social psychologists have long highlighted how individuals tend to conform to the actions and opinions of others, especially those they perceive as credible and knowledgeable (Cialdini, 2001). Influencers, by virtue of their established personas and rapport with their followers, tap into this psychological tendency. When influencers endorse OTT content, they effectively offer a stamp of approval that resonates deeply with their audience.

3.2 Collaborations Between Influencers and OTT Platforms or Content Creators

The marriage between influencers and OTT media is not a mere happenstance but a strategic collaboration fostering a win-win situation. Influencers gain access to high-quality content to enrich their feeds and cater to their followers' preferences. Simultaneously, OTT platforms and content creators tap into the influencers' established fan base, benefiting from their credibility and ability to bridge the gap between the content and the target audience.

These collaborations are a manifestation of what Bandura's social cognitive theory elucidates - people learn not only through direct experience but also through observing others (Bandura, 1986). In this context, influencers become role models whose endorsements elevate the perceived value of the content. This integration of observational learning and social endorsement contributes to the potency of influencer marketing on Instagram, where content consumption is often driven by identification with these digital role models.

3.3 The Impact of Influencer Marketing on Audience Engagement and Subscription

Initial engagement metrics only partially determine the effectiveness of influencer marketing. Its true power lies in the potential to convert mere engagement into sustained subscriptions and viewership. A study by Lin and Lu (2011) on the role of social influence in new media adoption underscores this phenomenon. They found that individuals are more likely to adopt new technologies and services when they perceive them as popular among their social circles. In influencer marketing, the influencer's endorsement acts as a virtual peer approval, influencing their followers to explore and subscribe to the promoted OTT content.

Instagram's user-friendly interface aids this process, allowing influencers to seamlessly integrate links to OTT platforms and content in their posts and Stories. This strategic fusion of social influence and technology integration aligns with the principle of compatibility in the technology acceptance model (Davis, 1989). The transition from engagement to action becomes seamless when the endorsement is delivered through a platform the audience already uses and trusts.

The world of influencer marketing on Instagram transcends the boundaries of conventional advertising. The influencers' aura of credibility and Instagram's immersive interface fosters an environment where endorsements translate into more than just fleeting attention. The psychology behind social proof and observational learning underscores the potency of influencer-driven OTT content promotion. Additionally, the strategic alignment between influencers and content creators, grounded in social cognitive theory, forms a collaboration that bridges the gap between content and audience. The psychological principles of conformity and the technology acceptance model reveal the mechanism through which influencer endorsements on Instagram translate into sustained audience engagement and subscriptions, ultimately redefining the dynamics of content promotion in the OTT media landscape.

4. INSTAGRAM MONETIZATION OPPORTUNITIES FOR OTT PLATFORMS AND CONTENT CREATORS

The correlation between Instagram's monetisation features and over-the-top (OTT) media has opened up new avenues for advertisers and content creators. By leveraging influencer endorsements and well-planned user engagement, brands can establish a genuine and compelling connection with their intended audience. Moreover, integrating psychological concepts such as Congruity and... (please provide the missing phrase to complete the sentence) can help optimise the impact of marketing efforts.

4.1 Leveraging Instagram's User Base for Additional Revenue Streams

In the dynamic realm of digital media, the juncture of creativity and commerce has evolved into an intricate landscape, necessitating innovative strategies for financial sustenance. For Over-the-Top (OTT) platforms and content creators, this terrain has unveiled a treasure trove of opportunities within Instagram's sprawling ecosystem. The symbiosis between Instagram's staggering user base and the captivating narratives of OTT media creates a robust foundation for augmenting revenue streams.

Drawing inspiration from the Attention Economics theory, posited by Davenport and Beck (2001), where attention is scarce in the information age, Instagram has become the nexus where users allocate their attention. This allocation spawns engagement and, consequently, the potential for monetisation. Tapping into this resource, OTT platforms and content creators weave compelling narratives that capture users' attention, laying the groundwork for revenue diversification.

4.2 Influencer Endorsements, Sponsored Posts, and Product Placements on Instagram

The emergence of the digital influencer economy has unveiled a novel avenue for revenue generation – influencer endorsements, sponsored posts, and product placements. This phenomenon, deeply intertwined with Instagram's culture, has become a pivot for OTT entities to monetise their offerings seamlessly. Influencers act as intermediaries, bridging the gap between content creators and their target audience. Influencers catalyse a cascade of engagement by aligning their persona with a specific OTT content piece, triggering a spiral of interest and curiosity.

This symbiotic relationship is akin to the Elaboration Likelihood Model (ELM) in persuasion psychology (Petty & Cacioppo, 1986). Influencers serve as peripheral cues tangentially associated with the OTT content, heightening users' engagement levels. These endorsements, supported by influencers' credibility, trigger peripheral processing where users form attitudes based on the influencer's recommendation. Though less cognitively demanding, this peripheral processing enhances the likelihood of users exploring the endorsed OTT content. Consequently, OTT platforms and creators capitalise on this engagement, effectively monetising their offerings.

4.3 Examples of Successful Monetization Strategies on Instagram

Tangible instances of successful monetisation underscore the efficacy of this symbiotic approach. Netflix's partnership with influencer Lele Pons to promote their original movie "The Kissing Booth" illustrates the power of influencer endorsements. Pons' massive following and target demographic alignment exponentially amplified the movie's reach. This scenario resonates with the Congruity Theory (Osgood & Tannenbaum, 1955), where the compatibility between the influencer's persona and the endorsed content enhances persuasiveness. The alignment between Pons' youthful, relatable image and the movie's target audience created a harmonious resonance, magnifying engagement and monetisation.

Moreover, Amazon Prime's strategic utilisation of Instagram for product placements accentuates the intersection of commerce and creativity. Amazon Prime taps into the art of subtle persuasion by embedding its offerings within relatable, everyday scenarios. The psychological phenomenon of the Mere Exposure Effect, as elucidated by Zajonc (1968), dictates that familiarity breeds preference. Amazon Prime's products seamlessly integrated within Instagram feeds elicit repeated exposure, fostering a sense of familiarity that subsequently translates into consumer preference. This strategic assimilation of products into relatable narratives presents an innovative monetisation avenue for OTT platforms.

OTT platforms and content creators can monetize Instagram through audience engagement, influencer collaboration, and product integration.The Attention Economics theory elucidates Instagram's status as a podium where attention is allocated, serving as the cornerstone for revenue diversification. Influencer endorsements, drawing inspiration from the Elaboration Likelihood Model, strategically steer user engagement toward monetisable content. Real-world examples, embracing psychological theories like Congruity and Mere Exposure, highlight the success of influencer partnerships and product placements. As the digital landscape evolves, the symbiotic relationship between Instagram's monetisation avenues and OTT media expands the boundaries of creative and financial innovation.

5. INSTAGRAM USER-GENERATED CONTENT AND FAN COMMUNITIES

User-generated content (UGC) and fan communities have had a significant impact on the digital media landscape, especially on platforms like Instagram. UGC is a powerful tool for brands, as almost 80% of people say it influences their buying decisions. Fan communities, fostered by Instagram and other platforms, have grown into tightly-knit, participatory cultures that promote deeper connections and have a significant impact on the success of Over-the-Top (OTT) media by enhancing engagement and a sense of belonging. The intersection of UGC and fan communities has democratised content creation, with audiences becoming active contributors and co-creators of content instead of passive consumers. This shift has also changed the way brands engage with their audiences, focusing on active fans and creating fun, engaging content to boost customer loyalty and attract new people. Instagram has a significant impact on UGC, with 79% of people saying it highly influences their buying decisions. Due to its visual nature, Instagram is a critical space for brands to get creative and connect with their audiences through UGC. As of 2023, Instagram has 2 billion monthly active users, making it the fourth most used social media platform.

5.1 The Role of Instagram in Fostering User-Generated Content Around OTT Media

Instagram's transformative impact on media consumption has been underscored by its role in ushering in an era of user-generated content. User-generated content (UGC) is a testament to the empowerment of audiences, turning them from passive consumers into proactive contributors. Instagram's visually immersive nature and user-friendly interface have offered the perfect canvas for users to showcase their creativity and passion for their favourite OTT content. This co-creative process has not only fortified the bond between content creators and viewers. Still, it has also provided content creators with a treasure trove of authentic, diverse, and engaging material.

As posited by Jenkins (2006), the cognitive theory of participatory culture elucidates the transformative power of UGC and fan communities. It emphasises that media consumers are no longer passive recipients but active participants who create and circulate content. Instagram, with its user-driven interface, has propelled this theory into reality. The platform's visual centricity facilitates a seamless transition from passive consumption to active co-creation. This engagement contributes to OTT content's visibility and enhances its resonance as fans inject their interpretations and creativity into the narrative.

5.2 Examples of Fan Communities and Their Contributions to the Success of OTT Content

The emergence of fan communities on Instagram has transcended mere fandom, evolving into veritable hubs of creativity, camaraderie, and knowledge exchange. An illustrative example is the "Game of Thrones" fandom, where Instagram has served as an expansive gallery of fan art, episode analyses, and collaborative discussions. Such fan-driven initiatives provide an ecosystem where the passion for a particular OTT series metamorphosis into a rich tapestry of content, amplifying the series' reach far beyond its original episodes.

Intriguingly, research by Hsu and Wang (2018) explores how fan communities contribute to the immersive experience of OTT media. Their study reveals that fan participation enhances emotional engagement and connection to the content. Through its visual and interactive features, Instagram bolsters this immersive experience by allowing fans to showcase their emotional investment through visual expressions and engage in spirited conversations with fellow enthusiasts.

5.3 Strategies Employed by OTT Platforms and Content Creators to Encourage and Engage with Fan Communities on Instagram

OTT platforms and content creators have not merely observed the rise of fan communities on Instagram but have actively harnessed and nurtured them. They have employed ingenious strategies encompassing direct engagement, content sharing, and participatory campaigns. One standout approach is the OTT "takeovers," where cast members or creators temporarily control an OTT platform's Instagram account. This strategy merges behind-the-scenes insights with fan interactions, creating a palpable sense of inclusion.

Cultivating fan communities has become an art of reciprocity. OTT platforms and content creators increasingly acknowledge the creative contributions of fans, often showcasing their artworks, analyses, and theories on their official accounts. This acknowledgement fosters a sense of validation and belonging, transforming fans into brand ambassadors who amplify content organically.

These strategies have deep-rooted psychological underpinnings. The self-determination theory (SDT), as highlighted by Deci and Ryan (1985), underscores the significance of autonomy, competence, and relatedness in human motivation. By fostering fan communities on Instagram, OTT platforms and content creators address these fundamental human needs. The autonomy to express creativity, the competence to contribute meaningfully, and the relatedness within the community create a holistic engagement loop.

Instagram has undoubtedly emerged as a fertile ground for merging user-generated content and fan communities, infusing a new dimension into the digital media arena. The participatory culture fostered by Instagram successfully transforms audiences into co-creators, generating a rich and diverse collection of authentic content. Fan communities thrive as epicentres of passion and creativity, effervescently manifesting this participatory culture. OTT platforms and content creators, attuned to this paradigm shift, have woven innovative strategies that reciprocate engagement, effectively nurturing a mutually beneficial ecosystem. This profound interplay between content creators, platforms, and fans on Instagram is a testament to the platform's role in amplifying the success of OTT media through democratised engagement and immersive connection.

6. INSTAGRAM DISCOVERABILITY AND TREND SPOTTING

With the abundance of content available on Over-The-Top (OTT) platforms, it is easy to feel overwhelmed and lost. Fortunately, content curation algorithms have been developed to solve this issue. By analysing user behaviours, interests, and preferences, these algorithms recommend content that aligns with their tastes. This enhances the user experience and encourages viewers to consume more content. As a result, these algorithms have become crucial in boosting content visibility and keeping up with market trends. Harness the power of content curation algorithms to revolutionise your viewing experience and discover new content aligned with your interests.

6.1 Instagram's Discovery Features and Their Impact on OTT Media

In the contemporary digital landscape, the deluge of content has given rise to the critical challenge of discoverability. As the Over-the-Top (OTT) media domain burgeons with a surfeit of offerings, the role of Instagram as a catalyst for discoverability has emerged as a pivotal force. Instagram's intrinsic design, characterised by its visual appeal and interactive features, bolsters its potency as a discovery platform. The essence of Instagram's architecture, fostering the rapid consumption of visual content, aligns harmoniously with the immersive nature of OTT media.

Drawing insights from the Information Foraging Theory proposed by Pirolli and Card (1999), the discovery process can be likened to animals foraging in an information-rich environment for food. Instagram, acting as the digital terrain, assists users in their "foraging" by presenting bite-sized visuals that are aesthetically pleasing and serve as navigational cues. This aligns seamlessly with OTT media, where captivating visuals are the vanguard of content immersion. Instagram's discoverability features cater to the inherent human preference for easily digestible stimuli, enhancing the probability of unearthing relevant OTT content.

6.2 Hashtags, Trends, and Amplifying OTT-Related Content on Instagram

The ubiquity of hashtags within the Instagram ecosystem has metamorphosed from a mere labelling mechanism to a dynamic tool of content categorisation, community formation, and, significantly, trend amplification. With their ability to amalgamate diverse content under a common umbrella, hashtags become instrumental in augmenting the discoverability of OTT media. The strategic utilisation of specific hashtags ensures that OTT-related content infiltrates users' exploration trajectories, transcending follower networks and venturing into broader, trend-driven explorations.

Trendspotting, an intricate art honed by modern marketers and content creators, has found a haven on Instagram. In an era where cultural trends ebb and flow like digital tides, Instagram serves as an observatory for identifying these shifts. The concept of trend spotting is akin to the Diffusion of Innovations theory posited by Rogers (1962), which elucidates the process by which new ideas disseminate within a society. Instagram's Discover page, algorithm-driven recommendations, and trending hashtags collectively epitomise the diffusion process in the digital realm. By proactively leveraging these tools, OTT content curators can ride the wave of trends, ensuring their content remains relevant and resonant.

6.3 Case Studies Highlighting Successful Discoverability and Trend-Spotting on Instagram

Examining tangible instances that spotlight Instagram's efficacy in discoverability and trend spotting reinforces its standing as a harbinger of content visibility. A standout example is the meteoric ascent of K-dramas, particularly within Western audiences. Instagram became the cauldron where fan-driven hashtags flourished into vibrant communities, such as #KdramaAddict or #KoreanDrama. This burgeoning community, propelled by shared experiences and enthusiasm, amplified the discoverability of K-drama content. As per Hennig-Thurau et al. (2004), this phenomenon aligns with the concept of Electronic Word of Mouth (eWOM), where user-generated content fuels the viral spread of information. Instagram's inherent virality fosters the exponential growth of content trends, propelling OTT media into the global consciousness.

Furthermore, Spotify's integration with Instagram stories offers another intriguing case study. The seamless integration of music streaming into Instagram stories, accompanied by the interactive 'swipe up' feature, led to an organic surge in music discovery. This fusion of platforms echoes the principles of Cross-Media Convergence, as explained by Jenkins (2006), where different media systems intersect and collaborate to enrich user experience. Similarly, OTT media can strategically partner with Instagram to channel users from visually captivating snippets to full-fledged content, effectively crossing the convergence bridge.

The interplay between Instagram's discovery mechanisms and the proliferation of OTT media presents a fascinating nexus of influence. Like the nuances of human information foraging, Instagram's design principles seamlessly align with the immersive nature of OTT content consumption. The dynamic use of hashtags and trend-spotting strategies amplifies the visibility of OTT offerings within a crowded digital landscape. Concrete case studies accentuate Instagram's transformative role in catapulting trends and content into the mainstream. As the digital ecosystem burgeons, this alliance between Instagram's discoverability tools and the OTT media domain paints a promising picture of enhanced content visibility and resonant trends.

7. CONCLUSION

The voyage through this exploration has uncovered the profound interplay between Instagram and the ascendancy of Over-the-Top (OTT) media. As the digital landscape evolves, the synthesis of these two juggernauts underscores the potency of collaboration in reshaping content consumption and interaction paradigms. Instagram's visually immersive ecosystem, fortified by its billion-strong user base, has emerged as a veritable powerhouse in propelling the growth of OTT media. The findings of this study manifest in a harmonious narrative: Instagram's visual-centricity aligns seamlessly with the captivating narratives of OTT content, crafting a resonant synergy that elevates both platforms. The art of visual storytelling finds a dynamic stage on Instagram, where content creators and OTT platforms deftly weave narratives that engage, anticipate, and immerse the audience.

Additionally, influencer marketing has evolved into a driving force, capitalising on Instagram's ecosystem to extend the reach of OTT content. Furthermore, user-generated content and fan communities have birthed immersive experiences, fostering audience loyalty and enhancing content resonance. Instagram's discoverability mechanisms amplify OTT media's visibility, carving paths to viral trends. Lastly, monetisation avenues galore for OTT platforms and content creators, with influencer endorsements and product placements emerging as influential strategies.

This exploration's implications cascade into OTT media's and Instagram's future, heralding an era of innovation and symbiotic evolution. OTT platforms and content creators are poised to hone visual storytelling techniques further, capitalising on Instagram's dynamic formats and interactive features. The partnership between influencers and OTT entities is poised for refinement, considering the growing sophistication of influencer marketing strategies. Moreover, the emergence of user-generated content as a critical driver in audience engagement signifies the potential for a paradigm shift in content co-creation. Instagram's role as a trendsetter and content amplifier is bound to evolve, potentially influencing the very content production dynamics of OTT platforms. Monetisation, a linchpin in content sustainability, will witness an augmentation of strategies, necessitating a delicate balance between commerce and content quality.

This exploration paves a path towards a holistic engagement strategy for OTT platforms and content creators. Visual storytelling and influencer collaborations should remain at the forefront, meticulously orchestrated to cater to diverse audience segments. Engaging with fan communities can foster a sense of ownership, deepening loyalty and commitment. Leveraging Instagram's discoverability features mandates strategic deployment of hashtags, trends, and algorithmic mechanics. Moreover, monetisation strategies must be well-calibrated to align with content ethos, ensuring authenticity and user trust. Users of Instagram can benefit from actively participating in content campaigns driven by over-the-top (OTT) media, engaging with fan communities, and contributing to trend amplification. By curating their digital experience and interacting with others, they can shape the trajectory of content development.

To conclude, the ever-changing relationship between Instagram and OTT media demonstrates a story of mutual progress, interaction, and development. The outcomes and suggestions of this investigation emphasize the transformative potential of these platforms, both individually and together, in the continuously developing digital media terrain. As we come to the end of this exploration, it opens doors to a new phase in the evolving narrative of OTT media and Instagram's interdependent journey.

REFERENCES

Bandura, A. (1986). *Social foundations of thought and action: A social cognitive theory*. Prentice-Hall.

Brown, A. (2019). Changing the channel: How OTT is reshaping the media landscape. *Forbes*.

Brown, A. (2019). The role of Instagram in OTT video marketing: A Netflix case study. *Journal of Media Business Studies*, *16*(1), 42–54.

Brown, K. (2019). Leveraging Instagram for OTT media promotion: A new strategy. *Journal of Digital Media Management*, *7*(3), 275–289.

Brown, K. (2019). *On-demand: Exploring the impacts of OTT on traditional television*. MediaShift. [Link]

Cialdini, R. B. (2001). *Influence: Science and practice* (4th ed.). Allyn & Bacon.

Davenport, T. H., & Beck, J. C. (2001). *The Attention Economy: Understanding the New Currency of Business*. Harvard Business Press.

Davis, F. D. (1989). Perceived usefulness, perceived ease of use, and user acceptance of information technology. *Management Information Systems Quarterly*, *13*(3), 319–340. doi:10.2307/249008

De Cicco, T., Cangiano, F., & De Felice, M. (2019). Using hashtags for a purpose: The case of Instagram. *New Media & Society*, *21*(1), 1–20.

Deci, E. L., & Ryan, R. M. (1985). *Intrinsic motivation and self-determination in human behaviour*. Springer. doi:10.1007/978-1-4899-2271-7

Dijck, J. V. (2013). *The culture of connectivity: A critical history of social media*. Oxford University Press. doi:10.1093/acprof:oso/9780199970773.001.0001

Dijck, J. V. (2013). *The culture of connectivity: A critical history of social media*. Oxford University Press. doi:10.1093/acprof:oso/9780199970773.001.0001

Hennig-Thurau, T., Gwinner, K. P., Walsh, G., & Gremler, D. D. (2004). Electronic word-of-mouth via consumer-opinion platforms: What motivates consumers to articulate themselves online? *Journal of Interactive Marketing*, *18*(1), 38–52. doi:10.1002/dir.10073

Hill, C. (2020). Streaming Services Now Have Nearly 1 Billion Subscribers Globally. *Forbes*.

Hsu, C. L., & Wang, E. T. (2018). Understanding the psychological process underlying audience engagement with OTT content. *Internet Research*, *28*(5), 1209–1228.

Jackson, M. (2020). Building anticipation: How Netflix utilised Instagram Stories to promote "Stranger Things.". *Media and Communication*, *8*(2), 329–337.

Jackson, S. (2020). The influence of Instagram on OTT media marketing: A case study of Netflix's "Stranger Things.". *Journal of New Media Marketing*, *19*(2), 76–88.

Jenkins, H. (2006). *Convergence culture: Where old and new media collide*. NYU Press.

Johnson, L. (2019). *How to use Instagram's new algorithm to boost your reach*. Social Media Today. [Link]

Johnson, M. (2019). The Impact of Instagram on Modern Media Consumption. *Journal of New Media Studies, 3*(2), 45–59.

Johnson, S. K., Tullis, T. S., & Shaw, H. (2017). Browsing behaviours, information seeking, and cognitive load during learning from the Web. *Memory & Cognition, 45*(3), 422–436.

Jones, R. (2020). *Streaming Wars: Who will win the battle for your eyeballs?* BBC.

Jones, R. (2020). The Streaming Revolution: A Comparative Analysis of OTT Platforms. *Journal of Media Trends, 17*(3), 120–137.

Kaplan, A. M., & Haenlein, M. (2010). Users of the world, unite! The challenges and opportunities of Social Media. *Business Horizons, 53*(1), 59–68. doi:10.1016/j.bushor.2009.09.003

Krieger, M., & Systrom, K. (2012). *Instagram: From Zero to a Billion*. Stanford Business.

Lin, J. S., & Lu, H. P. (2011). Why people use social networking sites: An empirical study integrating network externalities and motivation theory. *Computers in Human Behavior, 27*(3), 1152–1161. doi:10.1016/j.chb.2010.12.009

Osgood, C. E., & Tannenbaum, P. H. (1955). The Principle of Congruity in the Prediction of Attitude Change. *Psychological Review, 62*(1), 42–55. doi:10.1037/h0048153 PMID:14357526

Paivio, A. (1986). *Mental representations: A dual coding approach*. Oxford University Press.

Petty, R. E., & Cacioppo, J. T. (1986). *Communication and Persuasion: Central and Peripheral Routes to Attitude Change*. Springer. doi:10.1007/978-1-4612-4964-1

Pirolli, P., & Card, S. (1999). Information foraging. *Psychological Review, 106*(4), 643–675. doi:10.1037/0033-295X.106.4.643

Roberts, H. (2017). *How Instagram is revolutionising audience engagement for creators*. Tubular Insights. [Link]

Roberts, H. (2020). Instagram as a storytelling platform: Leveraging visual content for brand narratives. *Journal of Social Media Strategy, 6*(1), 45–57.

Roberts, K. (2020). Instagram: A powerful platform for visual storytelling. *Journal of Contemporary Rhetoric, 10*, 89–97.

Roberts, S. (2017). From Follower to Fan: Investigating User Engagement in OTT Media through Instagram. *Media Studies Journal, 25*(4), 78–92.

Rogers, E. M. (1962). *Diffusion of Innovations*. Free Press.

Smith, J. (2020). *Visual storytelling on social media: The case of Disney*. Social Media Today.

Smith, T. (2018). Influencer Culture: The Changing Dynamics of Media Promotion. *Communication Review, 41*(2), 215–230.

Smith, T. (2018). Instagram's influence on visual storytelling. *Journal of Visual Communication, 17*(3), 297–315.

Smith, T. (2018). *OTT platforms and the power of visual storytelling*. The Drum.

Smith, T. (2020). Crafting visual narratives on Instagram: Disney+ case study. *Visual Media Journal, 23*(4), 489–505.

Statista. (2021). *Number of monthly active Instagram users from January 2013 to June 2021*. Statista.

Verma, M., & Kalorth, N. (Eds.). (2017). *Essays on Contemporary Media Theory and Practices: With an Introductory Article by Prof.* Denis McQuail on the Future of the Field of Communication. Amity University Rajasthan.

Williams, C. (2022). *The influencer economy: Understanding its impact on modern marketing*. Marketing Profs.

Williams, J. (2022). The Instagram Phenomenon: Exploring Visual Culture in the Digital Age. *International Journal of Visual Culture, 14*(1), 102–120.

Zajonc, R. B. (1968). Attitudinal effects of mere exposure. *Journal of Personality and Social Psychology, 9*(2), 1–27. doi:10.1037/h0025848

Zeigarnik, B. (1927). Das Behalten erledigter und unerledigter Handlungen. *Psychologische Forschung, 9*(1), 1–85.

Section 2
User Experience

Chapter 6
Impact of OTT Media on Advertising and Marketing

Munise Hayrun Sağlam
https://orcid.org/0000-0003-3847-1337
Yildiz Technical University, Turkey

Ibrahim Kirçova
Yildiz Technical University, Turkey

ABSTRACT

OTT media platforms (Netflix, Amazon Prime, Disney+Hotstar, etc.) are another logical TV development that transmits content via an Internet connection without the provider's influence or control over the content. The subject is essential because OTT media allows viewers to watch video content uninterruptedly, anywhere, anytime, and on any device, and content owners can build direct audience relationships independent of the video service provider. This chapter aims to understand the changes that developments in OTT media have brought to the marketing and advertising environment compared to traditional media and to draw attention to the increasing importance of advertising content for consumers and publishers. It discusses some of the practical benefits and issues exemplified for consumers and advertisers of this change in the media landscape: (1) the role of data in targeting consumers and the impact of brand image and loyalty gained on OTT platforms as a result of highly focused targeting, and (2) the power of OTT advertising agents to change consumers' behavior and data privacy concerns.

INTRODUCTION

With the acceleration of digitalization, OTT media services have become phenomenally widespread globally and locally (Chang & Chang, 2020). This chapter examines the impact of OTT media on marketing and advertising activities as another logical development of television. OTT - the acronym for Over-the-top - permanently replaces this system, as it refers to content delivered through an Internet connection without the provider's influence or control over the content. OTT media platforms offer consumers the most excellent possible flexibility as they can watch linear programs on any fixed or mobile device, regardless of their Internet access provider.

DOI: 10.4018/979-8-3693-0116-6.ch006

Previously, watching TV meant being available to watch scheduled programs at certain times. However, with technological advances and the popularity of personal devices such as smartphones, high-speed Internet, and new content platforms, a new method of watching a video called OTT has emerged that provides more flexible viewing options (Jain, 2021). OTT refers to consuming featured video content from linear television and the provider via the Internet. Over The Top is a symbol that goes beyond the Internet box and the television packages or channels offered by default (programs always travel physically through the Internet box) (Chen, 2019). OTT media platforms offer consumers the most excellent possible flexibility as they can watch linear programs on any fixed or mobile device, regardless of their Internet access provider. Exceptionally fast internet connections have made OTT accessible to all types of video formats, from feature films to YouTube tutorials.

According to the latest statistics released by The Diffusion Group, nearly half (42%) of television time is devoted to content provided by an alternative service, or "over-the-top" (OTT) content (Marketing Charts, 2020). As the popularity of this service grows, distributors are forced to offer a wide variety of quality content across multiple media. OTT has therefore shaken the broadcast industry by changing how viewers want to access video content (i.e., on multiple screens and in the context of multiple events) and with content owners now able to engage directly with viewers regardless of the service provider. This development has resulted in a general upheaval in the audio- visual landscape, with new players, new sources of revenue, and new information about the audience involved, enabling new ways for content to be distributed and consumed worldwide. It is essential to read the results of this change in the media environment correctly and understand how consumers perceive it regarding how advertisers do business legally, the improvement of their marketing activities, and the development of different advertising techniques.

OTT platforms aim to grow by focusing on local content, pricing flexibility, mobile access and understanding local culture. This requires a combination of strategies involving engaging users to establish a competitive presence and expand the user base. Netflix India's gamification-based strategy pushes viewers to play a role similar to the characters in the movie, ensuring they have an unforgettable experience with the brand. For example, Netflix India did exciting marketing campaigns for 'Red Notice'. They recently launched a store where customers can attempt to "steal" artifacts while dodging lasers and security as a promotion for Netflix India's action-packed Hollywood blockbuster movie 'Red Notice' (Shaw, 2021). In this highly secure 'Red Notice Shop' store, gifts were offered to those who can steal. Similarly, OTT platforms in India take care to diversify content based on language, genre, and audience. For example, a wide range of content is offered, from classic Bollywood movies to modern web series. OREO has collaborated with Netflix's Stranger Things to launch limited edition 'Oreo Red Velvet' in India. They released a special edition of red cookies to celebrate the upcoming release of "Stranger Things Season 4"(Kumari, 2022). They have also created an Instagram filter that turns your world upside-down, another fun way to engage with the show's fans.

In the past, television has always worked linearly and always through a middleman. Whether cable television, satellite television, or IPTV, a provider provides content via its infrastructure (Kim et al., 2017). With traditional television, for example, the cable provider lays the lines, and users can only see what the cable television is currently broadcasting. Precisely what that is and when it can be received has been, and to some extent still is, decided in a classic top-down system. However, OTT providers offer content to users via streaming. OTT services are therefore separated from infrastructure providers. The most well-known OTT providers in the market are Netflix, Amazon Prime, Hulu, DAZN, and Eurosport Player (IONOS, 2019). In order to receive streaming services, users only need an Internet connection and usually install the respective OTT provider's app. The requested content can be streamed through the app anytime, anywhere, and with any internet-enabled device.

OTT platforms have revolutionized the marketing landscape by offering online services (Palomba, 2022) that allow subscribers to stream audio-visual content using different devices. These platforms have revolutionized how people consume video content worldwide, as they offer the convenience of accessing content even on the go. OTT broadcasters allow users to watch TV shows and movies whenever they want on any device using streaming services such as Netflix, Amazon Prime, and Hulu (Palomba, 2022), while production companies are putting tremendous effort into creating quality, original content to meet the offerings of this growing demand. OTT technology also makes it possible to make phone calls and SMS messages with providers such as Skype and WhatsApp (Glossaire, 2023). In addition, OTT media providers once again demonstrated the increasing importance of user-generated content, and the understanding of advertising that differs individually has also accelerated the development of targeted and permission marketing. These permission marketing strategies can help OTT platforms build more profound and positive relationships with audiences. Personalization, in particular, helps viewers spend more time on the platform and maintain their subscriptions. Permission marketing activities on OTT media platforms aim to send updates, special offers, or new content announcements via mobile applications or email, with user permission, and conduct surveys or surveys to obtain user feedback. This is an effective strategy to attract new subscribers or retain existing subscribers.

The permission-based content distribution landscape has enabled the rise of OTT platforms, which offer both free and subscription-based services to access content. These platforms use different methods to trial their content. Subscription-based OTT platforms offer free trial periods, giving new users access to all content on the platform for a specified period. For example, Netflix and Disney+ offer new users a one-month free trial. Specific OTT platforms follow the practice of providing accessible content categories to users before granting full access. For instance, YouTube Premium requires a subscription to access its original content. At the same time, some videos can be watched by non-subscribers for free—furthermore, platforms such as IMDb TV offer free content. Some free OTT platforms support their content with ads, allowing users to access content for free. Other platforms offer free content categories and limited versions of the entire platform. Limited access to content is also available to free users (Sharma & Lulandala, 2023). Additionally, some OTT platforms offer free access deals during specific periods or holiday seasons. These methods help users to try the platform's content before deciding to subscribe. However, for these platforms to attract and retain users, it is crucial to increase the quality and variety of their content. Users can access VOD (Video on demand) and live video on multiple sites, and audio libraries on Spotify, podcasts, and online radio stations. SMS and internet-based voice calling apps like Facebook Messenger, Skype, Viber, and WhatsApp are also part of the OTT services. Over the past few years, mobile video has risen dramatically, with over 90% of internet video streams seen on mobile devices (Krishna & Sen, 2022).

In short, the most significant impact of OTT media services on advertising activities and marketing, in general, is hidden in the fact that user experience is the critical point. In its simplest form, OTT platforms know what the public wants to watch and how to watch it: they can offer recommendations on content, serve more targeted ads, etc., thereby creating a higher level of participation and expanding the market scope. Moreover, in recent years, many OTT platforms have been powered by artificial bits of intelligence capable of detecting the type of screen the user is connecting to and the internet speed. In this way, the platform can optimize the quality of the video according to the size of the screen and the speed of the connection (Chen, 2019). It can also make intelligent suggestions for content to watch based on the time of day, people who share the same interests as the user, ratings for the content the user is viewing, and more. These benefits trigger a positive brand image and sentiment towards the OTT media platform, resulting in long-term loyalty (Shim et al., 2022).

The purpose of this chapter is to focus on the consequences of the rise of OTT media services and examine their impact on marketing and advertising activities. The chapter explains how OTT media platforms replace traditional television by delivering content via an internet connection. Additionally, chapters focusing on advertising and marketing activities explain with examples how OTT media platforms provide advertising strategies and more personalized advertising opportunities for their target audience. It underlines the future importance of OTT services in the context of data privacy and ethical use, with insights into how user experience should be optimized, particularly with personalized advertising. Finally, it suggests OTT media research to shed light on future studies.

TRADITIONAL AND NEW GENERATION TELEVISION BROADCAST DISTRIBUTION METHODS (DTH VS. OTT)

OTT, TV and video revenue is expected to reach US$235 billion by 2028 (Statista, 2023). With the increase in subscription-based services, there is more demand for OTT media platforms in the future; OTT market is expected to drive growth from 2022 to 2030 with a CAGR of 26.42%. (Precedence Research, 2022). With this growth, dominant OTT players such as YouTube, Netflix, Amazon Prime, and Hulu are actively promoting global market entry and gaining access using their existing content from Disney, Apple, Warner Media, and HBO. The emerging OTT market is already a fierce battleground filled with strong competitors (Choi & Kim, 2020).

One benefit of using OTT rather than IPTV or DTH (Direct-to-Home) is the ability to customize advertisements based on the geographic location of the viewer's IP address (Arnold, 2018). Databases of OTT operators such as Netflix or Amazon are located on central servers. If a user decides to watch a particular movie in the stream, the data is sent to him in IP packets. The transmission takes place through the infrastructure of the Internet provider. It is only used by OTT as a means of transmission. There is no legal liability for the content used, as the Internet provider ultimately only undertakes the transmission of data packets (Kim et al., 2017). Generally, streaming storage-intensive content in HD quality requires a stable and high-performance Internet connection between the sender and receiver of OTT content. Because if the transmission rate is too low or the DSL network is overloaded, the quality of the stream may be lost, or the video may be interrupted (IONOS, 2019). However, there are no barriers to receiving OTT content under good network conditions. Also, unlike an OTT advertisement broadcast on a connected television device, it is impossible to interact with a conventional television. These new advanced ad formats can strengthen the advertising landscape by better-targeting consumers.

Satellite television providers offer DTH (Direct-to-Home) services. This service allows viewers to receive television programs directly into their homes using satellite dishes and satellite receivers. It provides access to television programs via satellite antenna without cable or other communication infrastructure (Nagaraj et al., 2021). For broadcasters, cost is a crucial factor, and satellite transmission provides a cost-effective point-to-multipoint network solution. Unlike other infrastructure transmission options, satellite transmission does not increase costs based on the number of users. This means broadcasters can reach many homes without incurring additional infrastructure transmission costs. While the initial investment may seem high, this setup provides immediate access to a large audience, making it an extremely efficient and reliable option for broadcasters.

MORE TARGETED CONSUMERS

From a regulatory perspective, OTT services for extensive use of personal and geocoded data are often seen as a competitive advantage for the OTT service provider. Through the reuse of audience information in planning, programming, and advertising, OTT allows publishers better to target consumers with accurate data for each individual. Using data on the characteristics and behavior of users of these services plays a vital role in increasing sales, primarily through online advertisements or website referrals (Arnold et al., 2018). Moreover, targeting online advertising content is very interesting because not only are entirely new requirements for measuring and predicting consumer behavior emerging in near real-time (Tefertiller, 2020) but also specifically for measuring advertising effectiveness. This way, the entire targeting process can be tuned in near real-time. In the context of programmatic advertising, if the public knows what they want to watch and how to watch it correctly, they can offer more accurate suggestions about the content and more targeted ads, etc., thus achieving a higher level of participation (Bush, 2016). Further adjustments to the target group extend to target group-specific optimization of ad content display.

The Role of Data in Targeting Consumers

New digital technology is emerging as a complement to traditional services, and others are replacing traditional services; that is, they are born to perform the same technological functions and emerge as substitutes for traditional services, massifying their intensive use. Telecommunications businesses are evolving, and with this, traditional telecommunications services are being abandoned, and other new providers are becoming responsible for providing these services.

These technologies work within the digital ecosystem, considering the trends in which end users accept their transactions. These trends are framed within the scope of personalization, where users always benefit from an excellent availability of content and information. This real-time flow of information and content is available to each user's preference, providing more focused resources for advanced marketing services that allow us to configure and choose what we want to consume and when with the combination of Smartphone and Internet technology

The fact that streaming services of the digital age connect and interact with customers in real time has revolutionized marketing and advertising tremendously. OTT platforms offer advanced analytics tools to identify audience based on data such as demographics, geographic location, viewing history, and preferences. Marketing activities can be carried out through content created specifically for certain audience segments. This approach allows companies to tailor their ads to a specific demographic rather than targeting a broad demographic and geography as traditional ads do.

In the context of programmatic advertising, bids can be customized with different targeting types and target group-specific optimization of ad content display. Behind this high customization are datasets where we leave our behavioral surplus (Zuboff, 2019). In short, this significant development in the media and entertainment industry is due to the ability of OTT platforms to offer viewing quality and diversity with richer content than traditional media consumption experiences (Singh et al., 2021).

For internet advertising to be designed by the target audience, it is necessary to correctly evaluate the target audiences of the potential buyers of the advertisement. To conduct the evaluation, it must utilize data from numerous sources and put it in context. By reusing audience information in planning, programming, and advertising, OTT allows publishers to target consumers with accurate data for each individual (Choi & Kim, 2020). At this point, online and offline data can be used for targeting. On the one hand, online data is the so-called registration data that the user consciously provides. The data provided by enrollment are mostly socio-demographic. On the other hand, data is generated from users' behavior on the Internet. The user generally influences collecting and using this data only following the opt-out procedure. For example, when Discount cards and similar customer loyalty systems are used, specific data may be transmitted for advertising purposes and thus for online advertising purposes without a consent statement unless the customer objects to it (Shim et al., 2022).

Another way to distinguish different data is by the unit of measurement. It can be first-party, second-party, and third-party data. First-party data refers to any data that a company collects directly from website visitors or customers, whether directly from an advertiser or publisher. In other words, the data belongs to the company (or party) that collected it. Some examples of first-party data include data in CRM, subscription data, survey data, behavioral data collected from company websites or apps, etc (BVDW, 2015).

First-party cookies refer to the way data is collected by a website or application. A cookie is actually a data file stored by the web browser. It remembers users so they do not have to log in every time they visit. Behavioral data is also collected through cookies and compared to information already collected about that user. Advertisers use first-party data to identify the ideal audience for targeting, work with publishers to determine which ad fits the ideal audience. They also use it primarily to personalize advertising content to create a direct connection with the interests of the target group and to make the customer journey as seamless and customized as possible.

Second-party data is data that another company has collected but that another company can access - either through purchase or through collaboration. An example of this would be if a clothing brand aimed at women decides to introduce a men's line and needs appropriate target groups to market to. If the purchased data contains personal information, it must be protected in the same way as first-party data containing personal information (BVDW, 2015).

Third-party data is sometimes referred to as external, aggregated, derived or purchased data. They are obtained indirectly from marketers, aggregators, or other sources. They do not come from the user or from his interactions or activities with a specific company (Singh & Kumar, 2023). Third-party data typically needs to be aggregated with lots of first-party data and other third-party data to provide value and sometimes consists of multiple data sets "stitched" together. This data may include information such as buy signals, e.g., whether someone wants to buy a new car. This also includes but is not limited to, demographic information, data collected using third-party tracking technologies, and many other types.

These data types can be used together to provide advertisers with the strongest and most accurate data sources. The combination of these types of data can help advertisers better understand their audience, expand their advertising reach, and improve their marketing efforts to achieve better engagement and loyalty. However, with the increasing importance of data privacy and regulatory compliance, advertisers must know what makes sense to protect their business from liability.

Engage with the Social Community on OTT Media Platforms

The TV market in North America currently has many active built-in OTT players. Netflix's success has significantly impacted the local TV industry, leading traditional providers to offer new OTT services and create original content in response (Kim et al., 2017). After the original content succeeds in attracting users to the platform, the second important task is to create a familiar feeling and attitude association with users exposed to similar content and ensure that they stay in interaction with each other. For example, Netflix's foray into the highly dynamic Indian OTT market has been a remarkable one. Upon Netflix's entry into the Indian market, they introduced international content. However, their campaign strategy was primarily focused on local demographics and imbued with a substantial amount of humor (Nafees, et al., 2021). Despite stiff competition from established players like Amazon Prime Video and Hotstar, Netflix quickly adapted to the unique preferences and challenges of the Indian audience. One of the key factors contributing to Netflix's success in India has been its focus on content localization. The streaming giant understood the importance of catering to India's diverse linguistic and cultural landscape and started producing a mix of Hindi and regional language content (Ramesh & Jaggi, 2022). This strategy paid off, with series like "Sacred Games" and "Delhi Crime" garnering immense popularity. Moreover, to provide a smooth user experience, Netflix focused on improving its streaming quality and content recommendation algorithms. It also allowed users to download content for offline viewing, which was a hit in a country with inconsistent internet connectivity.

Customer loyalty is a behavioral and emotional consumption continuum between a firm and its customers that focuses on customer interaction and participation (Habib et al., 2022). Hollebeek and Macky (2019) pointed out that it effectively obtains consumer engagement based on loyalty, creates brand communities, develops a positive brand image, and directs consumer purchase intention. Achieving high levels of engagement due to a commitment to OTT platforms mobilizes the industry, helping to create a more dynamic, focused, and diverse marketing environment. Moreover, it occurs when an increasing number of individual users of one platform side makes the platform more attractive to another (Arnold, 2018). Users of one platform side indirectly benefit if the number of platform users on their side continues to increase. Thus, more platform users are attracted to another platform side, making the platform more attractive.

Further, the impact of OTT media on marketing should go beyond the user's purchasing behavior to participate emotionally and physically in the service provider's activities (Vivek et al., 2012). Initiating marketing action for OTT media providers to build a community of users enables them to Develop a loyal customer base that is emotionally connected to the products/services offered by the company. At the same time, consumption values obtained by consumers will also support the formation of trust toward the brand. Chakraborty et al. (2023) suggest that trust between users of OTT platforms is influenced by various factors related to consumption, such as pricing, service quality, engaging content, and appealing promotional deals. Participation in such a trust-based community will also encourage the development of unique services, offering more different offerings and unique content packages and allowing consumers to share their opinions about the content (Dang et al., 2020). Currently, Well-Known OTT service providers create personalized content packages for their customers. They achieve this by reorganizing and merging their content libraries to include various offerings such as video, music, and game services (Gupta & Singharia, 2021). This approach provides customers with a unique and enhanced service experience. However, engaging with the content and social community on OTT platforms is crucial for users to derive significant value. This value directly affects their satisfaction and determines whether they will continue to use OTT services.

Recognizing India's inconsistent internet connectivity, both platforms have also allowed users to download content for offline viewing (Singh, 2020). Both platforms have been cautious about content that could be considered culturally insensitive or offensive, often editing or censoring content to avoid controversies. They have also used innovative marketing strategies such as promoting shows by tying them to cultural events and festivals, leveraging the popularity of local celebrities, and running interactive social media campaigns. Moreover, both platforms have invested in original soundtracks and music videos for their shows, recognizing the importance of music in Indian entertainment. They have also released content during major festivals and holidays to attract more viewers. All of these adaptations and strategies demonstrate how OTT platforms have tailored their offerings to cater to various segments of the Indian audience effectively. It is a dynamic and competitive market, and platforms continue to evolve their approaches to stay relevant.

In addition, considering that customers consume emotions and memory with extra interest and attention (Alsharif et al., 2021) and produce OTT media content individually, this will also support the advancement of more prosperous algorithm-based programmatic advertising. However, from the perspective of service providers, it is essential to focus on the critical factors that affect customers' decisions to continue doing business with them and consistent advertising content to remain competitive and ensure future sales flow continuity (Viswanathan et al., 2017). For sellers, the platform is attractive the more potential buyers use the platform because the higher the number of platform users, the more likely a service or product will be offered. However, OTT firms have long been interested in attractive strategies to attract consumers to their content and create engagement. However, today it has become their primary goal to increase their earnings by paying more consumers. Regarding this matter, to effectively gain more paying subscribers, companies must utilize market segmentation and targeted marketing techniques.

OTT Brand Image

A strong brand image for the OTT platform is crucial in today's digital age. As the competition heats up in the OTT media sector, consumers must develop positive feelings and attitudes towards the brand in their minds, to differentiate themselves, provide reasons for their preference, and most importantly, develop a culture that helps the organization maintain this value it provides for itself (Aaker, 2012; Keller, 2017). This requires all businesses to create a unique online presence. At this point, brand image is created through continuous advertising efforts and verified by customers' direct interactions with the brand (Aaker, 2012). Research has shown that digital marketing content and communication are essential for an effective online marketing strategy (Kala & Chaubey, 2018). They contribute significantly to a brand's image and influence consumers' purchasing behavior. To achieve this, OTT platforms should actively engage with consumers on social media platforms to stay updated with trends and build a positive brand image. Nowadays, numerous OTT platforms have collaborated with telecom providers to offer appealing deals, resulting in improved brand reputation and customer growth for the OTT platforms (Shah & Mehta, 2022). Social media and digital marketing are critical for boosting brand recognition and executing marketing campaigns on OTT platforms. Their strategic use is more prevalent than ever before. Instead of relying on traditional media, utilizing social media can lead to improved brand image and increased buying intention for marketers, following the lead of their competitors. These methods provide more measurable campaign results (Silvia, 2019). Ultimately, loyalty to the brand or company is aimed at a consistent digital brand image. OTT media platforms actively engage with consumers on social media platforms to ensure continued customer loyalty.

The rise in popularity and number of OTT service users can be attributed mainly to the partnerships between these businesses and telecom carriers. Social media, social commerce, and other forms of digital marketing as strategic tools to raise brand awareness and promote products and services are on the rise (Habib et al., 2022). Marketers can get better outcomes in terms of brand image, brand equity, and purchase intentions by following the methods of their competitors and employing social media and digital marketing instead of traditional or mass media. Campaign success can be more accurately gauged using these strategies.

IMPACT OF OTT MEDIA SERVICE ON ADVERTISING ACTIVITIES

Understanding the impact of OTT advertising on the marketing industry is crucial in identifying the new trends and features of the media industry. OTT services have revolutionized the traditional production, distribution, and consumption stages, and it is essential to recognize the innovations they bring to the marketing environment (Banerjee et al., 2014; Kim, 2015).

As the technology-driven consumer services industry has grown and networks have evolved, the ways we access entertainment and information have changed rapidly (Choi & Kim, 2020); Along with the growing popularity of OTT platforms, subscription-based services are becoming more common (Gupta & Singharia, 2021). In the past, we relied heavily on TV broadcasts for multimedia. Nevertheless, with the rise of internet smartphones and services like YouTube and Netflix, we can watch multimedia content from anywhere in the world without a TV. This is because of the simplicity and widespread availability of OTT internet protocol (IP) services (Kim et al., 2017).

OTT media platforms influence targeted advertising and permission marketing activities to improve consumer experience and engagement. The technology-driven targeting mentioned here is not only to thematically coordinate ads with specific target groups but also to ensure that the advertising material is displayed correctly and to control the number of impressions for an individual consumer (Arnold, 2018). However, the most vivid effect of OTT media on advertising activities is that it can determine the essential values of consumers and programmatically produce content based on these values. Also, adding consumption value benefits to marketing offers will support the development of existing services. The content creator must then consider an effective audience strategy to attract a new audience and build a lasting relationship based on the interests and specific needs of the users. For example, Netflix analyzes and recognizes its audience perfectly and manages to predict the type of content the user would like to watch (Kim et al., 2017). With this detailed analysis obtained by crossing different behavioral signals and indicators, such as ratings or the number of views, Netflix allows them to offer an enhanced and personalized user experience (Thomas, 2023).

When we consider pricing the most important revenue-generating marketing tool, pricing OTT services is another critical factor affecting media consumption. It has been found that the most effective strategy for pricing OTT media consumption is to determine pricing plans based on consumers' usage patterns. Because OTT services require much bandwidth, research suggests methods for estimating network consumption and pricing content delivery via a software-defined network (Oliveira et al., 2018). Consumers' OTT-service usage patterns must be determined quickly for plans based on network usage amount to work smoothly. For network and OTT providers to create successful pricing strategies, they must promptly and precisely determine which users are utilizing which OTT services and how much data they are consuming (Choi & Kim, 2020). This involves classifying all items and load-balancing accordingly. Therefore, to develop an effective plan, the initial step is to classify the OTT users.

On the other hand, data on the software and hardware used by the user and the bandwidth of the internet connection are needed to prevent long loading times in technical terms and to display the advertisement correctly. This data is transmitted automatically when a website is called up, thus enabling the advertisement to be adapted to the technical equipment of the consumer (Arnold, 2018). Some of this data can also be used to tailor advertisements to the topic, as, for example, the operating system used can be used to conclude the consumer's willingness to pay. In addition, lately, there has been a growing awareness of the distinction between paid and free OTT services that use mandatory ad tracking. This can be a nuisance for users and may affect their decision to pay for ad-blocking features depending on factors such as ad length, location, and the likelihood of skipping the ad (Shon et al., 2021).

When consuming OTT media content, such as placement on a web page, it is essential to draw the buyer's attention to a particular advertisement. If it is evident in which ad slot or between watched content an ad will be placed, the ad can be optically adapted to the medium, resulting in an improved ad effect. It also plays an important role when the ad is displayed, and adjustments can be made to improve its impact. A distinction must be made as to whether the point in time is seen as more effective overall or is tailored to a particular target group. If the ad is tailored to the target audience, it is called personalized advertising (Lorimer, 2013). The allocation of individual advertising messages to existing tags is now highly automated within the framework of so-called programmatic advertising. A critical success factor of programmatic advertising is the target group-specific control of advertising messages. Besides, OTT services use thumbnail images from videos to recommend movies and show to encourage users to watch content (Bong-Goon & Park, 2021). However, It is important to remember that even though OTT users can explore specific content, they may still feel overwhelmed by the sheer number of options on the platform. The way recommendation information is presented can affect consumers' attitudes and behaviors (Kim & Bae, 2016).

The programmatic ecosystem in OTT advertising is made up of demand (buy) and supply (Sell, 2014). The market also becomes more dynamic as pricing is based on real-time supply and demand for each ad impression (Busch, 2016). Efficiency in marketing is essential for companies to increase their profit figures. An effective marketing system requires bidirectional data flow analysis to reach the right audience at the right time, which is possible with accurate and sufficient information about potential customers. Integrating data management and technology in business processes increases efficiency and improves targeting (Busch, 2016; Grether, 2016). With this automated technique, publishers use their ad slots for advertising to advertisers who want to use this space to reach more potential customers (Alsabeeh & Issam Moghrabi, 2018).

Original content production is important to ensure the continuity of interaction on OTT media platforms. Using the OTT service, creators can generate a more stable income, scale their offerings, and reach a wider audience without directly depending on a single distribution platform. Thanks to the good analytics tools available on the platforms, the audience is targeted at a granular level, making it easy for them to engage and monetize the content. Content creators must then consider an effective audience strategy to attract a new audience and build a lasting relationship based on users' interests and specific needs. For example, Netflix analyzes and recognizes its audience perfectly and manages to predict the type of content the user would like to watch (Kim et al., 2017; Kour & Chhabria, 2022). The result is obtained by crossing different behavioral signals and indicators, such as rating or number of views. This detailed analysis allows them to provide an enhanced and personalized user experience (Thomas, 2023).

OTT Creates New Consumer Habits

OTT services are rapidly gaining popularity among today's consumers because they offer entertainment and ease of use, similar to traditional TV. Considering the range of content provided, it is a fact that these platforms will create new consumer habits by threatening traditional television networks (Tefertiller, 2020). Additionally, the competitive advantage of OTT services outperforms conventional TV options of all sizes (Chen, 2019). Today's generation of users (sometimes called "Generation Y") is an increasingly individualized customer generation that is content-oriented rather than brand-focused. As a rule, although not attractive to a particular content provider, Hulu receives a variety of content over the Internet from modern OTT streaming providers such as Netflix or YouTube, regardless of the origin of the content producer (Spacek, 2018). This may be due to media providers striving for liberation to receive and manage content in their way.

Moreover, OTT platforms have enabled users to take control of media consumption by allowing them to choose lower-cost content, unlike linear content on a traditional television set, which is often considered "background noise" (Steiner & Xu, 2020). OTT viewers choose what they want to watch. In this way, consumers freed from television restrictions increasingly watch video content on their smartphones, tablets, laptops, or game consoles, creating many opportunities for content owners to engage more on these platforms and devices (Palomba, 2021). It is valuable for OTT service providers to constantly pay attention to aspects that affect consumers' consumption behaviors, especially those that improve interaction and user experience in terms of delivering targeted marketing messages to consumers.

Since Generation Z grew up in the digital age, unlike other generations, it has different interests and consumption habits from traditional media. Considering their characteristics, such as making decisions much faster and trying to keep up with everything, the series broadcast on OTT media platforms are compatible with the media consumption habits of Generation Z (Ayten et al., 2019). Therefore, Generation Z may be interested in unconventional content that may interest them on OTT platforms. Moreover, they are motivated to watch certain media content regularly so that they can comment on the same topic while chatting with their peers (Nagaraj et al., 2021). True crime stories, series with mysterious and science fiction themes, documentaries about social justice, discussion programs, and activist content are viral among Generation Z (Singh, 2020). Generation Z consumers are masters of two screens at once, able to interact with social networks and manage fast-moving content while watching TV. In fact, new media consumption patterns, such as binge-watching and self-scheduling, called the "Netflix effect," have emerged among Generation Z viewers (Omukić et al., 2022). In this context, this generation is more interested in multimedia content, live game broadcasts, and content related to video games, as well as professional e-sports events (Sharma & Lulandala, 2023).

OTT services typically offer a free trial period, followed by the option for customers to continue using the service by subscribing and paying a fixed monthly fee. This subscription grants uninterrupted access to unlimited content on the streaming platform (Spacek, 2018). Users can enjoy free content from major OTT service providers by watching ads. However, one obstacle these providers encounter is that many consumers prefer to pay for online video services. However, the use of OTT has dramatically benefited the streaming industry, including video, music, podcasts, and audio. This increase in use is due to the ability to choose specific content, flexibility in packaging, wider availability on different devices, greater internet access, and lower costs (Mordor Intelligence, 2020).

Additionally, the growing demand for personalized content has led to significant adoption rates of OTT devices. In addition, gamers who offer OTT platform services no longer want to be seen as platforms that only provide access to movies and series but also invest in the production and licensing of their content. This scenario has resulted in direct competition within the traditional TV and OTT industry. With the deployment of advanced technologies on the platforms, the competition is getting more intense. In addition to providing messaging services, certain OTT applications offer similar features to those found on traditional broadcast channels. Many users share enjoyable videos, music, and local and international news with a large audience of other users who highly engage with the content. This wide range of applicability accelerates adoption. On the other hand, it has been found that the most valuable features for consumers in Ott media consumption are resolution, recommendation system, display option, and recommendation system (Kim et al., 2017).

The improvements that OTT media will experience in their advertising strategies due to the development of programmatic algorithms will continue until they achieve a near-perfect match between the audience and the advertisements. That is, algorithms expose viewers to advertisements for products and services that they habitually consume or are likely to consume, as well as products and services that meet their current needs, even if the individual is unaware that these products or services need or are available, or even know they are available. For example, ads for cheap, local accommodations are served to passengers affected by upcoming flight delays (White & Samuel, 2019). On the other hand, according to some researchers, programmatic advertising has been presented as a technology that can facilitate the development of micro-foundations that lead to unwavering commitment seeking, meaningful relationships, and much-lauded 'loyalty' (Chung et al., 2018). However, indiscriminate application of techno-social forms of marketing to the detriment of traditional forms risks exclusion, which affects 'relational fit' (Wang & Ding, 2017). The most significant disadvantage of this situation is that it reduces the sense of belonging to the brand or platform. As the frequency of implementation of the perfect close match (personification beyond customization) increases, consumers will be dominated by recommendations that give the most optimal choice offered by the platforms, as individuals will hand over control to algorithms that will consider the appropriate choices.

Data Privacy Concerns

OTT business models are data-centric business models that rely on data to create value for the consumer; as a result of this data value creation, services such as personalized online advertising on the Internet (Dorfer, 2018, p. 38). Personal data may be used to improve the quality of an OTT service, target advertising, or referral systems (Choi & Kim, 2020). This means that online advertising no longer only targets websites to be viewed; instead, Internet users are the focus of alignment (Gertz/McGlashan 2016, p. 58). The extensive use of personal data, especially by Over The Top (OTT) services, is always the focus of discussion (Choi & Kim, 2020). However, actual consumer behavior avoids typical criticisms of OTT services' data usage. Consumers often give their data with little thought to using an OTT service. This so-called personalized advertising poses new challenges for the advertising industry: the possibilities offered by personal data and the technological structures of the Internet in the context of data-driven marketing are changing the added value for online advertising (Arnold, 2018). Personal data is becoming a central resource with high-value potential for OTT media platforms, and personalized advertising is increasingly relevant to advertisers and Internet users as a tool of the platform's sales policy (Bründl et al., 2015).

OTT is the first characteristic recommendation system that has the most significant impact on the advertising activities of the media. Although people can access plenty of information online, it can be overwhelming and distracting. With the abundance of online sources, it is becoming increasingly difficult for consumers to find reliable information. Companies have taken notice of this issue and are now providing personalized recommendation services to assist people in discovering the products or content they need. (Jeckmans et al., 2013). Recommendation algorithms are commonly used in content platforms but typically only suggest the most popular or commonly searched content. Incorporating a personalized touch into the recommendation system can enhance the benefits for individuals. Customized recommendation services have become increasingly popular and successful in recent years. Amazon and Netflix report that over 35% of their sales come from these services and several OTT players have attempted to enhance their recommendation systems with greater complexity and accuracy.

RESULT

OTT media platforms are one of the players in the digital ecosystem that provides the most critical media service that changes the course of marketing and advertising activities and creates data-based value (Dorfer, 2018, p. 38). OTT is a platform that delivers film and television content through a high-speed Internet connection instead of cable or satellite providers. It includes content, services, and applications provided to end users through the open Internet. (Turner, 2019).

The intended uses may be diverse. Personal data may be used to improve the service's quality, show targeted advertisements specific to the target audience, or provide individual content recommendations. Data on the characteristics and behavior of users of these services can play an important role, especially for financing through online advertising. Pseudo-advertising and targeting of individual content recommendations or search results are often criticized. Actual consumer behavior is the exact opposite of this criticism. Consumers often reluctantly give up their data to use an OTT service, even though surveys indicate they value privacy and personal data protection. This behavior is commonly known as the "Privacy Paradox." Indeed, there needs to be more information about consumers' attitudes toward using their data, depending on the service used (Arnold, 2018).

Logically, compared to a basic search on the internet, an e-commerce platform typically demands more data to be entered by the user. Data collection, aggregation, and processing and their conversion into valuable data in personalized OTT advertising are assigned to data-driven value creation (Kollmann 2019). There is a complex relationship between data collection, quality of OTT service, and customer interest. A possible inconsistency in the minds of consumers between data protection statements and targeting options offered by OTT media services to their advertised customers will undermine trust in the platform. On the one hand, to better understand what role this data plays, it is crucial to discuss what data, how much, and in what ways, whether collected by the service itself or obtained through a data agent. On the other hand, the consumer's acceptance of such measures plays a decisive role. Such services cannot be successful in the long run if there is a lack of acceptance.

Creating positive purchase intentions for OTT platforms will ultimately strengthen consumer engagement and build trust and loyalty to the platform. The most crucial element that keeps a digital media offer alive is to increase participation by raising the quality of the customer experience. Therefore, the continuity of customers' participation in an OTT platform determines the long-term profitability of the participants (Kim & Lee, 2023). Understanding every aspect of the customer, from how consumers navigate the platform and what materials they like to see to predicting what content will appeal to the target audience, is vital for increasing engagement.

Advertisements on OTT platforms can effectively target users of any age, gender, education level, interests, and precise location data, using data from their behavior within apps or search history across various platforms (Grover, 2023). Businesses manage digital media marketing to reach customers and advertise with a more targeted and defined approach. As a result, OTT platforms must constantly seek new ways to retain their customers and develop more engaging content to differentiate themselves. However, newer and smaller OTT platforms may need more financial resources to explore new video content development; this makes it almost difficult to create and produce new content, exceptionally compatible with competing OTT platforms and devices.

OTT platforms and their various applications are expected to continue being used as a marketing tools for the mutual benefit of consumers and marketers. Although this scenario may seem like a marketing acumen with an excellent opportunity, the most threatening factor for the digital media marketing industry in the future in the context of OTT media is the data privacy risk and, thus, the lack of trust posed by the desire to access more data. The paradox must be carefully considered, on the one hand, to provide consumers with higher quality content; on the other hand, how to increase consumer confidence and create the intention to buy in the public interest (Arnold, 2018).

As local providers introduce their OTT models, the competition for subscribers and advertisers will intensify. Traditional TV ratings have already been on a downward trend. As a result of this fragmentation of services and content, the industry will need to undergo a redesign. On the other hand, soon, OTT media platforms saw India as having a vast potential to be tapped with its cultural diversity, young population, and increasing internet access. These platforms have gained a large audience in India by offering content that reflects the local culture and meets the audience's demands (Sharma & Lulandala, 2023). As the popularity of OTT media increases, especially in India, these platforms have found success by focusing on content and viewing behavior to more accurately understand India-specific content and audience preferences (Sadana & Sharma, 2021). Their interest in Hindi and the diversity of languages and dialects in the country also reflects Netflix's belief in the interest it receives in India. Netflix, on the other hand, aims to improve its value proposition to appeal to a broader audience while remaining a premium service in India. Moreover, Netflix has invested heavily in technology to improve user experience, offering various subscription plans and partnering with Indian filmmakers and production houses for content production (Krishna & Sen, 2022).

The result is a general upheaval in the audio-visual landscape with new players, new revenue streams, and new information about the relevant audience, leading to new ways to distribute and consume content worldwide (Chakraborty et al., 2023). Therefore, OTT media presents a more feasible marketing opportunity to encourage repeat purchases by providing enjoyable access to high-quality content that satisfies curious minds—the increased value derived from the monetary benefits of promotional offers. In addition, rapid developments in OTT media highlight that practitioners and marketers develop a deeper understanding of adding and retaining new customers. In this context, we can summarize the most important reasons for publishers to benefit from OTT ads to increase revenue generation, as it easily adapts to a young and rapidly growing global audience, Engaging and effective content formats, high visibility rates, data transparency and microtargeting, and reduced advertising costs (Lee et al., 2018). Furthermore, in today's digital age, having a strong brand image for the OTT platform is essential, and it requires all businesses to establish a unique online presence. As it is known, brand image is established by continuous advertising efforts and verified by customers' direct interactions with the brand (Aaker, 2012).

The digitization and online circulation of content production means not only the entry of new actors and the transformation of the consumption of cultural content but also a reformulation of the rules (Kim & Lee, 2023). This has led to an environment of extreme competition. Former creators have found themselves (thanks to the "dramatization" and "platformization" of culture) in younger companies with the ability to understand their audience (Gambarato, & Heuman, 2022). Thus, the price of media content depended on demand from consumers rather than the cost recorded on the supply side (Yim, 2013). Previously, content providers have mainly used a free, ad-supported model without direct payment from viewers. Nevertheless, with the emergence of OTT services, it's clear that consumers now prefer paying directly for content instead of relying solely on advertisers. This shows that the willingness to pay for content is becoming more critical.

Recommendations

This overall impact of OTT media on customer views will continue to be an essential issue that will continue to shape media consumption and marketing strategies. On the other hand, when user habits are examined, it becomes clear that OTT platforms have significantly changed traditional media content consumption patterns among consumers. Given the changing spectrum of sports content, it is a fact that more research is needed to more comprehensively examine the interests, habits, and viewing patterns of OTT consumers.

The paradoxes underlying personalized advertising include competing goals of gaining chance experiences for consumers without violating perceived data privacy (Samuel et al., 2021). OTT media service providers will commit to acquiring and using more comprehensive and personal data sets. On the other hand, a highly targeted, personalized ad will also increase data privacy concerns. As a result, it is also important to highlight that service providers may face challenges in overcoming perceptions regarding the ethical use of consumer data in the future.

Netflix's success in adapting to cultural diversity in India is a significant achievement in how OTT systems manage the balance between local and global content and cater to users' desires. Since the presence of cultural diversity will significantly affect the content creation process, it is helpful to conduct ethnographic studies to understand the consumption patterns of groups for more local content.

\The presence of increased competition in the OTT business, combined with the influx of additional market participants, has the potential to result in consolidation. More research is needed to explore the competitive dynamics and merger/continuation strategies used by large and small OTT platforms.

REFERENCES

Aaker, D. A. (2012). *Building Strong Brands*. Simon & Schuster.

Alsharif, A. H., Md Salleh, N. Z., & Baharun, R. (2021). Neuromarketing: Marketing research in the new millennium. *Neuroscience Research Notes*, *4*(3), 27–35. doi:10.31117/neuroscirn.v4i3.79

Arnold, R., Bott, J., & Hildebrandt, H. (2018). *Die Nutzung von Daten durch OTT-Dienste zur Abschöpfung von Aufmerksamkeit und Zahlungsbereitschaft: Implikationen für Daten- und Verbraucherschutz*. WIK: Diskussionsbeitrag, Nr.431.

Ayten, A., Bulat, S., & İnceismail, E. (2019). A Study of Generation Z Viewing Habits in Context of Uses and Gratification Theory: The Protector Netflix Series Case. *Communication and Technology Congress – CTC 2019.*

Bong-Goon, S., & Park, D. H. (2021). Effective Strategies for Contents Recommendation Based on Psychological Ownership of over the Top Services in Cyberspace. *Journal of Theoretical and Applied Electronic Commerce Research, 16*(4), 976–991. doi:10.3390/jtaer16040055

BründlS.MattC.HessT. (2015). Wertschöpfung in Datenmärkten. Eine explorative Untersuchung am Beispiel des deutschen Marktes für persönliche Daten. *Forum Privatheit.* doi:10.7892/boris.105186

Busch, O. (2016). The Programmatic Advertising Principle. In O. Bush (Ed.), *Programmatic Advertising The Successful Transformation to Automated, Data-Driven Marketing in RealTime* (pp. 3–16). Springer. doi:10.1007/978-3-319-25023-6_1

BVDW. (2015). *Zielgruppengenaues Targeting unter Nutzung von Online- und Offline-Daten.* BVDW. https://www.bvdw.org/presseserver/LeitfadenTargeting/leitfaden_targeting_zielgruppengenaues-targeting-unter-nutzung-von-online-und-offline-daten_2015.pdf

Chakraborty, D., Siddiqui, M., Siddiqui, A., Paul, J., Dash, G., & Dal Mas, F. (2023). Watching is valuable: Consumer views -Content consumption on OTT platforms. *Journal of Retailing and Consumer Services, 70,* 1031–1048. doi:10.1016/j.jretconser.2022.103148

Chang, P. C., & Chang, H. Y. (2020). Exploring the factors influencing continuance usage of over-the-top services: The interactivity, consumption value, and satisfaction perspectives. *International Journal of Technology and Human Interaction, 16*(4), 118–138. doi:10.4018/IJTHI.2020100108

Charts, M. (2020). *Consumers Are Streaming More Since the COVID-19 Outbreak – but What About Pay-TV On-Demand?* Marketing Charts. https://www.marketingcharts.com/television/tv-audiences-and-consumption-113253

Chen, Y. N. K. (2019). Competitions between OTT TV platforms and traditional television in Taiwan: A Niche analysis. *Telecommunications Policy, 43*(9), 101793, 1-10. doi:10.1016/j.telpol.2018.10.006

Choi, J., & Kim, Y. (2020). Time-Aware Learning Framework for Over-The-Top Consumer Classification Based on Machine- and Deep-Learning Capabilities. *Applied Sciences, 10*(23), 8476, 1-17. doi:10.3390/app10238476

Dang, V. T., Nguyen, N., & Pervan, S. (2020). Retailer corporate social responsibility and consumer citizenship behavior: the mediating roles of perceived consumer effectiveness and consumer trust. *Journal of Retailing and Consumer Services, 55*(1), 102082, 1-10. https://doi.org/ doi:10.1016/j.jretconser.2020.102082

Gambarato, R., & Heuman, J. (2022). Beyond fact and fiction: Cultural memory and transmedia ethics in Netflix's The Crown. *European Journal of Cultural Studies, 0*(0). Advance online publication. doi:10.1177/13675494221128332

Grover, S. (2023). *OTT vs CTV: Differences Explained for Publishers.* Adpushup https://www.adpushup.com/blog/ott-vs-ctv/

Gupta, G., & Singharia, K. (2021). Consumption of OTT Media Streaming in COVID-19 Lockdown: Insights from PLS Analysis. *The Journal of Business Perspective, 25*(1), 36–46. doi:10.1177/0972262921989118

Habib, S., Hamadneh, N., & Hassan, A. (2022). The Relationship between Digital Marketing, Customer Engagement, and Purchase Intention via OTT Platforms. *Journal of Mathematics, 22. Journal of Mathematics, 5327626*, 1–12. doi:10.1155/2022/5327626

Hollebeek, L. D., & Macky, K. (2019). Digital content marketing's role in fostering consumer engagement, trust, and value: Framework, fundamental propositions, and implications. *Journal of Interactive Marketing, 45*, 27–41. doi:10.1016/j.intmar.2018.07.003

Mordor Intelligence. (2021). *Marché Mondıal Over The Top (Ott) - Croıssance, Tendances, Impact du Covıd-19 et Prévısıons. (2023-2028)*. Mordor Intelligence. https://www.mordorintelligence.com/fr/industry-reports/over-the-top-market

Jain, K. (2021). The Rise of Ott Platform: Changing Consumer Preferences [IJMR]. *EPRA International Journal of Multidisciplinary Research, 7*(6), 257–261. doi:10.36713/epra2013

Jeckmans, A., Beye, M., Erkin, Z., Hartel, P. H., Lagendijk, R. L., & Tang, Q. (2013). Privacy in Recommender Systems. *Chapter in Book/Report/Conference proceeding*. London: Springer. 10.1007/978-1-4471-4555-4_12

Kala, D., & Chaubey, D. S. (2018). The effect of eWOM communication on brand image and purchase intention towards lifestyle products in India. *International Journal of Services Economics and Management, 9*(2), 143–157. doi:10.1504/IJSEM.2018.096077

Keller, K. L. (2017). Managing the growth tradeoff: challenges and opportunities in luxury branding. Advances in Luxury Brand Management. Springer.

Kim, M. S., Kim, E., Hwang, S., Kim, J., & Kim, S. (2017). Willingness to pay for over-the-top services in China and Korea. *Telecommunications Policy, 41*(3), 197–207. doi:10.1016/j.telpol.2016.12.011

Kim, S., & Bae, J. (2016). Cross-cultural differences in concrete and abstract corporate social responsibility (CSR) campaigns: Perceived message clarity and perceived CSR as mediators. *International Journal of Corporate Social Responsibility, 1*(6), 1–14. doi:10.1186/s40991-016-0009-1

Kollmann, P., Hill, M. E., Allen, R. C., McNutt, R. L. Jr, Brown, L. E., Barnes, N. P., Delamere, P., Clark, G., Andrews, G. B., Salazar, N., Westlake, J., Romeo, G., Vandegriff, J., Kusterer, M., Smith, D., Nelson, K., Jaskulek, S., Decker, R. B., Cheng, A. F., & Stern, S. A. (2019). Pluto's Interaction With Energetic Heliospheric Ions. *Journal of Geophysical Research. Space Physics, 124*(9), 7413–7424. doi:10.1029/2019JA026830 PMID:35860291

Kour, G., & Chhabria, B. (2022). Understanding platform strategies for consumer stickiness on OTT platforms. *Journal of Indian Business Research, 14*(4), 540–555. doi:10.1108/JIBR-04-2021-0122

Krishna, G., & Sen, A. (2022). The Global Entertainment Major Has Completed Five Interesting Years in India, Focussed on Its Premium Positioning. What Lies Ahead? *Business Today*. https://www.businesstoday.in/interactive/immersive/netflix-india-popular-ott-platform-in-india/

Kumari, S. (2022). *Indian OTT platforms rely heavily on marketing, or do they?* Best Media Info. https://bestmediainfo.com/2022/06/indian-ott-platforms-rely-heavily-on-marketing-or-do-they

Lee, C. C., Nagpal, P., Ruane, S. G., & Lim, H. S. (2018). Factors affecting online streaming subscriptions. *Communications of the IIMA*, *16*(1). doi:10.58729/1941-6687.1394

Nafees, L., Mehdi, M., Gupta, R., Kalia, S., Banerjee, S., & Kapoor, S. (2021). Netflix in India: Expanding to success. *Emerald Emerging Markets Case Studies*, *11*(2), 1–31. doi:10.1108/EEMCS-10-2019-0285

Nagaraj, S., Singh, S., & Yasa, V.R. (2021). Factors affecting consumers' willingness to subscribe to over-the-top (OTT) video streaming services in India. *Technology in* Society, *65*(C), 1-7. doi:10.1016/j.techsoc.2021.101534

Oliveira, T., Fiorese, A., & Sargento, S. (2018). *Forecasting Over-the-Top Bandwidth Consumption Applied to Network Operators.* In *Proceedings of the 2018 IEEE Symposium on Computers and Communications (ISCC)*, Natal, Brazil. 10.1109/ISCC.2018.8538539

Omukić, S., Činjarević, M., & Peštek, A. (2022). How "Netflix Effect'' is (Re)shaping the Media Consumption Patterns of Y-ers and Z-ers? Information Systems and Technologies. WorldCIST 2022. Springer, Cham. doi:10.1007/978-3-031-04819-7_54

Palomba., A (2022). Building OTT brand loyalty and brand equity: impact of original series on OTT services. *Telematics and Informatics, 66*(3), 101733, 1-14. doi:10.1016/j.tele.2021.101733

Prasad, S. S. (2022). Impact of OTT media on the society: Insights from path analysis. *Asia-Pacific Journal of Business Administration*, *14*(2), 185–198. doi:10.1108/APJBA-06-2021-0261

Ramesh, A., & Jaggi, R. K. (2022). The contemporary film public relations' ecosystem in India – from stars to stories. *International Journal of Indian Culture and Business Management*, *25*(1), 17–37. doi:10.1504/IJICBM.2022.120922

Sadana, M., & Sharma, D. (2021). How over-the-top (OTT) platforms engage young consumers over traditional pay television service? An analysis of changing consumer preferences and gamification. *Young Consumers*, *22*(3), 348–367. doi:10.1108/YC-10-2020-1231

Sell, A., Mezei, J., & Walden, P. (2014). Walden, P. An attitude-based latent class segmentation analysis of mobile phone users. *Telematics and Informatics*, *31*(2), 209–219. doi:10.1016/j.tele.2013.08.004

Shah, S., & Mehta, N. (2022). Over-the-Top (OTT) Streaming Services: Studying Users' Behaviour Through the UTAUT Model. *Management and Labour Studies*, *0*(0). doi:10.1177/0258042X221137438

Sharma, K., & Lulandala, E. E. (2023). OTT platforms resilience to COVID-19 – a study of business strategies and consumer media consumption in India. *The International Journal of Organizational Analysis*, *31*(1), 63–90. doi:10.1108/IJOA-06-2021-2816

Shaw, K. (2021). *Netflix India Launches The Red Notice Shop Turnıng Fans Into Shoplifters Via 22feet Trıbal Worldwıde Indıa.* Campaign Brief. https://campaignbriefasia.com/2021/11/29/netflix-india-launches-the-red-notice-shop-turning-fans-into-shoplifters-via-22feet-tribal-worldwide-india/

Shim, D., Lee, C., & Oh, I. (2022). Analysis of OTT Users' Watching Behavior for Identifying a Profitable Niche: Latent Class Regression Approach. *Journal of Theoretical and Applied Electronic Commerce Research, 17*(4), 1564–1580. doi:10.3390/jtaer17040079

Shon, M., Shin, J., Hwang, J., & Lee, D. (2021). Free contents vs. inconvenience costs: Two faces of online video advertising. *Telematics and Informatics, 56*, 101476. doi:10.1016/j.tele.2020.101476

Silvia, S. (2019). The importance of social media and digital marketing to attract millennials' behavior as a consumer. *Journal of International Business Research and Marketing, 4*(2), 7–10. doi:10.18775/jibrm.1849-8558.2015.42.3001

Singh, D. (2020). 8 shows that give us a peek into the gen-Z life, on Netflix and Disney+ Hotstar. *Vouge India*. https://www.vogue.in/culture-and-living/content/8-shows-that-give-us-a-peek-into-the-gen-z-life-on-netflix-and-disney-hotstar

Singh, S., Singh, N., Kalinić, Z., & Liébana-Cabanillas, F. J. (2021). Assessing determinants influencing continued use of live streaming services: An extended perceived value theory of streaming addiction. *Expert Systems with Applications, 168*(2), 1–16. doi:10.1016/j.eswa.2020.114241

Spacek, D. (2018). *Personalisierte Medien und Unterhaltung*. Walderwyss. https://www.walderwyss.com/user_assets/publications/2359.pdf

Stanimirovic, U. (2023). *What Is OTT: A Definitive Guide to Over-the-Top Streaming*. Target. https://target-video.com/what-is-ott/#8-how-is-ott-content-delivered

Steiner, E., & Xu, K. (2020). Binge-watching motivates change: Uses and gratifications of streaming video viewers challenge traditional TV research. *Convergence (London), 26*(1), 82–101. doi:10.1177/1354856517750365

Tefertiller, A. (2020). Cable cord-cutting and streaming adoption: Advertising avoidance and technology acceptance in television innovation. *Telematics and Informatics, 51*, 1-9. doi:10.1016/j.tele.2020.101416

Thomas, F. (2023). *Plateformes OTT: quel intérêt pour les créateurs de contenu?* JND. https://www.journaldunet.com/media/publishers/1520017-plateformes-ott-quel-interet-pour-les-createurs-de-contenu/

Turner, G. (2019). Approaching the cultures of use: Netflix, disruption and the audience. *Critical Studies in Television, 14*(2), 222–232. doi:10.1177/1749602019834554

Viswanathan, V., Hollebeek, L. D., Malthouse, E. C., Maslowska, E., Jung Kim, S., & Xie, W. (2017). The dynamics of consumer Engagement with mobile technologies. *Service Science, 9*(1), 36–49. doi:10.1287/serv.2016.0161

Vivek, S. D., Beatty, S. E., & Morgan, R. M. (2012). Customer engagement: Exploring customer relationships beyond purchase. *Journal of Marketing Theory and Practice, 20*(2), 122–146. doi:10.2753/MTP1069-6679200201

White, G. R. T., Samuel., A., Thomas R., & Jones P. (2021). Programmatic advertising: An exegesis of consumer concerns. *Computers in Human Behavior, 116*(1), 106657, 1-9. doi:10.1016/j.chb.2020.106657

Chapter 7
OTT Platforms From the Perspective of Critical Algorithm Studies:
The Algorithmic Paradox of the Audience

Elif Karakoç Keskin
https://orcid.org/0000-0002-2831-2247
Yeditepe University, Turkey

ABSTRACT

The perspective of critical algorithm studies, which focuses on the concerns that algorithmic mechanisms create or may create in the individual and social context emphasizes that it is important to examine the position of individuals who are currently using recommender systems. Recommender systems are one of the algorithmic structures aimed at keeping users constantly connected and interacting on digital platforms. It is thought that the digital togetherness enabled by media convergence necessitates a focus on recommendation systems within the data cycle of the digital platform ecosystem. This chapter attempts to focus on the effects at the intersection of algorithmic and social structures and problematize these effects in the context of OTT platforms within the framework of current concepts. Hence, the chapter focuses on describing the current state and potential concerns of personalization algorithms and recommendation systems on OTT platforms in relation to the basic conceptualizations of critical algorithm studies in the context of human-algorithm interaction.

1. INTRODUCTION

With the advancement of digital technology, the audience's communication and connection with the media, as well as the ways in which they consume media information, have changed. With digital broadcasting, the audience now has more control over time and space than they did with traditional broadcasters. The audience can now watch visual and/or audio media content anywhere, at any time, and on any device of their choice thanks to the benefits of the digital age. One instance of this is the Over-the-Top (OTT)

DOI: 10.4018/979-8-3693-0116-6.ch007

streaming media delivery system used by Video on Demand (VoD) services, which enables users to access videos without the need for a conventional video playback device.

It is critical in the VoD platform system, which aims to ensure that media content consumption is not interrupted, to maintain the audience's interest and loyalty to the platform, as well as to analyze the user's predictable persona with viewing data. Platforms in this regard benefit from recommender systems based on personalization content, and thus recommendation algorithms.

Broadcasting service providers also control the flow of content in order to direct the audience from VoD platforms to social media platforms, and from social media platforms to VoD platforms, in order to increase screen time, keep them engaged, and thus generate more revenue. The algorithms, which are activated by training the user's behavioral data, make recommendations that the user is likely to click on and possibly interact with. VoD platforms, which have become important components of today's media ecosystem, reach out to both existing subscribers and potential users via various social media platforms and make content recommendations.

In the algorithmic structure, the choices made by users to watch media content on digital platforms are addressed as behavioral data (Kara & McAleese, 2021, p. 4), and the algorithm is processed to provide recommendations for each user and guide the user's decisions. Recommendation algorithms use a database of user preferences (Breese et al., 1998) to predict content that a user might like, find interesting and useful (Burke, 2002), and are able to direct users to that content.

Providing services worldwide, VOD platforms such as Netflix, Amazon Prime, and Disney Plus offer users a variety of content ranging from movies, television series, television programs, and documentaries (Zengin, 2020, p. 169). Users can thus watch content whenever and wherever they want. They also encounter content for their predictable behavioral data with the conditions provided by recommendation systems. Netflix, for example, "trains" audiences to comprehensively mark content, using personalization-driven recommendation systems to provide users with a personalized video library and recommendations to ensure that users continue to watch or subscribe (Bhaskar, 2016). Aside from Netflix, many VoD platforms are investing more and more in machine learning-based recommender systems in order to retain current consumers and attract new ones.

Through VoD platforms, the audience has far more control over what they watch, how they watch it, and how long they watch it than in the traditional watching process. However, it is also paradoxically controlled by the algorithmic structure of the platform through its behavioral data within the framework of recommender systems adopted as one of the business models of the platform ecosystem.

Critical algorithm studies (CAS) have been motivated by the working principle of recommender algorithms, which is based on collecting, processing, and analyzing user data to train the algorithms and then using this data to provide new recommendations to users.

The working principles of algorithms and their functioning as decision mechanisms in the processes of data collection, storage, and analysis are examined in critical algorithm studies, which focus on the concerns that algorithmic structures create or may create in individual and social contexts. Accordingly, the power of algorithmic systems (Moats & Seaver, 2019) that influence users' decision-making processes in the digital environment provide a foundation for studies on the potential effects and risks of algorithms, algorithm-based systems, and data science tools on social life.

Critical algorithm studies address the need for an academic field of study (O'Neil, 2017) that assumes the responsibility of understanding and critiquing the role of technology, particularly algorithms that are responsible for many decisions in social life. This perspective enables the questioning of algorithms not only as codes containing digital instructions but also as guiding mechanisms that construct individual and social outcomes. Most economic and social behaviors in the digital age leave digital footprints that can be used for forecasting and prediction (Blazquez & Domenech, 2018, p. 111). The fact that algorithms serve as recommendation mechanisms for users via the process of machine learning or make decisions on their behalf in processes inherent to users reveals the perspective of critical algorithm studies that use data and/or algorithms from the informatics world.

Since algorithms are assumed to be value-laden and are removed from the perspective of technological determinism, critical algorithm studies have evaluated how algorithms relate to society and the individual using conceptualizations of critical media theories like capital accumulation, ownership structure, power, and surveillance. They have also sparked the development of new ideas regarding the interaction between humans and algorithms. Critical algorithm studies focus on the risk typologies of platforms that include algorithm-driven recommender systems and allow us to discuss the activity of audiences using these platforms in light of the concepts of algorithmic power, algorithm-mediated surveillance[1], algorithmic consent[2], algorithmic imaginary[3], and, within this, algorithmic paradox[4].

Based on these, it is considered crucial to address the position of behavioral data of users who have watched via video-on-demand (VOD) services. This leads to algorithmic power through recommender and personalization algorithms, which are two of the main drivers of consumption. Indeed, algorithmic structure is inevitable from the first step to the last step in the online world. As a result, it is expected that a critical algorithm studies perspective for today's digital environment, where the use of VoD platforms and the time spent on these platforms is constantly increasing, will contribute to field discussions.

In this context, the book chapter will address the audience's continuing position in the algorithmic structure as they engage with algorithms within the constraints of VoD platforms, using the conceptual framework of critical algorithm studies. Therefore, it is aimed to provide theoretical suggestions for the studies to be applied in user-centered studies conducting in the relevant perspective.

1.1 Personalization Algorithms and Recommendation Systems on Digital Platforms

Personalization, which appears as a reference point affecting consumption activities and includes the processes of profiling, segmentation, targeting, filtering, tailoring, mass personalization, and one-to-one marketing (Wind & Rangaswamy, 2001, p. 5; Vesanen & Raulas, 2006, p. 6), can be expressed as personalizing the message for the individual who receives it. (Vesanen, 2007, p. 410). In this sense, with the acceptance of personalization to create both cognitive and emotional trust in users (Desai, 2017, p. 16), the stopping points of consumption activities continue to progress by using different tools and intermediaries in communication with the target audience in the historical trace inherent in technological developments. Algorithmic systems have become one of the most popular tools for data-driven business models.

When analyzed in the context of consumption practices and taking into account the amount of big data in the online world, personalization—the process of designing a website to meet the needs and preferences of specific users—has become crucial for platform creators and managers because it allows them to engage with the user, comprehend their behavior, and stay one step ahead of them (Hussein et al., 2013). At this point, the main element of algorithms that provide personalization in the context of today's technology is creating models that contain information about individual preferences that determine user behavior in a complex web-based system environment (Shinde & Kulkarni, 2012, p. 1381).

Customers/users, social media data, point of sale data, and Internet of Things data are seen as elements of the data ecosystem that enrich users' profiles and enable the determination of personalization strategies. Accordingly, researchers have drawn attention to the importance of demographic, geographic, psychographic, and behavioral data in determining individual user personas (Kotler et al., 2021, p. 164). At this point, it is possible to say that machine learning algorithms have become important parts of the consumption industry by contributing to personalization processes. This is because algorithms are used to extract a profile from all the actions of the internet user in the online world and to offer new content for this profile. For instance, romantic comedy movies will be the majority of the recommended film content for a user on a VoD platform if the user has viewed, liked, or added these movies to their list.

The personalization effect is achieved by delivering content in formats and media appropriate to the user's profile, context of use, and preferences. At this point, personalization is achieved through the use of algorithms and data collection schemes that predict and recommend content that matches users' interests (Chorianopoulos, 2008, pp. 1–5). From this perspective, the strategies implemented within the framework of personalization include the processes of accessing, storing, and reprocessing data.

As Diakopoulos (2015) emphasizes, personalization algorithms, as decision mechanisms based on machine learning, derive their power from the fact that they are decision makers in the processes of prioritizing, classifying, associating, and filtering content in the online space. Therefore, personalization algorithms that work on which elements should be highlighted for the user are directly related to the aim of attracting the user's attention to the relevant digital platform for a long time in a sustainable way. This is because the more time the user spends on the relevant platform (for the personalization algorithm process), the more behavioral data or digital traces they will leave. Therefore, digital platform owners or advertisers who see internet users as potential consumers tend to use personalization effectively based on the conclusion that users' purchase motives are triggered by personalized content (Schafer et al., 1999; Hyken, 2017; Konstantoulaki et al., 2019; Bugeja, 2020).

With the big data environment affecting more and more people's daily lives, how to extract useful information from data has become a crucial issue. Hence, recommender systems help to solve the problem of information overload by providing personalized services to users through algorithms using data mining techniques and have been applied to many industrial fields (Huang et al., 2015). This is because it becomes difficult or impossible for users to filter irrelevant products, compare alternatives, and choose the best option without the support of the system. According to Javed et al. (2021) recommender systems are collections of software tools and methods that provide users recommendations in an effort to keep them interested. Recommendation in the online context refers to the algorithmic adapted presentation of content streams on the digital platform based on user feedback, as opposed to a strictly chronological order. As a result, algorithmic recommendation systems are the basis for online recommendation in this process.

For instance, recommendation systems at Google are used for various purposes, including personalizing search results to show links that generate revenue for Google. Google, through its Adworks and Adsense services, highlights ads in line with consumers' preferences, showing the most relevant content for the user for any word search (Løkke, 2020, p. 71). On sites such as YouTube, Facebook, Twitter, and Instagram, recommendation systems provide a personalized stream of content for each user, enabling continued engagement with the platform and increasing advertising revenues. Netflix uses personalization-driven recommendation systems to provide users with a personalized video library and to offer more viewing recommendations to keep users watching or subscribing. Amazon uses a recommendation system to respond to predicted user requests to encourage them to buy products from Amazon rather than elsewhere. In this way, Amazon is able to improve the matching of products with consumers and manage its inventories efficiently while providing customized recommendations (Chase, 2013). In the web, where the use of personalization-based recommendation systems increases interaction and encourages consumption, it is predicted that platforms such as TikTok, where content is almost exclusively offered by recommendation systems, will become more popular (Cobbe & Singh, 2019, p. 10). Based on all of these, a lengthy list of recommendations that users might come across on digital platforms—such as those for television shows or movies, books, music, investments, friends, food and drink, apparel, and accessories—can be created.

Intertwined goals such as personalization of content, targeted advertising, and continuous platform usage are the expressions of the outputs that emerge from the algorithmic inputs of recommendation systems. Algorithms are inevitably modeled on visions of the social world, and the outcomes are influenced by commercial processes or agendas (Beer, 2017, p. 4). Considering this context in which algorithms are influenced or affected, it is necessary to underline that algorithms are an integral part of the social world. This is because algorithms are becoming increasingly important in terms of participation in public life as "decision-makers in the selection of the most relevant information for individuals". The fact that algorithms serve as tools for user recommendations or act as decision-makers for users in tasks that are essential to user behavior highlights the importance of the critical algorithm studies approach, which draws data and/or algorithms from the information environment. Algorithmic choice emerges when knowledge is given to the algorithm (Gillespie, 2014, p. 191), and algorithmic decision-making quality (Diakopoulos, 2015, p. 40) gains the upper hand. Large tech companies like Alphabet, Amazon, and Meta, in particular, have gained significant influence in predicting how users will access information, socialize, watch, and purchase content by gathering, processing, analyzing, and categorizing user data and then offering users personalized recommendations (Løkke, 2020, pp. 70–71).

Recommendation is also one of the factors that influence individuals' decision-making in offline social processes. For example, when deciding to watch a movie, the movie to watch can be chosen based on the recommendations of a friend. However, in the online world, recommendations work differently than they do offline. This difference is related to the demand for the recommendation. Because the user's preferences and behaviors already exist in the online world, the recommendation is determined and presented to him or her based on the relationality of these preferences and behaviors without the need for a request. Therefore, the recommendations formed within the possibilities of the digital world are presented to the user in a way that focuses on personal preferences and includes interactions without requiring the user's effort.

Recommender systems rely on various types of input. The most appropriate way for the system to succeed is through explicit feedback, where users directly express their interest in the content, such as by rating it with stars, adding it to the watch list, adding it to favorites, liking it, etc. In the absence of explicit feedback, implicit feedback types are utilized. Implicit feedback includes viewing history, streaming activities, browsing history, and long views (Koren et al., 2022, p. 92). Therefore, recommendation systems on VoD platforms can be defined as algorithmic structures that provide appropriate personalized content for the user through prioritization, classification, and filtering processes.

Recommendation systems commonly use content-based (focusing on the user profile based on the user's preferences on platforms and the item characteristics of the content they prefer) (Pazzani & Billus, 2007; Mobasher, 2007; Javed et al., 2021), collaborative (focusing on item characteristics based on the user's similarities with other users) (Herlocker et al., 2000; Papagelis & Plexousakis, 2005), and hybrid techniques (adopting the strengths of content-based and collaborative filtering) (Burke, 2002; Thorat et al., 2015; Koren et al., 2022). In addition to these basic techniques, specific recommendation systems based on popularity, demographic filtering, knowledge, utility, social networking, and deep learning

(Colombo-Mendoza vd., 2015; Mu, 2018; Tarus vd., 2018; Burke, 2002; Rakshit vd., 2022) can also be mentioned. These techniques play an important role in determining the content that a user of any digital platform will watch, affecting the way the user consumes content and interacts with both themselves and other users on all digital platforms they use.

1.2 OTT Platforms and Algorithmic Recommender Systems

Online video content has become increasingly popular as the population of digital media has grown enormously in parallel with advances in web technologies. In this context, the global streaming video market has shown remarkable growth, especially in the last decade. In 2022, OTT video revenues reached an estimated USD 154 billion, and by April 2023, the number of OTT video users worldwide had reached approximately 3.5 billion. The highest share of OTT revenues is generated by SVOD channels that adopt the subscription service principle (Statista, 2023, parag.1-3).

VoD platforms are a media delivery system that allows users to access videos without a traditional video playback device by using an OTT streaming system, which enables the delivery of audio and/or visual content streamed over the internet instead of a traditional cable or satellite subscription without the involvement of an internet service provider at the point of control or distribution (Özel, 2020, p. 120). VoD systems are basically divided into three categories: Subscription Video on Demand (SVOD), Transactional Video on Demand (TVOD), and Advertising-based Video on Demand (AVOD).

SVOD platforms, where the viewer receives video services on condition of subscription, can be exemplified as Netflix, Hulu, Amazon Prime, Disney Plus, Apple TV and HBO Max. TVOD platforms where video service is received per transaction, that is, the viewer pays for the content they choose, have options such as Apple iTunes, Sky Box Office, Amazon Video Store (Gallier, 2021).

AVoD platforms, which include ad-based video services, are usually offered to the viewer as freemium, but the viewer watches advertisements while watching the content. YouTube, Vimeo, Crackle, and Dailymotion are examples of this type of video on demand. In addition to this freemium service, YouTube, one of the most preferred AVoD platforms worldwide, also offers premium subscribers the option to watch ad-free videos. Of course, YouTube is also a video-sharing website. In this context, YouTube allows users to share videos and interact with other users.

According to the Digital 2023 April Global Statshot Report, YouTube, Netflix, Amazon Prime Video, and Disney Plus are among the top 10 most used video-centric applications worldwide (Datareportal, 2023). One of the common features of the most preferred VoD platforms worldwide is that they use algorithmic recommendation systems based on the principle of personalization.

The business models implemented by platforms in this developed market to maintain their current position and sustain their users' interactions in order to take them further use personalization algorithms and thus the mediating role of recommendation systems.

Based on the way digital content is consumed, VoD video streaming platform owners use personalization algorithms and recommendation systems to create value in the digital platform ecosystem.

Today, many digital platforms utilize mixed approaches to recommendation systems. For instance, Netflix's recommendation systems specifically consider factors like location (country and region), the kind of device being used to watch the video, time, national, religious, and cultural holidays; attention (the user's focus on watching the video or playing it in the background); friends who are watching the video with; weather; seasonality; and the user's regular activities (like commuting). In this context, in addition to user and item characteristics, various contextual features are also important in creating recommendations that can receive fast and efficient interactions (Adomavicius et al., 2022, p. 212).

VoD platforms have similar interfaces and use similar techniques in terms of recommendation systems. While it is not possible to access all the technical details about the working principles of the platforms' recommendation systems, studies focusing on the relationship between the platform and the audience provide information about the functioning of the recommendation systems on these platforms. In this sense, Netflix is the most frequently encountered platform in the relevant literature, as it is the most widely used VoD platform.

Netflix sorts the entire video catalog (or subsets selected by genre or other filtering) in a personalized way for each member profile (Gomez-Uribe & Hunt, 2015, p. 15). Netflix recommends a homepage, videos (including "top picks" for the user), and video categories. At the end of each video, further viewing is recommended. Each video is assigned a personalized "match" percentage, indicating the user's estimated interest. Users can provide feedback on each video in the form of "like" and "dislike" buttons (Cobbe & Singh, 2019, p. 9). Bhaskar (2016) emphasized that Netflix "trains" viewers to tag content comprehensively. Netflix uses personalization-driven recommendation systems to provide users with a personalized video library and more viewing recommendations to keep them watching or subscribing. A comparison of user interfaces on Netflix reveals that the same content is presented to people with different tastes with different banners, in different categories, or under different lists (Özel & Özay, 2021).

Among VoD platforms, it is worth mentioning YouTube, as it is also one of the most visited social media platforms worldwide. YouTube, as one of the platforms that makes extensive use of personalization-based recommendation systems, automatically plays the most relevant video that matches the user's digital traces on YouTube (behavioral data such as viewing history, search history, behavioral data such as video liking, sharing, commenting, etc.) after a video that a user is watching ends. The literature on YouTube recommendation systems highlights the worry that the platform's algorithms may make it easier for users to access extremist content. The literature has raised concerns on how to strike a balance between users actively looking for harmful content and recommender systems that point people toward content they might not otherwise encounter. (Yesilada & Lewandowsky, 2022, p. 2).

Briefly said, recommendation systems, while differing in how they operate and serve different objectives, essentially aim to maintain the flow of media content consumption while also gaining deeper insights into their audience. This system allows the user to pursue a path that occasionally leads to binge-watching, with every second they spend on the platform providing data for recommendation algorithms.

Based on all these, it is possible to say that the recommendation systems adopted by VoD platforms in their business models position the viewer in an algorithmic cycle within the scope of changing viewing practices.

With various new media platforms operating through personalized algorithms and recommendation systems, the viewer has much more control over what to watch, how to watch, and how much to watch compared to the traditional viewing process. These new and variable mediums also allow viewers to consume large amounts of content through binge-watching (Conlin et al., 2016, p. 152).

Therefore, OTT platforms have not only transformed the global media landscape but also changed viewing behaviors and provided a lens into the algorithmic systems that are effective in this change process. This has also allowed for the discussion of algorithmic recommendation systems within the conceptual framework of critical algorithm studies, with the goal of maintaining the relationship and exchange that users build with the platforms that provide them with video streaming services gradually. As a result, it motivated conversation about where viewers fit into the algorithmic route.

1.3 The Position of OTT Audiences with Key Concepts of Critical Algorithm Studies

With the increase in the amount of data in the internet world working simultaneously with digital platforms, the decision-making effect of algorithms in the digital environment has become increasingly important in the field of social sciences. The critical perspective, which focuses on the choices made by the algorithm, the working principles that bring about these choices, the algorithm-based business models of digital platforms, and the user positioned opposite the process, has made the evaluation of algorithms inevitable. Opinions (Dourish, 2016; Seaver, 2017), which have moved the boundaries of the term algorithm from purely technical boundaries to social boundaries based on social interaction, have led to the development of this perspective.

Critical algorithm studies correspond to the need for an academic field of study (O'Neil, 2017) that takes responsibility for understanding and critiquing the role of technology and especially algorithms, which are responsible for many decisions, in social life. This perspective that the social sciences bring to data science enables the questioning of algorithms not only as codes containing digital instructions but also as guiding mechanisms that construct individual and social outcomes. In the digital age, most economic and social behaviors leave digital footprints, which are being used for prediction and forecasting purposes (Blazquez & Domenech, 2018, p. 111). In addition, the fact that algorithms work as recommendation mechanisms for users through the machine learning process or make decisions on behalf of users in processes inherent to users has expanded the focus of critical algorithm studies. Within this framework, critical algorithm studies offer insights into the circumstances that put audiences in a paradoxical cycle within VoD platforms.

1.4 Algorithmic Power

In the conjuncture that shifts from the traditional media environment to the digital environment, power relations in imaginations regarding ownership structures are also made meaningful with algorithmic structures. Thus, the idea of a society where power is increasingly in the hands of the algorithm is formed (Bucher, 2018, p. 33). What is considered important to express at this point is that the hegemonic effects of the content presented to individuals through the media in social, cultural, economic, and political frameworks are realized regardless of traditional and new media environments. In this respect, the assumption that enables the association of algorithms and power is that algorithms have become an effective driving force for power that operates with various components in the digital environment.

In this sense, Beer's (2009) concept of algorithmic power helps to make sense of the important role of algorithms in governing contemporary societies through codes and algorithms. Drawing on Lash's concept of "post-hegemonic" forms of power, Beer (2009, p. 994) emphasized "power through algorithms", arguing that the algorithms underlying social media platforms have the capacity to shape social and cultural formations and directly influence individual lives. In his study, Beer (2009) focuses on the power of algorithms in shaping auditory and cultural experiences within the framework of user profiles, based on the example of Last.FM, a music sharing platform. Beer (2009) states that listeners who visit www.last.fm and create a playlist for their favorite music provide a user profile for the algorithms to be trained on. Thus, this user profile enables the algorithmic system to organize itself. As the depth of information held about the user increases, this playlist more accurately matches and predicts the user's tastes. *"This is undoubtedly an expression of power, not of someone having power over someone else, but of the software making choices and connections in complex and unpredictable ways in order to shape the everyday experiences of the user"* (Beer, 2009, p. 997). Of course, algorithms derive this power over knowledge formation from the behavioral data of internet users. The algorithmic manifestations of internet users' own digital footprints are the algorithmic manifestations of which content will or will not stand out on any digital platform. Today, due to the seamlessness of digital platforms' interfaces and users' implicit trust in algorithms, the values and ideologies embedded in algorithms inevitably seep into users' research and content (Bakke, 2020). This is because the content that users encounter is listed by algorithms according to a set of inclusion, exclusion, and ranking criteria.

This system, which prioritizes any content for a user and tries to determine what to see and even what to consume, supports the idea of a form of power structured through algorithms.

Bucher (2018) theorizes the concept of algorithmic power based on Foucault's understanding of relational and generative power. The underlying assumption in this theorization is the effort to evaluate algorithms in the context of their social effects, taking them out of their purely technical meaning, which also forms the periphery of critical algorithm studies. For this very reason, he describes algorithmic systems as a field of power and a set of strategies within this field of action. Just as statistics enable the management of populations in Foucault's account of security, algorithms function as management tools that direct the flow of content and the practices of users to this or that region or activity (Bucher, 2018, p. 38).

In this sense, algorithmic power is also about how, when, and under what conditions algorithms and different aspects of them become available to certain actors. Bucher (2018) discusses algorithms in relation to power as a social issue and argues that algorithms essentially produce new ways of organizing the world. In this respect, the main argument for algorithmic power stems from how algorithmic systems shape the orientations of individuals.

In the historical process, technological efforts to make machines smarter have led to human-machine interaction built on algorithmic systems. Every user who performs internet experiences on digital platforms transfers the traces of these experiences to data pipes, referring to Ong's (2012) expression of information pipes. Users' digital traces, i.e., personal and behavioral data, have also become the raw materials for new content, products, and services to be offered to the user on digital platforms that use algorithms. In this sense, according to Han (2019), power in the age of big data is smart power. Indeed, Foucault (2019, p. 74) described the exercise of power as directing behavior and ordering possible outcomes. This idea sheds light on the relationship between recommendation algorithms and behavioral data. Indeed, in the age of artificial intelligence, it is possible to say that data is one of the knowledge identities that power pursues.

For this reason, Pasquale (2018, p. 9), in a description inherent to the digital environment where algorithms are built, likens the contemporary world to a one-way mirror, not a peaceful kingdom of private walled gardens. Pasquale (2018), in his Black Box Society, examines the secrecy behind algorithms, starting from the problematic fact that while institutional actors have information about the smallest details of individuals' daily lives, users do not know how this information is used to influence their decisions.

Considering all this, it is possible to emphasize thinking about algorithms in relation to the notion of power as a key method for making sense of how algorithms shape users' choices and how they relate to institutional structures.

Beer (2019) argues that data analytics in the digital environment are part of power structures, value production, and economic infrastructures, and therefore the relationship between capital and power should be focused through the lens of platform capitalism. In this respect, understanding the impact and dominance of algorithmic power on the individual and society requires understanding the context of capitalism inherent in the consumption process and surveillance related to the circulation of data. It is possible to say that the greatest wealth of the power established through algorithms is the power to access and use user data.

As Srnicek (2017) emphasizes, capitalism in the digital age has turned to data as a way to sustain economic growth and vitality in the face of a stagnant manufacturing sector. Algorithms are part of the interaction between content, platform logic, and user behavior data. In particular, these algorithms work in the context of recommendation systems. Therefore, they are designed to recommend highly interactive content (Saurwein & Spencer-Smith, 2021, p. 226). This chapter, which critically evaluates the algorithms of platforms using recommendation systems, starts from the assumption that platforms essentially act with a business logic.

The use of algorithms guided by recommendation systems has become much wider. In addition, technology companies have increased the value of their companies through the economic benefits of platformization across a variety of social media platforms, VoD platforms, and mobile apps. Many digital platforms use recommendation algorithms to determine what a user should see on their platform based on data about what the user has already viewed, purchased, or done. This process, which is intertwined with platformization, highlights predictable consumption practices, especially for internet users who use more than one digital platform. In this respect, it is possible to say that the business models of platforms that tend towards predictable consumption practices are in the nature of ensuring the continuation of a capitalist system structured on user data.

1.5 Data Surveillance

With the understanding of datafication, the idea of a network society has developed in the direction of a datafied society. Data provides key inputs to the various methods of analysis used by individuals, institutions, and businesses to understand and explain the world. These inputs contain powerful utility and high value that shape people's lives in terms of innovations, products, policies, and knowledge generation. For this reason, data has become a vital resource for the world. According to van Dijck (2017), datafication keeps everything under the sun at the heart of the networked world by transforming it into a data format. Data also feeds many applications used on various digital platforms and is therefore at the center of media practices.

As a reflection of the digital traces of Internet users, the attractiveness of data in various sectors continues to increase continuously. As Zuboff (2019) emphasizes, in the age of surveillance capitalism, individuals' experiences on the internet are sources of raw materials for a new economic order that demands them as free raw materials for forecasting and sales practices. In this context, issues such as accessing data, analyzing data, and using data in necessary ways cause these data sets, which are expressed as economic value, to become one of the important discussion topics for critical perspective in the social sciences. In this respect, it is possible to say that the digital traces that users leave "freely" and "voluntarily" in digital media environments in line with their digital movements are the most effective data sets that increase the power of economic capital and ensure its continuity.

Users' digital traces remain hidden in large datasets, and their lives are reflected in the digital network. The digital ecosystem, which turns Internet users into data subjects, also reveals that traditional surveillance practices are being reshaped. Because, in traditional surveillance practices (to go back to the beginning), while there is a visual perspective dependency in Bentham's panopticon, thanks to big data, the digital panopticon enables a 360-degree view of its inhabitants (Han, 2019, p. 63). Han's views provide remarkable grounds for understanding the active role of users in this panoptic order and the mutual relationship that digital platforms establish with users through surveillance practices. According to Han, in this order, users contribute to the formation of the digital panopticon by voluntarily submitting themselves to the panoptic gaze. In this respect, the dialectic of freedom in the digital environment becomes visible in that the user is both the perpetrator and the prisoner of the panoptic order.

While these basic conceptualizations reveal different understandings of surveillance, they converge on the view that surveillance has become commonplace at the level of life in general. Today's surveillance society has moved away from its panoptic underpinnings and is in an environment where it is given through algorithmic curation. It is inevitable to imagine the surveillance big brother of Orwell's 1984 dystopia with the big data created by algorithmic systems that infiltrate users' online activities and subject them to analysis for various purposes. This is because surveillance has become a business model for technology companies that aim to keep or direct users within this experience cycle by collecting users' behavioral data and, more specifically, by spying on users' internet experiences, preferences, likes, shares, etc. Recommendation systems also play an important role in these business models. At this point, it is useful to refer to Gary T. Marx's (2002) study on traditional surveillance and new surveillance processes in relation to these surveillance practices and data relationality. According to Marx, in new surveillance, data collection to obtain personal data is often integrated into routine activities and automated through the use of machines.

In capitalist business models based on data surveillance, personal information has become the primary resource to be exploited and commodified, and thus a new and highly effective logic of accumulation has emerged. In a surveillance capitalist environment, users have become part of a data-intensive economy in which they produce their own data through the digital labor process, produce it as datafied commodities, and buy back the information produced about them from this data. As in the case of recommendation systems, the personalization environment created with users' collected data aims to show selected content to users with predictive algorithms, to get users to click on ads or other paid content, or to persuade them to stay engaged with the platform (Cobbe & Singh, 2019).

In this respect, it is possible to say that the user, surrounded by recommendation algorithms, is free but conditioned in their choices (Cheney-Lippold, 2011, p. 178). Of course, the condition is the preferences carried by the data that the user will provide indirectly or directly, willingly or unwittingly, for the digital environment experience that the user expects. From this point of view, it would be useful to mention the concepts of algorithmic paradox and imagined affordance.

1.6 Imagined Affordance and the Algorithmic Paradox

Digital platforms relate to the user with their features and content, especially their interfaces. The interaction between the user and the platform enables the user to be better recognized by the algorithms, thereby shaping their inferences about imagined affordances through the algorithm suggestions presented to them (Blinded for Review). Nagy and Neff (2015) use the concept of imagined affordances to describe the complex relationship between the user and the platform interface, focusing on the user's perceptions, beliefs, and expectations of the platform, especially within the scope of the suggestions presented to him or her, based on the idea that it would be insufficient to locate the action possibilities of a social media platform with a set of features. As Markham et al. (2018) emphasize, the imagined affordances created through algorithms are essentially related to the complex relationship between the platform and the user created by the ambiguities of algorithms. Indeed, according to Fouquaert (2019, p. 13), paradoxically, users have a vague understanding of how algorithmic processes work and their effects, despite being aware that algorithmic processes take place within the framework of their behavioral data.

At this point, the concept of the algorithmic imaginary can be emphasized. According to Butcher (2017), although it is difficult to know exactly how algorithms work, personalized algorithm experiences have the potential to illuminate how algorithms make the imaginary possible under which conditions. In other words, the algorithmic dream emerges from the user's beliefs, experiences, and expectations of the algorithm (Schulz, 2022). In this context, it is thought that it is possible to say that the behavior of the user adopting the algorithm finds a field of action within the framework of imagined affordance.

A mental estimate of a user's ability to interact with an interface is known as imagined affordance. For instance, on a video-on-demand platform, the user interface displays commands like "play," "add to list," "save," and so on. Conversely, imagined affordances are less obvious and are determined by the designer's objectives as well as the user's perceptions and expectations. As the user spends more time on the VoD platform, the algorithmic suggestions that are displayed to them modify their perceptions of the imagined affordance within this network of relationships.

For users, the black box has an important place in the formation of the algorithmic paradox. Because the ambiguity of how and for what purpose the algorithms are processed or how they are finalized does not clarify the users' focus on the control of their data.

The order based on the capitalist economy surrounds users with a circle of positivity surrounded by "like" feedback, free from all kinds of negativity. It is possible to say that the communication between man and machine is based on positivity. In that case, it would not be wrong to state that it is the price of the delusion of positivity and freedom that platforms provide to the user that makes individuals' preferences consumable. Fouquaert and Mechant (2021) also reported that the fact that the advantages perceived by users in terms of the platform are more dominant than the disadvantages prevent a change in usage habits, thus creating an algorithmic paradox.

"Algorithm paradox is derived from the privacy paradox, which is the discrepancy between an individual's intentions to value their privacy and how they actually behave in the online environment" (Shin, 2023, p. 48). For instance, a study (Barth & de Jong, 2017) found that even while people are aware of the threats to their privacy when using the internet, they nevertheless frequently give up personal information to receive personalized services. The researchers' idea of the privacy paradox, which they employed to explain this predicament, highlights users' propensity to engage in privacy-compromising activities online, creating a contradiction between their attitudes about privacy and their real behavior.

So from the user's perspective, the algorithmic paradox involves the contradiction of disclosing their data and having control over their data in order to benefit from personalized platform services. These two far-flung structures point to a much more risky situation, especially for users who are not algorithm-aware. On the other hand, the nature of the business model of media platforms also points to a paradox (Shin, 2023, p. 48). In this case, the algorithms used by VoD platforms are powered by user data. For instance, a user agrees to the terms and conditions as soon as they utilize any VoD platform. A lot of websites, including Netflix, Amazon, and others, make it clear that user information is gathered and might be shared via third-party links. In general, these data collection methods are offered to give users better service. In order to obtain better services, individuals willingly give their privacy to the digital world. The paradox of internet users being surrounded by algorithms is this contradiction.

Through recommendations made by platforms, users can find new audio and video content. But it can also have the unintended effect of making people less open-minded or preventing them from discovering new interests. Put differently, recommendation systems employ algorithms to direct users toward specific patterns of thought or consumption. In addition, this is the cause of the damaging echo chamber and filter bubble effects that lead to polarization and dedifferentiation in society. Users of the platform are put in a paradoxical situation where algorithms have the ability to manipulate them. This highlights how important it is to have a critical mindset and be aware of algorithms and ethical behavior in the digital world.

2. FOR FUTURE STUDIES

Behavioral data is at the heart of the digital world. As a matter of fact, the conceptualizations at the focus of critical algorithm studies are based on the trivets of data providers, data users, and algorithms. Critical algorithm studies, which basically focus on the relationship between these three components, focus on economic, cultural, and social elements at the point of sustaining this relationship. Because, inherent in the consumption practices of internet users, the aim of increasing the profit maximization of technology companies and the parties in cooperation with these companies causes them to see user data as an economic value, Therefore, practices aimed at ensuring that the user or viewer remains constantly connected in the digital environment include algorithms that create this environment by predicting the environment that the user may want based on his or her own preferences. In addition to the economic purpose, the various purposes nurtured by the party developing the algorithms also ensure that the digital environment is guided by algorithms.

Recommendation systems play an important role in the sustainability of user and algorithm interaction in the OTT ecosystem. These algorithmic systems adopted by platform owners in their business models affect the agenda of the conceptual framework that critically evaluates algorithms. When taking into account the present and future implications of algorithms in the social domain, this line of reasoning raises a number of issues. This conceptual framework problematizes the algorithmic establishment of power on digital platforms, data commodity and capitalist practices on platforms, data surveillance, and the position of digital media inhabitants and media experiences surrounded by algorithmic systems within the context of all these main topics, with regard to the issue of media ownership in critical communication studies.

In today's world, where the number of OTT users worldwide reaches higher numbers every year, the business models based on personalization and recommendation systems used by VoD platforms to manage the algorithm-user interaction, especially VoD platforms, create certain exposures in users' viewing experiences. For this reason, it is thought that defense mechanisms to be developed against algorithmic systems that have the power to manage the content consumption behavior of viewers are important. Therefore, within the algorithmic structures that envelop the digital environment more and more strongly every day, viewers' having more control over their behavior and approaching algorithmic influences on their decisions more critically are areas of struggle that should be focused on despite the risk typologies emphasized by Critical algorithm studies. In this regard, it is important to draw attention to the areas of ethics, algorithm awareness, and algorithm literacy in algorithmic systems.

In the context of all these, the following recommendations can be made for future research and strategic steps focusing on the risk typologies that constitute the concept of Critical algorithm studies:

- Identifying users' experiences with recommendation systems through research designed specifically for VoD platform types, taking into account sample diversity and research methods,
- Interdisciplinary research on VoD users' experiences with recommendation systems, taking into account the risk typologies of algorithms in various fields within the scope of the social sciences,
- Conducting interdisciplinary research to determine the level of algorithm awareness and literacy of VoD users within the scope of their demographic characteristics and digital capital and their defense mechanisms against the risks posed by algorithms,
- Designing and conducting projects and research in collaboration with media professionals and algorithm developers that will be the source of regulations focused on the formation of digital platform structures based on user autonomy, including ethical and responsible technologies,
- Bringing imagined affordance, algorithmic paradox, and algorithmic consent manufacturing to the field through research on user experience.
- In creating a culture of living with algorithms, it is recommended to design research that relates individuals' digital competencies and algorithm awareness.

REFERENCES

Adomavicius, G., Bauman, K., Tuzhilin, A., & Unger, M. (2022). Context-aware recommender systems. In F. Ricci, L. Rokach, & B. Shapira (Eds.), *Recommender systems handbook* (pp. 211–250). Springer. doi:10.1007/978-1-0716-2197-4_6

Bakke, A. (2020). Everyday googling: Results of an observational study and applications for teaching algorithmic literacy. *Computers and Composition*, *57*, 1–16. doi:10.1016/j.compcom.2020.102577

Barth, S., & de Jong, T. D. M. (2017). The privacy paradox – Investigating discrepancies between expressed privacy concerns and actual online behavior – A systematic literature review. *Telematics and Informatics*, *34*(7), 1038–1058. doi:10.1016/j.tele.2017.04.013

Beer, D. (2009). Power through the algorithm? Participatory web cultures and the technological unconscious. *New Media & Society*, *11*(6), 985–1002. doi:10.1177/1461444809336551

Beer, D. (2017). The social power of algorithms. *Information Communication and Society*, *20*(1), 1–13. doi:10.1080/1369118X.2016.1216147

Beer, D. (2019). The data gaze: Capitalism, power and perception: Society and space series. *Sage (Atlanta, Ga.).*

Bhaskar, M. (2016, September 30). In the age of the algorithm, the human gatekeeper is back. *The Guardian.* https://www.theguardian.com/technology/2016/sep/30/age-of-algorithm-human-gatekeeper

Blazques, D., & Domenech, J. (2018). Big data souces and methods for social and economic analyses. *Technological Forecasting and Social Change*, *130*(C), 99–113. doi:10.1016/j.techfore.2017.07.027

Breese, J. S., Heckerman, D., & Kadie, C. (1998). Empirical analysis of predictive algorithms for collaborative filtering. *In Proceedings of the Fourteenth Conference on Uncertainty in Artificial Intelligence,* (pp. 43-52). Publication History.

Bucher, T. (2017). The algorithmic imaginary: Exploring the ordinary affects of Facebook algorithms. *Information Communication and Society*, *20*(1), 30–44. doi:10.1080/1369118X.2016.1154086

Bucher, T. (2018). *If...Then: Algorithmic power and politics*. Oxford University Press. doi:10.1093/oso/9780190493028.001.0001

Bugeja, S. M. (2020). *The influence of web personalisation on the consumer's decision-making process* [Unpublished doctoral dissertation, L-Università ta' Malta, Malta].

Burke, R. (2002). Hybrid recommender systems: Survey and experiments. *User Modeling and User-Adapted Interaction*, *12*(4), 331–370. doi:10.1023/A:1021240730564

Chase, C. W. Jr. (2013). Using big data to enhance demand-driven forecasting and planning. *The Journal of Business Forecasting: Methods & Systems*, *32*(2), 27–34.

Cheney-Lippold, J. (2011). A New Algorithmic Identity. *Theory, Culture & Society*, *28*(6), 164–181. doi:10.1177/0263276411424420

Chorianopoulos, K. (2008). Personalized and mobile digital TV applications. *Multimedia Tools and Applications*, *36*(1-2), 1–10. doi:10.1007/s11042-006-0081-8

Cobbe, J., & Singh, J. (2019). Regulating recommending: Motivations, considerations, and principles. *SSRN*, *10*(3), 1–49. doi:10.2139/ssrn.3371830

Colombo-Mendoza, L. O., Valencia-García, R., Rodríguez-González, A., Alor-Hernández, G., & Samper-Zapater, J. J. (2015). RecomMetz: A context-aware knowledge-based mobile recommender system for movie showtimes. *Expert Systems with Applications*, *42*(3), 1202–1222. doi:10.1016/j.eswa.2014.09.016

Conlin, L., Billings, A. C., & Averset, L. (2016). Time-shifting vs. appointment viewing: The role of fear of missing out within TV consumption behaviours. *Communicatio Socialis*, *29*, 151–164.

Datareportal (2023, April). *digital 2023 April global statshot report*. https://datareportal.com/reports/digital-2023-april-global-statshot

Desai, D. (2017). *A study of design aspects of web personalization for online users in India*. (Corpus ID: 64977506) [Doctoral dissertation, Gujarat Technological University Ahmedabad]. Semantic Scholar.

Diakopoulos, N. (2015). Algorithmic accountability. *Digital Journalism (Abingdon, England)*, *3*(3), 398–415. doi:10.1080/21670811.2014.976411

Dourish, P. (2016). Algorithms and their others: Algorithmic culture in context. *Big Data & Society*, *3*(2), 1–11. doi:10.1177/2053951716665128

Foucault, M. (2019). *Özne ve İktidar* (I. Ergüden & O. Akınhay, Trans.). Ayrıntı.

Fouquaert, T. (2019). *The Algorithm Paradox: knowledge of versus attitudes towards curation algorithms*, [Unpublished master dissertation, Ghent University, Belgium].

Fouquaert, T., & Mechant, P. (2021). Making curation algorithms apparent: A case study of "Instawareness" as a means to heighten awareness and understanding of Instagram's algorithm. *Information Communication and Society*, *25*(12), 1–21.

Gallier, E. (2021). *SVOD vs TVOD vs AVOD: What's the Best Content Delivery System?* Harmonic Inc. https://www.harmonicinc.com/insights/blog/svod-vs-tvod-vs-avod-whats-the-best-content-delivery-system/

Gillespie, T. (2014). The relevance of algorithms. media technologies: Essays on communication. In T. Gillespie, P. J. Boczkowski, & K. A. Foot (Eds.), *Materiality and society* (pp. 167–193). MIT Press.

Gomez-Uribe, A. C., & Hunt, N. (2015). The Netflix recommender system: Algorithms, Business Value, and Innovation. *ACM Transactions on Management Information Systems*, *6*(4), 1–19. doi:10.1145/2843948

Han, B. C. (2019). *Psikopolitika: Neoliberalizm ve yeni iktidar teknikleri* (H. Barışçan, Trans.). Metis.

Herlocker, L. J., Konstan, A. J., & Riedl, J. (2000). Explaining Collaborative Filtering Recommendations. *CSCW '00: Proceedings of the 2000 ACM conference on Computer supported cooperative work.* ACM. 10.1145/358916.358995

Huang, Y., Cui, B., Zhang, W., Jiang, J., & Xu, Y. (2015). TencentRec: Real-time stream recommendation in practice. *In Proceedings of the 2015 ACM SIGMOD International Conference on Management of Data- SIGMOD'15.* Association for Computing Machinery.

Hussein, W., Ismail, R. M., Gharib, T. F., & Mostafa, M. G. M. (2013). A personalized recommender system based on a hybrid model. *JUCS -. Journal of Universal Computer Science*, *19*(15), 2224–2240. doi:10.3217/jucs-019-15-2224

Hyken, S. (2017, October 29). Personalized customer experience increases revenue and loyalty. *Forbes.* https://www.forbes.com/sites/shephyken/2017/10/29/personalized-customer-experience-increases-revenue-and-loyalty/#3852914d4bd6

Javed, U., Shaukat, K., Hameed, A., Iqbal, I., Mahboob, F., Alam, T., & Luo, S. (2021). A Review of Content-Based and Context-Based Recommendation Systems. [iJET]. *International Journal of Emerging Technologies in Learning*, *16*(03), 274–306. doi:10.3991/ijet.v16i03.18851

Kara, B. B., & McAleese, S. (2021). *Algorithmic awareness: conversations with young canadians about artificial intelligence and privacy.* MediaSmarts. https://mediasmarts.ca/sites/default/files/publication-report/full/report_algorithmic_awareness.pdfBlinded for Review.

Konstantoulaki, K., Rizomyliotis, I., & Papangelopoulou, A. (2019). Personalised content in mobile applications and purchase intentions: An exploratory study. *Business and Management Studies*, *5*(4), 13–23. doi:10.11114/bms.v5i4.4571

Koren, Y., Rendle, S., & Bell, R. (2022). Advances in collaborative filtering. In F. Ricci, L. Rokach, & B. Shapira (Eds.), *Recommender systems handbook* (pp. 91–142). Springer. doi:10.1007/978-1-0716-2197-4_3

Kotler, P., Kartajaya, H., & Setiawan, I. (2021). *Pazarlama 5.0 insan için teknoloji* (T. Gezer, Trans.). Nişantaşı Üniversitesi Yayınları.

Løkke, E. (2020). *Mahremiyet Dijital Toplumda Özel Hayat. (D. Başak, Çev.).* Koç Üniversitesi Yayınları.

Markham, A., Stavrova, S., & Schlüter, M. (2018). Netflix, imagined affordances, and the illusion of control. In T. Plothe & A. M. Buck (Eds.), *Netflix at the nexus: Content, practice and production in the age of streaming television* (pp. 29–46). Peter Lang.

Marx, G. T. (2004). What's new about the "new surveillance"?: Classifying for change and continuity. *Surveillance & Society*, *1*(1), 9–29. doi:10.24908/ss.v1i1.3391

Moats, D., & Seaver, N. (2019). "You social scientists love mind games": Experimenting in the "divide" between data science and critical algorithm studies. *Big Data & Society*, *6*(1), 1–11. doi:10.1177/2053951719833404

Mobasher, B. (2007). Data Mining for Web Personalization. Brusilovsky, P., Kobsa, A., Nejdl, W. (eds) The Adaptive Web Methods and Strategies of Web Personalisation. Lecture Notes in Computer Science içinde (s.90-136). Springer. doi:10.1007/978-3-540-72079-9_3

Mu, R. (2018). *A survey of recommender systems based on deep learning*. Digital Object Identifer., doi:10.1109/ACCESS.2018.2880197

Nagy, P., & Neff, G. (2015). Imagined affordance: Reconstructing a keyword for communication theory. *Social Media + Society*, *1*(2), 1–9. doi:10.1177/2056305115603385

O'Neil, C. (2017, November 14). The ivory tower can't keep ignoring tech. *The New York Times*. www.nytimes.com/2017/11/14/opinion/academia-tech-algorithms.html

Ong, J. W. (2012). *Sözlü ve yazılı kültür: Sözün teknolojileşmesi* (S. Postacıoğlu Banon, Trans.). Metis.

Özel, S. (2020). Talebe bağlı video servisleri çağında Netflix etkisi. *İnsan& İnsan*. *7*(26), 115-138.

Özel, S. & Özay, D. (2021). Yeni medya ortamlarında izleyici seçimi ve öneri algoritmaları. *İlef Dergisi*, *8*(2), 297-324.

Papagelis, M., & Plexousakis, D. (2005). Qualitative analysis of user-based and item-based prediction algorithms for recommendation agents. *Engineering Applications of Artificial Intelligence*, *18*(7), 781–789. doi:10.1016/j.engappai.2005.06.010

Pasquale, F. (2015). *The black box society: The secret algorithms that control money and information*. Harvard University Press. doi:10.4159/harvard.9780674736061

Pazzani, M. J., & Billsus, D. (2007). Content-Based Recommendation Systems. Brusilovsky, P., Kobsa, A., Nejdl, W. (eds) The Adaptive Web Methods and Strategies of Web Personalisation. Lecture Notes in Computer Science içinde (s.325-341). Springer. doi:10.1007/978-3-540-72079-9_10

Rakshit, P., Saha, S., Chatterjee, A., Mistri, S., Das, S., & Dhar, G. (2022). A Popularity-Based Recommendation System Using Machine Learning. In H. K. Deva Sarma, V. Piuri, & A. K. Pujari (Eds.), *Machine Learning in Information and Communication Technology. Lecture Notes in Networks and Systems* (Vol. 498). Springer.

Saurwein, F., & Spencer-Smith, C. (2021). Automated trouble: The role of algorithmic selection in harms on social media platforms. *Media and Communication*, *9*(4), 222–233. doi:10.17645/mac.v9i4.4062

Schafer, J. B., Konstan, J., & Riedl, J. (1999). Recommender systems in e-commerce. *In Proceedings of the 1st ACM Conference on Electronic Commerce,* (pp. 158-166). Association for Computing Machinery
Schulz, C. (2022). A new algorithmic imaginary. *Media Culture & Society*, *45*(3), 451–681.

Seaver, N. (2017). Algorithms as culture: Some tactics for the ethnography of algorithmic systems. *Big Data & Society*, *4*(2). doi:10.1177/2053951717738104

Shin, D. D. (2023). *Algorithms, Human and Interactions: How Do Algorithms Interact with People? Designing Meaningful AI Experiences*. Routledge.

Shinde, K. S., & Kulkarni, U. (2012). Hybrid personalized recommender system using centering-bunching based clustering algorithm. *Expert Systems with Applications*, *39*(1), 1381–1387. doi:10.1016/j.eswa.2011.08.020

Srnicek, N. (2017). *Platform capitalism*. Polity Press.

Statista (2023). *Video streaming worldwide - statistics & facts*. Statista. https://www.statista.com/topics/7527/video-streaming-worldwide/#topicOverview

Tarus, K. J., Niu, Z., & Mustafa, G. (2018). Knowledge-based recommendation: A review of ontology-based recommender systems for e-learning. *Artificial Intelligence Review*, *50*(21), 21–48. doi:10.1007/s10462-017-9539-5

Thorat, B. P., Goudar, M. R., & Barve, S. (2015). Survey on collaborative filtering, content-based filtering and hybrid recommendation system. *International Journal of Computer Applications*, *110*(4), 31–36. doi:10.5120/19308-0760

Van Dijck, J. (2014). Datafication, dataism and dataveillance: Big data between scientific paradigm and ideology. *Surveillance & Society*, *12*(2), 197–208. doi:10.24908/ss.v12i2.4776

Van Dijck, J. (2017). Foreword. In T. M. Schäfer & K. van Es (Eds.), *The datafied society studying culture through data* (pp. 12–13). Amsterdam University Press. doi:10.1515/9789048531011-002

Vesanen, J. (2007). What is personalization? A conceptual framework. *European Journal of Marketing*, *41*(5/6), 409–418. doi:10.1108/03090560710737534

Vesanen, J., & Raulas, M. (2006). Building bridges for personalization – a process model for marketing. *Journal of Interactive Marketing*, *20*(1), 1–16. doi:10.1002/dir.20052

Wind, J., & Rangaswamy, A. (2001). Customerization: The next revolution in mass customization. *Journal of Interactive Marketing*, *15*(1), 13–33. doi:10.1002/1520-6653(200124)15:1<13::AID-DIR1001>3.0.CO;2-#

Yesilada, M., & Lewandowsky, S. (2022). Systematic review: YouTube recommendations and problematic content. *Internet Policy Review*, *11*(1), 1–22. doi:10.14763/2022.1.1652 PMID:36466439

Zengin, F. (2020). Akıllı makine çağı sinemasına giriş: Sinema sanatında yapay zekâ teknolojilerinin kullanımı. *İletişim Çalışmaları Dergisi*, *6*(2), 151- 177.

Zuboff, S. (2019). *The Age of Surveillance Capitalism: The Fight for a Human Future at the New Frontier of Power*. Public Affairs.

ENDNOTES

1. Algorithm-mediated surveillance refers to a form of surveillance based on algorithmic curation in which users' behavioral data is collected and analyzed in a given digital environment. Algorithm-mediated surveillance has become part of a data-driven economy.
2. In today's digital platform ecosystem, it is possible to say that the various consent notifications that users encounter almost every moment have come to an automatic form of consent with the motive of not being able to benefit from the relevant service or uses at the point where users accept or reject them without questioning. This situation gives rise to algorithmic consent manufacturing (Treré, 2016, p. 130).
3. The algorithmic imaginary emerges in the user's beliefs, experiences, and expectations about the algorithm (Schulz, 2022). In this context, it is possible to say that the manufacturing of algorithmic consent within the framework of imaginary possibilities finds a field of action that exceeds the right to privacy.
4. Users of algorithm-driven technology experience a dichotomy between benefits and drawbacks due to the opaque and intricate black box working principles of algorithms.

Chapter 8
Advancing Personalization and Recommendation Algorithms in the OTT Industry:
Enhancing User Experiences and Driving Engagement

Ruth Neyah
Vellore Institute of Technology, India

M. Vijayakumar
https://orcid.org/0000-0002-1079-5383
Vellore Institute of Technology, India

ABSTRACT

In order to deliver customised content and improve user experiences, over-the-top (OTT) providers must adopt efficient customization and recommendation algorithms as the OTT sector continues to grow. The objective of this chapter is to investigate the developments, difficulties, and best practises relating to personalization and recommendation algorithms in the over-the-top environment. The significance of customization and recommendation algorithms in the over-the-top OTT business will be covered in the proposed chapter. The proposed chapter seeks to provide readers interested in customisation and recommendation algorithms within the OTT business with useful information and helpful advice. It will discuss how the OTT market is changing and provide practical advice to OTT service providers looking to improve their users' user experiences via sophisticated personalisation and recommendation algorithms.

1. INTRODUCTION

The Over-The-Top (OTT) industry has gone through a seismic shift in the recent years, which has revolutionised the way that people consume media content and transformed the landscape of the entertainment industry. OTT platforms, which are characterised by their ability to deliver a diverse array of media content directly to consumers over the internet, have not only disrupted traditional models of media

DOI: 10.4018/979-8-3693-0116-6.ch008

distribution but also redefined the very nature of viewer engagement (Brian & Robert,2020).OTT platforms are characterised by their ability to deliver a diverse array of media content directly to consumers over the internet. The idea of personalization, which adapts content suggestions to the preferences of each individual user to produce a viewing experience that is unique to that user, is at the centre of this transformation. This study will investigate the mechanisms, benefits, challenges, and future prospects of enhancing user experiences and driving engagement through advanced personalization techniques. The purpose of this research is to investigate the pivotal role that personalization and recommendation algorithms play in the OTT industry.

The rapid growth of over-the-top (OTT) platforms has resulted in an unprecedented volume of media content becoming readily accessible to users at any time and from any location. However, this abundance has also presented a challenge, which is the task of locating content that, amidst the vast ocean of options, resonates with individual preferences. In response to this, recommendation algorithms have emerged as essential tools for users to utilise in order to efficiently navigate the content maze that exists today. These algorithms make use of user data, such as viewing history, preferences, and interactions, in order to generate recommendations for content that is specifically suited to each individual user (Yousaf,2020). Not only does this personalization make it easier to find content, but it also increases user engagement by providing them with options that are pertinent to the areas in which they are most interested. As a consequence of this, OTT platforms are increasing the amount of money they invest in the development of more refined recommendation algorithms in order to provide content suggestions that are more accurate and relevant (Kwon, Y et al.,2021).

The advantages of providing users with personalised recommendations for content go far beyond the convenience factor. A sense of connectivity and loyalty between the viewer and the platform can be fostered by enhancing the user experience. A successful personalization strategy gives users the ability to craft their own entertainment experience, which in turn results in longer engagement sessions and higher levels of user satisfaction. Additionally, as users find content that resonates with them, they are more likely to explore a platform's extensive library, find hidden gems, and even sample genres that they might not have otherwise considered. This is because users become more likely to do so as they find content that resonates with them. Therefore, the implementation of advanced personalization techniques helps drive user engagement and retention, which in turn contributes to the expansion of the over-the-top (OTT) industry as a whole.

The pursuit of effective personalization, on the other hand, is not without its obstacles. An ongoing challenge consists in finding a happy medium between providing personalised content recommendations and protecting the privacy of individual users. Ethical questions are raised as a result of the fact that platforms are collecting and analysing user data in order to improve their recommendation algorithms. This makes it necessary to take a transparent approach to data usage and provide users with control over their information. In addition, the "filter bubble" effect, in which users are only shown content that is in line with their existing preferences, raises questions about the potential for limiting serendipitous content discovery and narrowing perspectives. To ensure that personalization improves user experiences without inadvertently stifling diversity and exploration, addressing these challenges is essential and must be a top priority.

When we look into the future, we can see that the personalization and recommendation algorithms that will be used in the OTT industry will undergo remarkable development. It is anticipated that as technology continues to advance, machine learning and artificial intelligence will play crucial roles in playing a pivotal role in the further refinement of these algorithms (Hallur et al.,2023).The incorporation of contextual information, such as the time of day, location, and mood of the user, may result in highly personalised content recommendations that are in line with the context in which the viewer is currently situated. In addition, methods of collaborative filtering, social interactions, and even physiological responses could be utilised to improve algorithm accuracy, thereby expanding the scope of user personalization.

In conclusion, the development of the OTT industry has completely rethought the methods by which users access and consume media content, putting a greater emphasis on the significance of personalization and recommendation algorithms. In the field of over-the-top (OTT) content delivery, personalization can be broken down into a complex landscape that this study will investigate. This study aims to shed light on how advanced personalization techniques can elevate user experiences, foster engagement, and shape the trajectory of the ever-evolving OTT ecosystem. This will be accomplished through an exploration of mechanisms, benefits, challenges, and future possibilities. As we delve deeper into this complex realm, our ultimate goal is to unearth insights that will contribute to scholarly discourse as well as practical implementations in the OTT industry (Sharma, N.,2021).This will, in turn, make the lives of users more fulfilling in an era where there are an infinite number of content possibilities.

1.1 Understanding Personalization and Recommendation Algorithms

Personalization and recommendation algorithms have emerged as the linchpin of enhancing user experiences and driving engagement within the Over-The-Top (OTT) industry. This is because the contemporary digital landscape features an unprecedented abundance of content that competes for the attention of users. The term "personalization" refers to the process of adapting content and experiences to the specific preferences of each individual user. This enables platforms to produce an environment that is more pertinent and curated. In conjunction with this idea, recommendation algorithms make use of user data in order to make content suggestions for users, thereby assisting users in navigating the vast content repository that is made available on OTT platforms. These algorithms play a significant role in shaping patterns of user engagement and fostering a sense of connectivity between viewers and platforms.

The efficiency of various personalization and recommendation algorithms is dependent on the complex interaction of a variety of different components and methods. First and foremost, the collection of data serves as the basis upon which these algorithms are constructed (Niko,2022). User interaction data, such as viewing history, search queries, and interactions with content, can provide extremely useful insights into a user's preferences. One of the primary methods, known as collaborative filtering, evaluates a user's actions and preferences in relation to those of other users who are similar to that user, and then makes content recommendations that are founded on these group decisions.

Filtering information based on the content itself is another method that evaluates the intrinsic qualities of both the content and the user's preferences. Platforms make recommendations for content based on the viewer's historical preferences by analysing metadata such as the genre, actors, and themes associated with the content. These approaches are combined into a single method known as a hybrid method, which draws on the advantages of both approaches to generate recommendations that are both more precise and comprehensive.

In addition, matrix factorization and deep learning models are becoming increasingly popular. Matrix factorization techniques decompose the user-item interaction matrix to uncover latent factors that drive preferences, allowing for more nuanced recommendations to be generated as a result. Deep learning models, which are powered by neural networks, have the ability to capture complex patterns in user behaviour and content attributes, which results in an increase in the accuracy of suggestions.

A dynamic cycle that reshapes the way audiences interact with OTT platforms is set in motion by the intricate interplay between personalization, recommendations, and user engagement. Through the use of personalization, viewers can have an experience that is unique to them and that resonates with them, which increases the likelihood that they will find content that is relevant to their interests. Users' engagement deepens as they come across content that speaks to them on a personal level; this helps to foster a sense of emotional investment in the platform. The way in which personalization and recommendation algorithms approach the "paradox of choice" is a particularly good example of the synergy that exists between the two. Because there is such a large content library that users can access, there is a possibility that they will become overwhelmed and stop using the platform (Zhang,2023).The recommendations function as navigational guides, compiling a manageable selection of content that is in accordance with the preferences of the users. This not only makes it easier to find content, but it also lessens the mental strain associated with making decisions, which increases the likelihood that engagement will be maintained.

In addition to this, the efficiency of recommendation algorithms is dependent on the presence of ongoing feedback loops. The algorithms keep track of how users engage with the content that has been recommended to them and use this information to improve subsequent suggestions. This iterative process refines recommendations over time, thereby creating a positive feedback loop that leads to increased engagement and relevance.

In turn, active participation from users is essential to the success of a platform. Increases in engagement metrics, such as longer viewing sessions and increased interaction frequency, are directly correlated with increases in user retention rates. Users have a greater tendency to feel that platforms are responsive to their individual preferences when they are provided with personalised content recommendations. A cycle of continuous improvement is maintained when users invest more time and attention into a platform, which in turn generates more data that provides valuable insights that enable further algorithm refinement (OKUMUŞ, M. Sami.,2023).

Platforms are able to provide personalised content recommendations that are meaningful to individual viewers by utilising these algorithms, which are powered by cutting-edge methods and an extensive range of data points. Personalization and recommendations have a complex relationship with one another, which results in the formation of a dynamic cycle that increases user engagement, strengthens emotional connections with the platform, and reduces the amount of content that is available (Shin,2022). These algorithms are poised to evolve as the OTT landscape continues to change, and they will leverage emerging technologies to further refine their accuracy and impact. The transformative potential of data-driven strategies is illustrated by the symbiotic relationship that exists between personalization, recommendations, and user engagement. These three factors will have a significant impact on the future of media consumption and content delivery (Shin,2022).

1.2 Data Collection and User Profiling

Strategies for collecting and analysing user data have emerged as critical components in the ever-evolving world of the over-the-top (OTT) industry. These components are responsible for shaping personalised experiences and optimising content recommendations. Understanding user behaviour, preferences, and engagement patterns requires a solid foundation, which can be provided by these strategies, which are supported by robust data collection mechanisms and sophisticated analytics (Wong,2015).

Multiple touchpoints spread out across the user journey are the essential components of data collection. A wealth of information can be gleaned from usage data, which includes a user's viewing history, search queries, interactions with content, and engagement metrics, among other things. These kinds of data can be gathered from users' interactions with the platform, whether those interactions take the form of overt actions (such as likes, ratings, and reviews) or covert actions (such as the amount of time spent on content and patterns of browsing). Data generated by users, such as their profiles and their social interactions, can also provide useful clues for the purposes of personalization (Kalorth,2018).

The application of data analysis techniques is critical to the process of transforming raw data into insights that can be acted upon. The purpose of descriptive analytics is to provide an overview of user behaviours by summarising historical data. On the other hand, predictive analytics utilise algorithms to forecast future user actions based on historical patterns. The process of providing recommendations on actions to take in order to improve user experiences is known as prescriptive analytics. These methods, when combined with models of machine learning, make a contribution to the refinement of personalization strategies and the acceleration of user engagement.

The generation of accurate user profiles and segmentation is an essential component to the success of algorithms that provide personalization and recommendations. Platforms are able to differentiate users according to their preferences, behaviours, and demographic information when they make use of data insights. One strategy involves grouping users into distinct segments based on their shared behaviours. This makes it possible to provide content recommendations that are specifically tailored to the preferences of each individual segment.

In the process of creating user profiles and user segments, machine learning algorithms are an extremely important factor. The formation of homogenous clusters is made easier by the use of collaborative filtering techniques, which locate users who have preferences and behaviours that are similar to one another. A content-based filter makes use of the attributes of the content to determine the preferences and interests of the user. These methods are combined in hybrid approaches, which then capitalise on the qualities that are unique to each method to produce more accurate user profiles.

However, the collection and utilisation of user data raises a number of complex ethical considerations, despite the fact that the potential benefits of data-driven personalization are enormous. Because of privacy concerns, responsible data handling practises are required. These practises must respect the autonomy of users and protect sensitive information. Finding a happy medium between the two goals of personalization and privacy requires open and honest communication regarding the practises of data collection, usage, and sharing.

The importance of obtaining informed consent and providing users with control over their data is highlighted by regulatory frameworks such as the General Data Protection Regulation (GDPR) and the California Consumer Privacy Act (CCPA), both of which are based in the state of California. Platforms have a responsibility to take measures to anonymize and aggregate user data in order to prevent individual users from being singled out. To prevent unauthorised access, data encryption and secure storage are two of the most important preventative measures that can be taken.

The implications of ethics go beyond merely complying with the law and encompass a wide range of issues, such as the "filter bubble" effect. Recommendations that are overly personalised could, unintentionally, restrict users' exposure to a variety of perspectives, thereby limiting the scope of their worldview. It is essential, in order to lessen the impact of this effect, to strike a balance between the accidental discovery of content and the receiving of personalised recommendations.

Additionally, data biases have the potential to unintentionally perpetuate stereotypes as well as inequalities. If historical data reflects existing biases in a society, then recommendation algorithms may inadvertently reinforce those biases when making suggestions regarding content. In order to address these biases, it is necessary to make a concerted effort to locate and correct discriminatory patterns in the design of data and algorithms.

The development of accurate consumer profiles and divisions is the key to the success of personalised content recommendations, and effective data collection mechanisms and analytics techniques are the foundation upon which these are built. An approach that places a high priority on user consent, data security, and fairness in algorithmic decision-making is necessary because privacy concerns and ethical implications require a meticulous approach. Not only does this ensure the uninterrupted expansion of the OTT industry, but it also upholds the principles of user empowerment and ethical technology deployment in this age of digitalization.

1.3 Advanced Recommendation Algorithms

The Over-The-Top (OTT) industry relies heavily on collaborative filtering as a foundational component for producing accurate content recommendations. This strategy makes use of the preferences and actions taken collectively by a user community in order to generate individualised recommendations. The fundamental idea is that users who have shown a tendency to behave in ways that are consistent with their interests or preferences in the past are likely to continue doing so in the future.

The terms "user-based" and "item-based" refer to the two primary approaches that are included in collaborative filtering. User-based collaborative filtering identifies other users whose preferences are comparable to those of the target user and then recommends content that these other users have found enjoyable. Item-based collaborative filtering, on the other hand, focuses on identifying similar items based on user interactions and recommends items that are comparable to those with which the user has previously interacted. The availability of historical interaction data is critical to the success of collaborative filtering, which relies on that data. Ratings, likes, and viewing histories of the user may be included in this data (Kumar,2022).

Consideration of the content's inherent qualities is at the heart of content-based filtering, which works in tandem with collaborative filtering. This method seeks to gain an understanding of the characteristics of the content by analysing aspects of it such as the genre, actors, and directors, as well as keywords. When these attributes are aligned with the preferences of the user, content-based filtering generates recommendations for items that are compatible with the user's previous interactions and preferences.

There are numerous benefits associated with using content-based filtering, in particular in circumstances in which user interaction data is limited. It is especially useful in circumstances in which novel content or preferences specific to a niche market need to be catered to. However, the efficacy of content-based filtering is contingent on the quality and richness of content metadata. Content metadata is the foundation for aligning content attributes with user preferences, so its quality and richness are essential.

Due to the limitations of individual filtering methods, the way has been cleared for the development of hybrid algorithms that combine collaborative and content-based methods. The purpose of hybrid algorithms is to take advantage of the positive aspects of each technique while minimising the negative aspects of each. Switching, weighting, and combining are the three primary classifications that can be applied to these distinct types of algorithms.

Depending on the circumstances, switching hybrid algorithms will either use collaborative filtering or content-based filtering to make their decision. In order to combine the recommendations of collaborative filters and content-based filters, weighting hybrid algorithms give different weights to the outputs of each type of filter. The creation of a unified set of recommendations can be accomplished by combining hybrid algorithms, which directly merge the outputs of both approaches. In circumstances characterised by complex and multidimensional patterns of user behaviour, hybrid algorithms prove to be particularly useful. These algorithms provide more accurate and varied recommendations by combining the insights gained from collaborative filtering and content-based filtering. As a result, they are able to cater to a wider range of user preferences.

1.4 Contextual Personalization in OTT

In the rapidly evolving landscape of the Over-The-Top (OTT) industry, the pursuit of increased personalization has led to the incorporation of contextual information such as time, location, device, and user behaviour. Specifically, the quest for enhanced personalization has led to the incorporation of these factors. OTT platforms are able to provide users with a more personalised and interesting experience that has the potential to have a deeper level of resonance if they make use of the contextual cues (Samriti et al.,2020).

The preferences of users are significantly influenced not only by the time of day but also by the day of the week. Platforms are able to optimise their recommendations by gaining a better understanding of when users are most active or when they engage with particular categories of content. A viewer who watches in the morning might be more interested in news or educational programming, while a viewer who watches in the evening might lean more towards entertainment.

The geographical setting of users is taken into consideration when location-based personalization is applied. This can be utilised to make recommendations for content that is pertinent to a particular region, such as regional news or shows that are culturally relevant. Additionally, language preferences and subtitle selections can be adapted based on location data if it is available.

The experience that a user has while watching content on a platform is affected by the device that they use to access the platform. It is possible to personalise recommendations according to the capabilities of the device, the size of the screen, and the user behaviour associated with specific devices. For instance, a viewer on a mobile device may prefer content that is shorter, while a viewer watching TV may enjoy watching films that are longer (Friederich,2023).

An understanding of individual preferences can be gained through the analysis of user interactions and engagement patterns. Platforms are able to make recommendations that are more tailored to the preferences of users if they monitor the genres, actors, and topics with which users engage most frequently.

Utilising contextual information in order to produce individualised experiences is materialised through the use of adaptive user interfaces (AUIs). These interfaces adjust themselves dynamically based on the context of the user, ensuring that interactions are consistent across all devices and improving the search for content. For instance, a user who accesses the platform on a smartphone might be presented with a streamlined and mobile-friendly interface, whereas a user who accesses the platform on a smart TV might come across an immersive layout.

Adaptive interfaces are able to optimise the delivery of content based on the capabilities of the device. For instance, an adaptive interface can send high-definition content to devices that are capable of displaying it, while simultaneously sending content with a lower resolution to devices that have fewer display options. Platforms are able to prioritise specific sections of content when they understand the context of the user. For example, during the evening hours, an adaptive interface may display genres that are typically associated with relaxation or entertainment in a prominent manner.

By taking into account the viewer's location as well as their language preferences, OTT platforms are able to provide content in the viewer's native language as well as accurate subtitle options. OTT platforms are aware that users do not constitute a single, homogenous group, and they understand that personalization must be extended to different user segments in order to accommodate a wide range of preferences. The process of segmenting users involves classifying them into subgroups according to a variety of criteria, including genres, languages, demographics, and viewing histories.

By categorising users according to their preferred genres, platforms are able to provide content recommendations that are tailored to individual preferences. It's possible that users who frequently watch action films will receive recommendations for other genres that are similar. It is essential, when speaking to an international audience, to accommodate a variety of linguistic preferences. The viewing experience can be made more welcoming by enabling platforms to categorise users according to the languages they prefer and then providing them with content presented in those languages.

Demographics: When conducting demographic segmentation, important considerations like age, gender, and cultural background are taken into account. It's possible, for instance, that the content suggestions for adolescents won't be the same as those for mature adults. Platforms are able to provide users with a curated collection that is congruent with their preferences because the content catalogue can be adapted to cater to specific user segments. In conclusion, the utilisation of contextual information within the OTT industry represents an essential step towards the delivery of personalised and engaging experiences.

Insights gained from contextual cues such as time, location, device, and user behaviour enable platforms to adapt user interfaces, optimise content delivery, and personalise recommendations. Personalization for different user segments ensures that a wide range of preferences can be accommodated, while adaptive user interfaces produce individualised interactions that are tailored to the user's specific circumstances. Redefining how users interact with and experience content on OTT platforms is poised to be made possible by leveraging contextual information to elevate personalization, which is continuing to evolve alongside the industry as a whole.

1.5 Real-time Personalization and Dynamic Recommendations

Platforms are leveraging real-time data and adaptive algorithms to provide content recommendations that cater to individual preferences even in the dynamic environment of live events, as audiences increasingly demand personalised experiences. Platforms are leveraging real-time data and adaptive algorithms to provide content recommendations that cater to individual preferences even in the dynamic environment of live events, as audiences increasingly demand personalised experiences.

Personalization can be difficult to accomplish when dealing with live streaming and event-based content like sporting events, concerts, and live news broadcasts. As opposed to content that has been pre-recorded, these events take place in real time, which requires algorithms to instantly adapt their recommendations as user interactions and content continue to develop. In addition, there is a lack of historical interaction data for events that are currently taking place, which makes it difficult to accurately predict the preferences of users (Periaiya et al.,2023).

During live events, user interactions such as clicks, likes, and comments are tracked and monitored by algorithms that operate in real time. These interactions shed light on the preferences of the user population at large and help direct recommendation development. Techniques of collaborative filtering, which are based on the exploitation of collective preferences, may be adapted for use in real-time settings by locating users who are presently observing the same event and recommending content on the basis of their concurrent actions.

In order to make recommendations that are more accurate, algorithms perform real-time analysis of dynamic contextual information such as a user's location, device, and social connections. A user who is currently present at a live sporting event, for instance, may be given access to real-time statistics and analysis. Platforms collect immediate feedback from users during live events, including ratings and comments from users of the platform. This feedback is incorporated into recommendation algorithms so that suggestions can be refined for the event that is currently taking place as well as for future engagements. In order to keep up with the ever-changing nature of live events, real-time recommendations need to be delivered as quickly as possible (Singh et al.,2023). Requiring dependable infrastructure and carefully crafted algorithms are prerequisites for reducing latency.

Massive data streams are produced as a result of the high number of user interactions that occur during live events. In order to effectively manage this deluge of data, you will need data processing methods that are both efficient and scalable. The need for real-time data collection, which is a prerequisite for real-time personalization, raises privacy concerns for end users. Platforms are obligated to maintain data usage transparency and comply with applicable privacy regulations. Distributed computing and advanced optimisation strategies are required in order to scale real-time algorithms so that they can accommodate large user bases and a number of events happening at the same time.

Recommendations made in real time are extremely reliant on accurate contextual data. Inaccuracies can result in suggestions that aren't aligned properly, which can negatively impact the user experience. Personalization strategies need to be tailored specifically to the type of live event being held. Flexibility is required in order to adapt algorithms to a wide variety of events, ranging from sports to news. Real-time personalization algorithms are causing a revolution in the OTT industry by making it possible to make individualised recommendations for live streaming and event-based content. These algorithms adapt their recommendations in the midst of unfolding events by utilising real-time user interactions, dynamic context, and immediate feedback.

1.6 Evaluation and Metrics for Personalization

When it comes to measuring the efficacy of personalization algorithms and making certain that platforms are in line with user preferences, engagement metrics, and overarching business objectives, key performance indicators (KPIs) play a pivotal role. CTR stands for click-through rate. The click-through rate, or CTR, is the percentage of users who click on recommended content relative to the total number of recommendations. When the CTR is high, it shows that users find the recommendations to be relevant and appealing. The conversion rate is the percentage of users who not only click on recommendations but also take the desired action, such as signing up for a subscription or making a purchase. This can be tracked using the percentage of users who convert. This KPI reflects the influence that the recommendations have beyond engagement on the behaviour of the user.

The length of time that users spend interacting with content that has been recommended can provide valuable insight into the content's relevance and quality. View durations that are longer are indicative of higher levels of user satisfaction and successful personalization. The percentage of users who leave a platform after viewing a single piece of recommended content is measured by the "bounce rate." A lower bounce rate is an indication that recommendations are successfully keeping users interested in the content. The churn rate is a measurement that determines how many users unsubscribe from the platform or stop using it. When users find content that is in line with their preferences, effective personalization should lead to a reduction in churn, which is the loss of customers.

Methodologies such as A/B testing are absolutely necessary when it comes to determining the efficacy of personalization strategies and optimising recommendation algorithms. As part of these experiments, various iterations of content recommendations are being shown to specific subsets of users, and their level of engagement is being analysed. In A/B testing, several key metrics are used, including the following:

A/B testing focuses heavily on metrics such as click-through rate (CTR), conversion rate, and view duration. When these metrics are compared across a variety of recommendation algorithms, it is possible to gain insight into which strategy drives higher levels of engagement. The level of engagement with personalised content can be determined by monitoring the actions of users, such as the amount of time spent scrolling, clicking, and otherwise interacting with recommendations.

When designing recommendation interfaces, it is helpful to visualise where users click and where their attention is focused in order to determine the best placements and designs. The delicate challenge that recommendation algorithms face is striking an effective balance between the needs of the user, the potential for serendipity, and the goals of the business. Even though personalised recommendations are designed to cater to the preferences of users, an excessive amount of personalization can lead to the formation of filter bubbles and reduce users' exposure to a variety of content. To achieve this delicate equilibrium, it is necessary to take into consideration the following factors:

1. It is essential to incorporate serendipitous recommendations that introduce users to new genres or topics in order to broaden their horizons and prevent content from becoming stale. The recommendations have to be in line with the business objectives of the platform, such as boosting the number of subscribers or driving up the amount of money made from advertisements.
2. Satisfaction of the User: User feedback and sentiment analysis provide insights into whether or not recommendations genuinely enhance user experiences and cater to the preferences of the users. Giving users the ability to customise their personalization settings and being transparent about how their data is used are two ways to earn users' trust and give them more agency. It is important for algorithms to strike a balance between catering to well-established user preferences and investigating fresh material that may be relevant but has not previously been interacted with (Shri, C et al.,2023).

In conclusion, the successful evaluation of personalization strategies is contingent on the existence of well-defined key performer indicators that measure user behaviour as well as engagement and conversion rates. The use of A/B testing methodologies makes experimentation and the optimisation of algorithms easier. In order to strike a balance between user satisfaction, serendipity, and business objectives, recommendation algorithms need to be approached with nuance.

1.7 Successful Personalization and Recommendation Strategies

Leading over-the-top (OTT) service providers have been at the forefront of developing innovative methods to cater to the preferences of individual users, curate content libraries, and revolutionise the way audiences engage with digital media. This research delves deep into the strategies that prominent OTT service providers have used in the past, highlighting the valuable lessons learned, difficult challenges overcome, and innovative approaches that have reshaped the industry (Ahlawat, R., & Ahlawat, P.,2023).

Personalization based on user data has been an area in which Netflix has been an innovator. Netflix uses sophisticated recommendation algorithms to tailor content suggestions to individual users by carefully analysing user behaviour, viewing history, and preferences regarding different types of content. The "Recommended for You" feature utilises a combination of collaborative filtering and content-based filtering, which results in an extremely personalised experience of content discovery. The success of Netflix has taught the company many valuable lessons, including the significance of data granularity, the need for ongoing algorithmic improvement, and the significance of user feedback in the process of refining recommendations (Burroughs,2019).

Amazon Prime Video makes the most of Amazon's comprehensive ecosystem by integrating data about customers' browsing habits, purchase histories, and Prime memberships in order to provide a more personalised experience. The "Watch Next TV and Movies" feature provides a seamless connection between the recommendations provided by Prime Video and the wider interactions that users have with Amazon. The takeaway from this is the significance of cross-platform integration in the delivery of comprehensive and individualised experiences, making use of the wealth of data collected across a variety of touchpoints (Sindhu & Vani,2021).

Disney+ stands out in the market by capitalising on its well-known brand identity and providing subscribers with access to a sizable catalogue of fan-favorite programming. It makes use of content curation and recommendation algorithms to expose users to both classic songs and recently released music. The success that Disney has experienced demonstrates the importance of having a distinct brand identity as well as the synergy that can be created between recommendation algorithms and curated content collections.

Personalization that is effective must be accomplished without violating the users' right to privacy and in a manner that is consistent with ethical standards for the use of data. The challenge that persists today is finding the optimal balance between data protection and personalization of content. An overabundance of personalised recommendations may result in the "filter bubble" effect, in which users see only content that is consistent with their already-held preferences, thereby reducing the opportunities for accidental discovery. The most effective strategies include components that provide users with access to a variety of content.

The fragmentation of content becomes a challenge as over-the-top (OTT) providers increase the amount of original content they offer. This void must be filled by recommendations, which should ensure that users are made aware of and have access to a diverse range of content options. It is essential to strike a balance between the complexity of recommendation algorithms and the transparency offered to users. The most successful service providers have discovered methods to explain recommendations to users, which has helped to foster trust and engagement.

Some platforms are refining their recommendations by incorporating contextual information such as the time of day, the location of the user, and the type of device they are using. This strategy improves relevance and has a greater resonance with the users' current circumstances. Real-time data analysis is being used during live events to provide personalised content recommendations that are in line with the context of the event that is currently taking place as well as user preferences. Some platforms are employing AI-driven content creation in order to tailor content to individual preferences in order to improve user experience. This makes it possible to personalise promotional materials and artwork in a way that caters to the preferences of individual users (Chan-Olmsted,2019). OTT providers are engaging users on a deeper level by introducing interactive elements and allowing users to make choices that influence the narrative. This creates a viewing experience that is both one-of-a-kind and highly personalised for each individual user.

The industry's leading OTT providers have experimented with a wide variety of successful personalization and recommendation strategies, each of which presents its own set of unique learning opportunities, obstacles, and innovations. The industry is constantly changing in response to the demands of users for content experiences that are more seamless, engaging, and relevant. We gain insights into the dynamic interplay of data analytics, algorithmic sophistication, and creative content curation that will define the future of personalised content consumption by looking into the business strategies of industry giants such as Netflix, Amazon Prime Video, and Disney+.

1.8 Trends And Advancements in Personalization Algorithms

When making content recommendations, algorithms are increasingly taking into account contextual factors such as time of day, location, and the type of device being used. This current trend improves the usefulness of suggestions by bringing them into alignment with the immediate circumstances of users. Platforms are providing content recommendations during live events that adapt to ongoing contexts and user preferences by utilising real-time data analysis. By taking this approach, engagement and a sense of immediacy are both boosted. The use of sophisticated machine learning models and artificial intelligence is radically altering the personalization industry. Deep learning algorithms are able to accurately capture the nuances of user behaviour and preference, which in turn leads to more precise content recommendations (Singh, N et al., 2022).

Some platforms are introducing interactive elements and content that allows users to choose their own adventure, which gives users the ability to shape the narrative. Users have agency over the content that they choose to consume thanks to this level of content personalization. While the implementation of personalization algorithms can lead to improved user experiences, ethical considerations and user privacy must be given careful attention at every step of the process. It is of the utmost importance to strike a balance between the advantages of personalization and the protection of user rights and data.

Users have the right to be fully informed about the data collection practises that are being used, and they must have the option to opt in or opt out of features that involve personalization. Transparent communication fosters trust among users and gives them more agency. Individuals can be prevented from being identified by taking the necessary precautions to have their data aggregated and anonymized. This maintains the user's privacy while allowing for enhanced levels of personalization.

When only the data that is absolutely necessary to provide personalised experiences is collected, the risk of data misuse and an invasion of user privacy is significantly reduced.

Compliance with Regulations: Adhering to data protection regulations such as the GDPR and the CCPA guarantees that user data is handled in an ethical and responsible manner.The challenges that are presented by personalization algorithms need to be addressed in order to ensure that content recommendations are fair and effective.

The process of generating accurate recommendations can be difficult when there are new users or items with limited interaction data. In order to find a solution to this issue, various platforms are turning to hybrid methods, which combine content-based and collaborative filtering techniques with information that is contextual. The perpetuation of stereotypes or the exclusion of certain user groups can both be the result of discriminatory recommendations that are caused by biased algorithms. Auditing algorithms to ensure that they are fair and including diverse training data are both strategies that can be used to mitigate the effects of this challenge.

Recommendations that are too personally tailored have the potential to create content echo chambers. Users are more likely to experience content that is unexpected and enriching if the level of personalization is balanced with the amount of exposure to diverse content.

As the OTT industry continues to develop, personalization algorithms are becoming increasingly important to the process of reimagining how content is consumed. A dedication to providing individualised engagement is reflected in a number of developing trends, including contextual personalization, real-time recommendations, integration of AI, and interactive content (Shin,2020). The importance of ethical considerations and user privacy cannot be overstated, which highlights the requirement to find a middle ground between personalization and data protection. It is essential, for the continued development of personalised content delivery, to find solutions to problems such as the cold-start problem and concerns regarding algorithmic fairness.

2. CONCLUSION

The chapter that focuses on the significance of developing personalization and recommendation algorithms for the Over-The-Top (OTT) industry highlights the transformative role that these strategies play in improving user experiences and driving engagement. Platforms have the ability to foster deeper connections with users, encourage longer viewing sessions, and ultimately boost user satisfaction by providing content recommendations that are customised to individual preferences. The use of personalization algorithms makes it possible for platforms to provide users with individualised content discovery experiences. Algorithms are able to accurately predict and suggest content that is in line with individual preferences when they take into account user interactions, viewing history, and contextual data.

The effective presentation of content that resonates with viewers is a key driver of user engagement that can be achieved through personalization. This results in increased levels of user satisfaction, decreased rates of user churn, and increased total time spent on the platform. In order to obtain useful insights, advanced algorithms make use of data provided by users. Platforms are able to improve their content acquisition strategies, develop their own original content, and enhance their recommendations when they have a better understanding of viewing patterns and content preferences.

Enhancing personalization by including contextual information like time, location, and device type is possible by incorporating this data. This real-time adaptation ensures that recommendations are aligned with the immediate circumstances of users, which enhances the user experiences of those users. This chapter also discusses potential obstacles in the field of personalization, such as the "filter bubble" effect, concerns regarding data privacy, algorithmic bias, and the requirement for transparent algorithmic decision-making. In order to ensure that personalization practises are ethical and fair, it is essential to address these challenges.

It is impossible to overstate how important it is to make strides in personalization and recommendation algorithms in order to improve user experiences and engagement. This chapter emphasises how these strategies provide a pathway to create meaningful interactions between users and content, which will shape the future of media consumption (Luca,2015).

These algorithms improve content discovery, encourage continuous viewing, and cultivate brand loyalty by providing users with content that is tailored specifically to their preferences. By catering to the specific inclinations of individual users, personalization algorithms foster a feeling of connectedness. This increases the user's level of engagement, which in turn increases the likelihood that they will return to the platform multiple times and interact with it for longer periods of time.

Effective personalization strategies are aligned with business goals, thereby increasing content consumption, decreasing churn, and possibly increasing subscription rates or advertising revenues. Striking a Balance It is essential to strike a balance between personalization and algorithmic fairness. It is necessary to design algorithms in a way that eliminates bias and ensures diverse recommendations that are tailored to each user type. The ethical treatment of user data is extremely important. Building trust requires over-the-top (OTT) service providers to place a higher emphasis on user consent, anonymization, and transparent data usage practises.

In order to gain insights into user preferences and behaviours, it is necessary to collect and analyse a wide variety of user data. This includes the user's viewing history, interactions, and contextual information. Constantly experimenting with new ideas and making adjustments to existing algorithms in order to achieve greater precision and relevance in recommendation systems. This chapter highlights the importance of advancing personalization and recommendation algorithms not only as a technological pursuit but also as a strategic imperative for over-the-top (OTT) service providers. To ensure the success of these strategies, it is essential to personalise the content discovery experiences offered, boost user engagement, and construct user trust through the use of responsible data practises. As the landscape of OTT services continues to shift, content providers who are able to successfully implement personalised experiences stand to gain a competitive advantage by delivering content interactions that are engaging, relevant, and memorable.

REFERENCES

Ahlawat, R., & Ahlawat, P. (2023). AN ANALYSIS OF THE ROLE OF OVER-THE-TOP (OTT) PLATFORMS IN THE CHANGING FACE OF INDIA'S FILM AND TELEVISION INDUSTRY. [IJMR]. *EPRA International Journal of Multidisciplinary Research*, *9*(11), 378–386.

Burroughs, B. (2019). House of Netflix: Streaming media and digital lore. *Popular Communication*, *17*(1), 1–17. doi:10.1080/15405702.2017.1343948

Chan-Olmsted, S. M. (2019). A review of artificial intelligence adoptions in the media industry. *International Journal on Media Management, 21*(3-4), 193-215.

Friederich, F., Palau-Saumell, R., Matute, J., & Meyer, J.-H. (2023). Digital natives and streaming TV platforms: An integrated perspective to explain continuance usage of over-the-top services. *Online Information Review*. doi:10.1108/OIR-03-2022-0133

Hallur, G., Aslekar, A., & Prabhu, S. (2023). Digital Solution for Entertainment: An Overview of Over the Top (OTT) and Digital Media. *Digital Entertainment as Next Evolution in Service Sector: Emerging Digital Solutions in Reshaping Different Industries,* 35-53. Research Gate.

Kalorth, N. (2018). *Social Media Experiences and Narratives Formation of Opinions in the Age of Post–Truth*. Research Gate.

Kumar, M. K., & Gangwar, R. (2022). Necessity of OTT Regulation in Indian Context. *Bayan College International Journal of Multidisciplinary Research*, *2*(2), 78–90.

Kwon, Y., Park, J., & Son, J. Y. (2021). Accurately or accidentally? Recommendation agent and search experience in over-the-top (OTT) services. *Internet Research*, *31*(2), 562–586. doi:10.1108/INTR-03-2020-0127

Luca, M. (2015). User-generated content and social media. In *Handbook of media Economics* (Vol. 1, pp. 563–592). North-Holland.

Okumuş, M. S. (2023). The Audience Struggle between Television, Cinema, and OTT Platforms: The Case of Netflix and Disney+ In Turkey. *Turkish Online Journal Of Design Art And Communication*, *13*(1), 108–123. doi:10.7456//11301100/008

Ott, B. L., & Mack, R. L. (2020). *Critical media studies: An introduction*. John Wiley & Sons.

Pajkovic, N. (2022). Algorithms and taste-making: Exposing the Netflix Recommender System's operational logics. *Convergence (London)*, *28*(1), 214–235. doi:10.1177/13548565211014464

Periaiya, S., & Nandukrishna, A. T. (2023). What drives user stickiness and satisfaction in OTT video streaming platforms? A mixed-method exploration. *International Journal of Human-Computer Interaction*, 1–17. doi:10.1080/10447318.2022.2160224

SamritiD.SharmaP. (2020). OTT-existing censorship laws and recommendations. SSRN 3735027.

Sharma, N. (2021). *OTT Channels and their marketing strategies* [Doctoral dissertation, School of Petroleum Management].

Shin, D., Hameleers, M., Park, Y. J., Kim, J. N., Trielli, D., Diakopoulos, N., Helberger, N., Lewis, S. C., Westlund, O., & Baumann, S. (2022). Countering algorithmic bias and disinformation and effectively harnessing the power of AI in media. *Journalism & Mass Communication Quarterly*, *99*(4), 887–907. doi:10.1177/10776990221129245

Shin, D., Lim, J. S., Ahmad, N., & Ibahrine, M. (2022). Understanding user sensemaking in fairness and transparency in algorithms: Algorithmic sensemaking in over-the-top platform. *AI & Society*, 1–14. doi:10.1007/s00146-022-01525-9

Shin, D., Rasul, A., & Fotiadis, A. (2022). Why am I seeing this? Deconstructing algorithm literacy through the lens of users. *Internet Research*, *32*(4), 1214–1234. doi:10.1108/INTR-02-2021-0087

Sindhu, M., & Vani, C. (2021). *The OTT (Over the Top)*. Platforms and Movie Watching Experience of the Audience.

Singh, K. K., Makhania, J., & Mahapatra, M. (2023). Impact of ratings of content on OTT platforms and prediction of its success rate. *Multimedia Tools and Applications*, 1–18.

Singh, N., Arora, S., & Kapur, B. (2022). Trends in over the top (OTT) research: A bibliometric analysis. *VINE Journal of Information and Knowledge Management Systems*, *52*(3), 411–425. doi:10.1108/VJIKMS-12-2021-0316

Wong, S. (2021). *Over The Top TV (OTT), Big Data and The Future Of Predictive Buyer Analytics.* Research Gate.

Yousaf, A. (2021). A cross-country analysis of the determinants of customer recommendation intentions for over-the-top (OTT) platforms. *Information & Management, 58*(8), 103543.

Zhang, Yu. (2023). Research on media communication methods in the context of intelligent algorithms. *International Conference on Mathematics, Modeling, and Computer Science (MMCS2022).* SPIE. 10.1117/12.2670491

Chapter 9
The Art and Science of User Engagement:
Personalization and Recommendations in the OTT Era

Nitesh Behare
https://orcid.org/0000-0002-9338-8563
Balaji Institute of International Business, Sri Balaji University, India

Daman Jeet
IBS Hyderabad, The ICFAI Foundation for Higher Education, India

ABSTRACT

This chapter explores the importance of personalization and recommendation algorithms in OTT era, emphasizing their role in enhancing content discovery and customizing user experiences. Crucial techniques like collaborative filtering and content-based filtering underpin these algorithms, which ensues personalized user experiences. Recommendation algorithms shape media consumption patterns, content discovery, influencing user behavior, cross-platform consumption and binge-watching habits. This chapter also paid attention to acknowledging ethical considerations like privacy concerns and algorithmic bias. Additionally, it also explores the challenges and opportunities for content creators in catering to algorithmic preferences, along with significance of balancing effective ad targeting and user privacy in personalized advertising. Improving and assessing recommendation algorithms using different metrics and feedback loops is important, however future trends concentrate on contextual personalization and adaptive experiences, enhancing user's entertainment journey.

1. INTRODUCTION

The way people engage with streaming video in the ever-evolving entertainment industry has been completely transformed by Over-The-Top (OTT) media. Every OTT platform works on a data-driven paradigm, gathering consumer data to gain valuable insights into audience behaviour. For strategic decision-making, this analytical data serves as cornerstone, from content development to targeted marketing campaigns. Recommendation algorithms play an essential role in augmenting the overall viewers' experience by

DOI: 10.4018/979-8-3693-0116-6.ch009

proposing contents tailored to individual preferences. These algorithms not only engage the viewers but also ensures they discover new content that resonates with their unique interests.

We are inflowing in an era of content democratization, where OTT stands as a driving force, restructuring the way viewers consume, create and interact with media. In this dynamic landscape of entertainment, personalization and recommendation algorithms are fundamental in delivering a rich and captivating entertainment experience while fuelling the growth of the OTT industry (Yeole, Saha, & Bhaisare, 2022).

1.1. The Evolutionary Impact of Personalization and Recommendation Algorithms

Personalization and recommendation algorithms have had a transformational impact in changing digital media consumption over the years. These algorithms have reshaped the way we access, find, and interact with content, creating a significant influence not just on the media and entertainment industries, but also on our daily lives. Enhancing content discovery is one of the most significant ways these algorithms have impacted digital media consumption. Traditionally, consumers had to hunt huge content libraries, which sometimes resulted in decision fatigue and dissatisfaction. Personalization algorithms have completely altered the scene (McKinnon, 2022). These algorithms analyse user behaviour and preferences, making tailored content suggestions that align with individual interests. In turn, it simplifies the content discovery process and introduces users to a broader range of content. Users are no longer restricted to popular or trendy selections; instead, they may discover specialized or lesser-known contents that resonates to their own preferences. As a result, the digital media ecosystem has turned as more assorted and accessible.

Another significant influence of these algorithms is the customisation of user experiences. Based on previous interactions, each user's dashboard and content recommendations are personalized (Chandra, Verma, Lim, Kumar, & Donthu, 2022). These algorithms not only keep consumers interested, but they boost their overall satisfaction. Users are shown such contents that are tailored to their interests, building a bond with the digital platforms they use. This sense of personalization encourages consumers to return frequently, increasing user retention and platform loyalty (Liang, 2007).

Decision fatigue has been greatly decreased by customization algorithms (Furey, 2023). With so much contents available on so many platforms, people may become overwhelmed when picking what to watch, listen to, or read. Personalized recommendations make this process easier by providing information that matches the user's tastes. This not only streamlines the user experience but also encourages users to explore more relevant content they might not have considered otherwise. By frequently offering content that reverberates with individual users, platforms will be able to maintain user's interest and extend the time users spend on their platforms. Longer user engagement has a direct influence on the success of content providers, as it results in higher subscription rates, improved ad views and enhanced overall revenue (Saxena, 2023).

Personalization is critical in encouraging people to subscribe to subscription-based platforms (Haleem, Mohd, Mohd, Ravi, & Rajiv, 2022). These platforms can persuade users that a subscription is a worthwhile investment by displaying the contents that are relevant to their interests. This, in turn, leads to long-term revenue sources. Data-driven insights have also emerged as a vital consequence of these algorithms.

1.1.1. Growing Global and Domestic Prominence of OTT

1.1.1.1 Indian OTT Industry

The landscape of digital media consumption has changed, with consumers seeking more than simply traditional services. Original content has emerged as the key in attracting and maintaining customers, ranging from web series to exclusive documentaries and features. This shift in consumer behaviour compels OTT platforms to develop, spending heavily in content production in order to appeal to a diversified audience with varying interests. The investment of Rs. 3,300 crore underscores the industry's commitment to elevating the content quality and diversity available on OTT platforms. This allocation is not merely a financial decision; it symbolizes a strategic move to tap into the immense potential of original content to drive subscriber growth and revenue. As we navigate through this digital era, original content stands tall as the cornerstone that will shape the future trajectory of the OTT industry. The substantial investment by key players reflects a collective vision to not only meet but exceed the expectations of an increasingly discerning audience, ensuring that the OTT landscape continues to be vibrant, innovative, and irresistibly engaging (IndianExpress, 2018).

Figure 1. Media and telecommunication prediction
(https://www.impactonnet.com/cover-story/the-rs-5000-cr-opportunity-for-ott-platforms-in-india-6074.html)

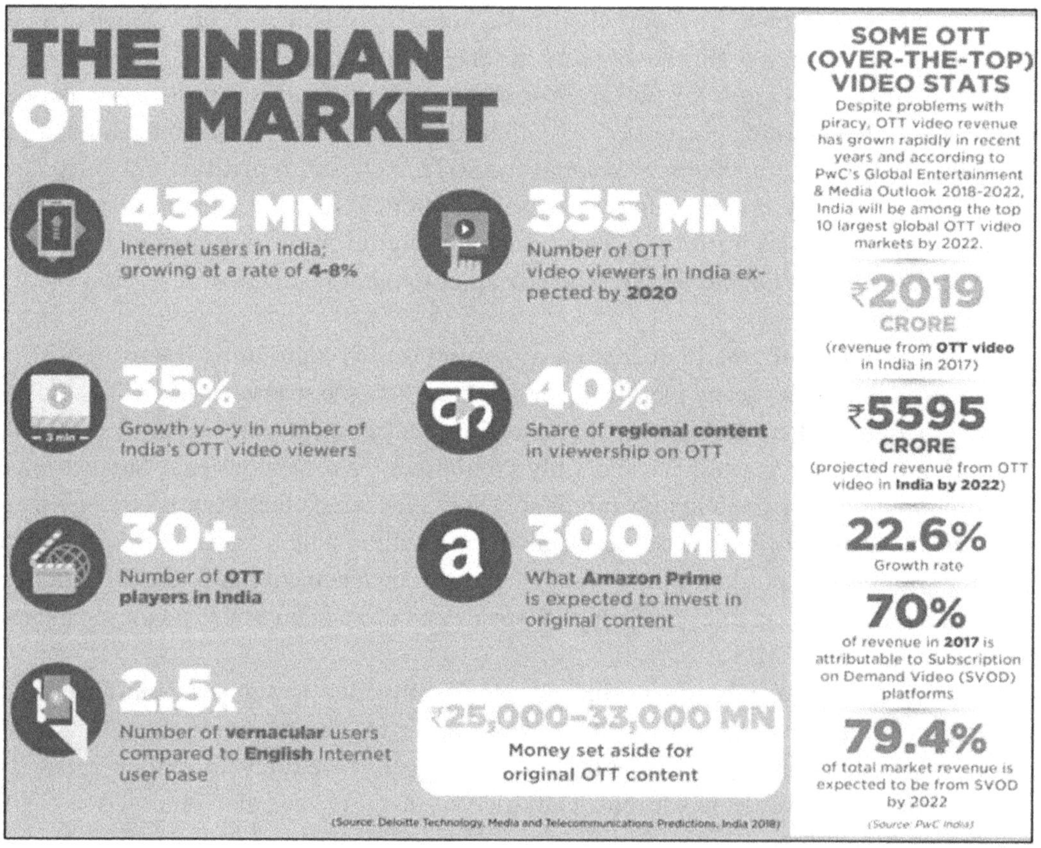

In 2019, the dynamics of the Indian streaming market have undergone a notable transformation. Amazon Prime and Netflix, which were once catching up, now find themselves at the forefront, a shift accelerated by the impact of the coronavirus pandemic. According to data from JustWatch, during Q2 of 2020, both Netflix and Amazon Prime claimed a substantial fifth of the market each (Buchholz, International Brands Rise to the Top of Indian Streaming Market, 2020), while the collaboration between Disney+ and local player Hotstar secured a 17 percent share. This marks a significant departure from 2019 when Hotstar alone commanded nearly 30 percent of the market, with Amazon Prime and Netflix holding modest shares of 10 and 5 percent, respectively (See Figure 2).

Figure 2. International brands rise to the top of Indian streaming market
(https://www.statista.com/chart/23009/market-share-streaming--ott--platforms-in-india/)

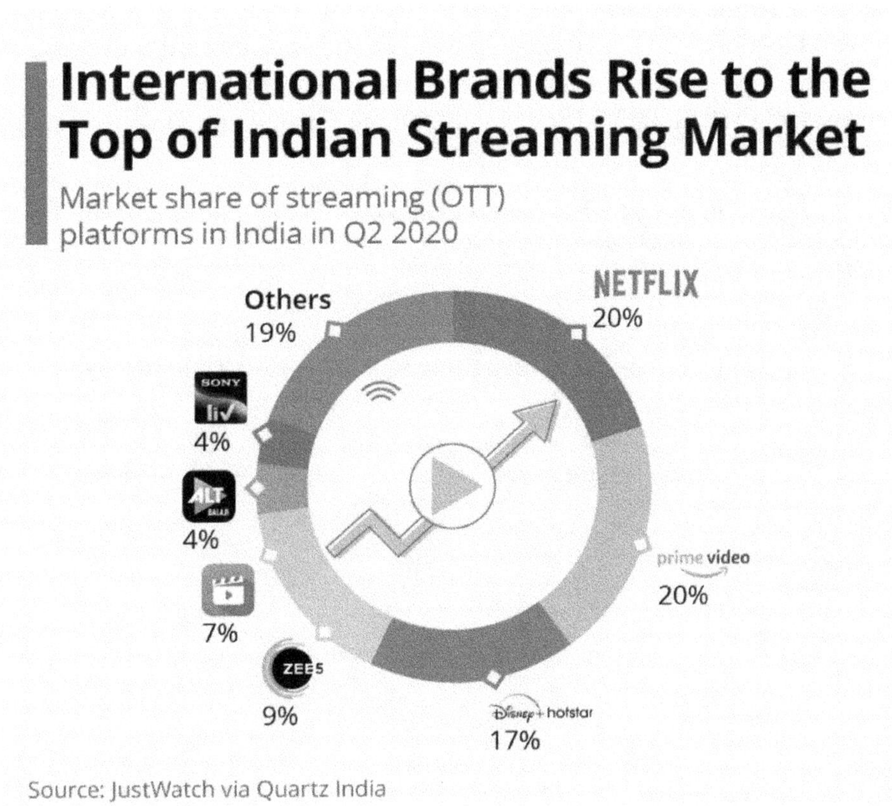

This platform has become a focal point for the release of new Bollywood productions, either as original content or as an alternative avenue while cinemas remain closed (Welle, 2021). Despite the ascendancy of international players, the Indian streaming market retains its fragmented nature. Local brands, numbering several, continue to command nearly half of the market share, reflecting a diverse and competitive landscape. The interaction between global OTT giants and local platforms, coupled with the changing consumer's dynamics brought about by the pandemic, underscores the evolving nature of India's streaming industry (Lidhoo, 2022).

1.1.1.2 Global OTT Industry

The worldwide OTT market has transformed from a small market to a powerhouse within the larger media and entertainment environment. Fuelled by increasing internet penetration, the demand for on-the-go content, and the proliferation of smart devices, OTT platforms have become essential to how audiences consume media worldwide (Koka, 2023). Universally renowned players like Netflix, Amazon Prime Video, and Disney+ have extended their footprint, tapping into diverse markets and reshaping traditional broadcasting models. The adaptability and ease that OTT services provide, allowing consumers to access a large selection of content at any time and from any location, are driving the industry's expansion (Buchholz, 2020).

Original content has occurred as a cornerstone for success, with major investments being made to produce elite series, films, and documentaries. This not only attracts subscribers but also fosters brand loyalty. The global OTT industry, valued in the billions, continues to redefine how content is created, distributed, and consumed, challenging traditional television and cinema. The integration of advanced technologies like 5G networks, artificial intelligence, and virtual reality augurs a promising future. As the industry evolves, the global OTT landscape is set to continue its upward trajectory, offering unparalleled content diversity, personalized experiences, and a transformative influence on the media and entertainment ecosystem (M&M, 2022) (Statista, 2023)(See Fig 3, 4 and 5).

Figure 3. Secondary research, expert interviews and markets and markets analysis *(https://www.marketsandmarkets.com/Market-Reports/over-the-top-ott-market-41276741.html)*

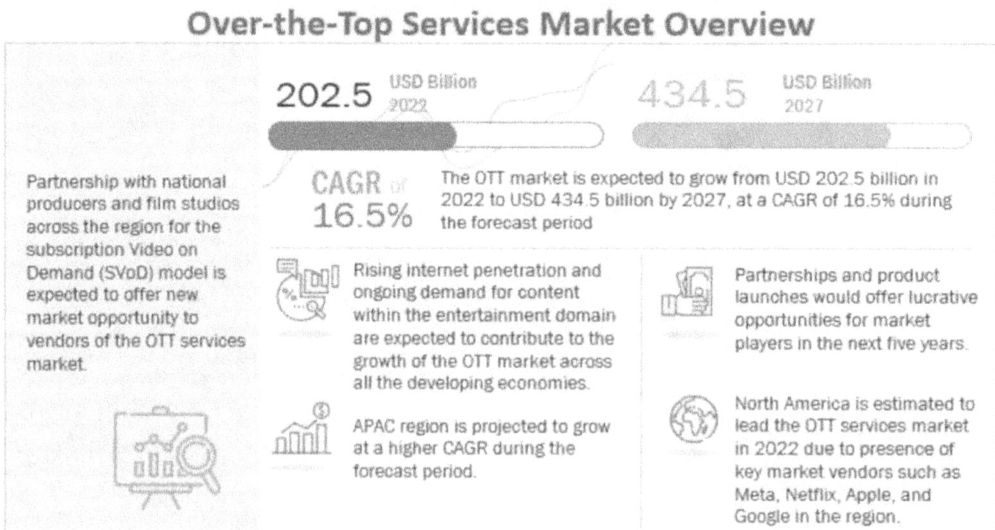

1.2. Significance of Personalization and Recommendation Algorithms in the OTT Era

In the era of OTT, personalization and recommendation algorithms have emerged as significant components, revolutionizing the way content is discovered, delivered and consumed. These technologies

Figure 4. Change in revenue
(https://www.statista.com/outlook/amo/media/tv-video/ott-video/worldwide#revenue)

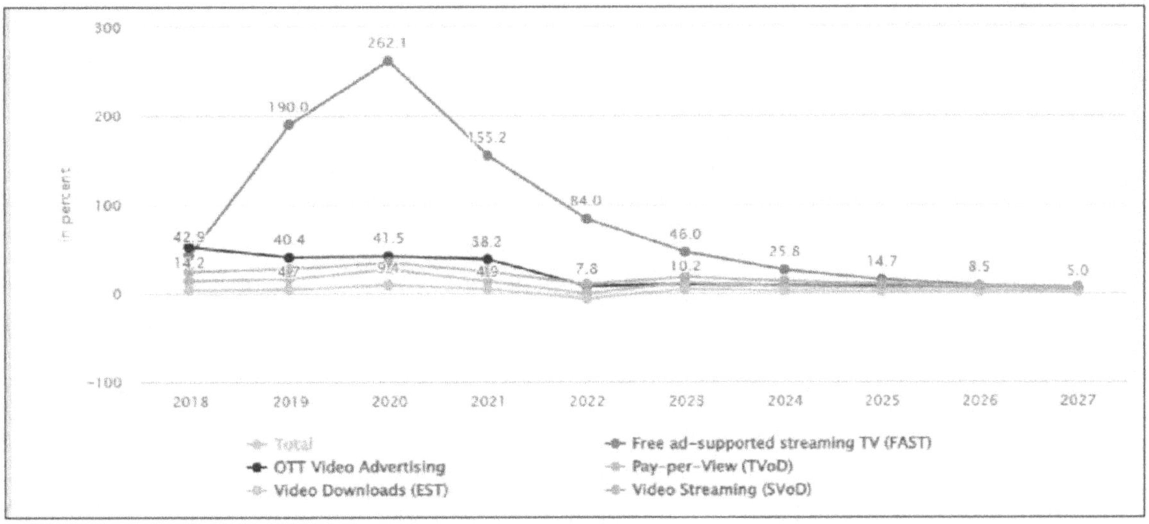

Figure 5. Average revenue per user, globally
(https://www.statista.com/outlook/amo/media/tv-video/ott-video/worldwide#revenue)

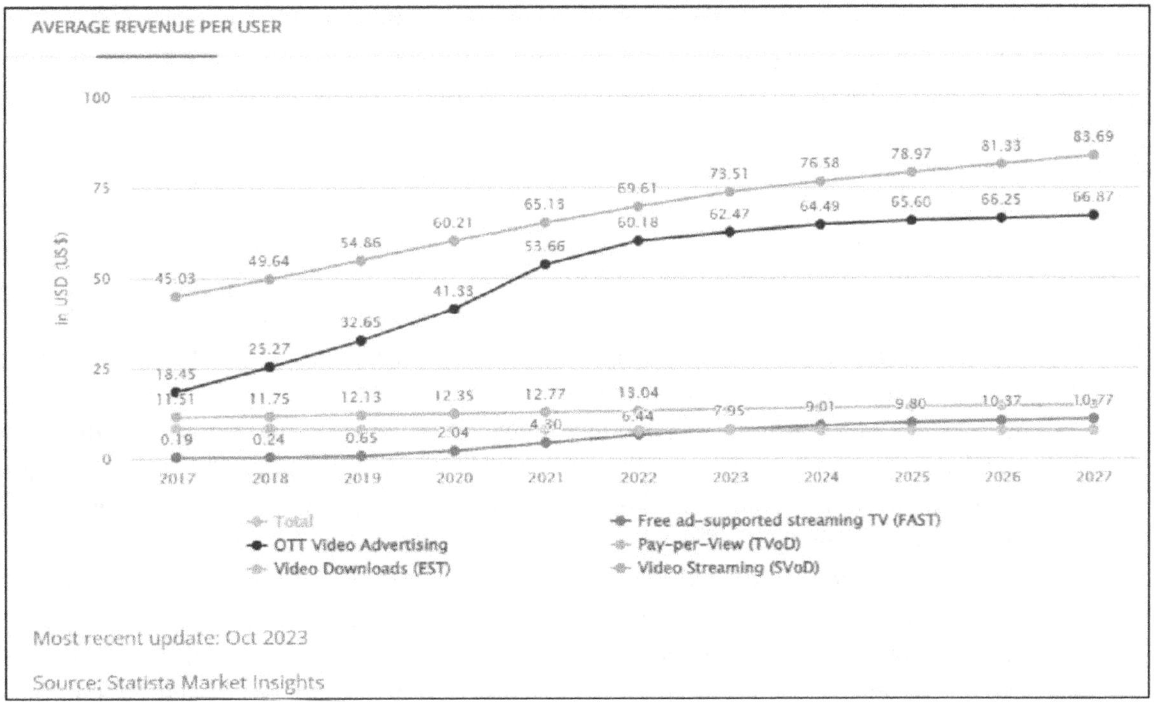

leverage user data to curate personalized experiences, enhancing user satisfaction and driving customer (viewer) engagement. The significance of personalization and recommendation algorithms can be further understood through the following aspects:

i. Hyper-Personalized Content: Personalization algorithms enable OTT platforms to understand preferences of individual users, their viewing habits and demographics. By analysing such crucial data, OTT platforms can create personalized content recommendations customised to each user's unique interests (Gokul, 2022). This hyper-personalization ensures that users are presented with content which are most likely to reverberate with them, leading to increased user satisfaction, content consumption and ultimately retention (Services, 2022).
ii. Monetization Opportunities: By understanding user preferences and their behaviour, these algorithms facilitate targeted advertising (Moore, 2023), allowing platforms to deliver relevant ads to specific user segments. This precise targeting improves effectiveness of the advertisement by increases user engagement and maximizes revenue potential for both platforms and advertisers (Crowly, 2023). Furthermore, personalized recommendations can drive users towards premium content options, pay-per-view events, or subscription upgrades, further boosting revenue streams (Start, 2023).
iii. Seamless Content Discovery: Content discovery becomes a significant challenge for users as abundance of content available on OTT platforms. Recommendation algorithms address this issue by offering curated suggestions based on a user's previous viewing history, ratings and feedback. By showcasing appropriate and diverse content options, these algorithms help users to explore and discover new shows, movies, or genres that align with their preferences, promoting serendipitous content discovery and expanding their viewing horizons (Vijayanagar, 2021).
iv. Increased User Engagement: OTT platforms can capture consumers' attention and keep them engaged for longer periods by surfacing content that aligns with their interests. This increased engagement translates into more time spent on the platform, higher content consumption and a higher likelihood of users exploring additional offerings, leading to improved user loyalty and reduced churn rates (Bambha, 2023).
v. Content Discovery and Exploration: Content discovery can be overwhelming for users as vast amount of content available on OTT platforms (Conviva, 2021). By suggesting content based on their viewing history, preferences and popular trends, recommendation algorithms help users navigate this vast library (Indian Retailer, 2022). These algorithms facilitate content exploration, enabling users to discover shows, movies, or genres they might not have considered otherwise. Content Discovery and Exploration enhances user engagement and drives them to spend more time on the platform, increasing content consumption (Algolia, 2022).
vi. Retention and Customer Loyalty: OTT platforms keep users engaged and satisfied, reducing the likelihood of churn by consistently providing personalized content recommendations. When users find relevant and appealing content effortlessly, they are more likely to stay loyal to the platform, leading to increased customer satisfaction and long-term user retention (Sumeet, 2023).
vii. Data-Driven Insights and Decision-Making: To gain insights into user behaviour, content performance and market trends, OTT platforms can leverage this data. These data-driven insights enable producers, content creators and platform operators to make informed decisions about content acquisition, production, marketing strategies and investment in original programming, optimizing resource allocation and enhancing the overall content offering (Allam & Thrideep, 2023).

viii. Competitive Advantage: Platforms that excel at delivering accurate and relevant content recommendations are more likely to attract and retain users as compared to those with generic or less effective recommendation systems. A superior personalized user experience distinguishes leading OTT providers, enhances brand perception, and positions them as preferred choices for consumers seeking personalized and curated content (Balki, 2021).

2. UNDERSTANDING PERSONALIZATION AND RECOMMENDATION ALGORITHMS

OTT businesses are rigorously using personalization and recommendation algorithms. These algorithms leverage user data to understand customer demographics, their preferences and their viewing habits. By analysing this crucial information, OTT platforms can curate personalized content recommendations and enhancing customer engagement (Sharma A., 2023). Recommendation algorithms help users to discover new shows, movies or genres based on their interests whereas personalization algorithms enable the delivery of hyper-targeted content (Globallogic, 2021). Leading platforms like Amazon Prime, Netflix and Hulu are heavily investing in AI and ML to retain existing consumers (Minzheong, 2021) and recognizing consumer in understanding their interests, content searching patterns, viewing habits and genre preferences are crucial for success of OTT (Arti, 2021). Machine-learning personalization uses predictive analytics and algorithms to vigorously showcase the most relevant content to each visitor (Canet, 2022). It empowers OTT platform to uniquely deliver personalized recommendations for content and exclusive one-to-one experiences. By leveraging machine learning in the OTT industry, next-generation platforms can endorse categories, special offers, brands and more, providing a scalable way to achieve personalized experiences (Srinivasan, 2023).

Profoundly, AI/ML-powered personalization includes "delivering right content to the right user at the right time across all touchpoints, ensuring a seamless and customized experience" (Balki, 2021).

There are numerous use cases for machine learning in the media and entertainment industry:

i. Personalized Marketing Campaigns: Tailor offers and messages based on real-time user interactions and behavioural insights.
ii. Customer Sentiment Analysis: Analyse customer behaviour to determine positive and negative sentiments, providing valuable information for personalized recommendations (Cooltrack, 2021).
iii. Cognitive personalization: It utilizes cognitive computing technologies and methods to offer personalized individual experiences. It comprises harnessing the power of machine learning algorithms and artificial intelligence (AI) to understand and interpret user preferences, their behaviours and perspective with the purpose of delivering tailored content, recommendations or interactions (Cooltrack, 2021).
iv. Personalized Recommendations: Analyse diverse data sources to enable users to make customized content choices and predict user behaviour.
v. Customer Segmentation: Transform customer data into actionable user segments, allowing for targeted and personalized strategies to convert users into subscribers (Miguel Alves Gomes, 2023).

vi. Media Metadata Tagging: Automate the creation of rich metadata indexes, including objects, scenes, activities, faces, etc., extracted from audio-visual content and integrate them into digital and media asset management systems (Ben Lutkevich, 2022).
vii. Automated Compliance Marking: Detect potentially inappropriate content to avoid compliance issues in global markets and enhance brand safety for advertisers. (Robert Amor, 2021)

In the digitally advanced world success of any OTT platform is based on various factors like content, the way of presentation, user interface and user experience. Therefore, in this competitive world, precise analysis of consumer behaviour and AI/ML-based personalized recommendations play a substantial role in addressing these factors. Personalization helps OTT brands to handle marketing challenges like minimizing customer acquisition costs, delivering individualized recommendations, improving conversion rates, boosting average user content consumption and enhancing consumer engagement and customer lifetime value (CLTV).

2.1. Integration of AI and Big Data

The integration of AI and big data analytics became crucial for OTT recommendation algorithms. AI-driven engines processes enormous datasets to offer more personalized, timely, and engaging content suggestions. These historical developments replicate how recommendation algorithms have developed hand in hand with the growth of OTT platforms. This integration has not only transformed how viewers discover and engage with content but have also influenced advertising, content creation, and the overall user experience in the OTT industry (Nvidia, 2022) (Kasula, 2020).

2.2. The Role of Personalization in OTT Platforms

The abundance of content can also generate new challenges for users in determining relevant and engaging content and this is where the *personalization* comes into picture.

2.3. Definition and Functioning of Personalization and Recommendation Algorithms

Personalization algorithms/recommendation algorithms analyse user data to forecast and offer "content recommendations" in synchronization with individual tastes. These algorithms function by collecting and analysing user information like past viewing history, genre preferences, ratings and interaction patterns (Alam & Khusro, 2020). Then these algorithms leverage such data to generate personalized recommendations which cater to the unique preferences of each user. Recommendation algorithms uses collaborative filtering and content-based filtering to generate personalized suggestions to their consumers. Collaborative filtering analyses behaviour and preferences of similar kind of users to make recommendations. Then by comparing preferences and patterns of a targeted user, collaborative filtering can recognize such contents which an individuals are likely to find appealing. On the other hand, Content-based filtering emphases on analysing attributes of the content itself such as genre, story plot, summaries, directors and actors to match user preferences with specific content characteristics (Martinez & Costa-Montenegro, 2010).

2.4. Role of Machine Learning and Artificial Intelligence in Enhancing Algorithms

In improving personalization and recommendation algorithms, machine learning and artificial intelligence are integral components which enable algorithms to continuously learn, adapt and develop over time. Recommendation algorithms can dynamically adjust and upgrade their suggestions based on user feedback and behaviour by leveraging machine learning models. This allows personalization and recommendation algorithms to become more precise and personalized in their recommendations (Zhang, Lu, & Jin, 2021). On the other hand, Artificial intelligence techniques like Natural Language Processing (NLP) and Computer Vision, also play a crucial role in enhancing algorithms. NLP empowers algorithms to analyse and understand literal data, like user reviews, descriptions and comments, to gain deeper insights into user preferences. Whereas, Computer Vision allows algorithms to analyse visual content, like, video thumbnails and images, to extract valuable information and make content recommendations based on visual similarities (Necula & Păvăloaia, 2023).

2.5. Benefits of Personalized User Experiences in Content Discovery and Engagement

In today's digital age, where attention span of individuals is fleeting and contents are abundant, personalized user experiences have occurred as a powerful tool for content discovery and user engagement in the OTT industry (Menon, 2020). By harnessing huge amount of data generated by users, personalized user experiences offer many benefits that revolutionize the way user interact with content. Personalization in OTT platforms brings numerous benefits like enhancing relevancy by delivering highly personalized content recommendations based on user preferences and demographics. This leads to proficient content discovery on OTT platform, facilitating users to explore wide array of relevant shows and movies (Booth, 2020). Personalization intensifies user engagement that results in higher content consumption, longer viewing sessions and greater satisfaction. It also brings up users' loyalty and retention as they receive consistent and personalized recommendations. Furthermore, personalization empowers the discovery of niche and serendipitous contents which also save user's time and augmenting their horizons.

By considering diverse interests and preferences of users, OTT platforms can ensure wide range of content from different cultures, perspectives and genres which helps to encourage diversity in the content ecosystem and offers more inclusive and enriching viewing experience to the users (Schweidel, et al., 2022).

3. ENHANCING USER EXPERIENCE THROUGH PERSONALIZATION

Personalization has revolutionized the dynamics of entertainment industry by offering pivotal strategy for improving the user experience. By customizing content recommendations as per individuals' preference and interests (Lindecrantz, 2020), personalization offers various benefits which considerably influence user satisfaction, engagement and overall enjoyment. One of the key benefits of personalized recommendations is the ability to assist users to discover new and relevant content (Chandra, Verma, Lim, Kumar, & Donthu, Personalization in personalized marketing: Trends and ways forward, 2022). In an era of ICT, where contents are overloaded, where content libraries are readily available and users often struggle to find relevant contents which aligns with their interests. Personalized recommendations streamlines the content discovery process to quickly find something they are likely to enjoy which helps in reducing frustration and enhancing overall viewing experience (Netflix, 2019). These personalized recommendations, by eliminating the need to manually search for content, also save users valuable time. By leveraging user data, algorithms can understand individual viewing habits, preferred genres, directors, cast, story plot and other factors that contribute to personal taste. This enables OTT platforms to deliver content recommendations that are highly relevant and engaging for each user, resulting in a more satisfying and enjoyable viewing experience.

Personalizing contents to individual preferences comprises collecting and analysing data to create personalized profiles. OTT platforms collect data from user activities like viewing history, likes, ratings, and users' feedback. Recommendation algorithms use machine learning and AI to examine user profiles to engender personalized recommendations based on past viewing experience, ratings, genre preferences and context (Altexsoft, 2021). These recommendations are accessible through OTT interfaces like homepages, playlists and feeds. Moreover, personalization fosters long-term customer engagement and loyalty. Many studies have proven that users who regularly receive recommendations aligned with their interests are more likely to stay engaged, return for more content and remain loyal. The ability to interact with recommendations, provide feedback, and customize preferences empowers users, increasing engagement and satisfaction. Personalized interfaces and emotional connections formed through recommendations create a more immersive and enjoyable user experience (Malhotra, 2020).

4. RECOMMENDATION ALGORITHMS: MECHANISMS AND TECHNIQUES

At the core of modern digital platforms, content recommendation algorithms are driving personalized experiences and assisting users to discover relevant content. These algorithms influence various techniques to examine user data and generate personalize recommendations. Such algorithms that generate content recommendations, focuses on content-based filtering and collaborative filtering approaches. In addition, it delves into the role of artificial intelligence and machine learning techniques in the systems of recommendation and highlighting their impact on improving recommendation accuracy and personalization.

4.1. Collaborative Filtering Approach

In recommendation systems, Collaborative filtering is a widely used technique that leverages the collective behaviour of users to make recommendations (Roy, Introduction To Recommender Systems- 1: Content-Based Filtering And Collaborative Filtering, 2020). It undertakes that consumers who have agreed in the past on their preferences are expected to agree again in the future. Collaborative filtering can be further divided into two categories:

i. User-Based Collaborative Filtering: This approach identifies similar users based on their preferences and generates recommendations by examining the content liked or consumed by those similar users. For example, if User X and User Y have similar viewing histories and preferences, the system might recommend content that User Y has enjoyed to User X (Koren & Bell, 2015).
ii. Item-Based Collaborative Filtering: In this approach, recommendations are made based on the resemblance between items themselves (Burke, O'Mahony, & Hurley, 2015). The algorithm

identifies items which are alike to the ones the user has interacted with in the past. For example, if User X has rated Movie A highly recommended, the system may recommend other movies that users with similar tastes have also highly rated (Roy, Introduction To Recommender Systems- 1: Content-Based Filtering And Collaborative Filtering, 2020).

4.2. Content-Based Filtering Approach

This approach focuses on *attributes of the content* to make recommendations that uses various characteristics of content, like story plot, genre, directors, actors, or textual descriptions, to recognize similarities and generate recommendations (Kharwal, 2023). By examining the attributes of the contents which users have previously shown interest in, the algorithm can endorse similar contents which align with their preferences. For example, if a user frequently watches thriller contents, the algorithm may suggest other thriller movies/contents or TV shows (Gemmis, Lops, Musto, Narducci, & Semeraro, 2015) (Roy, Introduction To Recommender Systems- 1: Content-Based Filtering And Collaborative Filtering, 2020).

4.3. Hybrid Approaches

Hybrid recommendation systems combine collaborative filtering and content-based filtering approaches to leverage the strengths of both methods. The aim is to provide more accurate and diverse recommendations by overcoming the limitations of each individual approach (Chiang, 7 Types of Hybrid Recommendation System, 2021) (Harsoor, 2023).

4.3.1 Machine Learning and Artificial Intelligence Techniques in Recommendation Systems

AI and ML have completely transformed recommendation systems, allowing users to get more accurate and personalized content recommendations. These approaches use complex algorithms based on huge datasets to intensify recommendation accuracy and customisation. Some of the key machine learning and AI techniques employed in recommendation systems include:

i. Deep Learning: Deep learning approaches, such as neural networks, have shown to be quite effective in recommendation systems. These models can extract complicated patterns and representations from user input automatically, enabling more accurate predictions and tailored suggestions (Sarker, 2021).
ii. Natural Language Processing (NLP): Textual data, such as user reviews, comments, and descriptions, can be analysed and understood using NLP algorithms. Recommendation algorithms can obtain a better grasp of user preferences and give more contextually appropriate recommendations by extracting insights from this content (Khurana, Koli, Khatter, & Singh, 2022).
iii. Reinforcement Learning: By allowing recommendation algorithms to learn and change based on user feedback, reinforcement learning techniques may be used to optimize them. The algorithm can monitor user interactions with recommended contents and alter its suggestions as needed to maximize user happiness and engagement (Afsar, Crump, & Far, 2021).
iv. Context-Aware Recommendations: Contextual information, such as time, location, or device, may be used by machine learning algorithms to offer context-aware suggestions. A recommendation system,

for example, might propose various types of contents throughout the day vs the evening, or promote mobile-friendly content to consumers accessing the platform via a mobile device (Zheng, 2022).

v. Hybrid Approaches: Recommendation algorithm every so often employ a blend of diverse techniques to boost accuracy in the recommendation. Hybrid approaches leverage the strengths of multiple algorithms, like content-based filtering and collaborative filtering, to overcome the limitations in the recommendations and deliver more comprehensive and accurate recommendations (Ano & Morisio, 2017).

The integration of artificial intelligence and machine learning techniques into recommendation algorithm has expressively enriched their ability to capture subtle patterns, understand user preferences and subsequently deliver highly personalized suggestions on the content. These techniques allow algorithms to learn and adapt from users' feedback, resulting in continuous improvement and more precise recommendations over time.

5. SHAPING MEDIA CONSUMPTION PATTERNS

The proliferation of recommendation algorithms and advent of digital platforms have considerably influenced the way users consume media. Recommendation algorithms play a pivotal role in shaping media consumption patterns, binge-watching behaviour, influencing content discovery and paradigm shift from conventional linear consumption to personalized experiences which has empowered users, allowing them to have more control over their content consumption journey and fostering a sense of individualization. Recommendation algorithms become game changer in revolutionizing content discovery, empowering users to discover a broader range of content offerings which align with their interests and preferences. This shift has also presented opportunities for niche market exploration, content diversity and personalized advertising. Personalized experiences will remain at the forefront of media consumption, creating a more engaging, satisfying and immersive user experience as recommendation algorithms continue to evolve and improve (Dhiman, 2023) (Sharma, Sreen, & Baishya, 2023).

5.1. Influence of Recommendation Algorithms on User Behaviour

Recommendation algorithms revolutionize content discovery by curating personalized recommendations, expanding users' horizons to a broader range of shows, movies, and genres they might not have discovered through traditional browsing methods (Vatsal, 2021). Furthermore, they introduce unanticipated content discovery, surprising users with recommendations aligned with their interests, fostering exploration and delight in the discovery process (Wang, 2018). Furthermore, recommendation algorithms drive increased content consumption by managing users through a continuous stream of tailored recommendations. As users engross with recommended content and provide feedback, the algorithms improve their suggestions, encouraging users to spend more time on the platform and explore a wider range of content (Chen & Chan, 2023). Conversely, there is a potential downside, as these algorithms can unintentionally contribute to filter bubbles and echo chambers, regulating exposure to diverse viewpoints and reinforcing existing preferences, potentially impacting the diversity of content consumed (Kitchens, Johnson, & Gray, 2020).

5.2. Impact on Content Discovery, Binge-Watching, and Cross-Platform Consumption

These algorithms have fuelled the popular binge-watching trend by delivering unified, personalized content which encourages users to consume multiple episodes or entire series in one sitting. Moreover, recommendation algorithms empower cross-platform consumption, allowing users to flawlessly changeover between devices while receiving consistent and personalized recommendations based on their viewing history and preferences. This ensures a continuous and personalized experience, allowing users to enjoy their preferred content across different platforms without interruptions.

5.3. Examining the Shift from Traditional Linear Consumption to Personalized Experiences

The landscape of media consumption has undergone a profound shift from traditional linear programming schedules to a more personalized and user-centric model, fuelled by the advent of digital platforms and recommendation algorithms. This transformative change encompasses several key aspects. First, on-demand viewing has become a norm, liberating users from fixed broadcasting schedules and allowing them to access content at their convenience, enhancing their overall viewing experience (Krings, 2023). Second, recommendation algorithms personalize user experiences by tailoring content recommendations, fostering a sense of ownership and empowerment as users feel understood by OTT platforms (Werd, 2021). Third, these algorithms facilitate the discovery of diverse content and niche markets by analysing user preferences, enabling platforms to surface and promote content tailored to specific interests and previously overlooked genres (Shim, Lee, & Oh, 2022). Fourth, recommendation algorithms empower users by giving them control over their content consumption journey through active engagement and feedback, creating a sense of user involvement in shaping content recommendations. Fifth, the advertising landscape has been transformed as algorithms deliver targeted and personalized advertisements, aligning with individual user interests and preferences (IBM, 2021). Lastly, the shift towards personalized experiences generates valuable data and insights for content creators and platforms, empowering them to make informed decisions based on user behaviour and preferences (Indian Retailer, 2022). This paradigm shift has not only revolutionized how content is consumed but has also empowered users, diversified content offerings, and provided actionable insights to content creators and platforms.

5.4. Evaluating Metrics for Measuring Recommendation Effectiveness

To measure the efficacy of recommendation algorithms, it is crucial to consider different metrics that capture various aspects of user engagement and content discovery. Following are some commonly used metrics for evaluating recommendation effectiveness:

i. Click-Through Rate (CTR): The percentage of people that click on a recommended item after seeing it is measured by CTR. A high CTR implies that the recommendations are capturing the user's attention and encouraging further investigation. (Wordstream, 2022).
ii. Conversion Rate: Conversion rate is the percentage of people who interact with a recommended contents and complete the intended activity, like purchasing, subscribing to a service, or viewing

a video. A greater conversion rate suggests that the recommendations are effectively impacting user engagement and behaviour.

iii. View Time: View time measures the duration of user engagement with a recommended item. Longer view times indicate that users find the recommended content engaging and are more likely to consume the content in its entirety.

iv. Diversity: Diversity measures the variety of content recommended to users. It assesses whether the recommendations cover a broad range of genres, styles, and formats, ensuring that users are exposed to diverse content options rather than being limited to a narrow set of preferences.

v. Novelty: Novelty measures the extent to which recommended items are different from what users have already consumed. Higher novelty suggests that the recommendations are introducing users to new and unfamiliar content, expanding their content consumption horizons.

vi. Serendipity: Serendipity measures the degree to which recommendations surprise and delight users by suggesting unexpected content. It assesses the algorithm's ability to introduce users to content they may not have actively sought but still find interesting and engaging.

vii. User Feedback and Satisfaction: Collecting user feedback through surveys, ratings, or user satisfaction metrics provides valuable insights into the effectiveness of recommendations. Positive feedback and high user satisfaction indicate that the recommendations are meeting user expectations and contributing to an improved content discovery experience.

6. CHALLENGES AND ETHICAL CONSIDERATIONS

In the digital era, recommendation systems have become an integral part of our online experiences, guiding users towards digital content and products which aligns with their preferences. In content personalisation and recommendation systems, Challenges and Ethical Considerations include a range of important factors out of which user's privacy and data protection are paramount, as it must be handled responsibly. Algorithmic prejudice poses a risk to diverse content representation which is potentially emphasizing existing biases and limiting experience to the different perspectives (Salman, 2023). Accountability, equality and transparency are important as it ensures users to understand how recommendations are generated and avoid discrimination. Authorizing users with the control over their recommendations helps to address concerns of overreliance on algorithms. Also evading echo chambers and filter bubbles and regularly assessing and improving recommendation systems are important to endorse ethical standards and create a positive user experience.

6.1. Privacy Concerns and Data Protection in Personalization Algorithms

Striking a delicate balance between personalization and privacy stands as a paramount challenge for recommendation systems. In today's digital ecosystem, users have become acutely conscious of the collection, storage, and utilization of their personal information (Hickman, 2023). Nowhere are these concerns more salient than in the realm of recommendation systems. Users concern about exposure of the data, their profiling and probable misuse of their personal data (Fu, Chen, Gao, & Li, 2023).

6.1.1. Algorithmic Bias and its Implications for Diverse Content Representation

The occurrence of algorithmic bias in recommendation systems poses serious problems, particularly when it comes to the representation of varied information and opinions. These prejudices can emerge in a variety of ways, including gender, socioeconomic class, ethnicity, and cultural preferences. If recommendation algorithms are not carefully constructed and trained, they may accidentally favour specific types of information, resulting in biased suggestions and restricted coverage of varied opinions (Belenguer, 2022). The consequences of algorithmic bias go beyond simple content suggestions. They have the potential to exacerbate and prolong social imbalances and underrepresentation by reinforcing existing prejudices and excluding underrepresented groups. Several actions must be done to solve this issue and guarantee that recommendation algorithms provide a more equal and inclusive portrayal of material.

First and foremost, it is critical to promote diversity and inclusion in the creation of these algorithms. This entails bringing together people from diverse backgrounds to assist develop the suggestions and decision-making processes. It is also critical to incorporate different points of view into the training datasets. It aids algorithms in comprehending and reflecting a greater range of cultural, social, and demographic factors. Audits should be performed on a regular basis to discover and minimize bias in recommendation algorithms (Forum, 2018). Transparency is also important, since consumers should be able to change their content choices and understand how suggestions are made. By implementing these standards, the industry will be able to strive toward more responsible recommendation systems that really represent the diversity of information and opinions in our globalized and interconnected society. (Akter, et al., 2022).

6.2. Addressing Transparency, Fairness, and Accountability in Recommendation Systems

In a recommendation system, transparency, fairness and accountability are key considerations. Transparency comprises giving clear explanations of the recommendation process, data sources involved, algorithms used and metrics guiding the recommendations. On the other hand, fairness ensures recommendations not to favour particular entities/contents and offer equal opportunities for diverse content. OTT platform must vigorously assess algorithms for biases and discriminatory patterns. Whereas, accountability includes establishing mechanisms for reporting concerns, user feedback and requesting explanations for recommendations which fosters trust in OTT platform and user and also promotes transparency and fairness (Deldjoo, Jannach, Bellogin, Difonzo, & Zanzonelli, 2023).

7. CONTENT PRODUCTION IN THE ERA OF PERSONALIZATION

With increase in the personalized recommendations, powered by sophisticated algorithms, content creators find themselves piloting a landscape where customising their work to the individual preferences is utmost priority. In the era of personalization, content production is seriously influenced by the strategies employed for content curation in OTT platforms. Content creators are expected to use several tactics like audience insights, metadata optimization, trend analysis and collaborative partnerships in order to capitalize on the reach and impact of their content. The crucial challenge lies in maintaining the right balance between human curation and algorithmic recommendations to ensure a diverse and high-quality content library which caters to a wide range of interests and perspectives. Additionally, providing customization options and user control is critical as it enables users to curate their own personalized experiences, leading to enhanced user satisfaction and cultivation of a loyal user base. By embracing such strategies and considerations, content creators and OTT platforms can thrive in the era of personalization, delivering engaging and personalized content experiences to audiences worldwide (Eklund, 2022).

Personalized recommendations have transformed content consumption by customizing suggestions to individual preferences which can create opportunities and challenges, both, for content creators. By studying user data, content creators can foster their contents for amplified visibility and better customer engagement. Personalization also allows for fostering a sense of community, exploration of niche topics and building a loyal fan following. Conversely, the pressure to adapt to algorithmic preferences can stifle creativity, leading to prescribed content. Furthermore, an algorithmic recommendation may create filter bubbles and limiting exposure to diverse perspectives. Hence, to navigate such landscape, creators should strike a balance between meeting audience expectations and pushing their boundaries. On the other hand, leveraging insights in the data and seeking feedback from the consumers helps to refine content while maintaining artistic integrity (Haleem, Mohd, Mohd, Ravi, & Rajiv, 2022). Collaboration with other creators and experts broadens reach and promotes originality. Content curation is crucial for fostering user satisfaction and OTT platforms employ strategies to present personalized recommendations.

In the digital media consumption algorithmic recommendations have revolutionized the content discovery, however human curation remains crucial. Human curators add expertise, personalization and diversity to content collections, encouraging inclusivity and ensuring quality. Collaboration between curators and algorithms can creates a comprehensive experience. OTT Platforms can offer personalized playlists genre/topic preferences and content filters. Consumer feedback and unambiguous preferences enhance algorithms and improve recommendations. By enabling users to shape their content discovery, platforms enhance satisfaction, encourage consumer engagement and foster loyalty. For delivering a personalized experience, balance between algorithmic recommendations and user agency is essential (Eg, Tønnesen, & Tennfjord, 2023).

Furthermore, human touch in content curation can helps to bridge the gap between data-driven recommendations and emotional connection that users seek. Human curators can curate content based on current events, emerging trends, and cultural nuances offering more contextual and timely content experience. They have capability to curate thematic collections, create compelling narratives and present content in such a way that resonates deeply with users. This human element enhances a layer of trust and authenticity, facilitating users that feel connected to the curated content and fostering a robust bond between OTT platform and its users. Eventually, the collaboration between human curators and algorithms ensures a personalized content discovery journey which combines the best of both worlds - the scale of algorithms and efficiency, and the human expertise and creativity that adds depth and emotional resonance to the recommendations (Juetten, 2021).

8. PERSONALIZATION AND ADVERTISING

In terms of advertising on OTT platforms, personalization become important strategy in today's advertising landscape which allow brands to deliver targeted messages to their consumers based on their content preferences and behaviours. By customising ads to individual interests, advertisers can capture consumers' attention, improve conversion rates and increase engagement. Conversely, personalization also poses many challenges in balancing effective ad targeting and user privacy. Advertisers must be transparent about data collection practices and acquire user consent to respect privacy concerns. Ad-blocking tools and consumer demand for privacy further complicate personalized advertising. Despite these challenges, in the advertising industry, personalized ad experiences considerably influence revenue models. Targeted ads maximize campaign effectiveness, leading to the higher conversion rates and enhanced return on investment. By leveraging data-driven insights, advertisers can optimize their ad targeting strategies, apportion budgets effectively and generate higher revenue and cost efficiency (Marcus, 2023).

9. EVALUATING AND IMPROVING RECOMMENDATION ALGORITHMS

In recent years, recommendation algorithms have become integral part of digital customer experiences, guiding users through vast content libraries on OTT platforms. However, effectiveness of these recommendation algorithms depend on continuous improvement, rigorous evaluation and incorporation of user feedback. Metrics and evaluation methods are important in gauging the performance of recommendation algorithms. In this context many key metrics are commonly used and every metric provide valuable insights into different aspects of the system's performance. Some of the most widely used metrics include Precision, F1 score, Recall, Normalized Discounted Cumulative Gain (NDCG), Mean Average Precision (MAP) and Area Under Receiver- Operating Characteristic Curve (AUC-ROC) (Kasula, Netflix Recommender System — A Big Data Case Study, 2020).

Precision metrics measures the proportion of relevant items amongst the recommended ones, whereas recall gauges the proportion of relevant items which are successfully recommended. F1 score combines both precision and recall into a single metric, providing a balanced measure of recommendation quality. MAP metrics and NDCG metrics consider the ranking of recommended items and the relevance of those items to users, providing a more nuanced evaluation of recommendation lists. On the other hand, AUC-ROC measures the performance of binary recommendation tasks like *click predictions* (Kanstrén, 2020).

To assess recommendation algorithms technically, there are two key methods: First, *Offline evaluation*, that uses historical data and predefined evaluation metrics to evaluate algorithm's performance. Though *Offline evaluation* allows quick testing and comparison of different algorithms but may not fully capture real-time performance and user interaction. Second, *Online evaluation*, such as A/B testing, comprises conducting experiments by arbitrarily assigning users to different recommendation algorithms and evaluating their performance based on specific metrics. *Online evaluation* offers more accurate insights into the algorithm's performance in real-world scenarios but it needs a larger user base and longer testing periods (Zangerle & Bauer, 2022).

Feedback loops play an essential role in the continuous improvement of recommendation algorithms. These loops include gathering feedback from user, analysing it and integrating the insights into algorithmic updates. By examining user reactions and interactions, algorithms can adjust recommendations and ensures that they remain relevant and useful over time. Feedback loops enable algorithms to reiterate and improve their performance based on user feedback and augmenting the overall user experience (Zhang, Lu, & Jin, 2020).

User testing is another important method that involves directly observing users as they interact with the recommendation system. This approach provides valuable qualitative insights into user behaviours, preferences and frustrations. Through user testing, designers and developers can identify pain points, usability issues and areas where recommendations may fall short of user expectations. This information can be used in refining algorithms, develop the relevance and quality of recommendations enhance the overall user experience. It is crucial to note that user testing and user feedback should reflect the diversity of the user base to ensure inclusivity and avoid bias. Taking into account the preferences and needs of a wide range of users that helps to create recommendation systems which are more inclusive and cater to different user segments effectively.

10. FUTURE TRENDS AND INNOVATIONS

The landscape of personalization and recommendation algorithms is constantly evolving as technology continues to advance day by day. These technological advancements shaping the future of personalized experience of consumers and providing them tailored content by enhancing their overall engagement. Some of key trends and innovations in this field include advances in personalization and recommendation algorithms, contextual personalization, cross-platform personalization and emergence of OTT 2.0 (Strategus, 2021) (Banerjee, 2022).

10.1 Advances in Personalization and Recommendation Algorithms

These days, personalization and recommendation algorithms are becoming sophisticated, leveraging cutting-edge technologies like artificial intelligence(AI), Machine Learning(ML) and Natural Language Processing(NLP). These technological advancements empower algorithms to better understand consumer behaviours and their preferences, resulting in more relevant and accurate recommendations. One important trend is the use of deep learning algorithms which process huge amounts of data and extract complex patterns and allowing for more nuanced understanding of consumer preferences. These models can capture multifaceted relationships between content attributes, consumer behaviours and contextual factors which leads to highly personalized recommendations. Another emerging trend is the integration of real-time data and real-time personalization. Real-time personalization enhances immediacy and relevance of recommendations, keeping users engaged and satisfied (Pandey, 2023).

10.2 Contextual Personalization and Adaptive Experiences

Contextual personalization emphases on delivering appropriate content based on specific context where users interact with platforms. This interaction includes factors like time of day, device type, location and even environmental conditions. By considering contextual information, algorithms can provide more relevant and timely recommendations to the consumers (Storyly, 2023). Adaptive experiences creates personalised environment which maximizes user engagement and satisfaction (Storyly, What is content personalization?, 2023).

10.3 Cross-Platform Personalization and Recommendations

With propagation of devices and platforms, users expect seamless and reliable personalized experience across different channels. Cross-platform personalization aims to deliver personalized recommendations which surpass individual platforms and devices. To achieve cross-platform personalization, algorithms need to consider consumer data from multiple sources and synchronize recommendations across platforms

(Robosoft, 2022). This empower users to seamlessly do transition between devices and continue their personalized experiences. For instance, a user may start watching a show on their smartphone and later resume it on their smart TV, with the algorithm recommending relevant content based on their viewing history regardless of the device (Taylor, 2022).

10.4 OTT 2.0

OTT 2.0 is the next phase of current OTT media services which characterized by enhanced personalization, user engagement and interactivity. OTT 2.0 is based on the foundation of OTT 1.0, which introduced on-demand streaming and content delivery outside traditional broadcast channels. OTT 2.0 emphases on offering hyper-personalized experiences to users which comprises personalised recommendations based on leveraging real-time data, granular user preferences and incorporating interactive elements like polls, quizzes and personalized playlists. By offering highly personalized and interactive experiences, OTT 2.0 aims to increase loyalty, user engagement and monetization opportunities (Kapoor, 2023).

The future of OTT 2.0 lies in advanced personalization and recommendation algorithms, utilizing deep learning and real-time data integration to deliver more accurate and relevant content recommendations. Contextual and cross-platform personalization will further enhance user experiences, leading to hyper-personalized and interactive experiences in the OTT landscape (Sharpe, 2020).

11. CONCLUSION

Consumer Engagement in terms of Personalization and Recommendations has shed light on the profound impact of OTT on media consumption and production, both globally and domestically. Personalization and recommendation algorithms are at the core of OTT platforms, tailoring content to individual preferences and interests. Through personalized experiences, these algorithms successfully elevate consumer engagement and satisfaction by employing various techniques, like collaborative filtering and content-based filtering, combined with artificial intelligence and machine learning. The chapter shade lights on the role of recommendation algorithms in content discovery, binge-watching, influencing user behaviour and cross-platform consumption. Personalized experiences has replaced traditional linear consumption and made content discovery more efficient and user-centric. Moreover, this chapter has addressed ethical considerations surrounding personalization algorithms, comprising data protection, privacy concerns and algorithmic bias. Transparency, accountability and fairness are crucial in ensuring diverse content representation and user trust in recommendation systems.

In this dynamic landscape of media and entertainment industry, leveraging personalization and recommendation algorithms responsibly will be essential in offering users with satisfying and enriching content experiences, however, also respecting privacy of consumer and ensuring fair representation of diverse content. As OTT era endures to evolve, it is crucial for content creators and OTT platform to work collaboratively to harness the full potential of personalization and recommendation algorithms while upholding ethical principles and augmenting user engagement in the ever-changing media landscape.

REFERENCES

Adjust. (2023). *What is over-the-top (OTT)?* Adjust. https://www.adjust.com/glossary/ott-over-the-top/: https://www.adjust.com

Afsar, M. M., Crump, T., & Far, B. (2021). Reinforcement learning based recommender systems: A survey. *Information Retrieval*. doi:https://doi.org//arXiv.2101.06286 doi:10.48550

Akter, S., Dwivedi, Y. K., Sajib, S., Biswas, K., Bandara, R. J., & Michael, K. (2022, May). Algorithmic bias in machine learning-based marketing models. *Journal of Business Research, 144*, 201–216. doi:10.1016/j.jbusres.2022.01.083

Alam, I., & Khusro, S. (2020). *Tailoring Recommendations to Groups ofViewers on Smart TV: A Real-Time ProfileGeneration Approach*. IEEE. doi:10.1109/ACCESS.2020.2980206

Algolia. (2022). *What is content discovery, and how can you make it easier for your users to find what theywant?* Algolia. https://www.algolia.com/blog/ux/what-is-content-discovery-and-how-can-you-make-it-easier-for-your-users-to-find-what-they-want/

Allam, J., & Thrideep, N. (2023). *Why Video Streaming Platforms Should Embrace AI and Analytics*. Themathcompany. https://themathcompany.com/blog/why-video-streaming-platforms-should-embrace-ai-and-analytics

Altexsoft. (2021). *Recommender Systems: Behind the Scenes of Machine Learning-Based Personalization*. Retrieved from https://www.altexsoft.com: https://www.altexsoft.com/blog/recommender-system-personalization/

Angel One. (2023). *India's media and entertainment industry: A sector on the rise*. Retrieved Nov 02, 2023, from https://www.angelone.in: https://www.angelone.in/blog/india-media-entertainment-industry-a-sector-on-the-rise

Ano, E. C., & Morisio, M. (2017, November). Hybrid Recommender Systems: A Systematic Literature Review. *Intelligent Data Analysis, 21*(06), 1487–1524. doi:10.3233/IDA-163209

Arthofer, F., Kon, M., Lee, E., Rose, J., & Hardarson, Á. (2016). *The Future of Television: The Impact of OTT on Video Production Around the World*. Retrieved Jul 15, 2023, from bcg.com: https://www.bcg.com/publications/2016/media-entertainment-technology-digital-future-television-impact-ott-video-production

Arti. (2021). *Netflix or Amazon Prime: Who Uses AI and Machine Learning Better?* Retrieved Jul 12, 2023, from https://www.analyticsinsight.net: https://www.analyticsinsight.net/netflix-or-amazon-prime-who-uses-ai-and-machine-learning-better/

Axinom. (2021). *Metadata: Key to Value Generation in OTT*. Retrieved from axinom.com: https://www.axinom.com/article/metadata-in-ott

Balki, B. (2021). *OTT Personalization- An AI/ML Game-Changer*. Retrieved Jul 14, 2023, from www.globalligic.com: https://www.globallogic.com/wp-content/uploads/2021/02/OTT-Personalization.pdf

Bambha, M. (2023). *My own personal space: AB testing OTT experiences for user engagement, inclusion and growth*. Retrieved Jul 24, 2023, from timesofindia.com: https://timesofindia.indiatimes.com/blogs/voices/my-own-personal-space-ab-testing-ott-experiences-for-user-engagement-inclusion-and-growth/?source=app&frmapp=yes

Banerjee, D. (2022). *OTT Platforms – Trends to Look Out for in the Next Five Years*. Retrieved from https://www.muvi.com/: https://www.muvi.com/blogs/ott-platforms-trends-to-look-out-for-in-the-next-five-years

Belenguer, L. (2022). AI bias: Exploring discriminatory algorithmic decision-making models and the application of possible machine-centric solutions adapted from the pharmaceutical industry. *AI and Ethics*, *2*(4), 771–787. Retrieved October 28, 2023, from https://link.springer.com/article/10.1007/s43681-022-00138-8. doi:10.1007/s43681-022-00138-8 PMID:35194591

Ben Lutkevich. (2022). *digital asset management (DAM)*. Retrieved from TechTarget.com: https://www.techtarget.com/searchcontentmanagement/definition/What-is-digital-asset-management

Benjamin Habegger, O. H. (2014). *Personalization vs. Privacy in Big Data Analysis*. Retrieved from https://www.researchgate.net/publication/295121842_Personalization_vs_Privacy_in_Big_Data_Analysis

Bhattacharyya, D. R., Kohli, D. S., & More, D. R. (2020). Change In Consumption Habits Of Entertainment During Lockdown And The Role Of OTT Platforms. *Ilkogretim Online - Elementary Education, 19*(4), 4686-4695. doi:10.17051/ilkonline.2020.04.764875

Booth, J. (2020). *Visions for 2020: Key trends shaping the digital marketing landscape*. Retrieved Jun 30, 2023, from https://blogs.oracle.com/: https://blogs.oracle.com/advertising/post/visions-for-2020-key-trends-shaping-the-digital-marketing-landscape

BrandEquity. (2021). *How the pandemic emerged as a blessing for India's OTT industry*. Retrieved Jul 10, 2023, from brandequity.com: https://brandequity.economictimes.indiatimes.com/news/digital/how-the-pandemic-emerged-as-a-blessing-for-indias-ott-industry/84056159

Buchholz, K. (2020). *International Brands Rise to the Top of Indian Streaming Market*. Retrieved Nov 01, 2023, from Statista: https://www.statista.com/chart/23009/market-share-streaming--ott--platforms-in-india/

Buchholz, K. (2020). *International Brands Rise to the Top of Indian Streaming Market*. Retrieved Nov 01, 2023, from https://www.statista.com: https://www.statista.com/chart/23009/market-share-streaming--ott--platforms-in-india/

Burke, R., O'Mahony, M. P., & Hurley, N. J. (2015). Robust Collaborative Recommendation. In L. R. Francesco Ricci, *Recommender Systems Handbook* (pp. 961-995). Springer. Retrieved Jul 12, 2023, from https://link.springer.com/book/10.1007/978-1-4899-7637-6

Canet, L. (2022). *Churn It Down: How Media Companies Can Use AI To Keep And Win Subscribers*. Retrieved Jul 12, 2023, from www.forbes.com: https://www.forbes.com/sites/googlecloud/2022/06/13/churn-it-down-how-media-companies-can-use-ai-to-keep-and-win-subscribers/?sh=26c37c733744

Chandra, S., Verma, S., Lim, W. M., Kumar, S., & Donthu, N. (2022). Personalization in personalized marketing: Trends and ways forward. *Psychology and Marketing*, *39*(8), 1529–1562. doi:10.1002/mar.21670

Chandra, S., Verma, S., Lim, W. M., Kumar, S., & Donthu, N. (2022, May). Personalization in personalized marketing: Trends and ways forward. *Psychology and Marketing*, *39*(8), 1529–1562. doi:10.1002/mar.21670

ChenG.ChanT. Y. (2023). The Effects of Diversity in Algorithmic Recommendations on Digital Content Consumption: A Field Experiment. SSRN. https://papers.ssrn.com/sol3/papers.cfm?abstract_id=4365121 doi:10.2139/ssrn.4365121

Chiang, J. (2021). 7 Types of Hybrid Recommendation System. *Medium*. https://medium.com/analytics-vidhya/7-types-of-hybrid-recommendation-system-3e4f78266ad8

Chong, D. (2020). *Deep Dive into Netflix's Recommender System*. Towards Data Science. https://towardsdatascience.com: https://towardsdatascience.com/deep-dive-into-netflixs-recommender-system-341806ae3b48

Conviva. (2021). *Why Content Discovery in OTT Matters*. Conviva. https://www.conviva.com/why-content-discovery-in-ott-matters/

Cooltrack. (2021). *What is Cognitive Personalization?* Cooltrack. https://www.clootrack.com: https://www.clootrack.com/knowledge_base/cognitive-personalization

Crowly. (2023). *Decoding Mobile Ad Networks: Your Key to Successful App Marketing*. App Samurai. https://appsamurai.com: https://appsamurai.com/blog/decoding-mobile-ad-networks-your-key-to-successful-app-marketing/

Deldjoo, Y., Jannach, D., Bellogin, A., Difonzo, A., & Zanzonelli, D. (2023). Fairness in recommender systems: Research landscape and future directions. *User Modeling and User-Adapted Interaction*. doi:10.1007/s11257-023-09364-z

DhimanB. (2023). A Paradigm Shift in the Entertainment Industry in the Digital Age: A Critical Review. Preprints. doi:10.20944/preprints202306.1115.v1

Eg, R., Tønnesen, Ö. D., & Tennfjord, M. K. (2023). A scoping review of personalized user experiences on social media: The interplay between algorithms and human factors. *Computers in Human Behavior Reports*, *9*, 100253. doi:10.1016/j.chbr.2022.100253

Eklund, O. (2022). Custom thumbnails: The changing face of personalisation strategies on Netflix. *Convergence (London)*, *28*(03), 737–760. doi:10.1177/13548565211064520

Endavo. (2023). *What is OTT?* Endavo. https://www.endavomedia.com: https://www.endavomedia.com/what-is-ott/

ET. T. E. (2023). India's entertainment & media industry revenues to reach $73.6 bn by 2027: Report. *The Economic Times*. https://economictimes.indiatimes.com/industry/media/entertainment/media/indias-entertainment-media-industry-revenues-to-reach-73-6-bn-by-2027-report/articleshow/101863251.cms

ETCFO. (2019). How OTT Platforms, 5G Technology will impact Entertainment Industry. *Economic Times.* https://cfo.economictimes.indiatimes.com/news/media-advertising-entertainment-industry-the-moment-of-becoming-and-the-future/71805710

ETtimes. (2021). OTT platforms – the challenges of balancing creativity with customer centricity. *ET Times.* https://brandequity.economictimes.indiatimes.com/news/digital/ott-platforms-the-challenges-of-balancing-creativity-with-customer-centricity/86111079

Fdokumen. (2022). *OTT Personalization - GlobalLogic.* Fdokumen. www.fdocumen.id: https://fdokumen.id/dokumen/9562f_ott-personalization-globallogic.html

FMI. (2020). *OTT Content Market.* Future Marketimng Insights. https://www.futuremarketinsights.com/reports/over-the-top-ott-content-market

Fu, X., Chen, N., Gao, P., & Li, Y. (2023). Privacy-Preserving Personalized Recommender Systems. *SRN.* https://papers.ssrn.com/sol3/papers.cfm?abstract_id=4202576

Furey, M. (2023). *How Reelgood is Putting an End to Decision Fatigue.* Reel Good. https://data.reelgood.com/how-reelgood-is-putting-an-end-to-decision-fatigue/

Gemmis, M. d., Lops, P., Musto, C., Narducci, F., & Semeraro, G. (2015). Semantics-Aware Content-Based Recommender Systems. In L. R. Francesco Ricci, *Recommender Systems Handbook* (pp. 119-159). Springer. https://link.springer.com/book/10.1007/978-1-4899-7637-6

Globallogic. (2021). *How to Elevate Your OTTThrough Predictive Personalization.* Globalogic.

Gokul, M. (2022). *Personalization In The OTT Space For Better Recommendations And Smarter Video Analytics.* Argoid. https://www.argoid.ai/blog/personalization-in-the-ott-space-for-better-recommendation-and-smarter-video-analytics

Haleem, A., Javaid, M., Asim Qadri, M., Pratap Singh, R., & Suman, R. (2022). Artificial intelligence (AI) applications for marketing: A literature-based study. *International Journal of Intelligent Networks, 3*(1), 119–132. doi:10.1016/j.ijin.2022.08.005

Harsoor, S. (2023). Recommendation Systems: An Overview. *Medium.* https://medium.com/@sharanharsoor/recommendation-systems-an-overview-a9ff7d32b043

Hickman, M. (2023). *The Power of Personalized Marketing: AI, Customer Behaviour, and Recommender Systems.* LinkedIn. https://www.linkedin.com: https://www.linkedin.com/pulse/power-personalized-marketing-ai-customer-behaviour-systems-hickman/

IBEF. (2021). *OTT Video - Small Screen, Big Play.* IBEF. https://www.ibef.org/research/india-study/ott-video-small-screen-big-play

IBEF. (2022). *Media and Entertainment Industry Report.* IBEF. https://www.ibef.org/industry/entertainment-presentation

IBM. (2021). *How AI is changing advertising?* IBM. https://www.ibm.com: https://www.ibm.com/watson-advertising/thought-leadership/how-ai-is-changing-advertising

Indian Retailer. (2022). *How Data Analytics is Driving Personalization?* Indian Retailer. https://www.indianretailer.com/article/technology-e-commerce/digital-trends/how-data-analytics-driving-personalization

Indian Retailer. (2022). *How Digital Marketing Can Help in Increasing Consumer Engagement*. Indian Retailer. https://www.indianretailer.com/article/technology-e-commerce/digital-trends/how-digital-marketing-can-help-increasing-consumer

IndianExpress. (2018). Original content to drive growth for Rs 3,300cr investment in OTT services: Report. *India Express*. https://indianexpress.com: https://indianexpress.com/article/technology/tech-news-technology/original-content-to-drive-growth-for-rs-3300cr-investment-in-ott-report-5029883/

ITConvergence. (2023). *The Role of Machine Learning in Recommendation Systems*. IT Convergence. https://www.itconvergence.com/blog/the-role-of-machine-learning-in-recommendation-systems/

Jackson, D. (2017). The Netflix Prize: How a $1 Million Contest Changed Binge-Watching Forever. *ThrillList*. https://www.thrillist.com: https://www.thrillist.com/entertainment/nation/the-netflix-prize

Jain, M. K. (2021). THE RISE OF OTT PLATFORM: CHANGING CONSUMER PREFERENCES. [IJMR]. *EPRA International Journal of Multidisciplinary Research*, *7*(6), 257–262. doi:10.36713/epra2013

Juetten, M. (2021). Content Curated With A Human Touch: Bookshlf. *Forbes*. https://www.forbes.com/sites/maryjuetten/2021/09/07/content-curated-with-a-human-touch-bookshlf/?sh=2eabbc6f435b

Kanstrén, T. (2020). *A Look at Precision, Recall, and F1-Score*. Towards Data Science. https://towardsdatascience.com/a-look-at-precision-recall-and-f1-score-36b5fd0dd3ec

Kapoor, S. (2023). OTT 2.0 — India is ready. *Times of India*. https://timesofindia.indiatimes.com: https://timesofindia.indiatimes.com/blogs/voices/ott-2-0-india-is-ready/

Kasula, C. P. (2020). *Netflix Recommender System — A Big Data Case Study*. Towards Science Data. https://towardsdatascience.com/: https://towardsdatascience.com/netflix-recommender-system-a-big-data-case-study-19cfa6d56ff5

Kasula, C. P. (2020). *Netflix Recommender System — A Big Data Case Study*. Towards Data Science. https://towardsdatascience.com/netflix-recommender-system-a-big-data-case-study-19cfa6d56ff5

Kharwal, A. (2023). *Content Based Filtering and Collaborative Filtering: Difference*. The Clever Programmer. https://thecleverprogrammer.com/2023/04/20/content-based-filtering-and-collaborative-filtering-difference/: https://thecleverprogrammer.com/2023/04/20/content-based-filtering-and-collaborative-filtering-difference/

Khurana, D., Koli, A., Khatter, K., & Singh, S. (2022). Diksha Khurana, Aditya Koli, Kiran Khatter & Sukhdev Singh. *Multimedia Tools and Applications*, *82*, 3713–3744. doi:10.1007/s11042-022-13428-4 PMID:35855771

Kitchens, B., Johnson, S. L., & Gray, P. (2020). UNDERSTANDING ECHO CHAMBERS AND FILTER BUBBLES: THE IMPACT OF SOCIAL MEDIA ON DIVERSIFICATION AND PARTISAN SHIFTS IN NEWS CONSUMPTION. *Management Information Systems Quarterly*, *44*(4), 1619–1649. doi:10.25300/MISQ/2020/16371

Koka, V. (2023). The shift towards digital: A thriving OTT market. *Times of India*. https://timesofindia.indiatimes.com/blogs/voices/the-shift-towards-digital-a-thriving-ott-market/

Koren, Y., & Bell, R. (2015). Advances in Collaborative Filtering. In L. R. Francesco Ricci, *Recommender Systems Handbook* (pp. 77-118). Springer. https://link.springer.com/book/10.1007/978-1-4899-7637-6

Krings, E. (2023). *VOD Streaming – What It Is and How It Works with OTT*. DAcast. https://www.dacast.com/blog/vod-streaming/

Liang, T.-P., Lai, H.-J., & Ku, Y.-C. (2007). Personalized Content Recommendation and User Satisfaction: Theoretical Synthesis and Empirical Findings. *Journal of Management Information Systems*, *23*(3), 45–70. doi:10.2753/MIS0742-1222230303

Lidhoo, P. (2022). Was Bollywood saved by OTT during the pandemic? For many producers, the answer is a big Yes. *Business Today*. https://www.businesstoday.in: https://www.businesstoday.in/trending/entertainment/story/was-bollywood-saved-by-ott-during-the-pandemic-for-many-producers-the-answer-is-a-big-yes-348410-2022-09-28

Lindecrantz, E. (2020). *Personalizing the customer experience: Driving differentiation in retail*. McKinsey and Company. https://www.mckinsey.com/industries/retail/our-insights/personalizing-the-customer-experience-driving-differentiation-in-retail

Malhotra, S. (2020). *Recommendation Engines for OTT Platforms To Personalize Streaming*. Artificial Intelligence. https://artificialintelligence.oodles.io: https://artificialintelligence.oodles.io/blogs/recommendation-engines-for-ott-platforms/

Marcus, C. (2023). *OTT Advertising: How to Advertise on Streaming Service*. Color Matics. https://www.colormatics.com/article/ott-advertising-how-to-advertise-on-streaming-service/

Martinez, B. B., & Costa-Montenegro, E. (2010). A hybrid content-based and item-based collaborative filtering approach to recommend TV programs enhanced with singular value decomposition. *Information Sciences*, *180*(22), 4290–4311. doi:10.1016/j.ins.2010.07.024

McKinnon, I. (2022). *Consumer Insights And The Evolution of Personalized Website Recommendation Systems*. Rosetta. https://rosetta.ai: https://rosetta.ai/blog/consumer-insights-and-the-evolution-of-personalized-website-recommendation-systems

Menon, D. (2020). *Reduced Attention Spans In The Digital Age*. LinkedIn. https://www.linkedin.com/pulse/reduced-attention-spans-digital-age-deepak-menon/

Miguel Alves Gomes, T. M. (2023). A review on customer segmentation methods for personalized customer targeting in e-commerce use cases. *Information Systems and e-Business Management*, *21*(3), 527–570. doi:10.1007/s10257-023-00640-4

Minzheong, S. (2021). A Comparative Study on Over-The-Tops, Netflix & Amazon Prime Video:Based on the Success Factors of Innovation. *International Journal of Advanced Smart Convergence*, *10*(01), 62–74. doi:10.7236/IJASC.2021.10.1.62

M&M. (2022). *Over the Top Market by Type (Game Streaming, Audio Streaming, Video Streaming, and Communication), Monetization Model (Subscription-based, Advertising-based, and Transaction-based), Streaming Device, Vertical and Region - Global Forecast to 2027*. M&M. https://www.marketsandmarkets.com/Market-Reports/over-the-top-ott-market-41276741.html

Moore, A. (2023). *Increase Your Website's Ad Revenue with Ad Exchanges: A Step-by-Step Guide*. EZAOIC.

Muralidharan, G. (2020). *Personalization in the OTT Space for Better Recommendation and Smarter Video Analytics*. LinkedIn. https://www.linkedin.com: https://www.linkedin.com/pulse/personalization-ott-space-better-recommendation-video-muralidharan/

MyStory. (2023). *EVERYTHING YOU NEED TO KNOW ABOUT OTT TECHNOLOGY*. Mystory. https://yourstory.com/mystory/everything-you-need-to-know-about-ott-technology

Naresh, S. (2021). Smart Recommendation System For OTT platforms. *Medium*. https://medium.com/mobiotics/smart-recommendation-system-for-ott-platforms-f0e79b8e520

Necula, S.-C., & Păvăloaia, V.-D. (2023). AI-Driven Recommendations: A Systematic Review of the State of the Art in E-Commerce. *Applied Sciences (Basel, Switzerland)*, *13*(9), 5531. doi:10.3390/app13095531

Netflix. (2019). *How Netflix's Recommendations System Works?* Netflix https://help.netflix.com/en/node/100639

Nvidia. (2022). *Recommendation System*. Nvidia. https://www.nvidia.com: https://www.nvidia.com/en-us/glossary/data-science/recommendation-system/

Pajkovic, N. (2021). Algorithms and taste-making: Exposing the Netflix Recommender System's operational logics. *Convergence (London)*, *28*(1), 214–235. doi:10.1177/13548565211014464

Pandey, R. (2023). *The Future is Now: How AI and Machine Learning are Revolutionizing the Software Industry*. LinkedIn. https://www.linkedin.com: https://www.linkedin.com/pulse/future-now-how-ai-machine-learning-revolutionizing-software-pandey-/

Polaris, M. R. (2023). *Global Over the Top (OTT) Market Projected to Grow USD 2,228.36 Billion By 2032, at 27.0% CAGR: Polaris Market Research*. Global News Wire. https://www.globenewswire.com/en/news-release/2023/04/11/2644610/0/en/Global-Over-the-Top-OTT-Market-Projected-to-Grow-USD-2-228-36-Billion-By-2032-at-27-0-CAGR-Polaris-Market-Research.html

Ramesh, M. (2023). Indian OTT market set to reach ₹30,000 crore by 2030. *The Hindu- Business Line*. https://www.thehindubusinessline.com/news/indian-ott-market-set-to-reach-30000-crore-by-2030/article66760012.ece

ResearchAndMarkets. (2023). *OTT Streaming Global Market Report 2023: Major Players Include Facebook, Netflix, Amazon, Microsoft, Google, Apple, Hulu, Tencent, Rakuten and YouTube*. Globenewswire. https://www.globenewswire.com/en/news-release/2023/04/07/2643207/28124/en/OTT-Streaming-Global-Market-Report-2023-Major-Players-Include-Facebook-Netflix-Amazon-Microsoft-Google-Apple-Hulu-Tencent-Rakuten-and-YouTube.html

Researchwire. (2022). Trends in OTT technology — How AI and ML are transforming content production and delivery. *Research Wire.* https://www.researchwire.in/resources/trends-in-ott-technology-how-ai-and-ml-are-transforming-content-production-and-delivery/

Robert Amor, J. D. (2021). The promise of automated compliance checking. *Developments in the Built Environment, 5*(1), 100039. doi:10.1016/j.dibe.2020.100039

Robosoft. (2022). *Building cross-platform OTT apps: best practices in design & development.* Robosoft. https://www.robosoftin.com/blog/cross-platform-ott-apps-design-development

Roy, A. (2020). *Introduction To Recommender Systems- 1: Content-Based Filtering And Collaborative Filtering.* Towards Data Science. https://towardsdatascience.com: https://towardsdatascience.com/introduction-to-recommender-systems-1-971bd274f421

Roy, A. (2020). *Introduction To Recommender Systems- 1: Content-Based Filtering And Collaborative Filtering.* Towards Data Science. https://towardsdatascience.com: https://towardsdatascience.com/introduction-to-recommender-systems-1-971bd274f421

Salman, H. (2023). Unraveling the Power of Recommendation Systems: Personalization in the Digital Age. *Medium.* https://medium.com: https://medium.com/@hanifesalman0/unraveling-the-power-of-recommendation-systems-personalization-in-the-digital-age-a85623f111a9

Sarker, I. H. (2021). Deep Learning: A Comprehensive Overview on Techniques, Taxonomy, Applications and Research Directions. *SN Computer Science, 2*(420), 420. doi:10.1007/s42979-021-00815-1 PMID:34426802

Saxena, P. (2023). *Driving Engagement and Loyalty: The Impact of Social Media Marketing.* AdLift. https://www.adlift.com/in/blog/driving-engagement-and-loyalty-the-impact-of-social-media-marketing/

Schweidel, D. A., Bart, Y., Inman, J. J., Stephen, A. T., Libai, B., Andrews, M., Rosario, A. B., Chae, I., Chen, Z., Kupor, D., Longoni, C., & Thomaz, F. (2022). How consumer digital signals are reshaping the customer journey. *Journal of the Academy of Marketing Science, 50*(6), 1257–1276. doi:10.1007/s11747-022-00839-w PMID:35221393

Sharma, A. (2023). *OTT VS Traditional TV: The Battle for Viewership.* Next Gen IOTs. https://nexgeniots.com/ott-vs-traditional-tv-the-battle-of-viewership/

Sharma, A., Sreen, N., & Baishya, K. (2023). Identifying gratification behind the consumption of the OTT platforms in an emerging market: A means-end theory approach. *Marketing Intelligence & Planning, 41*(5), 593–612. https://www.emerald.com/insight/content/doi/10.1108/MIP-12-2022-0558/full/html?skipTracking=true. doi:10.1108/MIP-12-2022-0558

Sharpe, I. (2020). *OTT 2.0: understanding the importance of interactivity and engagement.* TVB Europe. https://www.tvbeurope.com/media-delivery: https://www.tvbeurope.com/media-delivery/ott-2-0-understanding-the-importance-of-interactivity-and-engagement

Shim, D., Lee, C., & Oh, I. (2022). Analysis of OTT Users' Watching Behavior for Identifying a Profitable Niche: Latent Class Regression Approach. *Journal of Theoretical and Applied Electronic Commerce Research, 17*(4), 1564–1580. doi:10.3390/jtaer17040079

Skyquestt. (2022). *Global OTT market insights*. Skyquestt. www.skyquestt.com: https://www.skyquestt.com/report/over-the-top-ott-market

Srinivasan, A. (2023). *Covid-19 fuels AI platforms causing cloud providers to invest*. LinkedIn. https://www.linkedin.com/pulse/covid-19-fuels-ai-platforms-causing-cloud-providers-aarthi-srinivasan/

StartIO. (2023). *Maximizing Revenue in 2023: Proven Strategies for App Monetization – Statistics, Models and Best Practices*. StartIO. https://www.start.io/blog/maximizing-revenue-proven-strategies-for-app-monetization-statistics-models-and-best-practices/

Statista. (2022). *OTT Video - Worldwide*. Statista. https://www.statista.com/outlook/amo/media/tv-video/ott-video/worldwide

Statista. (2023). *OTT Video - Worldwide*. Statista. https://www.statista.com: https://www.statista.com/outlook/amo/media/tv-video/ott-video/worldwide

Storyly. (2023). *What is content personalization?* Storyly. https://www.storyly.io/glossary/content-personalization

Strategus. (2021). *12 New Developments In Ott Platforms For 2022*. Strategus. https://www.strategus.com/blog/new-developments-ott

Sumeet, S. (2023). *Stay One Step Ahead: AI-Driven Tactics for OTT Customer Retention*. LinkedIn. https://www.linkedin.com/pulse/stay-one-step-ahead-ai-driven-tactics-ott-customer-retention-shah/

Suriati, S., Dwiastuti, M., & Tulus, T. (2017). Weighted hybrid technique for recommender system. *International Conference on Information and Communication Technology (IconICT)* (pp. 1-8). IOP. https://iopscience.iop.org/article/10.1088/1742-6596/930/1/012050

Taylor, K. (2022). *What is Cross-Channel Personalization?* Hitechnectar. https://www.hitechnectar.com/blogs/cross-channel-personalization/

Vatsal. (2021). *Recommendation Systems Explained*. Towards Data Science. https://towardsdatascience.com: https://towardsdatascience.com/recommendation-systems-explained-a42fc60591ed

Vijayanagar, K. R. (2021). *How do Content Recommendation Engines Work?* OTT Verse. https://ottverse.com/what-is-content-video-recommendation-engines-ott-vod/

Wang, C.-D. (2018). Serendipitous Recommendation in E-commerce using Innovator-Based Collaborative Filtering. *IEEE Explore*, (pp. 2168-2275). IEEE. doi:10.1109/TCYB.2018.2841924

WE Forum. (2018). *How to Prevent Discriminatory Outcomes in Machine Learning*. WeForum. https://www3.weforum.org: https://www3.weforum.org/docs/WEF_40065_White_Paper_How_to_Prevent_Discriminatory_Outcomes_in_Machine_Learning.pdf

Welle, D. (2021). How India's Covid Crisis Has Changed Bollywood? *Outlook India*. https://www.outlookindia.com/website/story/entertainment-news-how-indias-covid-crisis-has-changed-bollywood/390387

Werd, S. (2021). *Personalization as a tool to retain users of your OTT service*. Jump Data Driven. https://www.jumpdatadriven.com/personalization-as-a-tool-to-retain-users-of-your-ott-service/

Wordstream. (2022). *Click-Through Rate (CTR): Understanding Click-Through Rate for PPC*. Wordtream. https://www.wordstream.com/click-through-rate

Yeole, D. S., Saha, D. L., & Bhaisare, P. C. (2022). A study on User Perspective on OTT platform in India. *Journal of Positive School Psychology*, *6*(3), 7351–7366.

Zangerle, E., & Bauer, C. (2022). Evaluating Recommender Systems: Survey and Framework. *ACM Computing Surveys*, *55*(08), 1–38. doi:10.1145/3556536

Zhang, Q., Lu, J., & Jin, Y. (2020). Artificial intelligence in recommender systems. *Complex & Intelligent Systems*, *7*(1), 439–457. https://link.springer.com/article/10.1007/s40747-020-00212-w. doi:10.1007/s40747-020-00212-w

Zhang, Q., Lu, J., & Jin, Y. (2021). Artificial intelligence in recommender systems. *Complex & Intelligent Systems*, *7*(1), 439–457. doi:10.1007/s40747-020-00212-w

Zheng, Y. (2022, January 17). Context-Aware Collaborative Filtering Using Context Similarity: An Empirical Comparison. *Information (Basel)*, *13*(1), 42. doi:10.3390/info13010042

Section 3
Psychological and Social Implications

Chapter 10
FOMOphobia:
The Psychological Drivers of OTT Media Consumption Through Social Comparison, Self-Esteem, and Anxiety

Sridevi Gopakumar
https://orcid.org/0000-0001-6704-6183
Loyola Institute of Business Administration, India

Madhava Priya Dananjayan
Loyola Institute of Business Administration, India

ABSTRACT

In the era of social media, where users have easy access to a constant stream of updates about their peers' lives, individuals may dread missing out on social events, experiences, or opportunities. This phenomenon is known as fear of missing out. The present research examines the underlying psychological factors that influence the consumption of over-the-top media, with a particular emphasis on the influence of social comparison, self-esteem, and anxiety. Through qualitative research methods, including interviews and systematic coding procedures, the research uncovers the psychological implications of media consumption habits. The findings highlight the detrimental effects of social comparison on individuals' self-esteem, leading to heightened anxiety and the emergence of FOMOphobia. These insights emphasize the urgent need for tailored interventions and media literacy programs to mitigate these adverse effects.

1. INTRODUCTION

The advent of social media has ushered in a paradigm shift in the way individuals communicate, connect, and consume media content. The widespread adoption of platforms such as Facebook, Twitter, Instagram, and Snapchat has transformed the social landscape, facilitating instantaneous sharing of personal experiences, updates, and interactions. Concurrently, the rise of over-the-top (OTT) media platforms, such as Netflix, Zee5, Hotstar and Amazon Prime Video, has revolutionized the entertainment industry,

DOI: 10.4018/979-8-3693-0116-6.ch010

providing on-demand access to a vast array of movies, TV shows, and original content. Social media platforms have become an integral element of billions of users' daily lives around the globe. People can now share photos, videos, thoughts, and opinions with their social network, including friends, family, and acquaintances. This interconnectedness has nurtured a sense of virtual community, allowing people to remain informed, engaged, and connected regardless of their geographical location. In addition, social media has enabled the cultivation of online personas and the creation of carefully curated digital identities, spawning new forms of self-expression and social interaction.

Meanwhile, the presence of OTT media platforms has changed the way people consume entertainment material. These platforms provide a wide variety of streaming alternatives, enabling users to watch their favourite TV series, movies, and documentaries whenever and wherever they choose. Individuals may now engage in binge-watching sessions and tailor their media consumption experiences because to the proliferation of internet-connected gadgets such as smartphones, tablets, and smart TVs. The advent of social media and the dominance of OTT media platforms have resulted in a tremendously immersive and fascinating digital ecosystem. India had approximately 451 million unique visitors to the over-the-top (OTT) video platform YouTube in April 2022 as shown in Figure 1. YouTube was predominantly an OTT video platform supported by advertisements and had the highest number of unique visitors among streaming platforms during that time period. MX Player had the second-highest number of unique visitors in the South Asian market, far behind the market leader (comScore, 2022). These platforms have not only influenced how people engage with and consume media, but they have also given birth to new modes of information distribution, cultural exchange, and entertainment consumption. This revolution has repercussions that go beyond simple technology improvements, affecting societal dynamics, personal connections, and human well-being.

Figure 1. Number of unique visitors of video over-the-top (OTT) platform in India in April 2022, by platform (in millions) (comScore)

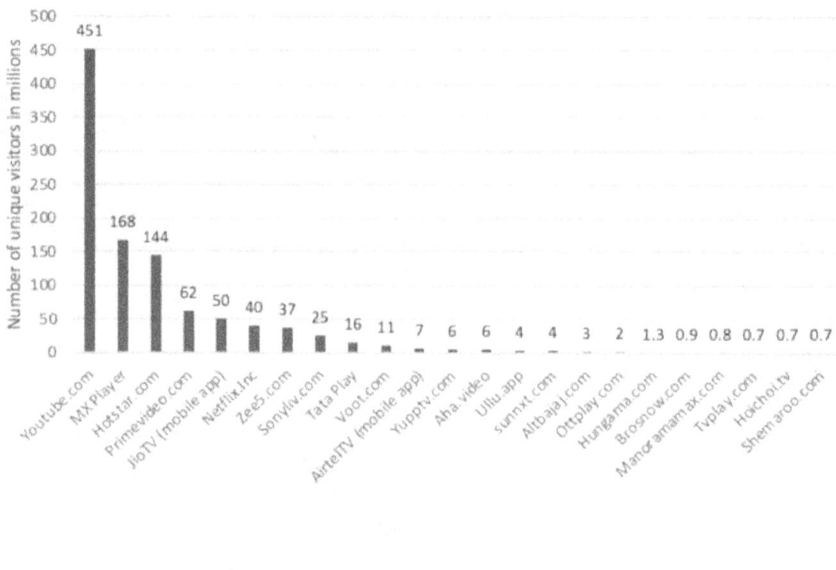

The psychological phenomenon known as the fear of missing out (FOMO) has gained significant relevance in contemporary times, particularly in the context of social media. The phenomenon under consideration is characterized by a sense of unease and concern that is experienced by individuals who perceive themselves as being deprived of potentially beneficial experiences that others may be enjoying. FOMO is a result of individuals' desire to maintain social connections with their peers and stay informed about the latest developments, news, and trends. Social media platforms have been instrumental in contributing to the sensation of FOMO among their users. The continuous influx of updates from various sources such as acquaintances, relatives, celebrities, social media personalities, and unknown individuals can generate a perception of ceaseless engagement and stimulation. This perception may result in increased levels of anxiety among individuals who perceive themselves as being excluded or left behind.

Empirical studies have demonstrated a noteworthy correlation between extensive engagement with social media and heightened feelings of loneliness (Primack et al., 2017). Notably, research findings have indicated that augmented technology usage can detrimentally impact the mental well-being of adolescents (Przybylski & Weinstein, 2017). Moreover, excessive utilization of social media platforms has been associated with elevated rates of depression among young adults in the United States (Lin et al., 2016). These discoveries highlight the potential negative consequences of excessive social media usage on individuals' psychological health, emphasizing the need for further examination of the intricate relationship between technology, social media, and mental well-being.

In order to comprehend the intricate dynamics underlying FOMOphobia, it is imperative to explore the psychological motivators that drive this phenomenon. Understanding this link is essential to understanding the possible effects of OTT media on the mental health and general wellbeing of social media users. The uniqueness of this chapter derives from its comprehensive framework that considers the interplay between social comparison, self-esteem, and anxiety as catalysts for both FOMOphobia and OTT media consumption. The outcomes of this investigation will contribute to a more comprehensive understanding of FOMOphobia and establish a foundation for developing interventions and strategies to promote healthier media habits and alleviate the negative effects associated with excessive OTT media consumption.

2. THEORETICAL BACKGROUND

The prominence of social media and the accessibility of OTT platforms have resulted in an increase in behaviour driven by FOMOphobia, the fear of missing out in connection to excessive consumption of OTT media, marking it as an emergent concept in the digital era. Comprehending the impact of FOMOphobia on individuals' well-being and media consumption habits necessitates a comprehensive understanding of the psychological drivers that underlie this phenomenon.

2.1 Individuals' Psychological Well-Being and The Fear of Missing Out

The link between the utilization of social media platforms and individuals' psychological well-being has garnered significant attention among researchers in the recent past. The relationship between the utilization of social media platforms and mental health outcomes is multifaceted. Several research studies have indicated that the utilization of social media platforms may have detrimental impacts on individuals' mental well-being. Conversely, an opposing viewpoint posits that social media usage can yield beneficial outcomes. Analysis indicated that an excessive use of social media platforms has the potential to result in heightened levels of anxiety and depression (Keles et al., 2019; Iqbal et al., 2022; Ulvi et al., 2022). An elevated prevalence of social media usage was also found to be correlated with heightened susceptibility to feelings of isolation and self-harm (Twenge et al., 2018; Sadagheyani & Tatari, 2020). Contrary to negative perceptions, several studies have highlighted the potential positive impacts of social media on mental health. One study revealed that social media usage can foster social connectedness and alleviate loneliness (Lin et al., 2020). Similarly, another study demonstrated that engaging with social media platforms can enhance positive emotions and overall well-being (Popat & Tarrant, 2022).

FOMOphobia, a form of anxiety characterized by the fear of missing out on exciting or interesting events occurring in alternative locations, frequently triggered by social media posts, has been associated with heightened levels of media consumption. A few investigations have indicated that individuals exhibiting elevated levels of FOMO tend to exhibit a higher tendency for utilizing social media platforms, subsequently resulting in increased levels of excessive and obsessive use of OTT media content (Przybylski et al., 2013; Elhai et al., 2016; Dhir et al., 2018; Abi-Jaoude et al., 2020; Gori et al., 2023). FOMO is seen as a significant predictor of individuals' daily media use (Eitan & Gazit, 2023). Thus this phenomenon of FOMO significantly influences individuals' level of involvement with OTT platforms and their patterns of media consumption. Individual differences may also exert an influence on the impact of FOMO on OTT media consumption (Hamutoglu et al., 2020). One relevant study explored the role of personality traits in the relationship between FOMO and OTT media consumption. The researchers discovered that individuals exhibiting high levels of extraversion and neuroticism were more prone to experiencing FOMO and engaging in excessive OTT media consumption as a means of coping. This implies that the influence of FOMO on media consumption habits may be influenced by individual personality traits.

2.2 Social Comparison and FOMOphobia

Individuals ascertain their own social and personal worth by comparing themselves to others.

According to social comparison theory, individuals possess an intrinsic motivation to acquire precise self-assessments through the process of comparing themselves to others (Festinger, 1954). This phenomenon is also observed in the realm of media consumption, wherein individuals make choices regarding their preferred television shows or media content based on their perception of others' preferences and enjoyment. Social media platforms, by their very nature, facilitate social comparison. The findings of a study indicated an association between passive engagement with social media, specifically the act of scrolling through others' posts, and heightened social comparison tendencies, as well as a decline in overall well-being (Verduyn et al., 2017). Similarly, it was found that engaging in social comparison activities on the Facebook platform exhibited a positive correlation with heightened levels of envy, a sentiment closely linked to the phenomenon FOMO (Pradhan et al., 2023). Evidence also suggested that FOMO played a mediating role in the association between social comparison and problematic smartphone use (Valkenburg et al., 2021). It is important to note that smartphones serve as a primary device for OTT media consumption.

2.3 Self-Esteem and Media-Related Anxiety

Self-esteem is a psychological construct that plays a significant role in an individual's cognitive processes, affective experiences, and behavioral patterns. According to self-esteem theory, individuals who possess high levels of self-esteem typically exhibit a favorable perception of themselves, experience a sense of confidence in their capabilities, and possess a strong sense of self-worth. Conversely, individuals characterized by diminished self-esteem may encounter feelings of self-doubt, unfavorable self-perception, and apprehension towards rejection (Cast & Burke, 2002). FOMOphobia, which is marked by a persistent desire for connectivity and a fear of being excluded from social events or experiences, can be indicative of diminished self-esteem. Individuals exhibiting low levels of self-esteem may experience an intensified perception of exclusion and apprehension, resulting in an excessive dependence on media and OTT media consumption. Existing research indicates that individuals who possess a diminished sense of self-worth are more prone to encountering the phenomenon known as fear of missing out (Buglass et al., 2017; Uram & Skalski, 2020; Ahmed et al., 2021; Leung et al., 2021; Sekścińska & Jaworska, 2022). Moreover, it is possible that individuals who possess a higher level of self-esteem may engage in an excessive consumption of OTT media as a means of coping with negative self-perceptions and feelings of inadequacy. This behavior can further reinforce FOMOphobia, as individuals become increasingly dependent on media consumption to alleviate their fears of missing out.

The field of psychology has shown increasing interest in media-related anxiety, especially in light of the emergence of digital media and its pervasive impact on individuals' everyday experiences. This particular manifestation of anxiety is distinguished by the presence of emotions such as unease, concern, or fear that are elicited by the act of consuming media. Media-induced anxiety can arise from diverse origins, such as cyberbullying and exposure to disturbing events or content. Research has indicated that an overconsumption of media, specifically on social media platforms, has the potential to induce the FOMO, subsequently eliciting sensations of anxiety (Astleitner et al., 2023). In essence, this perception of experiencing a sense of exclusion can elicit emotions of anxiety and restlessness.

2.4 Age and Gender

The influence of age on media consumption patterns has been recognized as a noteworthy determinant. According to a study, it was observed that individuals belonging to younger age groups exhibited a greater tendency to partake in binge-watching activities on OTT platforms. This finding implies a heightened level of media consumption within this particular demographic. The aforementioned trend can be ascribed to the elevated level of digital literacy and technological proficiency observed among younger cohorts (Lim et al., 2015). Regarding gender, research has indicated that there are distinct variations in media consumption patterns between men and women. Research findings indicate that women exhibit a higher propensity for participating in social television viewing, wherein they utilize social media platforms to engage in discussions and share content related to the television programs they are currently watching (Tefertiller & Maxwell, 2018). Hence, it is possible that age and gender play a crucial role in the interaction between psychological factors in influencing individual media consumption behaviors.

While the existing literature provides valuable insights into the psychological factors that influence OTT media consumption, this investigation attempts to fill in several voids. First and foremost, the majority of studies have focused on analyzing these factors individually. There exists a necessity for conducting research that examines the interaction between psychological factors and demographic variables in shaping OTT media consumption behaviors. The conceptual model for the current investigation is represented in Figure 2 which visually illustrates the relationships between the dependent variable (FOMOphobia), independent variables (Social Comparison, Self-esteem, and Anxiety), mediating variable (OTT Media Consumption), and moderating variables (Age and Gender). Secondly, the current literature largely focuses on Western contexts. There is a lack of research exploring these phenomena in different cultural and societal contexts. This study contributes to filling this gap by examining these

Figure 2. Conceptual model

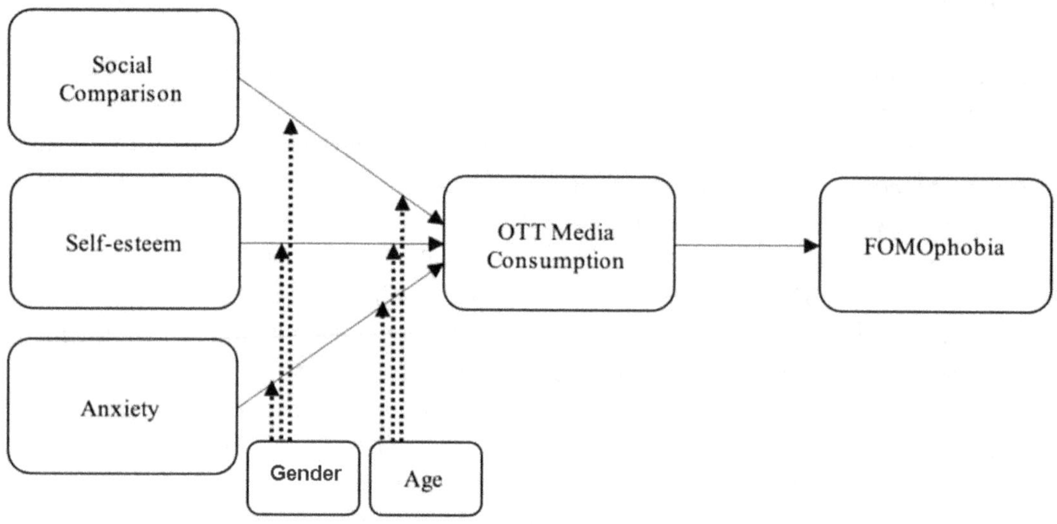

factors in a non-Western context, providing a more global perspective on OTT media consumption. By addressing these gaps, your study could contribute significantly to the literature on OTT media consumption, providing a more comprehensive and nuanced understanding of factors the driving this behavior in the era of social media.

3. RESEARCH OBJECTIVES

Firstly, it seeks to investigate how individuals perceive social comparison on social media platforms in relation to their use of OTT media platforms. This involves understanding the ways in which individuals compare themselves to others on social media in terms of the content they consume on OTT platforms. Secondly, the study aims to explore specific instances where social comparison influences participants' choice of OTT platforms or the content they watch. Additionally, the research aims to delve into the impact of seeing others' OTT media consumption experiences on social media and how it influences participants' viewing choices or preferences. It also aims to examine whether individuals feel pressure to watch certain shows or movies on OTT platforms based on others' discussions or recommendations on social media. Moreover, the research aims to explore the potential negative emotions, such as envy or dissatisfaction, that participants experience when comparing their media consumption habits to those of others on social media. It seeks to understand how these comparisons impact their self-esteem or sense of contentment. Finally, the study aims to gain insights into participants' active seeking of recommendations and opinions from others on social media before choosing content to watch on OTT platforms. It explores how this seeking behavior influences their decision-making process.

4. RESEARCH METHOD

The present investigation utilizes a qualitative research methodology, recognizing its applicability for examining modern occurrences, particularly when the contributing factors are unknown (Creswell & Creswell, 2018). This research aims to obtain a comprehensive understanding of the complex dynamics underlying the topic of FOMOphobia and its relationship with OTT media consumption by employing qualitative methods such as interviews. This methodology permits an in-depth exploration of the experiences, perceptions, and motivations of participants, casting light on the complex interplay between social comparison, self-esteem, anxiety, and media consumption in the context of social media. Through qualitative research, a deeper and more nuanced understanding of the psychological drivers of FOMOphobia can be accomplished, allowing for the development of targeted interventions and strategies to combat this phenomenon in the social media era.

4.1 Sampling and Data Collection

Purposeful sampling, which is also referred to as selective or judgmental sampling, is a research method that involves the deliberate selection of participants or cases based on specific criteria. The rationale behind selecting this approach is its pertinence in qualitative research, which endeavours to conduct a thorough investigation rather than achieving generalizability. The selection of participants was guided by specific criteria aligned with the research objectives, ensuring that individuals with relevant experiences and perspectives on FOMOphobia and OTT media consumption were included.

The determination of the sample size for semi-structured interviews is contingent upon several factors, such as the characteristics of the research phenomenon, the study's objectives with respect to the extent of coverage or comprehensiveness, and the intended level of data richness (Lakens, 2022).To identify potential participants, a preliminary screening was conducted based on characteristics including age, gender and social media engagement level. Through this procedure, individuals with probable FOMOphobia-related experiences and insights were identified. The final sample size of 26 participants was determined through iterative analysis of data saturation, where new insights and themes ceased to emerge from the interviews. Details of the research participants are provided in Table 1. Ethical considerations, such as informed consent and confidentiality, were maintained throughout the sampling process and data collection.

Open-ended interviews can yield rich and contextual data, thereby facilitating a comprehensive understanding of the psychological drivers and impacts associated with this emerging phenomenon and hence was chosen as the primary method of data collection for this study. The interview protocol was designed to elicit participants' experiences, emotions, beliefs, and behaviours related to FOMOphobia and OTT media consumption. Key topics that were explored included perceived social comparison on social media, self-esteem implications, anxiety triggers, coping mechanisms, and media consumption habits.

Participants were contacted through email with an overview of the research's principal goal and a request to participate in a 35-minute screen-recorded interview on Zoom. This ensured that their responses were accurately captured and during the interviews, detailed notes were also taken to complement the video recordings. The interviews were conducted in English and were semi-structured; a portion of the queries were designed to elicit an unbiased perspective from the participant, whereas other questions

Table 1. Research participants

Participant	Age Range	Gender	Qualification	Occupation	State of Residence
1	25	Male	Bachelor's	Software	Kerala
2	30	Female	Master's	Marketing	Delhi
3	22	Male	Bachelor's	Student	Karnataka
4	35	Female	Doctorate	Professor	Tamil Nadu
5	28	Male	Master's	Finance	Uttar Pradesh
6	40	Female	Bachelor's	Entrepreneur	Maharashtra
7	29	Male	Master's	IT	Gujarat
8	33	Female	Doctorate	Researcher	Maharashtra
9	26	Male	Bachelor's	Sales	West Bengal
10	31	Female	Master's	HR	Kerala
11	27	Male	Bachelor's	Media	Karnataka
12	29	Female	Master's	Designer	Delhi
13	23	Male	Bachelor's	Student	Tamil Nadu
14	36	Female	Doctorate	Psychologist	Maharashtra
15	24	Male	Master's	Consultant	Uttar Pradesh
16	42	Female	Bachelor's	Writer	Maharashtra
17	28	Male	Master's	Engineer	Karnataka
18	32	Female	Doctorate	Scientist	Tamil Nadu
19	25	Male	Bachelor's	Entrepreneur	Delhi
20	30	Female	Master's	Marketing	Maharashtra
21	21	Male	Bachelor's	Student	Karnataka
22	34	Female	Doctorate	Professor	Gujarat
23	27	Male	Master's	Finance	Maharashtra
24	39	Female	Bachelor's	Entrepreneur	Uttar Pradesh
25	29	Male	Master's	IT	Kerala
26	37	Female	Doctorate	Researcher	Tamil Nadu

sought for a more comprehensive response. During the initial phase of the interview, participants were queried regarding their personal background details. Subsequently, the participants' utilization of social media platforms was examined. Table 2 represents the social media usage habits of the 26 participants of the study. It includes the platforms they use, the frequency of use (e.g., daily, several times a week, once a week), and the average time spent on social media per day (in hours). The data indicates a diverse range of social media engagement patterns among the participants, characterized by varying levels of time spent and utilization of multiple platforms. Some individuals exhibit higher levels of engagement, spending more time and utilizing multiple platforms, while others demonstrate lower frequency and limited usage of platforms. The participants typically exhibited regular involvement with social media, either on a daily basis or multiple times per week, allocating an average of 2-4 hours per day to this activity. Instagram and Facebook were observed to be the most commonly utilized social media platforms, with

Table 2. Participants' social media usage habits

Participant	Social Media Platforms Used	Frequency of Use	Time Spent on Social Media (hours/day)
1	Facebook, Instagram	Daily	2
2	Twitter, LinkedIn	Several times/week	1.5
3	Instagram, Facebook	Daily	3
4	Snapchat, Facebook	Once a week	1
5	Instagram, LinkedIn	Several times/week	2.5
6	Facebook, Twitter	Daily	4
7	Instagram, LinkedIn	Several times/week	1.5
8	Twitter, Facebook	Daily	2.5
9	Snapchat, Instagram	Once a week	1.5
10	Facebook, LinkedIn	Several times/week	3.5
11	Instagram, Facebook	Daily	2.5
12	Twitter, LinkedIn	Several times/week	1
13	Instagram, Facebook	Daily	4
14	Snapchat, YouTube	Once a week	2.5
15	Facebook, Instagram	Several times/week	1.5
16	Twitter, Facebook	Daily	3
17	Instagram, LinkedIn	Several times/week	2
18	Snapchat, Facebook	Once a week	1.5
19	Instagram, LinkedIn	Several times/week	2.5
20	Facebook, Twitter	Daily	4
21	Instagram, LinkedIn	Several times/week	1.5
22	Snapchat, Facebook	Daily	3
23	Instagram, Facebook	Several times/week	2
24	Twitter, YouTube	Once a week	1.5
25	Instagram, LinkedIn	Several times/week	3
26	Snapchat, Facebook	Daily	2.5

LinkedIn and Twitter following suit in terms of popularity. Snapchat and YouTube experience reduced levels of usage.

The participants were also questioned regarding their previous media consumption patterns, including their favored genres, frequency of media consumption (such as daily, multiple times a week, or once a week), and their preferred over-the-top (OTT) platforms for content consumption. The analysis uncovers a wide array of genre inclinations, encompassing drama, comedy, action, thriller, fantasy, romance, documentary, and additional genres. The participants exhibit a consistent consumption pattern by regularly engaging with media content either on a daily basis or multiple times per week. OTT platforms such as Nctflix, Amazon Prime Video, Hotstar, YouTube, and SonyLIV are commonly cited as favored options. The evidence seen in Table 3 indicates that participants possess a diverse array of options and

Table 3. Participants' prior media consumption habits

Participant	Preferred Genres	Frequency of Media Consumption	Preferred OTT Platforms
1	Drama, Comedy	Daily	Netflix, Amazon Prime Video, Voot, MX Player, YouTube
2	Action, Thriller	Several times/week	Hotstar, SonyLIV, MX Player
3	Action, Fantasy	Daily	Netflix, Hotstar, ZEE5, YouTube
4	Documentary, Romance	Once a week	Amazon Prime Video, Netflix, MX Player
5	Comedy, Animation	Several times/week	JioCinema, SonyLIV, YouTube
6	Drama, Romance	Daily	Netflix, Amazon Prime Video, ZEE5
7	Thriller, Crime	Several times/week	Hotstar, Netflix, Voot, YouTube
8	Action, Adventure	Daily	JioCinema, Amazon Prime Video,
9	Comedy, Drama	Once a week	SonyLIV, Netflix, MX Player, YouTube, Hotstar,
10	Fantasy, Sci-Fi	Several times/week	Netflix, Hotstar, YouTube
11	Thriller, Comedy	Daily	Netflix, SonyLIV, ZEE5
12	Mystery, Thriller	Several times/week	Amazon Prime Video, Netflix, MX Player, YouTube
13	Comedy, Drama	Daily	Netflix, JioCinema, YouTube
14	Documentary, History	Once a week	SonyLIV, Amazon Prime Video, Hotstar, MX Player
15	Action, Adventure	Several times/week	Netflix, JioCinema, YouTube
16	Drama, Fantasy	Daily	Hotstar, Netflix, YouTube
17	Thriller, Crime	Several times/week	SonyLIV, YouTube, Netflix, ZEE5, MX Player
18	Comedy, Adventure	Once a week	JioCinema, Amazon Prime Video
19	Thriller, Drama	Several times/week	YouTube, Netflix, SonyLIV
20	Fantasy, Sci-Fi	Daily	Hotstar, Netflix, MX Player
21	Comedy, Drama	Several times/week	Netflix, SonyLIV, Voot, YouTube
22	Mystery, Thriller	Daily	Amazon Prime Video, YouTube
23	Drama, Sci-Fi	Several times/week	Netflix, Hotstar, MX Player, YouTube
24	Action, Adventure	Once a week	JioCinema, Amazon Prime Video,
25	Comedy, Thriller	Several times/week	SonyLIV, Netflix, MX Player
26	Romance, Mystery	Daily	Hotstar, Netflix, Voot

platforms for accessing their preferred genres, thereby highlighting the existence of a heterogeneous media landscape and diverse viewing habits among the participants.

In the next phase of the interview, the participant's comprehension and encounters pertaining to FOMOphobia were probed at. In particular their sentiments and emotions associated with the fear of missing out on media experiences and investigating how FOMOphobia influences their decisions and behaviors regarding OTT media consumption. The interview also delved into participants' perceptions and interpretations of content shared by others on social media and its impact on their self-perception, specifically exploring the concepts of social comparison and social media. Furthermore, the discussion examined the potential impact of FOMOphobia on individuals' self-esteem and sense of value. Instances where FOMOphobia led to heightened anxiety or worries were also discussed. Participants were invited to share their coping mechanisms for managing anxiety related to media consumption. Additionally, participants had the opportunity to contribute any further thoughts, experiences, or insights related to the research topic. The interview guideline functioned as a flexible framework, wherein the interviewers employed additional probing techniques and follow-up inquiries to further explore the participants' experiences and perspectives.

5. DATA ANALYSIS

The Zoom recordings underwent automatic transcription within the Zoom platform, followed by a subsequent review by the interviewer to ensure transcription accuracy. The data analysis process, as depicted in Figure 3, encompasses several sequential steps, this iterative and systematic approach guarantees the precision and dependability of the obtained findings. The researchers then immersed themselves in the data by reading and listening to interview transcripts multiple times. This phase was essential for familiarizing oneself with the content and grasping the nuanced responses of participants. The interviews were further analyzed and the data was coded using NVivo Pro software package (version 12; QSR International, Inc.; Burlington, MA, USA). The interview transcripts underwent a systematic coding procedure in order to identify significant units of data. This involved the initial assignment of codes to capture pertinent concepts and themes. Codes were devised for the purpose of illustrating distinct topics, concepts, or patterns found within the dataset. Codes that exhibit shared characteristics or represent similar ideas or concepts are classified into distinct categories.

Figure 3. Data analysis process

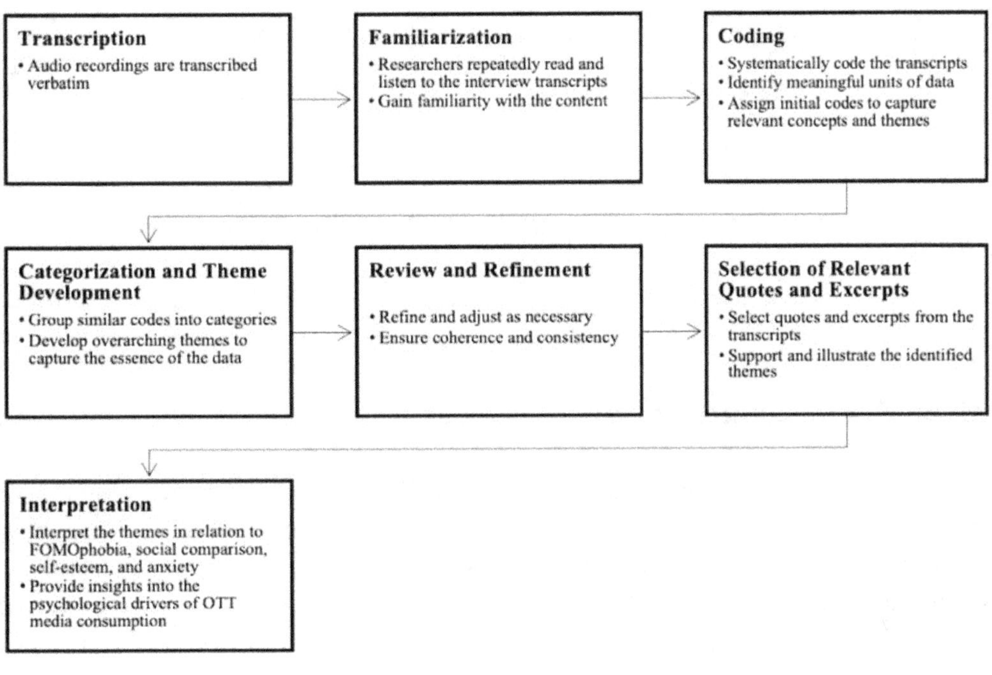

Themes subsequently emerged from these categories, reflecting the primary discoveries and trends observed. Following that, the identified themes were subjected to a process of review and refinement. The utilization of an iterative process in this study served to guarantee coherence and consistency in the identification of themes. The researchers engage in a rigorous assessment of the themes, carefully scrutinizing their relevance and congruity with the objectives of the study. Relevant quotations and excerpts from the interview transcripts are selected to support and illustrate the identified themes throughout the analysis. The final phase in the data analysis procedure entailed the interpretation of the FOMOphobia-related themes identified. The meticulous examination process guarantees that the conclusions are firmly based on the data and make a valuable addition to the current corpus of knowledge within the discipline.

6. FINDINGS

This section presents the findings that offer valuable insights into the connection between individuals' media consumption habits and their psychological well-being. The process commences with individuals being exposed to a diverse range of media content, subsequently leading to their inclination to engage in social comparisons. This comparison triggers emotional responses, including excitement, envy, dissatisfaction, insecurity, and self-doubt. These emotional reactions, in turn, impact individuals' self-esteem and anxiety levels. Those perceiving themselves as inferior to others may experience a decline in self-esteem, while the fear of missing out and anxiety arise from the pressure to conform to popular choices and avoid missing out on rewarding experiences or social interactions. Figure 4 depicts the interconnected stages and sheds light on the psychological implications of social comparison in the media context.

Figure 4. Process of social comparison and its impact on self-esteem and anxiety

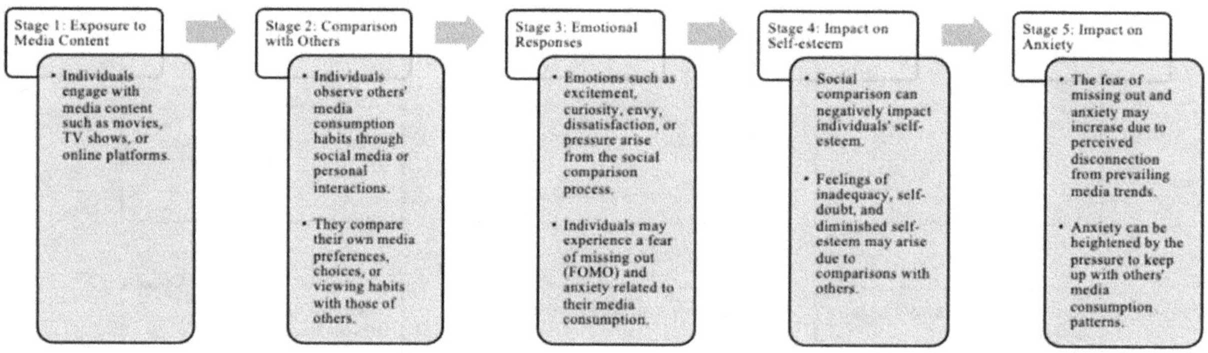

6.1 Perceived Social Comparison

In tandem with the rise of social media, the prevalence of OTT platforms for streaming movies, television programs, and other media content has increased substantially. Social media platforms have granted individuals with unparalleled opportunities to gain access to the lives and experiences of others. The continuous exposure to carefully selected portrayals of others' lives can result in an elevated perception of social comparison. Individuals frequently engage in the practice of comparing different facets of their existence, such as their patterns of media consumption, with those of their acquaintances, companions, and influential figures whom they actively follow.

Majority of the participants admitted that social media platforms frequently function as a breeding ground for the occurrence of social comparison. They described how they constantly compare themselves to others in terms of the content they consume on OTT platforms. This comparison encompasses factors such as popular shows or movies, genres, and viewing habits. In their reflections, the participants utilized phrases such as:

"I see people posting about their binge-watching sessions and it makes me feel like I should be watching more too. It creates this pressure to keep up with the trends and not miss out on what everyone else is talking about."(Participant 13)

"I've realized that social media promotes a certain kind of information that I should watch. When I see celebrities or close friends recommending a show, I often feel driven to follow the trend, even if it's not something I normally like."(Participant 21)

"What people find to be 'excellent' or 'popular' I'm more inclined to give the program or movie a go if there's a lot of talk about it online."(Participant 6)

When participants saw others sharing their OTT media consumption experiences on social media, they experienced various emotions. Certain individuals experienced a sense of excitement and curiosity, whereas others expressed sentiments of envy or dissatisfaction. The following excerpts from the interview underscore the emotional states expressed by the participants, including sentiments of envy, the influence of recommendations and discussions on social media, and the pressure to watch certain shows or movies due to the fear of missing out:

"If I see people raving about a particular show or movie, it piques my interest, I feel excited and I'm more likely to give it a try."(Participant 2)

"When I see others sharing on social media, it sometimes makes me feel a bit envious. I start questioning my own choices and wonder if I'm missing out on something better." (Participant 18)

"I have definitely felt the pressure to watch certain shows or movies on OTT platforms because they were trending or highly popular on social media. It made me curious and created a fear of missing out on the cultural conversation surrounding those media choices."(Participant 26)

The word cloud as seen in Figure 5 visually represents the emotions expressed by participants when discussing their experiences with social media and media consumption. The larger and bolder words in the cloud indicate the emotions that were more frequently mentioned. The analysis of the word cloud reveals that participants commonly expressed emotions such as envy, dissatisfaction, pressure, fear, anxiety, and stress. These emotions reflect the complex psychological dynamics at play, highlighting the potential impact on individuals' well-being and highlighting the need for further exploration and understanding of these experiences.

Figure 5. Emotional expression word cloud

A number of participants demonstrated a proclivity for actively seeking recommendations or opinions from others on social media platforms prior to making decisions regarding the content they consume. By actively seeking recommendations, participants hoped to discover new shows, movies, or genres that were popular or well-regarded by their social media peers: *"I always check what others are saying on social media before I decide what to watch on Netflix. If a show or movie is getting a lot of positive buzz and people are raving about it, I'm more likely to give it a try. I don't want to miss out on something everyone else is enjoying." (Participant 22).* Another participant revealed *"I follow a few influencers on Instagram who are really into movies and series. Whenever they recommend something, I take it as a cue to check it out. It's like having my own personalized guide to what's worth watching."(Participant 12).*

The participants believed that by aligning their decisions with those of others, they would make more informed decisions and avoid disappointment. This behaviour demonstrates the significance of social media as a platform for gathering insights and opinions about media content and the power of social comparison.

6.2 Self-Esteem

Self-esteem is a person's comprehensive evaluation and perception of their own value. It involves a person's beliefs regarding their abilities, worth, and significance. High self-esteem is characterized by a positive self-image, confidence in one's abilities, and self-acceptance. Individuals with low self-esteem, on the other hand, may struggle with self-doubt, a negative self-perception, and a lack of confidence in their abilities. The outcomes demonstrate that there exists a noteworthy association between social media usage and the evaluation of media consumption on OTT platforms, and the subsequent effect on individuals' self-esteem. Numerous participants conveyed sentiments of inadequacy, self-doubt, and diminished self-esteem when comparing their media preferences with those of their peers. The individuals' feelings of insecurity were made worse by the societal pressure to consume specific television shows or films, which was influenced by social media and driven by the fear of missing out. Several participants expressed as seen below an uncertainty regarding their own judgment and preferences in media, experiencing a desire for external validation, and questioning their level of knowledge or level of being "in the know:

"There was this one time when everyone was raving about a new series on an OTT platform. I felt compelled to watch it just so I could join in the conversations and not feel left out."(Participant 4).

"Sometimes I feel overwhelmed by the constant bombardment of recommendations and opinions on social media. It can be hard to filter through all the noise and find what genuinely interests me without feeling influenced by others."(Participant 6).

Interestingly, a small subset of participants voiced that they emphasized the importance of prioritizing their own preferences and interests over societal expectations. As revealed by one of the participants "*When I find myself judging myself or others based on the media they consume, I try to take a step back and remember that everyone's tastes are different. The most important thing is that I am happy and fulfilled with the media I consume."(Participant 20).* In the same vein, another noted "*I try to focus on the enjoyment I derive from the content I watch rather than how it compares to what others are watching."(Participant 14).* Thus a few emphasized the importance of prioritizing their own preferences and interests over societal expectations. By focusing on the enjoyment and personal value they derived from the content they watched, they were able to boost their self-esteem and maintain a positive outlook on their media consumption habits.

6.3 Anxiety and FOMOphobia

FOMOphobia, also known as the fear of missing out, is a psychological phenomenon that entails the experience of anxiety or apprehension when an individual perceives themselves as being deprived of rewarding experiences or opportunities in comparison to others. The participants articulated their encounter with a sense of obligation to consume specific television shows or films, driven by the apprehension of being excluded from conversations, regardless of whether these choices were congruent with their individual tastes. This pressure led to a persistent state of concern regarding the lack of alignment with others' media consumption patterns, thereby intensifying their fear of missing out (FOMOphobia) and anxiety. This perspective is widely held among the participants:

"Seeing others on social media discussing or recommending shows I haven't seen increases my anxiety. I feel a sense of urgency to catch up and be a part of the conversation."(Participant 1).

"Sometimes I find myself rushing through a series just to keep up with the conversation. I feel this pressure to watch it all quickly, and that anxiety can take away the enjoyment of the content. It's like I'm always in a race against time."(Participant 10).

"I remember feeling a knot in my stomach when a highly anticipated season of a popular show was released. Everyone was discussing it on social media, and I hadn't even caught up on the previous seasons. The fear of spoilers and not being able to join in on the excitement made me anxious."(Participant 24).

The manifestations of heightened anxiety or worries resulting from FOMOphobia can vary among individuals. Anxiety may be elicited in individuals upon encountering social media discussions or recommendations pertaining to popular shows or movies that they have not yet viewed. Individuals express concerns regarding their exclusion from conversations or their perceived disconnection from prevailing trends. The prevalent culture of binge-watching on OTT platforms has the potential to contribute to the development of FOMOphobia. Individuals may experience a sense of obligation to consume substantial quantities of content within a limited timeframe in order to remain informed and current. One of the participants claimed that *"Seeing people talk about how they finished an entire series in one weekend or discussing plot twists and cliff-hangers creates a sense of urgency in me."(Participant 3).* This type of pressure has the potential to result in increased levels of anxiety and a persistent apprehension regarding one's ability to keep pace with others. The observation was made that individuals may experience feelings of inadequacy when they perceive that others possess greater knowledge of current shows or trends on OTT platforms. This fear of making inadequate choices in their media consumption can generate anxiety and worry about not being "in the know."

When it comes to choosing what to watch, FOMOphobia can lead to impulsive decision-making. Individuals may feel compelled to watch a show or movie simply because others are talking about it, even if it doesn't align with their personal preferences. This can cause anxiety and regret if the content doesn't meet their expectations. The vast amount of content available on OTT platforms can trigger anxiety. Individuals may worry about making the "wrong" choice or missing out on hidden gems amidst the sea of options. This can create a sense of pressure and decision paralysis.

6.4 Age and Gender

Participants' preferred genres and frequency of media consumption varied across different age groups. Younger participants, particularly those in their early twenties, showed a preference for genres such as action, fantasy, and comedy. Older participants, on the other hand, leaned towards genres like drama and documentary. The frequency of media consumption also differed, with younger participants engaging in daily or several times a week, while older participants consumed media once a week. Gender differences were observed in participants' preferred genres and OTT platform usage. Male participants tended to favor action, thriller, and adventure genres, while female participants showed a preference for comedy, drama, and romance. The choice of OTT platforms also varied, with males leaning towards Netflix and Amazon Prime Video, and females favoring platforms like Hotstar and SonyLIV.

Results showed that younger participants, particularly those in their early twenties, were more susceptible to perceived social comparison on social media. They expressed a higher tendency to compare themselves to others in terms of the content they consume on OTT platforms. In contrast, older participants appeared to have a more balanced perspective and were less affected by social comparison. Another finding was that female participants showed a higher likelihood of experiencing negative emotions, such as envy or dissatisfaction, when comparing their media consumption habits to those of others on social media. This had a potential impact on their self-esteem. In contrast, male participants exhibited a relatively lower impact on self-esteem, suggesting that gender can influence the emotional implications of social comparison. Younger participants, especially those in their early twenties, reported a higher level of anxiety related to media consumption. They often felt a fear of missing out on rewarding experiences or opportunities compared to others. This heightened anxiety was associated with the rapid pace of content consumption and the desire to stay up to date with popular shows and trends. These insights highlight the nuanced relationships that exists, understanding these dynamics can contribute to the development of targeted interventions and strategies to mitigate the potential negative effects and promote healthy media consumption habits.

7. DISCUSSION AND IMPLICATIONS

The findings presented in the previous section shed light on the relationship between individuals' media consumption habits and their psychological well-being, specifically in terms of perceived social comparison, self-esteem, anxiety, and FOMOphobia. This discussion section will further explore these findings and provide insights into their implications. The prevalence of social media and the rise of OTT platforms have significantly influenced individuals' perception of social comparison. The results suggest that social media platforms frequently facilitate the emergence of social comparison, as individuals engage in comparing their patterns of media consumption with those of others. This comparison includes factors such as popular shows or movies, genres, and viewing habits. The participants revealed that they feel pressure to keep up with the trends and not miss out on what everyone else is talking about. A plethora of research has identified that people experience a wide range of emotions when they see others sharing their media consumption experiences (Matrix, 2014; Gupta & Singharia, 2021; Yue et al., 2022; Masciantonio et al., 2023; Periaiya & Nandukrishna, 2023). Participants expressed emotions ranging from excitement and curiosity to envy and dissatisfaction when seeing others share their OTT media consumption experiences on social media. This suggests that social media plays a crucial role in shaping individuals' perceptions of what they should be watching and the fear of missing out on culturally relevant content. The available evidence supports this assertion that social media plays a pivotal role in influencing individuals' perceptions regarding their viewing preferences and the apprehension associated with potential experiences of exclusion (Knobloch-Westerwick, 2014; Adams et al., 2016; Beyens et al., 2016; Burnell et al., 2019; Barry & Wong, 2020; Schmuck, 2021; Mundel et al., 2023). In addition, it was observed that individuals actively sought recommendations and sought the opinions of others on social media platforms prior to making informed decisions regarding the content they choose to consume. This behavior highlights the significance of social media as a platform for gathering insights and opinions about media content and emphasizes the power of social comparison in shaping individuals' choices.

The outcomes suggest a noteworthy correlation between the utilization of social media, assessment of media consumption on OTT platforms, and an individual's self-esteem. Several studies have revealed that excessive consumption can negatively affect self-esteem due to the constant exposure (Appel et al., 2016; Jang et al., 2018; Tandon et al., 2021; Faminiano & Yango, 2023; Sharma et al., 2023) .Participants expressed feelings of inadequacy, self-doubt, and diminished self-esteem when comparing their media preferences with those of their peers. The pressure to consume specific television shows or films influenced by social media and driven by the fear of missing out intensified these negative emotions. Interestingly, a subset of participants emphasized the importance of prioritizing their own preferences and interests over societal expectations. By focusing on the enjoyment and personal value they derived from the content they watched, they were able to boost their self-esteem and maintain a positive outlook on their media consumption habits. This suggests that individuals who are more resilient to the influence of social comparison and prioritize their own preferences may experience higher self-esteem.

FOMOphobia, or the fear of missing out, is a prevalent phenomenon among individuals who engage in media consumption (Tefertiller et al., 2019; Zhang et al., 2020; Hayran & Anik, 2021; Li et al., 2021;

Sadana & Sharma, 2021; Nata et al., 2022). Participants expressed a sense of obligation to consume specific shows or movies driven by the fear of being excluded from conversations and the anxiety of not being aligned with others' media consumption patterns. This led to a persistent state of concern and heightened anxiety regarding their ability to keep pace with others. The pressure to consume content quickly and the fear of spoilers further contributed to participants' anxiety. The vast amount of content available on OTT platforms also triggered anxiety and decision paralysis, as individuals worried about making the "wrong" choice or missing out on hidden gems.

Younger participants, particularly those in their early twenties, showed a higher susceptibility to perceived social comparison on social media. They exhibited a higher tendency to compare themselves to others in terms of the content they consume on OTT platforms. In contrast, older participants appeared to have a more balanced perspective and were less affected by social comparison. Gender differences were also observed, with male participants favoring action, thriller, and adventure genres, while female participants showed a preference for comedy, drama, and romance. Recent research has indicated that gender differences exist in the choice of OTT platforms as well suggesting that gender-specific preferences play a role in platform selection (Ghalawat et al., 2021; Nagaraj et al., 2021; Mulla, 2022)

By recognizing the impact of social comparison, fostering self-esteem based on personal preferences, and addressing FOMOphobia, individuals can develop healthier media consumption habits and protect their mental well-being in the digital age. It is crucial for individuals, as well as society as a whole, to promote a more critical and mindful approach to media consumption and to prioritize individual well-being over societal pressures and trends.

7.1 Implications For Researchers, Practitioners and Policymakers

The findings of this study hold significant relevance for researchers in the field of psychology and media studies. By shedding light on the impact of social media and FOMOphobia on individuals' psychological well-being, this study contributes to the existing body of knowledge. The identification of perceived social comparison as a common experience among participants provides a valuable starting point for further investigation into its underlying mechanisms and long-term effects. Researchers can delve deeper into understanding the role of social media platforms, content exposure, and individual characteristics in shaping social comparison processes. Furthermore, the findings regarding the link between social media usage, self-esteem, and evaluation of media consumption can inform future studies exploring the intricate relationship between media, self-perception, and psychological outcomes. Overall, this study offers valuable insights and directions for future research in the domain of social media and psychological well-being. The insights hold practical significance for professionals operating within the fields of mental health, counselling, and media literacy. The identification of specific emotions experienced by individuals during social comparison and media consumption can help practitioners tailor their interventions and support strategies accordingly. By recognizing the prevalence of negative emotions such as envy, dissatisfaction, and anxiety, practitioners can develop targeted interventions aimed at promoting emotional well-being and resilience. Additionally, the link between social media usage, self-esteem, and evaluation of media content highlights the importance of media literacy programs that empower individuals to critically evaluate and manage their media consumption. Practitioners can incorporate these findings into their practices, offering guidance and tools to help individuals navigate social media and mitigate the negative impact on their self-esteem and overall psychological well-being.

For policymakers who are interested in the welfare of individuals in the era of digital technology, the findings are significant. The identification of FOMOphobia as a significant concern suggests the need for policies and guidelines that promote healthier media habits and mitigate the anxiety associated with social media use. Policymakers can use these findings to inform the development of regulations and guidelines for social media platforms, encouraging responsible content creation and consumption. Additionally, policymakers can prioritize media literacy education in schools and community settings, equipping individuals with the necessary skills to navigate social media in a healthy and informed manner. By integrating these findings into policy initiatives, policymakers can contribute to creating a more supportive and balanced digital environment that safeguards individuals' psychological well-being.

7.2 Coping Mechanisms for Media-Related Anxiety

The psychological well-being of individuals can be negatively affected by media-related anxiety, which is influenced by factors such as perceived social comparison and FOMOphobia. Nevertheless, individuals have at their disposal various coping mechanisms that can be utilized to alleviate the impact of anxiety stemming from media exposure. The following strategies have been identified as potentially beneficial:

- Limiting media exposure: Setting boundaries on media consumption can be an effective coping mechanism. This includes establishing specific time limits or designated "media-free" periods to reduce the potential for information overload and constant exposure to social comparison triggers. Creating a balanced media diet that includes other activities, hobbies, and social interactions can also help reduce media-related anxiety.
- Self-awareness and mindfulness: Developing self-awareness about one's own triggers and emotional responses to media consumption is an important first step. Engaging in mindfulness practices, such as deep breathing, meditation, or grounding exercises, can assist individuals in maintaining present-moment awareness and effectively managing anxious thoughts and emotions that may arise during interactions with social media or media content.
- Critical media evaluation: Developing critical thinking skills and media literacy can empower individuals to evaluate media content more objectively. This involves questioning the motives behind media portrayals, understanding the impact of algorithms and media manipulation, and being mindful of the curated nature of social media. By critically evaluating media, individuals can make more informed choices and reduce the influence of social comparison on their well-being.
- Cultivating a positive mindset: Practicing positive affirmations, celebrating personal preferences and values, and reminding oneself that media consumption is a personal choice can contribute to a more positive mindset and improved self-esteem.

It is imperative to acknowledge that coping mechanisms can exhibit variability among individuals, necessitating a period of exploration to identify the most effective strategies. The utilization of various methodologies and the cultivation of self-patience are crucial factors in the process. Ultimately, the goal is to establish a healthy and balanced relationship with media that promotes well-being and reduces the negative impact of media-related anxiety.

8. FUTURE RESEARCH DIRECTIONS

Based on the findings of this study, there are several potential directions for future research that can further our understanding of the impact of social media and FOMOphobia on individuals' psychological well-being. Future research can explore the longitudinal effects of social media and FOMOphobia on individuals' mental health and well-being over an extended period of time. This could involve studying the long-term impact of social comparison, self-esteem, and anxiety on individuals' overall psychological functioning. Additionally, investigating the effectiveness of interventions and coping mechanisms specifically designed to mitigate media-related anxiety and promote healthy media consumption habits would be valuable. Moreover, exploring the influence of cultural and societal factors on individuals' susceptibility to social comparison and FOMOphobia can provide a deeper understanding of these phenomena across different contexts. Finally, examining the role of individual differences, such as personality traits and coping styles, in moderating the relationship between media consumption, social comparison, and psychological well-being would contribute to a more nuanced understanding of these complex dynamics.

9. CONCLUSION

Social media has become an indispensable element of contemporary life, transforming the way people communicate, exchange information, and view themselves and others. However, this study uncovers the darker side of this digital phenomenon, revealing the detrimental effects of social media and FOMOphobia on individuals' psychological well-being. The findings highlight the pervasive influence of social comparison, leading to negative emotions such as envy, dissatisfaction, and anxiety. The intricate relationship between social media usage, self-esteem, and evaluation of media content underscores the need for tailored interventions and media literacy programs to mitigate the adverse impact. These insights have far-reaching implications for researchers, practitioners, and policymakers, guiding future investigations, interventions, and policy initiatives aimed at fostering a healthier digital environment that protects individuals' psychological well-being. As social media continues to evolve, understanding and addressing these challenges become imperative to ensure a balanced and positive digital experience for all.

REFERENCES

Abi-Jaoude, E., Naylor, K. T., & Pignatiello, A. (2020, February 9). Smartphones, social media use and youth mental health. *Canadian Medical Association Journal, 192*(6), E136–E141. doi:10.1503/cmaj.190434 PMID:32041697

Ahmed, O., Nayeem Siddiqua, S. J., Alam, N., & Griffiths, M. D. (2021, February). The mediating role of problematic social media use in the relationship between social avoidance/distress and self-esteem. *Technology in Society, 64*, 101485. doi:10.1016/j.techsoc.2020.101485

Appel, H., Gerlach, A. L., & Crusius, J. (2016, June). The interplay between Facebook use, social comparison, envy, and depression. *Current Opinion in Psychology, 9*, 44–49. doi:10.1016/j.copsyc.2015.10.006

Barry, C. T., & Wong, M. Y. (2020, August 7). Fear of missing out (FoMO): A generational phenomenon or an individual difference? *Journal of Social and Personal Relationships*, *37*(12), 2952–2966. doi:10.1177/0265407520945394

Beyens, I., Frison, E., & Eggermont, S. (2016, November). "I don't want to miss a thing": Adolescents' fear of missing out and its relationship to adolescents' social needs, Facebook use, and Facebook related stress. *Computers in Human Behavior*, *64*, 1–8. doi:10.1016/j.chb.2016.05.083

Buglass, S. L., Binder, J. F., Betts, L. R., & Underwood, J. D. (2017, January). Motivators of online vulnerability: The impact of social network site use and FOMO. *Computers in Human Behavior*, *66*, 248–255. doi:10.1016/j.chb.2016.09.055

Burnell, K., George, M. J., Vollet, J. W., Ehrenreich, S. E., & Underwood, M. K. (2019, July 12). Passive social networking site use and well-being: The mediating roles of social comparison and the fear of missing out. *Cyberpsychology (Brno)*, *13*(3). Advance online publication. doi:10.5817/CP2019-3-5

Cast, A. D., & Burke, P. J. (2002, March 1). A Theory of Self-Esteem. *Social Forces*, *80*(3), 1041–1068. doi:10.1353/sof.2002.0003

Creswell, J. W., & Creswell, J. D. (2018, January 6). *Research Design: Qualitative, Quantitative, and Mixed Methods Approaches*.

Eitan, T., & Gazit, T. (2023, January). No social media for six hours? The emotional experience of Meta's global outage according to FoMO, JoMO and internet intensity. *Computers in Human Behavior*, *138*, 107474. doi:10.1016/j.chb.2022.107474

Elhai, J. D., Levine, J. C., Dvorak, R. D., & Hall, B. J. (2016, October). Fear of missing out, need for touch, anxiety and depression are related to problematic smartphone use. *Computers in Human Behavior*, *63*, 509–516. doi:10.1016/j.chb.2016.05.079

Faminiano, M. T., & Yango, A. R. (2023, June 9). Netflix viewing habit, grammatical competence, and academic self-efficacy of Selected Senior High School Students In Tagaytay City, Cavite. *Technium Social Sciences Journal*, *44*, 316–331. doi:10.47577/tssj.v44i1.8947

Festinger, L. (1954, May). A Theory of Social Comparison Processes. *Human Relations*, *7*(2), 117–140. doi:10.1177/001872675400700202

Ghalawat, S., Yadav, E., Kumar, M., Kumari, N., Goyal, M., Girdhar, A., & Agarwal, S. (2021). Factors Influencing Consumer's Choice of Streaming Over the top (OTT) Platforms. *Indian Journal of Extension Education*, *57*(03), 99–101. doi:10.48165/IJEE.2021.57323

Guest, G., Bunce, A., & Johnson, L. (2006, February). How Many Interviews Are Enough? *Field Methods*, *18*(1), 59–82. doi:10.1177/1525822X05279903

Gupta, G., & Singharia, K. (2021, February 1). Consumption of OTT Media Streaming in COVID-19 Lockdown: Insights from PLS Analysis. *Vision: The Journal of Business Perspective*, *25*(1), 36–46. doi:10.1177/0972262921989118

Hayran, C., & Anik, L. (2021, February 18). Well-Being and Fear of Missing Out (FOMO) on Digital Content in the Time of COVID-19: A Correlational Analysis among University Students. *International Journal of Environmental Research and Public Health, 18*(4), 1974. doi:10.3390/ijerph18041974 PMID:33670639

Iqbal, J., Asghar, M. Z., Ashraf, M. A., & Rafiq, M. (2022, July). Social Media Networking Sites Usage and Depression Among University Students During the COVID-19 Pandemic: The Mediating Roles of Social Anxiety and Loneliness. *Social Media + Society, 8*(3), 205630512211076. doi:10.1177/20563051221107633

Jang, W. E., Bucy, E. P., & Cho, J. (2018, August). Self-esteem moderates the influence of self-presentation style on Facebook users' sense of subjective well-being. *Computers in Human Behavior, 85*, 190–199. doi:10.1016/j.chb.2018.03.044

Keles, B., McCrae, N., & Grealish, A. (2019, March 21). A systematic review: The influence of social media on depression, anxiety and psychological distress in adolescents. *International Journal of Adolescence and Youth, 25*(1), 79–93. doi:10.1080/02673843.2019.1590851

Knobloch-Westerwick, S. (2014, July 14). *Choice and Preference in Media Use: Advances in Selective Exposure Theory and Research.* https://doi.org/ doi:10.1604/9780805855159

Lakens, D. (2022). Sample Size Justification. *Collabra. Psychology, 8*(1), 33267. Advance online publication. doi:10.1525/collabra.33267

Lin, L. Y., Sidani, J. E., Shensa, A., Radovic, A., Miller, E., Colditz, J. B., Hoffman, B. L., Giles, L. M., & Primack, B. A. (2016, January 19). ASSOCIATION BETWEEN SOCIAL MEDIA USE AND DEPRESSION AMONG U.S. YOUNG ADULTS. *Depression and Anxiety, 33*(4), 323–331. doi:10.1002/da.22466 PMID:26783723

Masciantonio, A., Résibois, M., Bouchat, P., & Bourguignon, D. (2023). Social Network Sites and Well-Being: Is it Only a Matter of Content? *Revue Internationale de Psychologie Sociale, 36*(1), 6. doi:10.5334/irsp.736

Matrix, S. (2014, June). The Netflix Effect: Teens, Binge Watching, and On-Demand Digital Media Trends. *Jeunesse: Young People, Texts. Cultures, 6*(1), 119–138. doi:10.3138/jeunesse.6.1.119

Mulla, T. (2022, April). Assessing the factors influencing the adoption of over-the-top streaming platforms: A literature review from 2007 to 2021. *Telematics and Informatics, 69*, 101797. doi:10.1016/j.tele.2022.101797

Mundel, J., Wan, A., & Yang, J. (2023, February 24). Processes underlying social comparison with influencers and subsequent impulsive buying: The roles of social anxiety and social media addiction. *Journal of Marketing Communications*, 1–18. doi:10.1080/13527266.2023.2183426

Nagaraj, S., Singh, S., & Yasa, V. R. (2021, May). Factors affecting consumers' willingness to subscribe to over-the-top (OTT) video streaming services in India. *Technology in Society, 65*, 101534. doi:10.1016/j.techsoc.2021.101534

Popat, A., & Tarrant, C. (2022, June 7). Exploring adolescents' perspectives on social media and mental health and well-being – A qualitative literature review. *Clinical Child Psychology and Psychiatry*, *28*(1), 323–337. doi:10.1177/13591045221092884 PMID:35670473

Pradhan, B., Kishore, K., & Gokhale, N. (2023, February 8). Social media influencers and consumer engagement: A review and future research agenda. *International Journal of Consumer Studies*, *47*(6), 2106–2130. doi:10.1111/ijcs.12901

Primack, B. A., Shensa, A., Sidani, J. E., Whaite, E. O., Lin, L. Y., Rosen, D., Colditz, J. B., Radovic, A., & Miller, E. (2017, July). Social Media Use and Perceived Social Isolation Among Young Adults in the U.S. *American Journal of Preventive Medicine*, *53*(1), 1–8. doi:10.1016/j.amepre.2017.01.010 PMID:28279545

Przybylski, A. K., Murayama, K., DeHaan, C. R., & Gladwell, V. (2013, July). Motivational, emotional, and behavioral correlates of fear of missing out. *Computers in Human Behavior*, *29*(4), 1841–1848. doi:10.1016/j.chb.2013.02.014

Przybylski, A. K., & Weinstein, N. (2017, January 13). A Large-Scale Test of the Goldilocks Hypothesis. *Psychological Science*, *28*(2), 204–215. doi:10.1177/0956797616678438 PMID:28085574

Sadagheyani, H. E., & Tatari, F. (2020, October 16). Investigating the role of social media on mental health. *Mental Health and Social Inclusion*, *25*(1), 41–51. doi:10.1108/MHSI-06-2020-0039

Sadana, M., & Sharma, D. (2021, April 8). How over-the-top (OTT) platforms engage young consumers over traditional pay television service? An analysis of changing consumer preferences and gamification. *Young Consumers*, *22*(3), 348–367. doi:10.1108/YC-10-2020-1231

Schmuck, D. (2021, September 1). Following Social Media Influencers in Early Adolescence: Fear of Missing Out, Social Well-Being and Supportive Communication with Parents. *Journal of Computer-Mediated Communication*, *26*(5), 245–264. doi:10.1093/jcmc/zmab008

Sekścińska, K., & Jaworska, D. (2022, April). Who felt blue when Facebook went down? - The role of self-esteem and FoMO in explaining people's mood in reaction to social media outage. *Personality and Individual Differences*, *188*, 111460. doi:10.1016/j.paid.2021.111460

Sharma, A., Sreen, N., & Baishya, K. (2023, June 6). Identifying gratification behind the consumption of the OTT platforms in an emerging market: A means-end theory approach. *Marketing Intelligence & Planning*, *41*(5), 593–612. doi:10.1108/MIP-12-2022-0558

Tandon, A., Dhir, A., Islam, N., Talwar, S., & Mäntymäki, M. (2021, November). Psychological and behavioral outcomes of social media-induced fear of missing out at the workplace. *Journal of Business Research*, *136*, 186–197. doi:10.1016/j.jbusres.2021.07.036

Tefertiller, A. C., & Maxwell, L. C. (2018, October 3). Depression, emotional states, and the experience of binge-watching narrative television. *Atlantic Journal of Communication*, *26*(5), 278–290. doi:10.1080/15456870.2018.1517765

Ulvi, O., Karamehic-Muratovic, A., Baghbanzadeh, M., Bashir, A., Smith, J., & Haque, U. (2022, January 11). Social Media Use and Mental Health: A Global Analysis. *Epidemiologia*, *3*(1), 11–25. doi:10.3390/epidemiologia3010002 PMID:36417264

Uram, P., & Skalski, S. (2020, December 10). Still Logged in? The Link Between Facebook Addiction, FoMO, Self-Esteem, Life Satisfaction and Loneliness in Social Media Users. *Psychological Reports*, *125*(1), 218–231. doi:10.1177/0033294120980970 PMID:33302798

Valkenburg, P. M., van Driel, I. I., & Beyens, I. (2021, December 31). The associations of active and passive social media use with well-being: A critical scoping review. *New Media & Society*, *24*(2), 530–549. doi:10.1177/14614448211065425

Verduyn, P., Ybarra, O., Résibois, M., Jonides, J., & Kross, E. (2017, January). Do Social Network Sites Enhance or Undermine Subjective Well-Being? A Critical Review. *Social Issues and Policy Review*, *11*(1), 274–302. doi:10.1111/sipr.12033

Yue, Z., Zhang, R., & Xiao, J. (2022, February). Passive social media use and psychological well-being during the COVID-19 pandemic: The role of social comparison and emotion regulation. *Computers in Human Behavior*, *127*, 107050. doi:10.1016/j.chb.2021.107050 PMID:34646057

Zhang, Z., Jiménez, F. R., & Cicala, J. E. (2020, September 13). Fear Of Missing Out Scale: A self-concept perspective. *Psychology and Marketing*, *37*(11), 1619–1634. doi:10.1002/mar.21406

KEY TERMS AND DEFINITIONS

FOMO (Fear of Missing Out): The pervasive sense of uneasiness and apprehension people feel when they think they are missing out on enjoyable experiences or chances compared to others.

FOMOphobia: The intense fear, dread, or anxiety of missing out on experiences, opportunities, or social connections amplified by social media.

Media-Related Anxiety: The emotional distress and apprehension experienced by individuals due to their media consumption habits and the fear of missing out on relevant content.

OTT Media Platforms: Digital streaming services that deliver video content over the internet directly to viewers, bypassing traditional broadcast or cable networks.

Psychological Well-Being: Nurturing the harmony between mind, emotions, and spirit to experience a state of optimal mental health and flourishing.

Self-Esteem: A person's subjective assessment of their own worth and value, including their thoughts, sentiments, and values, and how they feel about themselves.

Social Comparison: A mental process of assessing one's own worth in relation to that of others; it may lead to introspection, appraisal, and a sense of one's own place in the world.

Chapter 11
The OTT Syndrome:
Psycho-Social Impact of Binge-Watching

Aditi Singh Sharma
https://orcid.org/0000-0003-0705-8208
Amity University, Ranchi, India

ABSTRACT

OTT platform and binge-watching are the new buzzwords. Web series engage people through enticing stories and dramas. Content creators produce programs for binge-watchers. Human curiosity and the quest for instant gratification led to people watching episodes back-to-back. It is creating massive psycho-social impact. The effect can be seen mostly amongst the youth. Insomnia and eye disorders are the immediate side-effects. Long hours of isolation are creating loneliness, leading to myriad mental health issues. Students' academic performance is affected. Employers are reporting poor work performance by employees. The entire fabric of the family is getting stretched. Children are at great risk of getting exposed to things at an inappropriate age. The incidence of crimes inspired by the OTT content are being reported. Several studies and research are pointing towards severe detrimental consequences. There is an urgent need to address these issues. It is appropriate to term it OTT Syndrome.

1. INTRODUCTION

The end objective of all human endeavour is happiness. The human mind seeks happiness in all activities. Happiness for self and family is the utmost goal. The quest for happiness leads to indulgence in activities that have manifested itself in myriad ways. For eons gone by the world witnessed the emergence of several activities in the fields of art, music, culture, sports. For centuries gone by, the indulgence through physical activities was the norm across global societies. Thus people of all age groups especially the young took active participation in various activities that ultimately resulted in defining the culture of a group of people or society. Technological innovations over the past several centuries brought about significant alterations to the lives of people and the activities they indulged in.

People's pursuit for happiness and entertainment led to the development in the fields of arts and science. It led to the development of culture and sports. It led to the development of the defining characteristics

DOI: 10.4018/979-8-3693-0116-6.ch011

of a society. Although the process was gradual and slow; each society emerged with distinct identity. The exchange of ideas and culture was localized in nature. The civilizations that emerged defined the distinct characteristics.

Over the last two centuries, the developments in the fields of science and technology narrowed down the distances and eroded the barriers between societies. The development of means of travel led to cross cultural exchange of ideas and entertainment. The radio was a harbinger of a new era of entertainment that led to global exchange of ideas and provided a means of entertainment that involved a large audience. It involved the human mind and engaged people through listening and hearing. The development of the films and movies was a strong means of entertainment that could be consumed by a vast multitude of people unlike drama and theater. The emergence of television marked a significant phase that altered the way people consumed entertainment. People could now engage through the audio-visual mode from the comfort of their homes.

If there's one thing that defined families on a global scale; it was the family time spent in front of the television sets watching sitcoms, serials, sports, movies, cartoons, music channels, and news – the families would pull out the dinner trays and prep at the microwave before sitting down and spending quality time in front of the television sets for hours. Watching the latest must-see TV series is was the real pastime. It was the weekly ritual, and it was a cultural cornerstone by every means of the word. In India serials like the Ramayana, Mahabharata, Humlog garnered people's imagination and eyeballs; virtually bringing the entire nation to a standstill during the telecast hours.

The last two decades have brought about a paradigm shift in the way people indulge for entertainment. The emergence of the mobile technology has now enabled entertainment on the go. There is the added bonus of watching content whenever we want as and when desired.

The world no longer consumes digital content as a family, once a week, together around the television. Now there is content streaming across devices – mobiles, computers and televisions. Every individual member of a family is engaged on the digital content through various digital platforms and social media platforms. All this is shaping the need-it-now mindset and culture from the inside out.

1.1 OTT – Over-the-Top

OTT first appeared in the early 2000's, when internet speeds started to rapidly improve. The evolution of mobile technology from 3G to 4G and now 5G has accelerated the deep impact across the world. It has broken the generational barriers as millions of 8-to-80-year-olds are hooked onto the OTT platforms. There are now a host of OTT platforms streaming great shows and digital content. The OTT-On-The-Go is now a reality as people are compromising with the sleep hours to binge.

The video based content and its ease of access is impacting the lifestyles of the viewers. The acronym OTT stands for Over-the-Top. The term explains the new delivery method of films and television content over the internet. This content is available whenever we want, across many different devices, without the need for traditional broadcast, cable, or satellite TV providers. In simple terms, OTT streaming means paying an internet provider for internet access to watch Netflix, without paying for cable TV. OTT streaming is when premium content and a superior experience are made available by an OTT content platform, like Netflix, Disney+, Hotstar, Amazon Prime with the user not needing a cable TV subscription to watch. Because of this format, OTT content can be streamed on a variety of devices. The accessibility of OTT content is one of the many reasons it's so popular. To stream OTT, customers only need a high-speed internet connection and a connected device that supports apps or browsers. One can access OTT platforms in many ways, including via computer, phone, tablet, smart TV, or gaming console. One does not need a subscription to a TV service provider; but depending on the OTT platform, one may need a subscription to the OTT platform.

The world of video based entertainment has seen a significant transformation as a result of the spread of Smartphone based access and mobile internet connectivity. The ease of access through faster and affordable mobile internet services has led to people from all strata of society getting onboard social media and OTT platforms to view content. The world is now interconnected; unlike in the past. People from one part of the world are exposed to content from a global platform; this is impacting the social trends and culture of the society.

Mobile OTT Devices: Smartphones and tablets can download OTT apps to stream on-the go.

Personal Computers: Consumers can access OTT content from desktop-based apps or web browsers.

Connected TV Devices: The most common examples include Reliance TV, Apple TV

Game consoles: PlayStation, also often support OTT apps.

The OTT platforms have transformed the video consumption industry. People exercise the power and control over what they are watching, a convenient time to watch as per choice. The rapidly emerging technological developments are changing the way people consume online content. Netizens are in the driver's seat. Unlike other mediums of consuming video based content; consumers can find exactly what they want to watch and only pay for the content and services that they want. OTT offers the flexibility to adjust the according to the market for maximum uptake. Further, it opens the windows niche content platforms and communities to thrive.

The precursor to the OTT platforms can be the YouTube offerings. It is a social video platform that was originally designed to allow everyday consumers to share moments caught on video. YouTube has tried several times to enter the OTT market. It has met with limited success as the market clearly sees YouTube as a place for free content. The accessibility of OTT content is one of the many reasons it's so popular.

OTT is the ultimate platform for reaching the targeted audience directly with content and delivering a premium video experience that is under control entirely. With OTT, providers can get immediate user feedback through direct engagement and interaction.

With the advent and subsequent popularity of OTT, cable companies are getting the short end of the stick when it comes to new opportunities, and the demand for content is merely pushing these companies to consider different ways to market and deliver. Cable providers are still in the mix since many are providing internet services, and the main TV channel networks aren't giving up their broadcast streams, they're just also going after the OTT audience with digital streaming through apps, platforms, and more. Not only has OTT streaming changed the way we get television, but it's changed the way we watch it too.

OTT provides control on content, viewer experience, monetization, and most of all, data. People are often offended by ads. OTT platforms have opened up the possibility for ad-free content. This has been possible through Subscription Video-On-Demand (SVOD). SVOD involves a fixed rate monthly subscription for access to premium content. The other option is One-time purchases (TVOD). TVOD providers charge pay per view access to on demand files live streaming. There are other monetization strategies. Even if Advertising Video-On-Demand (AVOD) is the preferred model; OTT offers the mechanisms of targeted advertising. There is also the endemic content and control over the advertising and direct sponsorships. In 2022, 82% of all internet traffic came from video.

The OTT video streaming industry has registered a phenomenal growth in a very short span of time. Online video subscription sales that were around $10 billion in 2012 have crossed $50 billion. The varied formats include Subscription Video-On-Demand (SVOD) and Transactional Video-On-Demand (TVOD) services. SVOD involves a fixed rate monthly subscription for access to premium content. This is the case for services like Netflix and Disney+, where users can access curated content at any time with a monthly or yearly subscription. Some OTT platforms, like Amazon instead don't charge subscription fees to customers, instead generating revenue by showing their viewers ads while they're watching content or offering reduced-cost subscriptions with limited ads.

The recent developments have forced changes to relook at the demand for content. Instead of becoming extinct, the production houses are coming up with different ways to market and deliver. The cable providers continue to be part of the ecosystem by providing internet services.

The satellite channel networks are looking at becoming part of the OTT ecosystem by connecting to these companies and offering their services through their networks. TataPlay, Airtel TV, Reliance TV are also going after the OTT audience with digital streaming through apps. All this is possible because many people are consuming video content all the time.

The key components of the streaming channels are the content. It is the content that affects the psychology of the viewers. It leaves an indelible impact on the mind of the viewers. Producers are now in sync with the individual choices of the viewers. It is like a continuous quid pro quo between the producers and viewers. There is instant feedback available as millions of people are online through social media channels. A video can reach out to millions of people in an instant and there is news of videos going "viral". It is worth mentioning that several problems have been reportedly cropped up with issues pertaining to what is available on OTT platforms.

1.2 OTT Syndrome

The OTT syndrome can be defined as conditions that are being seen across netizens as a result of the excessive binge watching. The impact felt on physical and mental health is a major aspect of the syndrome. The syndrome can be studied in two aspects that characterize netizens.

Health Issues & Behavioural Issues

- a group of signs and symptoms that occur together and characterize a particular abnormality or condition (insomnia, physical ailments, postural issues)
- a set of concurrent things, such as emotions or actions, that usually form an identifiable pattern (loneliness, isolation, anxiety, depression)

2. LITERATURE REVIEW

There has been a rapid expansion in the way technological transformation and mobile technology has created a mass market for direct to device streaming of content. The Smartphone coupled with the fast internet services have changed the viewing habits and preferences of the end user. Internet TV, Video-on-demand (VOD) and OTT Platforms are the new norm. (Punathambekar & Kumar, 2012; Tryon, 2015).

There is a vast audience that has become accustomed to watching entertainment content through digital hand-held devices. (Laghate, 2018). The online streaming services have expanded during and in the post-COVID era. There is a significant difference that can be seen from the television and cinema halls experiences. The content is tailor made to suit the demands of the end viewers. Any study or analysis of the evolving audience and the viewing habits will have to deal with the difficult challenges. Traditional theories and approaches will need to be refined to accomplish a fair assessment. (Livingstone, 2003,2004, 2007).

The web series content provides the opportunity to experiment with flexible narrative structures. Most episodes converge at the end, creating curiosity in the minds of the viewers. There is an urgent need felt to watch the next episode. There is an urge to resolve narrative complexities. The viewer behaviour of lapping it all off in one go has given birth to the habit of watching the whole season at one time. This aspect can be known as 'binge watching'.

The television was a one way traffic which consumed peoples time and in return provided entertainment at fixed time shows. The viewing hours were limited as one had to be stationed in front of the television set to watch it. In many ways, this relationship is one-sided. The online streaming service on the other hand offers it viewers the choice of instant gratification by watching the entire episodes of a webs series in one go. (Sharma, 2016).

There has been a tremendous expansion in OTT platforms like Hotstar, Amazon Prime, Netflix, Disney+ Hotstar, have built a very large subscriber base in rural, semi-urban and urban areas. (Aadeetya, 2018). Most of these OTT platforms have captured the imagination of the netizens with global content and story lines (Joglekar, 2018).

"Internet Addiction Disorder" is a new phenomenon that is now being seen across all age groups and gender. There is a prevalence of this aspect in majority of the youth. A generation of people that grew up watching animated cartoons on television is now hooked onto the mobile based platforms. The youth are worst affected as it takes a heavy toll on their studies, their behaviour patterns, their socializing traits (Koravi, 2019).

Often times the global content exposes the impressionable minds. There are things shown that may be contrary to the ethics, values and culture of a society one is living in. This creates a conflict in the minds of the people that manifests itself in erratic behaviour patterns. (Koravi, 2019). It is of vital importance that the binge-watching leads to addiction to virtual content leading to disturbances in personal life. People acknowledge that binge-watching leads to anti-social behaviour, isolation, emotional distress and especially disturbed and inadequate sleep causing several health issues. (Dhanuka; Bohra, 2019)

Several studies have adopted a negative approach to the concept of binge viewing and its impact especially on the young people. There is a direct connect established between binge viewing and aggressive and unpleasant behaviour and emotions. The issues concerning depression, low self esteem, a dethatched behaviour, academic loss are highlighted by a number of studies and reports. Examples include (Stickney et al., 1999; Stice, Prensell, and Spangler, 2002; Sung, et al., 2005).

A lot of time is being invested in binge watching web series. The entertainment sought provided momentary pleasure. The viewers themselves negate any talk of negative effects of the new viewing experiences. The impact on academic grades and social lives is further downplayed upon by the viewers. (Peterson, 2016). Issues of sadness and loneliness were seen in most viewers. Studies further tend to highlight that watching web series and online video content on OTT platforms have affected people's attitudes, behaviour and affected social patterns across all age groups. (Sung et al., 2015). Several researches tend to indicate and suggest that excessive use of OTT platforms will ultimately affect mental health of people. OTT platforms used by students across the world have resulted in anxiety, despair, and depression symptoms. (Kircaburun and Griffiths, 2018) (Lissak and Mekler, 2019).

Several studies researched on the connection between OTT platform use and its effect on self-esteem and body image of the viewers. The impact on the impressionable minds is profound with idealized body pictures being floated on the social media including web series on the OTT platforms. (Cohen and Blaszczynski, 2015). The impact of advertising on the OTT platforms is profound and damaging for the young minds. (Fardouly et al.,2018).

Research has also been carried out over the impact of use of OTT platforms by students on their academic performance. According to a study high school students often multi-task on OTT platforms – using multiple devices at one time to view content are known to have performed poorly at academics. (Rosen et al., 2013). Further, researchers also discovered that even students attending under-graduate and post graduate programs faired poorly at academics due to the effect of excessive use of OTT based viewing and content. (Rosen et al., 2013; Rideout et al., 2019).

Several research studies have further evaluated the effect of OTT platforms on socialization and inter-personal interactions across various age groups and across all genders. According to a study, teenagers who spent a lot of time viewing content on OTT platforms had very poor face-to-face communication skills. Such people were also known to display very poor pro-social behaviour. However, according to a study in South Korea; use of OTT platforms was a positive mechanism to enhance social contact and social capital (Uhls et al., 2014; Lee and Kim, 2018).

2.1 Psycho Social Impact

OTT platforms are impacting the lives of millions of people across all age-groups and gender. It is generally perceived that the young people are more impressionable and tend to emulate behavior acquired through observations. The online streaming videos are affecting the behavior of people. It is creating a lasting and significant effect on human attitudes and social interactions. With each individual hooked on to the OTT content at a place and time convenient to them; the biggest casualty is the time available to delve into other pursuits. It has profound positive and adverse effects on the way social interactions are being carried out.

The most important aspect of web movies and web series is content. It is the content that attracts the attention of the viewers and also it is the content that leaves an impact on the minds of the viewers. The netizens are living in an age where content is available at the click of a button. It is relevant to study the factors affecting the contents of the online streaming platforms and to understand the new set of patterns of behavior of today's audiences that they are engaging in.

Further, the streaming content very rarely addresses social issues. The web series platforms are often found promoting alcoholism, smoking, tobacco, drugs, without highlighting the negative consequences. There have been several reported incidences of increase in crime "inspired" by content seen on streamed videos and web series.

Several crimes related to kidnapping, murder, assault, financial crimes, have been reported by investigations conducted by law enforcement agencies. Digital assessment of the crimes, have proven that those committing the crimes were involved in watching video content in the times prior to committing the crime.

The major side effect is being felt in the domain of personal health with untimely viewing hours leading to insomnia, obesity, and eye disorders. The content and its lack of regulation have ensured all types of videos reaching out to all age groups of viewers – the very young and old alike. Often, children are getting exposed to content that is age inappropriate.

Research has shown that there are many ways binge-watching might affect mental health. Binge-watching will increase anxiety, depression, and loneliness. Since binge-watching is a relatively new phenomenon, there hasn't been a lot of research into how it affects mental health. Some studies conducted in the developed world has established a high correlation between binge-watching and increasing negative psycho-social issues.

Other studies have found negative effects like increased fatigue, mood disturbances and insomnia. Many of these studies show correlation, rather than causation and it's easy to imagine that someone who is already depressed or anxious might spend more time binge-watching online content. There are several reasons to believe that binge-watching will negatively affect long-term mental health. More and more studies are being carried out to find out how people who binge-watch are more prone to insomnia and poorer quality sleep. The impact is being felt both in biological and psychological factors. In the long run, insomnia has been linked to a higher risk of major depression and anxiety disorders.

Biologically, the bright light from screens, especially in the blue spectrum, mimics daylight affecting quality of sleep. If one is exposed to this kind of light before bed, it may disrupt the circadian rhythm, making it harder to sleep.

Psychologically, a web series may impact the mind. The drama, tension, suspense, and action of web series lead to increase in heart rate, blood pressure, and adrenaline. When one finally tries to sleep one may feel like there has been a stressful or even mildly traumatic experience, which is not conducive to sleep. The sleep disruption takes a heavy toll on the mental health. Several studies have established that chronic and prolonged sleep deficit will quickly impair mental faculties such as attention, working memory, and emotional regulation.

Binge-watching tends to make people less physically inactive. People end up compromising on the time available for other activities. The inactivity is a pre curser to complication in physical health. Getting regular exercise or any physical activity is a critical part for keeping people happy. Health studies have established that moderate exercise improves mood by increasing levels of endorphins, serotonin, and BDNF, a neurotransmitter that grows neurons in certain parts of the brain. Physical activity creates a positive structural change in the brain that make one less vulnerable to stress and anxiety.

Binge-watching may just be a symptom of loneliness. It may also make one less likely to accept an invitation, reach out to friends, or even just leave the house. Socialization is a major casualty as people within the family are connecting with each other using social media even when they are under one roof. The social footprints is getting altered which is contrary to human nature. However, the corollary is that people cite social motivations for binge-watching. In order to make socially relevant conversations about a show with friends or colleagues people tend to engage on the OTT platforms. So in this limited way, binge-watching may have a pro-social silver lining.

In many ways, binge-watching is a double-edged sword. One may feel better while binge-watching a show. Later it might lead to feelings of significant letdown. People tend to idolize characters seen on the videos. This is emerging as an OTT Syndrome where people are displaying emotions that are leading to isolation and loneliness.

COVID-19 pandemic was the harbinger of unprecedented growth in the global OTT market. With the lockdown people were left with very few entertainment options. The only way to entertain themselves safely was in the confines of their homes with a digital device in hand. This is where OTT platforms came to the rescue. They were necessary then to alleviate loneliness and acted somewhat as a stress relief agent. But slowly and surely, even as the world came out of lockdown, the OTT market kept its hedonistic growth levels.

3. ANALYSIS AND FINDINGS

OTT platforms are completely changing the way people now consume media and entertainment. These platforms offer unmatched accessibility to other cultures, viewpoints, and genres. On-demand streaming content and the convenience of anytime anywhere viewership is a matter of debate for several reasons. The over-use of the digital media is raking up issues concerning with physical and mental health of people across all societies on a global scale.

There has been a massive spin-off on the production aspect of web series and other programs. The virtual world is creating its own content with producers being connected to the viewers. The netizens are a diversified lot with a global audience; yet most programs are able to establish a unique connect across the world.

Most content on the digital media web series are fresh with new concepts. There is lot of innovation and presentation style with and unique themes. The video on demand industry has evolved in the highly competitive digital market. They are also are being able to catch and retain the attention of the target audiences. The shows are completely different and most of the web series are psychologically appealing.

Priority is given to women centric plot development. Women are being portrayed in much dignified, progressive and realistic manner. The global audience has been exposed to content from across the world. Most realistic web series reflect on contemporary socio political aspects. The issues of economic exploitations and prevailing injustice based on caste, creed and gender are being covered more and more. Entertainment is provided along with strong theme. Various genres are getting covered by the web series and web movies,

The rapid expansion of the OTT services has transformed the video consumption industry. People are now experiencing a level of control never seen before. The platforms have a large fan base and strong subscriptions even is rural and remote areas. Smartphones and affordable internet on mobile is transforming the global digital world. Emerging Technology has changed the way people consume online content. Viewers are able to orchestrate their own viewing in terms of time, content, location, and devices used. The popularity of Internet distributed OTT services, together with the production of more innovative stories, have contributed to the popularization of a specific habit of viewing among audiences – 'binge-watching'. The contents streamed on the OTT platforms blends culture with strong storylines. The aid of technology helps attract a large number of viewers. Online platforms are interactive in nature, making them more popular among netizens, unlike their television or film counterpart, where viewers were mostly passive audiences.

The society is waking up to the issues being raised and its impact due to the inordinately excessive screen time. According to research, excessive screen time may have a detrimental psychological impact on a person's sleep, physical activity, anxiety, and loneliness. Viewers mostly watch the streamed content on mobile devices at an individual level. There is complete detachment to the world around. This is leading to lack of socialization and people getting isolated even within large families; as each member of the family is hooked onto their own OTT platform.

Children and young adults at the school and college going age are empowered with by smartphones. This was a result of the disruption due to the Covid pandemic. Education Technology companies offered a solution through learning on the digital platforms. Millions of families adopted the digital offerings in order to regulate and continue their child's education. It became easy and convenient for institutions to transmit education through the digital media platforms. A couple of years down the line the world is now waking up to the flip side of the coin. One issue of grave concern is the matter of age inappropriate viewership as the OTT platforms cannot filter out viewers on the basis of age.

Parents and guardians are burdened with the added responsibility to restrict smartphone use and screen time. This is leading to lot of behavioural issues and abnormal behaviour among young adults. There is a need to promote outdoor physical activity, and encourage social exchanges and interactions. The old world charm of the family investing time together in front of the television screens or going out to watch movies to a cinema hall is being lost. Time is at a premium and people are getting anxious and feeling left out of the game. All this has serious ramifications on the overall mental health of the individuals.

It can be concluded that the content on the OTT platforms have a deep impact on the psychology of the viewers. The viewers tend to identify with the characters and even end up aping them. The surrogate advertisements in the web series and web movies often tend to create unwanted desires that ultimately lead to frustration and depression.

3.1 Research Gap

Several studies are being undertaken at an academic level as well as at the research level on the usage trends and psychological implications of OTT platforms. There is still a sizable knowledge vacuum about the psycho social impact these platforms have on the viewers, especially the affect on young adults. More empirical research is required to examine the connection between the use of OTT platforms and outcomes related to mental health. Matters related to addiction, anxiety and depression are to be evaluated on a more detailed note. Further, there is need to carry out more study to determine the possible therapies and mitigation techniques for the detrimental psychological impacts due to OTT platform usage.

This topic involves multiple areas of research. It is significant to understand the media usage patterns and its impact on the viewers both psychologically and socially. The audience centric framework can be studied on the basis of viewing and gratification models. People use media for their entertainment. The behavior of the individual or a group of similar individuals can help in explaining and extrapolating the findings to study the psycho social impact. This will help in explaining how the media and content can be a source of influence on the audiences.

In the above chapter the discovery was made that a lot of people have various opinions regarding OTT platforms. One realizes the platform has given access to such a wide range of information to many people, in multiple areas. Most people are of the opinion that the OTT platforms are here to stay and will play a significant role in moulding the psycho social behavior of people in the society.

4. CONCLUSION

The OTT Syndrome is well and truly evident now. There are several aspects to this syndrome that are now identifiable. In the first place netizens are experiencing various physical and psycho-social impact of binge watching. There is the evidence of psychological aspects being felt amongst the youth especially. The aspects pertaining to behaviour – anxiety, stress and loneliness are being reported. Further, the impact felt on the family and society is profound. People are connected to each other on the digital platforms and social media. The need for physical socialization is eroding across all age groups. All this is affecting the socialization skills of the millennial kids. The development of the individual as a well rounded personality is definitely a major aspect of worry. Families are feeling the pinch as each member seeks to indulge in "my time" on the digital platforms.

REFERENCES

Ahmed, M. A. & Abdel, A. (2017). *New Era of TV Watching Behavior Binge Watching and its Psychological Effects.*

Bharat, D. & Pawan, S. M. (2021). Psychosocial impact of web series and streaming content: A study on Indian youth. *Global Media Journal.* https://www.global mediajournal.com/open-access/psychosocial-impact-of-web-series-and-streaming-content-a-study-on-indian-youth.php?aid=90530#6

Cohen, R., & Blaszczynski, A. (2015). Comparative effects of Facebook and conventional media on body image dissatisfaction. *Journal of Eating Disorders, 3*(1), 1–10. doi:10.1186/s40337-015-0061-3 PMID:26140215

David, A. S. & Moe, W. (2016). Binge Watching and Advertising. *Sage Journals.* https://journals.sagepub.com/doi/10.1509/jm.15.0258

Dhanuka, A., & Bohra, A. (2019) *Binge-Watching: Web-Series Addiction amongst Youth.* RSET. https://www.rset.edu.in/download/dsims/2_Binge_Watching_Web_Series_Addiction_am ongst_Youth.pdf

Fardouly, J., Diedrichs, P. C., Vartanian, L. R., & Halliwell, E. (2018). Social comparisons on social media: The impact of Facebook on young women's body image concerns and mood. *Body Image, 26*, 38–45. PMID:25615425

Kakkar, A., & Nayak, K. (2019). Analysis of Product Placement in Web Series and its Influence on Consumer Buying Behavior. *Journal of Business.* https://journalofbusiness.org/index.php/GJMBR/article/download/2755/2656/

Kircaburun, K., & Griffiths, M. D. (2018). Instagram addiction and the Big Five of personality: The mediating role of self-liking. *Journal of Behavioral Addictions, 7*(1), 158–170. doi:10.1556/2006.7.2018.15 PMID:29461086

Lee, S. Y., & Kim, M. S. (2018). Social capital and binge-watching on over-the-top content platforms. *Journal of Broadcasting & Electronic Media, 62*(2), 276–294.

Lissak, G., & Mekler, E. D. (2019). Youth online behavior and social media use in Israel: Analysis of associations with depressive symptoms. *The Journal of Adolescent Health, 64*(3), 334–340.

Rajpal, A. (2020). Web Series: A Look into an Emerging Industry. *Youth Inc. Magazine.* https://youthincmag,com/web-series-an-emerging-industry

Rideout, V. J., Fox, S., & Roberts, D. F. (2019). Young people's news habits: Examining the role of platforms, devices, and social networks. *Journal of Computer-Mediated Communication, 24*(5), 227–239.

Seonmi, L. (2021). *Examining factors influencing early paid over-the-top video streaming market growth: A cross-country empirical study.* MDPI.

Singh, S. (2018). *A study on factors leading to the adoption of OTT services among millennial consumers in India.*

Theodore, P. (2016). to binge or not to binge: A qualitative analysis of college students' binge-watching habits. *Fla Commun J, 44*, 77–88.

Yoon, H. S. (2018). *Motivations for binge-watching measure.* PsycTESTS Dataset.

Chapter 12
The Rise of OTT:
A Dynamic Shift Towards Binge Watching, an Increase for On-Demand Entertainment

Pritesh Pradeep Somani
https://orcid.org/0000-0002-0039-0358
Balaji Institute of International Business, Sri Balaji University, Pune, India

Nitesh Behare
https://orcid.org/0000-0002-9338-8563
Balaji Institute of International Business, Sri Balaji University, Pune, India

Ushmita Gupta
https://orcid.org/0000-0002-6442-1248
Balaji Institute of International Business, Sri Balaji University, Pune, India

Rashmi Darshan Mahajan
https://orcid.org/0000-0001-9082-6874
Balaji Institute of International Business, Sri Balaji University, Pune, India

Vishwanathan Hariharan Iyer
https://orcid.org/0009-0007-1469-2369
Balaji Institute of International Business, Sri Balaji University, Pune, India

Meenakshi Singh
https://orcid.org/0009-0006-9505-8214
Balaji Institute of International Business, Sri Balaji University, Pune, India

ABSTRACT

This study examines the influence of the rise of over-the-top (OTT) platforms leading towards binge watching, thereby analyzing their effect on the health of an individual and the increased demand for on demand entertainment. Users now have uninterrupted access to all the content shown, majorly due to availability of high-speed internet and affordable subscriptions. The ability to watch entire seasons or series at once has led to many health issues in connection with binge-watching. The study further looks at how the development of OTT platforms has led to an increase in the production of original content. The study also examines the ill effects of binge watching on human health and further solutions are proposed towards reducing the influence of binge watching. The future of binge watching will be determined by examining the patterns of striking a balance between linear and on-demand models while embracing technological advancements to offer an immersive and customized viewing experience.

DOI: 10.4018/979-8-3693-0116-6.ch012

1. INTRODUCTION

"Binge-watching is a guilty pleasure that we all indulge in. It's the ultimate form of relaxation and entertainment" – Anonymous

More the number of choices more is the confusion a person goes through and with lot to choose in hand leads to a different level of complexity and confusion. (Mehta,2022). Today we are living in world of instant. Today's generation wants everything super quick be it their work or their entertainment they are spoilt by the ample availability of choices. Apart from the regular source of entertainment like watching serials on T.V., catching a movie in a multiplex, some series on YouTube slowly and steadily a new but vast source of entertainment is catching up especially among the young generation i.e., the Over the Top (OTT) platforms offering vast source of entertainment across different genres spreading from Comedy, Romance, Action, Dark to anything under the sky in the world of entertainment is being sold under the umbrella of O.T.T. The increase in demand for varied entertainment has given rise to different O.T.T. platforms offering wide variety of content but shortage of time and other work commitment among people has given rise to 'Binge watching' which is a new phenomenon for the Indian audience who are witnessing the O.T.T. boost for the very first time.

1.1 Introduction to Binge Watching

(Boni, et al.,2017) The word "binge" is frequently associated with bad behaviour and is frequently used to refer to overindulgence and guilty pleasure. Binge-watching is a phenomenon that promotes sedentary behaviour, raises the risk of obesity, and disrupts healthy routines. The latest and prevalent 'binge' of society is binge-watching, which has established itself as a common way to consume media, including television and films. (Netflix Inc., 2018) Binge-viewing, which is defined as watching two to six episodes of a TV show in a single sitting, is a relatively new behavioural phenomenon. The emergence of numerous on-demand streaming platforms contributed to the rise in popularity of this activity. (Conlin, 2015) It is also important to note that binge-watching has been around for a while and is one of the old concepts and has traditionally taken the form of marathon T.V. viewing on V.H.S, D.V.D., D.V.R, or utilising the services on video on demand. In the modern world, binge-watching has become widespread, particularly among young people. The existence of various internet streaming services has increased people's propensity to consume content in big volume. Excessive binge resulted in a strong impact on mental health of person thereby resulting in severe anxiety, depression and loneliness among a person. Binge watching is also detrimental to social interactions. Long stretches in front of a screen might lead to loneliness and social isolation. Binge-watching among young people may lead to a lack of meaningful relationships and interpersonal interaction because they neglect their social lives. This results in loneliness feelings, which is a significant risk factor for depression and other mental health problems. (Yakimova, 2016) The culture of swift contentment has become prevalent today, and O.T.T. platforms have further added modern commercial angle to it. Due to the viewer's voluntary decision to watch maximum of the available content, binge-watching has become centre of attraction. Binge watching requires undivided attention of user and as a user they are aware about the time they going to put in but still they are putting that time. This results in a question given that binge-watching has become a part of their controlled routine, it begs the question of how it might damage their social welfare with others. Over and above all Wheeler (2015) stated As people come together to watch together as a group, binge-bonding sessions with peers can be a social side of binge-watching on the other hand the competitive part of binge-watching may be influenced by social pressures since people encounter them on a daily basis and sometimes it may lead to certain phenomena of FOMO (Fear of Missing out) if they are not able to express their views on certain part of discussion that may further lead to one or the other emotional damage either between their friendship or even their relationship. FOMO refers to the sense of missing a party, programme, concert, class, or other event that might cause you to be left out of a conversation or moment. (Conlin, Billings & Averset, 2016).

1.1.1 Types of Binge Watching

(Starosta, Izydorczyk and Lizińczyk, 2019) As we came across the concept of binge watching let us try to understand the different types of Binge watching. Broadly, binge watching can be divided in to six major categories namely the Classic Binger, the Thematic Binger, the Slow burner, the Social Binger, the guilty pleasure binger and the midnight Binger. Let us try to understand each one of them in detail.

1. **The Classic Binger:** This person is a original binge-watcher. They spend endless hours devoted to their screens, watching whole seasons of shows at a time. The classic binger possesses the amazing capacity to lose time and become engrossed in the narrative. They have a kick for suspense making every episode conclusion a happy moment for them.
2. **The Thematic Binger:** They like to investigate content centred on a certain genre or theme. They might go on a documentary binge or watch every superhero series on their smartphone or television sets. The fun part of this is exploring different viewpoints and stories within a selected category through a themed journey.
3. **The Slow Burner:** They are the opposite of Classic bingers. They enjoy every episode, reflecting carefully on the plot and characters. For them, quality is more important than quantity. With this method, they are in a better position to recognise the subtitles and features that they might miss during a binge-watching session.
4. **The Social Binger:** They enjoy watching marathons of series program or content with loved ones. It's a communal experience where talking, arguing, and laughing all play a crucial role in the watching process. Binge-watching of this kind fortifies relationships and produces priceless memories.
5. **The Guilty Pleasure Binger:** This kind of binge-watcher enjoys sinful things. They may be secretly fond of a corny series or a corny reality show. Even though the guilty pleasure binger is aware that the material is not sophisticated, they yet enjoy it.
6. **The Midnight Binger:** These nighttime binge-watchers find it impossible to resist staying up late to watch. Midnight viewing is enhanced by the silence and seclusion, nearly turning it into a magical ritual.

1.1.2 Motivation to Binge Watch

Cambridge Dictionary quotes Motivation refers to the enthusiasm towards the planned or unplanned activity. As far as Binge watching is concerned Pitman and Sheehan (2015) in their study quoted the real motivation behind binge watching is to effectively plan the manner in which the content can be consumed at the same time it is about watching a entire season or multiple episodes in one go. It was further found narration of the show plays a major role in keeping the audience glued to their smart phones or any other device used to stream the content. Further the peer pressure to stay updated with the latest happening also serve as a motivation towards consuming maximum content in the least possible amount of time. Students were more likely to binge-watch because of social interaction, escape from reality, ease of access to content, and the effectiveness of content providers' advertising (such as through viral content trailers). The more students binge-watch, the more likely they are to spend more time doing so in the future. (Panda and Pandey, 2017). Heaving a sigh of relaxation, feeling a sense of completeness meeting the cultural insights along with coming across the best content management experience plays a key role in motivating the viewers towards binge watching. (Steiner and Xu,2018)

2. REVIEW OF LITERATURE

There is a rapid growth in OTT services and their global reach platforms like Netflix, Amazon Prime have not only become household names but have also expanded their content libraries to cater to a diverse range of preferences. The basic reasons contributing towards success of OTT services comprise of affordability, convenience, and personalized content recommendations. (Smith,2018). There is an emergence of binge-watching as a dominant viewer habit in the age of streaming services further the need to craft engaging narratives that encourage viewers to watch "just one more episode" has reshaped the way stories are structured and paced. Johnson et al. (2019). (Jones, 2017) stated how the streaming giant has reshaped viewer habits, leading to a surge in binge-watching behaviours. He further opined Netflix's pioneering role in the rise of binge-watching. By releasing entire seasons of TV shows at once, Netflix disrupted traditional broadcasting schedules, allowing viewers to watch episodes at their own pace. OTT platforms like Netflix, Amazon Prime Video, Hulu, and Disney+ have amassed vast and diverse content libraries. They discuss how this proliferation has been driven by the need to cater to diverse viewer preferences. (Smith and Brown, 2020) further illuminated the factors driving this expansion, the effects on content creation, and the importance of content curation in the age of streaming. Johnson and White (2018) concluded how binge-watching serves as a form of escapism from the stresses and challenges of daily life. They stated how viewers often use binge-watching as a coping mechanism and a way to temporarily escape reality.

2.1 Health Issues Associated With Binge Watching

Many of the consumer take a pride in associating themselves with binge watching, watching series of episodes or movies one after another but it comes with its own share of problems and different health issues. There are enormous health issues associated with excessive binge viewing. Some of the issues are been listed below:

1. **Diabetes:** It is one of the serious illnesses which can result in life time dosage of insulin injection and restriction on the food intake too. Lengthy periods of inactivity and laying around on the couch increase the chance of developing diabetes. (Park,2015) Every hour of binge watching multiplies the probability of possessing diabetes by 3.4%. Any individual with a family history of diabetes needs to be more careful and avoid excessive binge watching of their favourite series or any movie.

2. **Screen addiction:** (Franssen, 2017) Every episode of a web series ends mostly with a cliff-hanger thereby serving as an invitation to continue watching one more episode even if they had decided for not having any additional screen timing for the series. Recognising and overcoming a screen addiction is not always simple. Dopamine is released in the brain when you feel like you have accomplished something, even something as simple as binge-watching a television. The boosting effects of the feel-good hormone help to fuel a feedback cycle that leads to screen addiction.
3. **Social isolation:** (Romans, 2022) Binge watching can ruin your current relationships be it family or friends and keep you from creating new ones. People encounter a series of problems when attempting to develop friendship or a social interaction with people, yet the majority overcome them to avoid the crippling effects of loneliness. Regular unattended exposure to binge watching can lead to a strong damage on social upbringing of an individual. More than required access to web series or any of the shows will ensure fictional characters will take the place of your social life once your binge-watching habit reaches a certain point and keep you content with it. The lives of fictional characters, however, cannot take the place of in-person encounters.
4. **Anxiety and Depression:** A report by (Karmakar, 2015) People binge watch a series or any movie with a basic purpose of killing boredom and cheering up themselves but on the other hand after watching a few episodes they feel more anxious and depressed as compared to those who have not watched even a single episode of the show. This alone should be enough motivation to avoid binge-watching TV, especially if you are already battling mental health issues.
5. **Self-Control issues:** When you binge watch, you are tempted to satisfy your desires right away, which might cause problems with self-control. This issue might show itself in other aspects of your life, such as your desire for rapid pleasure when it comes to shopping, eating, and other activities. Almost all the content provider like Netflix, Amazon prime, Hotstar release their content simultaneously which further motivate the people to watch more of content in one go.
6. **Cognitive Decline:** People who engage in hobbies like binge-watching may become distracted more easily and struggle to maintain the necessary levels of concentration to complete their day-to-day activities. The availability of one click entertainment has been made possible with the abundance of streaming media. There is no need of social interaction in order to survive. You are no longer needed to engage with your surroundings or other people in order to be stimulated. To avoid more mentally taxing activities, binge-watching may become a habit, which may rewire your brain and cause cognitive deterioration.
7. **Growing Belly Fat:** (Shah,2016) Approximately 90 minutes of binge-watching leads to an increase in belly fat of more than 3 inches. The same phenomena were not reported even with working on a laptop or even watching some T.V. program. Binge watching gets associated with long term health issues and other problems.
8. **Eye Strain:** It is well known fact that watching television increases eye strain. Instead of giving your eyes a break from watching TV, binge-viewing can cause a burning sensation, ocular tiredness, and blurriness. Mindless binge-watching keeps the brain active and aroused enough to prevent you from falling asleep. In other words, the more time you spend staring at the screen, the longer it will take you to turn it off, which could result in severe eye strain and restless nights.
9. **Reduction in physical activity and stamina:** (Albarrati,et.al, 2018) Poor muscle strength can lead to bad muscle health it further damages muscle health when sitting at one place for a long period of time.

2.2 Introduction to Over the Top

Over the Top (OTT) basically refers to any digital platform offering wide range of audio and video entertainment and streaming with help of Internet. (Wilbert, 2023) A few of the International streaming platforms like Amazon Prime, Netflix, HULU, HBO Max, Disney have made their presence felt in the Indian markets with excellent tailor-made content for the Indian audience. (Goncalves et al. 2014) stated O.T.T. refers to delivery of content to consumers through an open system with the help of Internet as a medium. (Erman et al., 2011, Sujata et. al., 2015) OTT streaming platforms provide on the go entertainment to people round the clock in the form of web series or movies which may or may not have witnessed theatrical release. (WHO, 2022) The previous few years have seen a dramatic change in the way entertainment is been consumed as a result of COVID-19 pandemic. Viewers were getting bored with the same content been seen again and again because the television was unable to create original programming as the entire industry was facing a complete lockdown. Another reason to avoid choosing mainstream media is the interruption of the content by commercials. Additionally, all movie theatres were closed at this time. Over the Top (OTT) video streaming became more popular as a result of this. This medium has presented itself to be more adaptable than conventional entertainment media and offers content that is immensely diverse. The ease of access and on-demand subscription service (SVOD) played a significant role in making the content improvement in this medium. (Sarkar, 2020) As OTT platforms expand, problems for content creators will also grow as they must provide consumers, especially millennials, with original material that is innovative and will compel them to subscribe to OTT channels and binge watch. (Tiwari, 2019) The number of OTT platforms are rapidly increasing in India. The availability of affordable data packs and a sizable consumer base appears to be the crux behind the driving factor to expand market penetration and develop a sizable clientele. The ongoing I.T. revolution and easy access to internet have served as a reason behind the superfluous growth of streaming services. The narrative was written four years ago in Indian setting after the COVID pandemic. The number of individuals utilising the internet services witnessed a rise, mobile providers came up with affordable 4G packs which further led to a boost in penetration of smart phones which further resulted in increase of OTT platforms.

3. PROFILE OF LEADING OVER THE TOP (O.T.T.) SERVICE PROVIDERS

3.1 Netflix

It is a well-known streaming service available worldwide which has put on offer a large selection of films, TV series, documentaries, and original content. A brief profile of Netflix is given below:

3.1.1 Background

It was found in 1997 by Reed Hastings and Marc Randolph in Scotts Valley, California, United States. During their initial days they started as an online rental platform wherein they use to deliver D.V.D. to people for a pre decided time duration. Later after 10 years they decided to start their streaming services enabling the users to stream the content through the help of internet.

3.1.2 Indian Journey

(Radia, 2016)The debut of Netflix in India has been intriguing and exciting. The streaming juggernaut first entered the Indian market in January 2016 offering three major plans starting with a basic plan of Rs.500, Rs.650 and Rs.800 respectively and has since made considerable progress towards being one of the top entertainment platforms in the country. In January 2016, Netflix made its formal debut in India, bringing a large selection of international content like Dexter, Orange is the new black, That 70's show, Marvel's Daredevil and Marvel's Jessica Jones, Narcos, Sense8, Grace and Frankie, and Marco Polo, etc for the Indian audiences. The first impression was not so receptive because established Indian streaming platforms were already offering range of content and the biggest challenge was overcoming the problem of piracy. Netflix started making investment across regional programming and forming alliances with Indian production companies to serve the diverse Indian audience.

3.1.3 Challenges in India

There were several obstacles in the way of Netflix's future expansion in the Indian market, but fending off competition is of top priority. (Damani, 2020) The competition was not just restricted to other OTT players but local DTH service provider like Taka Sky which was offering its own Television as well as Mobile app. at an affordable pricing. At the same time, they were also offering Video on Demand (VOD) services through which users were able to see any movie or show as per their choice and convenience at any given point. There were also some infrastructure problems. India had sluggish internet speed compared to the rest of the globe, despite inexpensive data availability. In fact, according to certain industry studies, India has the slowest broadband among the countries of the Asia-Pacific. A staggering 45% of internet users in India were able to get by with a connection speed of 1-3 Mbps, 30% with less than 1 Mbps, and fewer than 1% with just 50 Mbps, according to a poll.

3.1.4 Subscriber Base

(Bundhun,2023) in their research study found the total subscriber base of Netflix India stands at 6.1 million with many additions expected in coming year with the new and innovative content being added keeping in mind the exclusivity of Indian audience.

3.2 Amazon Prime

Amazon Prime is a subscription-based video on demand service offered by Amazon, one of the world's largest online retailers. Apart from providing video on demand it also offers services like early access to promotional schemes along with Quick delivery of goods. A Brief profile is presented below:

3.2.1 Background

Amazon launched Amazon prime in the year 2005. It was launched as a flagship program to offer fast delivery and offer a convenient yet customised shopping experience to people. It was an extension offered by Amazon which was offered as a complimentary service while marking their presence in India during their initial launch days. (Barraclough, 2016) They later added Amazon video as a service offering on demand access to various movies and shows across the world. During the initial phase of launch Amazon also offered access to Kindle at no additional cost. This was done just to ensure consumer become more aware about Amazon and Amazon Prime.

3.2.2 Indian Journey

(Agrawal, 2018) Post their entry in 2013 Amazon has expanded to different verticals like online music and video streaming. A few months after entry in the Indian markets as a one stop shopping destination they announced their entry as one stop entertainment destination too in the form of Amazon prime video offering exclusive access to movies along with original content of their own and also international content was made available to people. In 2017 they came up with their own streaming device Fire TV stick in competition with Google Chromecast. In order to cement their presence in the streaming industry and heart of people they came up with local flavour Indian content like Mirzapur, The Family man, Panchayat to name a few which helped them to gain strong publicity in the Indian market and further they plan to come up with more such original content to gather more subscribers from the Indian market.

3.2.3 Challenges in India

(Simon, 2021) The major challenge faced by Amazon was about content discovery as they were finding it difficult to recommend appropriate content to people. One thing that was a major worry for Amazon was that it lists show seasons separately rather than just showing the show once and including a submenu for seasons. It seems like an obvious method of inflating the homepage and search index to make it appear as though there is more material but, they are unable to offer any major content as compared to other players operating in the streaming industry.

Another challenge was in connection with padding, Prime under its recommendation menu was offering content which was nowhere related to the content which an user is presently streaming thereby it leads to break in the chain effect as consumer loose interest in the content that is been put on offer.

3.2.4 Subscriber Base

As of May, 2022 the total subscriber base of Amazon Prime stands at 13.6 million.

3.3 Disney + Hotstar

The present Brand was launched as Hotstar offering a broad selection of films, T.V. series, and original material owned and run by Disney along with local homegrown content was launched in India in the year 2015 as an independent streaming service provider. In the year 2019 parent body of Hotstar i.e., Star India was acquired by Disney and the brand was renamed as Disney + Hotstar. A brief profile is presented below:

3.3.1 Background

Disney + Hotstar has marked its presence across several nations, including Singapore, Malaysia, Thailand, Indonesia and India. They have put on offer variety of content across different property owned by

Disney such as Pixar, Marwel, Star-war and National Geographic. In addition to above they also offer original content produced and marketed by them on their own. It is available across multiple streaming platforms like Mobile, Desktop, Smart TV and also on the web browsers. Apart from Hindi content it has also put on offer local regional content in Marathi language too.

3.3.2 Indian Journey

It is well known as one of the largest streaming platforms of India. They have put on offer more than 1,00,000 hours of Television shows, movies and regional content in more than 18 languages at the same time covering major sporting events across the globe. (Rudra, 2023) Not only is Disney+ Hotstar setting the pace with its programming, but also with its solid technological foundation. The technology has raised the bar for video quality, ensuring uninterrupted playback even in the most constrained network conditions. They have ensured that there are no compromises made on audio-visual quality. Device-adaptive video streaming is now possible thanks to video technological advancements. This type of streaming adapts to the device being used and delivers the greatest video quality possible using the available bandwidth.

3.3.3 Challenges Faced

One of the major challenges faced during their growth was losing the streaming rights of Indian Premier League (I.P.L.) to rival streaming platform Jio which offered the streaming completely free of cost to any user accessing Jio Cinema. Another roadblock faced by them was the quality of content been offered by them to users, keeping in mind the content been offered across by other streaming platforms and Hotstar was finding it difficult to match the standards set by different players. At the same time across few of the instances they have also faced network outbreak where in users had experienced difficulties in streaming live sporting events. (Moneycontrol.com, 2023) To highlight an incident during the recently concluded Gavaskar Border Trophy played between India Australia in February, 2023 which was Exclusively streamed on Hotstar users had faced difficulty in streaming the live match for a record duration of more than 3 hours.

3.3.4 Subscriber Base

(Singh, 2023) As of May, 2023 the total subscriber base of Disney + Hotstar stands at 53 million

3.4 JioCinema

It is a popular and well-known streaming platform launched on 05th September, 2016 which is owned by Viacom 18 a majority owned subsidy of Reliance Industries which is a company operated by Mukesh Ambani. It allows the users to stream variety of content completely free of cost. A brief profile is presented below:

3.4.1 Background

The streaming platform Jiocinema allows Jio subscribers to stream different T.V. shows, Movies, Web series and the most recent addition being live sporting events. They offer content across multiple languages like English, Hindi, Marathi, Gujrati, Bhojpuri etc. (Pathak, 2019) At the same time users are given access to rich international content which is further made available in different regional languages to choose from thereby offering an enrich experience to the users.

3.4.2 Indian Journey

Jio made its presence felt in the streaming industry with a bang wherein they started as a streaming player showcasing old movies. Later they added live telecast of sporting events like FIFA, Cricket Worldcup and many other cricketing competitions across the globe. The latest addition to streaming on JioCinema was the 16th season of Indian Premier League which was made available to people without any subscription charges. It served as a blessing in disguise for JioCinema as it was able to add new subscribers as they made the streaming available for non Jio users too that too without any additional charges. The latest addition to JioCinema as a platform is the availability of premium Hollywood content which is been made available at a price of Rs. 999 per user which can be used to watch the premium Hollywood content across four devices at the same time.

3.5 Zee5

It is an Indian video streaming platform offering variety of content, including Television shows, movies and web series. It is owned, managed and operated by Zee Entertainment Enterprises Limited which is one of India's largest entertainment and media companies. The Usage of application is open for both premium as well as free content through their Television, Mobile or even their laptops. A brief profile is presented below:

3.5.1 Background

It allows the users to stream content in multiple language including Hindi, Marathi, English and many other regional languages too. It has put on offer different genres of movies, Television shows, web series along with exclusive and original Zee 5 content too.

3.5.2 Indian Journey

(Farooqui, 2022) Zee5 made their India Debut on 14th February, 2018 with the sole purpose of providing entertainment to people. It has put on offer more than 1,00,000 hours of digital content comprising of original shows, local as well international content to choose from and at the same time it has put on offer. They took the first mover advantage offering television shows to people through a Mobile or Desktop version. Looking at the journey of 5 years they are having major plans of expansion and growth in coming years. Their main focus area is on improving the quality of regional content so as to make it more easily accessible to people and making the content available in dubbed Hindi language too. Keeping their expansion ideology, they will continue to grow in the fiction as a genre but they are not planning to enter in to any of the non-fiction content as a business genre.

3.5.3 Challenges Faced

(Mitter, 2019) Inspite of being the pioneer not only in satellite television but also the first mover towards digital streaming with Ditto T.V. the first ever subscription video on demand service which allowed the users to experience live T.V., music and many more of such content across laptops or even their Blackberry based phones. Another major challenge was in connection with arrival of new platforms providing rich content and thereby leading to clutter in the market. Availability of original content was another challenge which Zee 5 was falling short as compared to other players operating in the market. They were lagging behind in proportion to content been offered by other streaming platform which was a grey area thereby leading towards lack of subscribers on the platform.

3.6 OTT and Data Consumption

(PTI, 2022) An Indian mobile user consumes approximately more than 11 G.B data per month excluding the WIFI usage at office and home. It is a stunning growth of more than 16% as compared to the usage's statistics figures for the year 2021 majorly due to availability of affordable data packs, easy access to smartphones and the ever-increasing content offered by OTT platforms. The data consumption in India is much higher as compared to global leader countries like China, USA, Germany. The average data price per G.B. in India is approximately Rs.7 which is quite less as compared to worldwide data consumption charges.

The video consumption has witnessed an exorbitant increase with availability of platforms like Netflix, Amazon Prime, Disney Hotstar etc to name a few. The average time spent across OTT platforms by a user in India is approximately 70 minutes while they approximately spend almost 40 minutes in a single seating.

3.7 Content Management

Content plays an important role in motivating the users towards selection of a streaming platform. If the availability of content is not relevant then there are major chances of users selecting some other streaming platform.

It can be interpreted from the Table 1.

a) There is no option to buy an Annual subscription for Netflix as a streaming platform whereas there is no option to buy monthly subscription for Disney + Hotstar.
b) Streaming platform like Netflix and Amazon prime do not offer any free content while users can have access to paid as well as free content on JioCinema, Disney + Hotstar and Zee5.
c) There was no provision of world digital premier of any new movie being premiered on Netflix while other platforms had the provision of allowing digital streaming premier.
d) Netflix and Zee5 are not telecasting any live sporting events while other three streaming platforms have telecasted one or the other live sporting event.
e) Jiocinema is the only streaming platform offering all the Indian content completely free of cost.
f) Amazon prime and Netflix offer animated content on their streaming platform while others are not offering any animated content.
g) There is no availability of Television programming on Amazon prime and Netflix while other streaming platform had the availability of streaming television serials.

Table 1. Programming distribution

Particulars	Amazon Prime	Netflix	Disney+Hotstar	JioCinema	Zee5
Original Movies	Yes	Yes	Yes	Yes	Yes
Regional Movies	Yes	Yes	Yes	Yes	Yes
International Content	Yes	Yes	Yes	Yes	Yes
Indian Television serial episodes	No	**No**	Yes	Yes	Yes
Live Sporting events	Yes	**No**	Yes	Yes	**No**
Cartoon content	No	**Yes**	No	No	No
Animated Movies	Yes	Yes	No	No	No
World Digital Premier	Yes	**No**	Yes	Yes	Yes
Availability of Free Content	No	No	Yes	Yes	Yes
Pricing (Annual plans)	Rs.1,499	N.A.	Rs.899	Free	Rs.699
Pricing (Monthly Plan)	Rs.299	Starting at Rs.199	N.A.	Free	Rs.99

Source: Primary data

Vocublary.com quotes *'Genre'* refers to specific type of content which a user may like to explore. There are different types of genres available across different streaming platforms. A streaming platform always wants to specialise in a particular Genre while being a common player across other content.

It can be interpreted from Table 2 different type of Genres been screened across all the streaming platforms. A detailed screening of all the stated five streaming platforms was done and it was found all of them have created their U.S.P. and are capitalising on the same.

Table 2. Genre and its availability

Particulars	Amazon Prime	Netflix	Disney+Hotstar	JioCinema	Zee5
Comedy	Yes	Yes	Yes	Yes	Yes
Romance	Yes	Yes	Yes	Yes	Yes
Horror	Yes	Yes	Yes	No	Yes
Science fiction	No	Yes	Yes	No	Yes
Drama	Yes	Yes	Yes	Yes	Yes
Mystery	Yes	Yes	Yes	Yes	Yes
Fantasy	Yes	Yes	Yes	No	Yes

Source: Primary data

JioCinema has presented itself as a free streaming platform which was earlier restricted to telecast of Bollywood or regional movies, later they added live sporting events like the world-famous FIFA World Cup and the latest addition to their kitty was the live streaming of Indian Premier League 2023. Post conclusion of I.P.L they have added different web series wherein they are offering one fresh episode every day at the same time there will be a premier of one movie every week. All these is been made available to users without any subscription fees or charges. The basic purpose behind this strategy is to ensure there is no reduction in number of subscribers post the conclusion of IPL. The strategy has proved quite helpful for Jiocinema as a platform and further it is offering the perfect competition to all the subscription based streaming platform and making them scratch their heads towards their future strategy.

Zee5 has presented itself as a streaming platform offering affordable family entertainment comprising of movies, web series and television shows. They have presented themselves as a player offering not only as a subscription-based service provider but also offering the facility of renting international content. The U.S.P. of Zee5 was the availability of premium content comprising of latest web series, movies and even the availability of Live T.V. They have offered two types of subscription Premium and Premium 4K, where in users subscribing to Premium 4K content were able to see the movies, web series along with television program.

Amazon Prime presented itself as a streaming platform offering the benefit of entertainment along with benefits like free home delivery of the shopping done through Amazon.co.in. They are well known for coming with exclusive content targeting the tier 2 and tier 3 cities of India. Web series like Mirzapur, The Family man and Panchayat were exclusively crafted for the Indian audience. At the same time, they have added Lionsgate play which is offering rich Hollywood content either on subscription on rental basis. It further allows a user to create profile in their account which allows different users to log in at the same time and watch content across different device thereby eliminating the need of password sharing.

Disney + Hotstar amassed itself as a streaming platform offering local as well as international content to users at a competitive pricing. Apart from offering plethora of content to people in terms of number of shows on offer or the variety of movies been made available to people. The U.S.P. of Disney + Hotstar stands in terms of number of languages offered in every show. It offers all it original shows and web series in 7 different languages ranging from Hindi, Marathi, Bengali, Tamil, Telugu, Malayalam and Kannada along with languages every show comes up with subtitles in English language. This is one of the major reasons behind having many subscribers to its credit.

Netflix is one of those streaming platforms which are famous for their international content. The U.S.P. of Netflix lies in its variety of content being offered by them. They boast themselves offering the maximum number of movies, web-series and T.V. shows as compared to their competitors fulfilling the requirement of different genres and fulfilling the requirements of large spread of audience. Another special part about Netflix is their recommendation part where in they are able to offer the best of the content looking at the search history of user thereby making the best of the setup for appropriate binge watching.

3.8 OTT and Binge Watching: Case Examples

Mr. A[1] is a marketing executive working with a Noida based company in Gurgaon. He was facing difficulties in breathing and performing day to day activities with ease leading to a hint of depression. He decided to consult doctors at BLK Max Super Speciality Hospital located in New Delhi complaining about depression and anxiety. Post diagnosis doctors were shocked and they came up with a strange illness which was creating major issues and concluded Mr. A was suffering from "Binge Watching Addiction" which is a recent phenomenon in last few years post the Covid-19 pandemic.

According to the consulting doctor Manish Jain, Arun believed he was facing depression and anxiety due to excessive work pressure and personal issues. After having discussion with his mother doctors realised Arun was involved in heavy binge watching and was facing sleep deprivation from a long period of time and this was resulting in him not being able to get up early on time. With passage of time this was resulting in anxiety and further it was leading to mental absenteeism at work place which was serving as an obstacle in his overall growth as a well performing employee. A simple harmless habit of watching movies or web series during travel turned in to a compulsive addiction and has become a bad habit leading to different health issues.

(Thomas, 2022) quotes In another case Mr. B[2], a 26-year-old man being admitted for excessive influence of video games addiction was found to be under the influence of addiction towards Netflix. Dr. Manoj Sharma who was treating the patient found the patient was under serious stress about his career prospects and was always comparing his career with that of his colleagues along with mounting pressure from parents along with the additional burden of a failed business. In order to keep away from stress, he started watching lots and lots of content on Netflix which helped him forget his worries for the limited period and then it became an addiction wherein he was watching either movies or some series on Netflix for more than 8 hours a day. With the increasing competition and mental pressure people find it quite easy for them to get involved in Binge watching and forget their worries for a limited period but on the other hand leading to more serious complication and health issues.

3.9 Suggestions Towards Reducing Binge

Excessive Binge watching can prove harmful not just for the human body but for the human mind too. It is necessary for an individual to reduce the number of hours spent across watching different content. Following are some of the suggestions which can be implemented in day-to-day life towards reducing the time spent across Binge watching and thereby contributing towards better health leading towards a better tomorrow

- Self-Discipline is the best form of Discipline, restricting self from watching not more than one episode of a series will keep the surprise element intact and prove beneficial towards avoiding health issues. This can be done by doing some other work like reading a book, taking a small nap or even speaking to friends or family member whenever you feel the urge to watch more than one episode per day of the content in order to keep the mind occupied in some other work.
- Avoid watching content under closed lights thereby keeping a track on watching habits so that sleeping hours are not compromised and the minimum required sleep for a healthy human body is met without any compromises.
- Don't fall for the peer pressure of watching a show or a movie just because everyone else is seeing the same as it leads to additional burden of watching a content without even being interested in watching the same thereby leading to mental trauma and anxiety.
- Disable the Autoplay feature while watching any of your favourite shows or series as it will stop the streaming service provider from streaming the episode directly. Further take a small break after every episode drink a glass of water or even take a small walk in the house as it will help in distracting the mind from binge watching back-to-back episodes.
- Try utilising the services of application blocker in mobile phone which will stop the users from exploring the application in between a certain time period. It may prove helpful in keeping away from binge watching shows and thereby saving ample amount of time and proving fruitful for health too.

- A user may try to ensure binge watching is not a stand-alone activity and is always performed with one or the work. The user can try to watch series or shows only during commute or during lunch and dinner break as it will keep the screen time to a lower level and will also serve the dual purpose of avoiding binge watching.
- Associate your Binge with a barter trade for doing something more productive like reading a book, newspaper, cleaning work at home, getting the groceries from the super market or even finishing any of the long pending work. You may watch one episode of a series or a movie only when you complete one of your pending tasks. These will prove helpful in completing the pending work and at the same time keeping self away from continuous binge watching.

3.10 Future of Binge Watching

(Adulla, n.d.) Gone are the good old days when entire family use to sit together and watch a General Entertainment Channel (GEC) like Star Plus, Color, Sony or even catch a movie together on a week-end. Today all the members of family are either glued to their mobile phone or laptop and stealing an episode from their hectic work schedule. With the users being spoilt for choices towards availability of different streaming platforms to choose from like Netflix, Amazon Prime, JioCinema and the access to loads of web series across different genres has given rise to people seeing several episodes of the series or an entire season of television show which has severely impacted the television industry in terms of programming been done and disbursed among the masses.

4. CONCLUSION

Binge watching is here to stay and on the contrary will become more intense with the passage of time. With ease of availability towards data pack and the penetration of OTT platforms along with rich content across ever genre, users are being lured towards spending more time across different O.T.T. platforms. Due to their on-demand nature, OTT platforms have been increasingly popular among the users and thereby encouraging them to explore more content. Binge watching has become a popular viewing habit which is been made possible by different OTT platforms. In order to fully immerse themselves in the narrative arcs and plots, viewers are encouraged to watch entire seasons or entire series at once. This has not only changed the way entertainment is been offered across different demographics irrespective of their age be the teenagers or even the senior citizens and it has also resulted in different health issues like severe headache, backpain along with a feeling of being away from people and being immersed either in the mobile screen or being glued to laptop thereby leading to poor social skills further affecting their relationship with their near and dear ones.

OTT platforms have changed the way entertainment is been consumed and has given a run for money to other entertainment platforms be it the Television, 70 mm movie watching or even the simple family get-together where people use to be together and have a healthy laugh together. The availability of 24 by 7 entertainment has made OTT a necessity across household apart from food, clothing and shelter.

OTT platforms have become an integral part of every one's life, be it during commute, weekends or even a lazy day at work place. OTT has helped people overcome boredom but at the same time it has also made the viewers addicted and thereby forcing them to watch more content which has resulted in increased screen timing leading to problems like obesity, reduced energy level. Binge watching is here to stay and the future of entertainment depends in balancing linear and on-demand models while embracing technology improvements that allow for a personalised and immersive viewing experience but also ensuring no compromises are made of health and last but not the least Binge watching is good till the time entertainment is concerned but never allow it to become an addiction or else the day is not far away where in we will be looking at Binge watching deaddiction centres need to come up towards solving problems of people.

REFERENCES

Adulla, S. (n.d.). *The Rise of Binge-Watching and its Impact on Television Consumption*. Revidd .https://www.revidd.com/blogs/the-rise-of-bi-nge-watc-hing-and-its-im-pact-on-televisionconsumption

Agarwal, M. (2018). *Prime Added Maximum Users In India In Its First Year In Amazon's History: Jeff Bezos*. Inc42 Media. https://inc42.com/buzz/prime-added-maximum-users-in-india-in-its-first-year-in-amazons-history-jeff-bezos/

Albarrati, A., Zafar, H., Alghadir, A. H., & Anwer, S. (2018). Effect of Upright and Slouched Sitting Postures on the Respiratory Muscle Strength in Healthy Young Males. *BioMed Research International*, *2018*, 1–5. doi:10.1155/2018/3058970 PMID:29682532

Barraclough, L. (2016). Amazon prime video now available in more than 200 countries. *Variety*. https://vari-ety.com/2016/digital/glo-bal/amazon-prime-video-now-available-in-more-than-200-countries-1201941818/

Binge Watching TV Linked to Higher Rates Of Depression And Anxiety. (2015). *Medical Daily*. https://www.medicaldaily.com/binge-watching-tv-linked-higher-rates-depression-and-anxiety-360776

Boni, M., Jambavalika, A., Roy, S., Naggar, J., & Shah, S. (2017). *The End of TV*. American Marketing Association.

Bundhun, R. (2023). How Netflix can capitalise on Indian Oscar wins to boost its subscriber base. *The National*. https://www.thenationalnews.com/business/2023/03/20/how-netflix-can-capitalise-on-indian-oscar-wins-to-boost-its-subscriber-base/#:~:text=Netflix%20subscriber%20numbers%20in%20India,firm%20Arthur%20D%20Little%20shows

Conlin, L., Billings, A., & Averset, L. (2016). Time-shifting vs. appointment viewing: The role of fear of missing out within TV consumption behaviours. *Communicatio Socialis*, *29*(4), 151–164.

Damani, V. (2022) 5 Key Challenges for Netflix in India. *TechApp*. https://techpp.com/2016/01/07/netflixindia-challenges/

Erman, J., Gerber, A., Ramadrishnan, K. K., Sen, S., & Spatscheck, O. (2011). Over-the-Top Video: The Gorilla in Cellular Networks. In J. Erman, A. Gerber, K. K. Ramadrishnan, S. Sen, & O. Spatscheck (Eds.), *Proceedings of the 2011 ACM SIGCOMM Conference on Internet Measurement Conference* (pp. 127-136). Association for Computing Machinery. 10.1145/2068816.2068829

Farooqui, M. (2022). *ZEE5 to increase originals by 2X, investment in content to be up by 50% in 2022.* Moneycontrol. https://www.moneycontrol.com/news/trends/entertainment/zee5-to-increase-originals-by-2x-investment-in-content-to-be-up-by-50-in-2022-8081711.html

Franssen, C. L. (2017). The Netflix Addiction: Why Our Brains Keep Telling Us to Press Play. *HuffPost.* https://www.huffpost.com/entry/the-netflix-addiction_b_8473094

Gonçalves, V. G., Evens, T., Alves, A. P., & Ballon, P. (2014). Power and Control Strategies in Online Video Services. At *the 25th European Regional Conference of the International Telecommunications Society (ITS).* ACM.

India Times. (2020). Always connected: Indians consume over 11GB data daily, spend 70 mins a day on OTT platforms. *The Economic Times.* https://economicti-mes.india-times.com/magazines/panache/always-con-nected-indians-con-sume-over-11gb-data-daily-spend-70-m-ins-a-day-on-ott-platfo-rms/articlesh-ow/74333875.cms

Johnson, M. A., & White, B. R. (2018). The Psychological Impact of Binge-Watching: Exploring Escapism and Emotional Attachment. *Journal of Media Psychology, 23*(3), 141–152.

Jones, P. C. (2017). The Impact of Netflix on Binge-Watching Habits: A Case Study. *International Journal of Communication, 11*, 2785–2803.

Kaatib, A. (2022). *How Too Much Binge-Watching Is Damaging Your Health.* MUO. https://www.makeuseof.com/tag/binge-watching-damaging-health/

Karmakar, D. (2015). Binge Watching TV Linked To Higher Rates Of Depression And Anxiety. *Medical Daily.* https://www.medicaldaily.com/binge-watching-tv-linked-higher-rates-depression-and-anxiety-360776

Mehta, B. (2022). Why do millennials prefer OTT platforms over traditional Theaters? *Agency Reporter.* https://www.agencyreporter.com/why-do-millennials-prefer-ott-platforms-over-traditional-theaters/

Mitter, S. (2019). After two unsuccessful attempts at video streaming, here's how ZEE cracked the OTT puzzle with ZEE5. *YourStory.com.* https://yourstory.com/2019/06/ott-zee5-original-content-partnerships-startups

Moneycontrol.com. (2023). Disney+ Hotstar faces outage amid the India-Australia test match. *Moneycontrol.* https://www.moneycontrol.com/news/business/disney-hotstar-faces-outage-amid-the-india-australia-test-match-10109821.html

Netflix, Inc. (2018). Netflix Declares Binge Watching is the New Normal. *PR News Wire.* https://www.prnewswire.com/news-releases/netflix-declares-binge-watching-is-the-new-normal-235713431.html

Panda, S., & Pandey, S. C. (2017). Binge watching and college students: Motivations and outcomes. *Young Consumers, 18*(4), 425–438. doi:10.1108/YC-07-2017-00707

Park, A. (2015). This Is What Binge-Watching TV Does to Your Health. *Time.* https://time.com/3767458/tv-binge-watching-health/

Pathak, P. (2019). JioCinema app: How to use, features and everything related to know. *India Today.* https://www.indiatoday.in/technology/features/story/jiocinema-app-how-to-use-features-and-everything-related-to-know-1423371-2019-01-04

Pittman, M., & Sheehan, K. (2015). Sprinting a media marathon: Uses and gratifications of binge-watching television through Netflix. *First Monday, 20*(10). doi:10.5210/fm.v20i10.6138

Press Trust of India. (2020, February 27). Always connected: Indians consume over 11GB data daily, spend 70 mins a day on OTT platforms. *The Economic Times.* https://economictimes.indiatimes.com/magazines/panache/always-connected-indians-con-sume-over-11gb-data-daily-spend-70-mins-a-day-on-ott-platforms/articleshow/74333875.cms

Radia, N. (2016). The Arrival Of Netflix In India: All That You Need To Know. *Inc42 Media.* https://inc42.com/resources/the-arrival-of-netflix-in-india/

Romans, C. (2022). *Try Out These 9 Apps to Help Alleviate Loneliness.* MUO. https://www.makeuseof.com/apps-alleviate-loneliness/

Rudra, N. R. (2023, April 19). *Disney+ Hotstar gets a new look; See what's changed.* Smartprix. https://www.smar-tprix.com/by-tes/disney-hot-star-ge-ts-a-new-lo-ok-see-whats-changed/

Sarkar, G. (2020). Indian OTT platforms dish out special fare for kids. *Indian Television.* https://www.indiantelevision.com/iworld/over-the-top-services/indian-ott-services-targetkids-with-special-fare-200601

Senal Group. (2022, May 19). Amazon Prime Video ramps up local originals in India. *Senal News.* https://senalnews.com/en/research/amazon-prime-video-ramps-up-local-originals-in-india

Shah, A. (2016). Belly up to the TV: Binge watching could lead to more stomach fat. *The Seattle Times.* https://www.seattletimes.com/life/wellness/belly-up-to-the-tv-binge-watching-could-lead-to-more-stomach-fat/

Shim, H., & Kim, K. J. (2018). An exploration of the motivations for binge-watching and the role of individual differences. *Computers in Human Behavior, 82,* 94–100. doi:10.1016/j.chb.2017.12.032

Simons, H. (2021). *Amazon Prime Video's biggest problem isn't content, it's everything else.* Android Authority. https://www.androidauthority.com/amazon-prime-video-problems-1228014/

Singh, M. (2023, May 10). *Disney's Hotstar loses 8.4 million subscribers as Ambani's JioCinema ascends.* TechCrunch+. https://techcrunch.com/2023/05/10/disney-hotstar-loses-8-4-million-subscribers-as-ambani-jiocinema-takes-off/?guccounter=1

Smith, J. (2018). Understanding Over-the-Top (OTT) Services: A Comprehensive Analysis. *Media Studies Journal, 35*(2), 215–230.

Starosta, J., Izydorczyk, B., & Lizińczyk, S. (2019). Characteristics of people's binge-watching behaviour in the "entering into early adulthood" period of life. *Health Psychology, 7,* 149–164.

Steiner, E., & Xu, K. (2018). Binge-watching motivates change: Uses and gratifications of streaming video viewers challenge traditional TV research. *Convergence (London).*

Sujata, J., Sohag, S., Tanu, D., Chintan, D., Shubham, P., & Sumit, G. (2015). Impact of Over the Top (OTT) Services on Telecom Service Providers. *Indian Journal of Science and Technology*, *8*(S4), 1–16. doi:10.17485/ijst/2015/v8iS4/62238

Team YourDost. (n.d.). 26-Year-Old Gurgaon Professional Diagnosed With 'Binge Watching Addiction.' *YourDost*. https://your-dost.com/blog/2017/08/binge-watc-hing-addi-ction.html?q=/blog/2017/08/binge-watching-addic-tion.html

Thomas, M. (2022). A clinic in India's Silicon Valley is treating its first case of Netflix addiction. *Quartz*. https://qz.com/india/1416875/bengalurus-nimhans-is-now-treating-netflix-addiction

Tiwari, V. (2019.). OTT Platforms: Their Revenue Model and Rise. *Insider*. https://insider.finology.in/investing/ott-platform-revenue-model

Wheeler, K. (2015). *The Relationships Between Television Viewing Behaviors, Attachment, Loneliness, Depression, and Psychological Well-Being*. [Honors College Theses, Georgia Southern]. https://digitalcommons.georgiasouthern.edu/honors-theses/98

Wilbert, M. (2023, June 15). *The 10 Best OTT Platforms + OTT Services in 2023*. Dacast https://www.dacast.com/blog/5-business-ott-platforms-for-over-the-top-video-content/

Williams, S. E. (2019). Challenges and Opportunities for Traditional TV Networks in the Era of OTT Dominance. *Journal of Broadcasting & Electronic Media*, *63*(2), 301–318.

World Health Organization [WHO] (2022, August). *WHO Coronavirus (COVID-19) Dashboard: Bangladesh*. WHO Health Emergency Dashboard.

Yakimova, N. (2016). *The Experience of Binge-watching Television Serials: A Phenomenological Description*. University Of Groningen.

ENDNOTES

1. In order to protect identity, name has been kept hidden, other things mentioned in case are true and original
2. In order to protect identity, name has been kept hidden, other things mentioned in case are true and original

Chapter 13
Effect of OTT Platforms on Juvenile Behavior:
Indian Perspective

Sheeba Khalid
https://orcid.org/0000-0002-9310-8621
Amity University, Lucknow, India

Malobika Bose
Amity University, Lucknow, India

Aradhana Yadav
https://orcid.org/0000-0002-5075-5327
Amity University, Lucknow, India

Adya Pandey
Amity University, Lucknow, India

ABSTRACT

Children are the nation's future-bearing shoulders. A country's kids must be on the correct path if it is to advance. But even if a child occasionally appears delinquent in nature and unfit for a community, a person's actions do not automatically exclude them from participation in society. Children have a delicate mind that may be guided in the appropriate direction for growth. This essay tries to analyze the factors that are leading to a rise in the use of technology by children in criminal activity. In some cases, technology that is meant to help them develop is turning out to be their enemy. The report also discusses several cybercrimes and how our legal system can prevent youngsters from committing them. The objective of this research is to investigate the impact of OTT platforms on the behavior of juveniles in the Indian context. The study aims to explore and understand the correlation between OTT platform usage and juvenile behavior, particularly focusing on potential links to criminal activities, cybercrimes, and the consumption of inappropriate content.

DOI: 10.4018/979-8-3693-0116-6.ch013

INTRODUCTION

What does modern childhood entail? Modern children's lives have unquestionably improved on a number of counts, due to increased public safety and assistance with both physical and mental health. Before they can walk or talk, many kids have access to cell phones and the countless options the digital world offers. In addition, children in the 21st century are reporting higher levels of stress and anxiety, and the pervasiveness of the digital world introduces new dangers like cyberbullying that follow them from the playground into their homes.

With the assistance of data, entertainment has become more personalized and portable in recent years. The introduction of OTT platforms has made numerous genres, languages, and production styles of programs freely accessible to the entire globe. Since the pandemic that began at the beginning of 2020, its utilization has increased.

The likes of Money Heist, Mirzapur, November Story, and Friends, among others, have been a constant source of entertainment for us to consume throughout the day. Due to the stark contrast of projections in the shows (such as offensive language, violence, and mindless but beautiful cinematography), it has begun to affect the lives of the young adults who are the largest consumers of these platforms. Psychologically, the amount of dread created by these shows is increasing abnormal mental health conditions such as stress, anxiety, and depression. It also effects the quality of logical and analytical thought that the human mind is able to conceive, conceptualize, and create with the capability's nature has bestowed upon humanity through evolutionary processes. (Anuradha Ishwaran, 2016)

"Nearly every action in today's technology-based world involves the internet. Life for most people has been increasingly digitised and connected to the internet. Due to the pandemic, this dependence on the internet has grown since last year. As things grow more ingrained in the digital age, students' higher education will increasingly be conducted online. According to United Nations International Children's Emergency Fund (UNICEF)1, one in three internet users are young, thus we may assume that one third of the population of the digital world is made up entirely of juvenile. We are evolving into an E-world, making us increasingly susceptible to dangers that go hand in hand with technological development. The notion of cybercrimes was created in response to this threat brought on by technological advancement. Under Indian law, the term "cybercrime" is not defined anywhere, although the information technology act of 2000 and the information technology amendment act of 2008 address numerous forms of cybercrime and the laws that apply to them.

There is no distinction between a youngster and an adult when it comes to access to technology and computers. Children today play a significant role in this technologically advanced society, which has an impact on their daily lives in the same ways that it does on adults'. The peer pressure that is currently consuming society is leading to an increase in visibility on social media platforms. These social media platforms do not distinguish between children and adults, so kids get access to the same information as adults have.

If used within acceptable bounds, all this exposure gives kids a chance to grow up in step with the fast-paced society. However, there are situations when technology is not exploited to one's advantage but is instead abused and used to harm others. Juveniles who misuse technology for their own ill-gotten profits commit cybercrimes including cyber-fraud and other types of online crimes. Cyber scams, cyberbullying, cyberstalking, identity theft, drug trafficking, digital piracy, cyber-suicides, cyber-theft, illegal hacking, and other sorts of cybercrimes are all commonly committed by young people. In addition to these well-known cybercrimes, fresh crimes are committed every day using technology.

The language and substance of OTT (over-the-top) platforms pose a severe threat to the creative and moral ideals of our nation. A number of crimes have occurred recently in which the perpetrators were inspired to do them after watching the web series. The content, language, and donation of shows on OTT (over-the-top) platforms such as Netflix, Disney Hotstar, Amazon Prime, Voot, MX Player, zee5, Alt Balaji, etc. have been a source of concern in recent years due to the many repercussions, particularly on the youth. These OTT platforms generate great profits at the expense of undermining Indian creative ideals and morality among the youth by offering cinema and television content replete with derogatory and obscene language and coitus sequences. It is estimated that the average Indian adolescent spends 8 hours and 29 twinkles per week watching internet video content, which is significantly more than the global average of 6 hours and 45 twinkles per week.

Relevant Theories and Concepts

In order to gain insight into the low prosecution and conviction rates for cyber-criminals in India, institutional and informal institutions must be examined. Previous scholars have acknowledged that economic activities and actors are embedded in formal and informal organisations. (Granovetter, M. (1985). The nature of cybercriminal operations matches perfectly with what Baumol [35] refers to as negative entrepreneurship. Baumol hypothesised that the distribution of productive, unproductive, and destructive entrepreneurs is a function of the rewards supplied by the society's game rules. These regulations are known as institutions. (Baumol, W. J. (1990)

In the past ten years, India's media landscape has undergone a technological revolution, promoting the mass market for specialty channels, content, and television technologies. Because of the new ways to interact with television media, primarily through smartphones, Internet TV, Video-On-Demand (VOD), and OTT platforms, viewing habits and platform preferences have changed. (Punathambekar & Kumar, 2012; Tryon, 2015)

In the future, OTT platforms benefited from the large audience that has become acclimated to viewing entertainment content on smartphones (Laghate, 2018). Now that they have entered the market, online streaming services have taken advantage of the situation. This internet video streaming differs significantly from conventional television in terms of its content, characteristics, and situations. It is still difficult to determine how much traditional media theories and methods can inform research on the evolving audience and their viewing habits. (Livingstone, 2003, 2004, 2007)

Several research studies suggest that adolescents' mental health may be negatively affected by their excessive use of over-the-top (OTT) platforms. An article, for instance, found that problematic OTT platform use among Turkish university students was associated with depressive and anxiety symptoms. Similar results were found in an article which discovered that Israeli adolescents who spend more time on OTT platforms have higher anxiety and depression levels. (Kircaburun and Griffiths, 2018, Lissak and Mekler, 2019)

An article has also examined the relationship between OTT platform usage and the self-esteem and body image of young people. According to a study, adolescents' body satisfaction and self-esteem decreased when exposed to idealized body images on social media (which frequently include content from OTT platforms). Cohen and Blaszczynski (2015) discovered that ad exposure on OTT platforms was associated with poor self-esteem and an unfavorable body image in adolescents. (Fardouly et al.,2018) (Cohen and Blaszczynski, 2015)

Joshi, Anushree (2019), In her research, discovered that the internet has popularised OTT services such as Netflix, Prime, etc., and people are eager to watch web series over 4G connectivity.

Dhanuka, Aditya, Bohra, and Abhilash (2019) have deduced from their investigation that youth are becoming increasingly addicted to web series. They have a negative impact on the mental, physical, and emotional wellbeing.

Aadeetya, S. (2018) asserts that the demand for on-the-go material on video streaming platforms is increasing among college students.

Qiu, Fan, and Cui, Yi. (2010) stated in their study that the viewer's behaviour is crucial when creating the streaming of videos due to the significant volatility and dynamism of consumer behaviour.

Kakkar, Alpana, and Nayak, Kalyani (2019) conclude that product positioning and placement play a significant influence in the development of web series for OTT platforms. People have begun to favour OTTs due to the strategic positioning of their products and content.

In India, especially in urban and semi-urban areas, television and movies are regarded as the most popular forms of entertainment. Without a question, these programmes have an enormous power and potential to influence the mental processes, attitudes, and behaviours of the individuals. It is commonly noted that young people, particularly children and adolescents, are inclined to remember phrases and songs from movies or television programmes, and that this has a lasting conscious and unconscious impact on their minds. Consequently, it plays a significant part in shaping the personality and character. But through these online platforms, primarily anti-national or anti-religious content is offered, which prompts an immediate response from the people; hence, it can be claimed that OTT platforms are promoting toxic culture among the youth.

The effect of OTT platform usage on the socialization and interpersonal interactions of young people has been the subject of numerous research studies. A study found that adolescents who used OTT platforms more frequently had poorer interpersonal communication skills and exhibited less prosocial behavior. In contrast, Lee and Kim (2018) found that the use of OTT platforms by South Korean adolescents may be a means for them to increase their social capital. (Uhls et al.,2014, Lee and Kim, 2018)

The effect of OTT platform usage on the academic performance of adolescents has also been investigated. According to a study by Rosen et al. (2013), high school students who frequently multitask on over-the-top (OTT) platforms — that is, use multiple devices simultaneously to watch videos — perform worse academically. In addition, a study found that adolescents' excessive use of OTT platforms was associated with lower academic achievement. (Rosen et al.,2013) (Rideout et al.,2019)

Numerous studies have demonstrated the negative effects of binge-watching web series and other forms of online streaming entertainment on adolescents. According to a study, bingeing is believed to be directly linked to negative emotions. Several studies have demonstrated the association between excessive viewing, body dissatisfaction, academic loss, depressive symptoms, and low self-esteem. Examples include (Stickney et al., 1999, Stice, Prensell, and Spangler, 2002, Sung, et al., 2005).

They set aside time to binge-watch web series and rewarded themselves in the process. The participants minimized or were unaware of the negative effects this novel viewing experience had on their grades, social lives, and schedule. (Peterson, 2006)

This article found that among 316 respondents between the ages of 18 and 20, binge-watching was linked to feelings of melancholy and isolation. Multiple studies demonstrate that binge-watching web series and online video content on OTT platforms has altered people's attitudes, behaviors, and social lives. (Sung et al.,2015)

Youths are more prone to imitate and adopt the behaviour of others since they can easily relate to what is portrayed on online platforms and other video content. Consequently, it causes numerous behavioural alterations in adolescents. It has a profound and lasting effect on their behaviour and thoughts. In addition, it has the following consequences: the entire process of youth socialisation is disrupted. Insomnia, depression, obesity, and eye disorders have grown in prevalence among adolescents. Additionally, the academic achievement of the youngsters has been impacted. Web content rarely addresses sexually transmitted illnesses and unintended pregnancies. The online series have become a forum for the promotion of alcohol, cigarettes, tobacco, drugs, and marijuana without emphasising their negative effects.

Numerous examples of youth committing crimes after being motivated by the programmes of such platforms have been reported recently, demonstrating their profound impact on young. Numerous crimes, ranging from kidnapping to murder, have been performed by youths who admitted in police custody that they attempted to emulate the crime after viewing the web series. Several of these occurrences are detailed below:

1. Let's begin with the infamous Ballabhgarh, Haryana murder. A third-year B.Com student was coming home following the exam. Suddenly, the accused Tausif shot her. Tausif admitted in police custody that he planned the murder after seeing the online series Mirzapur, in which Munna Bhaiya plays a character who shoots Sweetie in a one-sided love tale. This story influenced Tausif to have a one-sided affection for Nikita. He desired to wed her. Therefore, he awaited Nikita to take her outside of the campus. As soon as Nikita left college, Tausif began forcing her into a vehicle. Nikita, however, refused and complained. The accused then fatally shot Nikita. This information concerning Tausif's confession is available on the **Aajtak news channel's internet platform**.
2. In another incidence, according to the news website **TV9 Hindi**, the family of two Jamia Nagar, Delhi, boys called Nadeem and Aftab reported their abduction to the police. Southeast Delhi DCP RP Meena reported that these lads called their relatives using their own cell phones to inform them of their abduction. In addition to fabricating their own kidnapping story, they were also brazenly committing other crimes. In a chain-snatching case, these boys were apprehended via CCTV footage. In detention, they also admitted that the entire plot was inspired by a web series.
3. According to the website of the publication **Navbharat Times**, four young people devised an extortion scheme after viewing the web series. They initiated ransom calls to numerous parties. However, the UP police apprehended the suspect before they could obtain the extortion. They plotted to demand ransom after watching a crime-themed web series.

In light of this, it is essential to recognise that these Streaming platforms have global economic interests, but India provides a massive consumer base. Netflix and Amazon have a big market share in our nation, along with other platforms like hotstar, zee5, mx player, Alt Balaji, etc., and their accessibility and reach have risen over the lockdown time.

In order to protect the cultural values of the youth and foster a positive and healthy atmosphere, online platforms must be governed by appropriate rules and censored. The current government has often demonstrated its willingness to preserve Indian culture and values. In this regard, the Ministry of Information and Broadcasting (MIB) has stressed the need for OTT platforms to be regulated in order to streamline the sector and has held talks with several parties. The MIB recently notified the Information Technology (Guidelines for Intermediaries and Digital Media Ethics Code) Rules 2021 against this backdrop (Rules). The new regulations aim to strike a balance between self-regulation and government oversight. According to these regulations, OTT platforms must build a robust, three-tiered grievance resolution procedure. The initial level of regulation will be carried out by the OTT Platform itself via a grievance officer. The second level will consist of an institutional self-regulatory body composed of content publishers and their respective associations. This self-regulatory organisation would comprise of industry specialists led by a former Supreme/High Court judge or notable figure in the relevant sector. The third level consists of an inter-departmental committee established by the Ministry of Information and Broadcasting, which will provide oversight and hear appeals for decisions made at level two, or if MIB refers a complaint to the inter-departmental committee. The code of ethics issued under the Rules established classification rules for content based on the age of the viewer, themes, content, tone and impact, and intended audience. In addition to government restrictions and recommendations, it is the responsibility of every citizen to avoid using any content that pollutes the minds of adolescents and poses a grave threat to cultural values.

Exiting Applicable Legal Provisions Regarding Regulation of OTT Platforms

Despite the existence of bodies such as the Central Board of Film Certification, and is in charge of controlling the film production industry, and the Broadcasting Content Complaints Council, that tends to take customer complaint about non-news data broadcasted on TV, as well as statutes such as the Cinematograph Act and the Information Technology Act, which scans the contents shown in theatres and on cable TV, there aren't specific laws that governs digital content. It is vital to put certain statutes in place to equalize the playing field amongst movies that reach the general public via cinemas and films that reach individuals over the web.

According to a nationwide survey, the online media sector has a current audience of more over 17 crore via Ott services exclusively, with a valuation of INR 4000 crores. (Kumar,2020)According to statistics, the estimated duration an Indian user spends on OTT platforms has risen from 20 mins to 50 to an hour ever since Covid-caused epidemic. 49% of adolescents spend on average of 2-3 hours per day consuming online content. Based upon the evidence, it is reasonable to conclude that these OTT behemoths have a well-established following that is eager for supplementary content(Community, 2020).

With rising viewership and a growing need to appeal to a varied audience, it is becoming increasingly important to draw a distinction between originality and vulgarity. The use of aggression, sensuality, nudity, obscenity, violent words, and substances on such platforms has sparked several debates throughout the years. Be it the plea filed in the High Court of Delhi against series "Sacred Games" alleging that it slanders the former Indian Prime Minister Rajiv Gandhi's legacy, or the scandal over anti-women monologues or a rape scene in "Paatal Lok," or the turmoil over a kissing scene in a temple in "A Suitable Boy," which was alleged of negatively affecting religious sentiments, a variety of occasions which end up making policing in India difficult.

As a result, given the lack of a law dealing directly with digital material, the booming industry of these online platforms, and the developing content exhibited under the name of the director's 'creative space,' some type of control is required to keep people's beliefs from eroding.

Obscenity, as defined under Section 92 of the Indian Penal Code, is anything sensual or prurient that has the consequence of depraving or ruining someone. While these phrases are not specified in the IPC, the Courts have established the standard for determining whether something is 'obscene' or otherwise. The renowned Hicklin test of obscenity was set by the Supreme Court in 1965 in *Ranjit D. Udeshi v. State of Maharashtra ("Ranjit D. Udeshi v. State of Maharashtra," 1965)*, giving the term "obscene" a broad definition. Nevertheless, the term's reach has been restricted over time, and the Hicklin test has been abandoned by the Supreme Court. In the *Aveek Sarkar v. State of West Bengal ("Aveek Sarkar v. State of West Bengal," 2014) 4 SCC 257.)*, the Apex Court instead endorsed the American Roth approach, which permits obscenity to be assessed by adopting existing social norms from the perspective of an ordinary individual. It has been noticed that as society changes, what was formerly deemed obscene may not be regarded as obscene (Ray, 2020).

Though Section 292 of the IPC doesn't really specifically address obscenity on the web, rules have been laid forth under the IT Act that define penalties for posting or sending obscene content in electronic mode (India, 2017). Section 67B of the Statute puts emphasis on "punishment for representation of minors in sexually graphic act in digital form". Moreover, Section 69A authorizes the Central Government to implement regulations prohibiting accessibility to any material in the cause of India's sovereignty and integrity, cordial relations with foreign states, security of the state, or public order.

Section 295A of the IPC goes on to address conduct that are intentional and vindictive in nature, with the intent of hurting religious emotions of any class by demeaning its faith or its beliefs. However, the Supreme Court in *Ramji Lal Modi v. State of U.P*, has ruled that the provision only punishes acts of insult or attempts to insult carried out with the deliberate and malicious purpose to offend a class's religious beliefs ("Ramji Lal Modi v. State of U.P.," 1957).

Further legislation in effect include the Indecent Portrayal of Women (Prevention) Act, 1986, which outlaws immoral representation of women in publications, ads, cinema, artworks, and so on, and the Protection of Children from Sexual Offenses (POCSO) Act, which outlaws the sale & dissemination of child pornography.

Amended Information Technology (Intermediary Guidelines and Digital Media Ethics Code) Rules 2021

Following the realisation of the repercussions of OTT platforms, the Legislature has enacted a set of new guidelines to constrain questionable content and assist audiences in making better-informed choices about the content streamed online on such media platforms, that include Information Technology (Intermediary Guidelines and Digital Media Ethics Code) Rules 2021 **(India, 2021).** The Ministry of Information and Technology notified the new regulations vide order dated 25th February, 2021, that every social media platform, along with Ott services, were to abide by said rules by 26th May, 2021. According to Rule 3(2)(b), (c), (e), of the Information Technology (Intermediaries guidelines) Rules, 2021, no media platform will demonstrate, host, or publish any outrageous, sexually explicit, or potentially illegal content which may impact juveniles. According to Rule 3(2)(b), (c), (e), of the Information Technology (Intermediaries guidelines) Rules, 2021, no media platform will demonstrate, host, or publish any outrageous, sexually explicit, or potentially illegal content which may impact juveniles. According to Rule 3(3), the publisher need not broadcast or orchestrate the propagation of all such content on their mobile app or website. In such case, the users will be properly warned.

- In The new guidelines require OTT platforms to have a robust three-tier grievance resolution procedure. The OTT Platform will give the first degree of oversight via a grievance officer. The second level will consist of a self-regulatory entity made up of content publishers and their groups. An inter-departmental committee established at the third level by the MIB will offer supervision and consider appeals for decisions taken at level two or if the MIB sends a complaint to the inter-departmental committee.

- The Guidelines describe standards for material categorization based on the audience's age, topics, substance, character, and effect, among many other factors. It also demands OTT platforms to consider India's sovereignty, stability, and amicable connections.
- The content grading categories are "U" (appropriate for all ages), "U/A 7+" (suitable for people aged 7 and up), "U/A 13+" (suitable for people aged 13 and up), "U/A 16+" (suitable for people aged 16 and up), and "A" (suitable for people aged 16 and up) (restricted to adults). OTT platforms must incorporate access control techniques for material designated U/A 13+ or above.
- In only 24 hours of receiving complaints, intermediaries shall remove or limit access to anything that displays persons' private parts, depicts such individuals in complete or partial nudity or in a sexual act, or is in the nature of impersonation, including altered photographs. A grievance can be filed by either the party or someone acting on his or her behalf.
- On his website, software, or both, the intermediary is obligated to clearly declare the personal data and the use of personal information or data for its subscribers (as the case may be).
- Voluntary user verification is also provided for in the proposed Rules. Users who desire to validate their accounts voluntarily will be provided with an appropriate mechanism as well as a verifiable and recognised mark of verification.

Throughout the years, The growing use of social media for obscene material, discord, fraud, instigating violence, public order, anti-competitive behaviour, and other objectives has presented new hurdles to law enforcement authorities.

There has been much debate in recent years about whether content restriction on OTT platforms is necessary, and the Centre has now established rules for OTT players and social networking sites, which is a tremendous step towards governing the behaviour of online streaming services. The government is currently taking significant steps to establish regulatory procedures that will make social media platforms liable to the law while also protecting persons and organizations from exploiting them.

Challenges Associated With Regulation of OTT Platforms

The emergence of OTT platforms and the subsequent popularity of them has raised concerns regarding regulation of content as showed on these platforms. Regulation of OTT platforms possess a challenge for the authorities for they offer services to the users directly through internet bypassing cable or satellite services. Further the services through these platforms can be availed on demand wherein the user can view content at a time chosen by him. The manner in which services are made available and can be opted by user both differ from the other existing modes of entertainment(cable televisions and cinema) making it impossible to govern them as per the existing regulations available.(cable television, cinematographic.

PIRACY: A standardised practise prevailing among the digital platforms is the unauthorised use, storage and sharing of unsolicited content. Platforms engage in such activities usually to avoid paying the fees associated with purchasing legally the viewership rights. An example of such websites that allow user to download pirated versions of movies is the u TORRENT. Piracy has become both a menace and a challenge for the authorities to control. The cyber cells lack sufficient infrastructure and resources to track every digital device in their jurisdiction that may be involved in storage, usage and sharing of pirated content. Cyber cells are further constrained by the privacy laws. right to privacy is guaranteed as a fundamental right to the citizens. It shall be thus not feasible for the cyber cells to invade the personal devices of the users or track their devices without sufficient evidences. The statutory rights and procedural obstructions become one of the major challenges for the regulatory authorities to tackle the issue of piracy.

Cybercrime: In the process of subscribing to an OTT platform, people share their confidential information like bank details, credit card access, which has the potential to be misused and lead to cybercrime.

The provided information encompasses a wide range of studies and viewpoints regarding the influence of OTT platforms on the behavior of young people and societal issues. However, despite the extensive compilation of data and studies, there are still numerous areas of research that have not been adequately addressed:

Causality and Contextual Understanding: Although studies have found a correlation between the use of OTT platforms and detrimental effects on young people, there is a lack of comprehension regarding the cause-and-effect relationship and the specific contextual factors involved. An investigation of the chronological order and extent of influence could offer a more lucid understanding of how OTT content directly affects behavior.

Cultural and Regional Contexts: The influence of OTT platforms might vary considerably depending on cultural and regional disparities. The current research does not thoroughly investigate how various cultural origins may affect the impact of OTT content on the behavior of young people.

Long-term Consequences and Measures to Reduce Impact: Numerous research primarily examine the immediate or short-term effects. Examining the enduring consequences of excessive over-the-top (OTT) consumption on behavior, mental well-being, social interaction, and academic achievement could yield valuable insights for developing preventive measures or therapies.

Importance of Regulations and Media Literacy: Despite ongoing discussions and implementation of restrictions, there are still study gaps about the efficacy of these regulations in mitigating the impact of harmful content. Furthermore, it is necessary to investigate the impact of media literacy programs on equipping young people to actively and analytically interact with over-the-top (OTT) content.

Analysis of Diverse material: The studies primarily concentrate on the adverse effects of specific themes in the material. Examining a broader array of content categories and their diverse impacts on the behavior and perception of young people could enhance comprehension beyond the realms of violence and delinquency.

Comparative Analysis with conventional Media: There is a dearth of comprehensive research that juxtapose the influence of OTT platforms with that of conventional media such as television or cinema. Gaining a comprehensive understanding of the distinctions and commonalities in influence has the potential to yield significant insights.

By addressing these areas of research that have not been explored, we may improve our comprehension of the complex connection between OTT platforms and the behavior of young people. This, in turn, will help us develop more efficient policies and interventions to reduce any potential bad effects.

Objective: The objective of this research is to investigate the impact of Over-The-Top (OTT) platforms on the behaviour of juveniles in the Indian context. The study aims to explore and understand the correlation between OTT platform usage and juvenile behaviour, particularly focusing on potential links to criminal activities, cybercrimes, and the consumption of inappropriate content.

Method: A diverse sample of juveniles age 16-23 from various socio-economic backgrounds across Lucknow, Uttar Pradesh in India are selected.

Developed a structured questionnaire focusing on: OTT platform usage patterns, Behavioural aspects (attitude changes, impact on social interactions, academic performance). Exposure to inappropriate content (cyber pornography, violence, etc.) awareness and involvement in cybercrimes. Conduct surveys through both online and offline modes, utilizing schools, youth organizations, and online platforms to reach the target population.

Hypothesis: There is a positive correlation between juveniles in the 16-21 age group being exposed to Over-the-Top (OTT) content, especially content that includes violence and cyber delinquency themes, and their tendency to engage in cyber delinquent behaviors." The correlation is anticipated to be affected by variables such as social separation and alienation, as well as psychological effects, as assessed through an analysis based on questionnaires.

This hypothesis posits a potential correlation between exposure to specific content on OTT platforms and the increase in adolescent cyber-delinquent behaviors. The hypothesis posits that these behaviors may be influenced not only by the material itself, but also by social and psychological variables, which could intensify the impact even more. The focus was on evaluation of four factors, namely

1. Propagation of violence through OTT
2. Propagation of Cyber Delinquency
3. Social Distancing and Alienation
4. Psychological Impact.

Data Analysis and Evaluation

To analyse the impact of OTT content on increasing juvenile cyber delinquency the researcher collected the data from 201 respondents in the age group of 16-23 years. Most of the respondents were students of various educational institutions within the city of Lucknow. Before administering the questionnaire, the respondents were assured of their anonymity and non-disclosure of their identities. The focus was on evaluation of four factors, namely 1. Propagation of violence through OTT, 2. Propagation of Cyber Delinquency, 3. Social Distancing and Alienation, and 4. Psychological Impact. Each of these factors were analysed based on a set of five questions each. Below given is the analysis of the data thus collected based on the five factors.

*Table 1. Gender * age group crosstabulation*

Count					
		Age Group			**Total**
		16-18	**19-21**	**21-23**	
Gender	Male	60	14	19	93
	Female	18	61	29	108
Total		78	75	48	201

Factor One: Propagation of Violence

OTT platforms have added to the diverse taste for several series and shows among the youth and have led them on a highly engaging path of entertainment and information. The characteristics of OTT platforms

*Figure 1. Gender * age group crosstabulation*

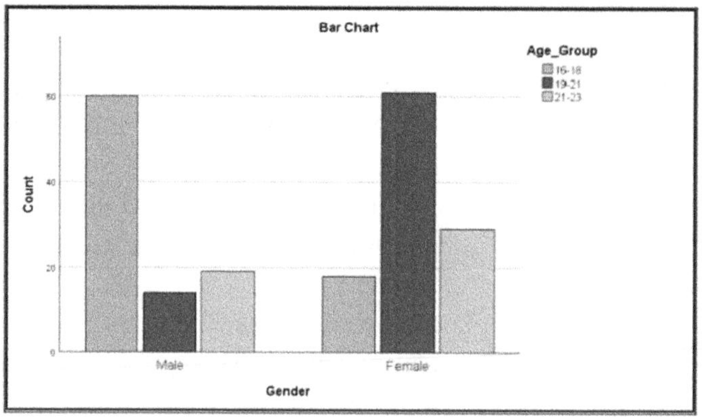

*Table 2. Gender * education crosstabulation*

Count					
		Education			Total
		Intermediate	Bachelor	Masters	
Gender	Male	30	44	19	93
	Female	7	81	20	108
Total		37	125	39	201

*Figure 2. Gender * education crosstabulation*

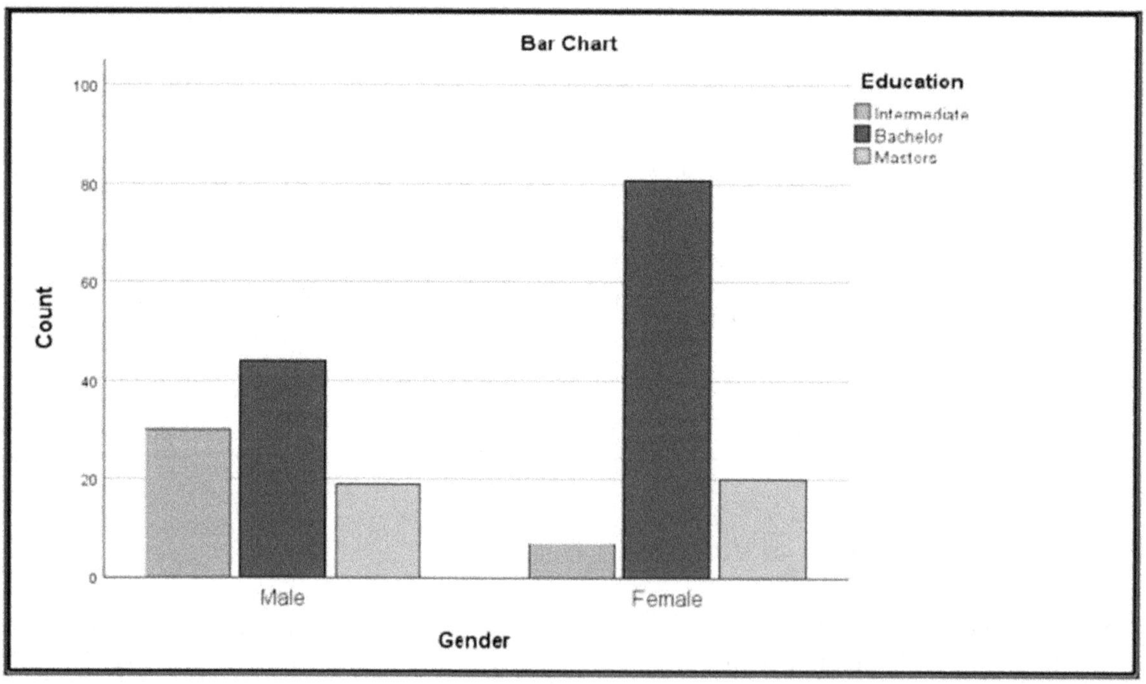

being cost-effective and convenient have contributed to their popularity. Further, they confer autonomy to the viewer as to the content they wish to see, deciding what one wants to see and at what time, has added on to the popularity of these platforms. It is observed that these platforms are used to depict anti-national and anti-religious content. As most of the series made available on OTT are designed on binge-watching, continuous watching has a deep impact on the minds of the viewers of which youth constitute the major portion. Spreading negative culture amongst the youth. (Kumari Astuti, Shristy Kamal, Zainab Imam and Runa, 2022)

Looking at the above responses it can be deduced that majority of the respondents agree with the fact that the content of the OTT platforms in India is more violent and abusive than regular television content. Majority of them were agreed that in the name of creative freedom and freedom of expression

Table 3. F1_1: OTT content contains abusive, violent, and narcotic elements in comparison to regular TV content

Correlations				
		Gender	**Age Group**	**F1_1**
Gender	Pearson Correlation	1	.348**	.005
	Sig. (2-tailed)		<.001	.945
	N	201	201	201
Age Group	Pearson Correlation	.348**	1	.023
	Sig. (2-tailed)	<.001		.750
	N	201	201	201
F1_1	Pearson Correlation	.005	.023	1
	Sig. (2-tailed)	.945	.750	
	N	201	201	201
**. Correlation is significant at the 0.01 level (2-tailed).				

Table 4. OTT contents are exploiting the term 'freedom of expression' without adequate responsibility

Correlations				
		Gender	**Age Group**	**F1_2**
Gender	Pearson Correlation	1	.348**	-.058
	Sig. (2-tailed)		<.001	.415
	N	201	201	201
Age Group	Pearson Correlation	.348**	1	-.009
	Sig. (2-tailed)	<.001		.900
	N	201	201	201
F1_2	Pearson Correlation	-.058	-.009	1
	Sig. (2-tailed)	.415	.900	
	N	201	201	201
**. Correlation is significant at the 0.01 level (2-tailed).				

Table 5. F1_3: OTT content has the power to manipulate public opinion

Correlations				
		Gender	**Age Group**	**F1_3**
Gender	Pearson Correlation	1	.348**	.237**
	Sig. (2-tailed)		<.001	<.001
	N	201	201	201
Age Group	Pearson Correlation	.348**	1	.110
	Sig. (2-tailed)	<.001		.119
	N	201	201	201
F1_3	Pearson Correlation	.237**	.110	1
	Sig. (2-tailed)	<.001	.119	
	N	201	201	201
**. Correlation is significant at the 0.01 level (2-tailed).				

Table 6. F1_4: OTT platforms deliberately create controversial content to make their content famous

Correlations				
		Gender	**Age Group**	**F1_4**
Gender	Pearson Correlation	1	.348**	.306**
	Sig. (2-tailed)		<.001	<.001
	N	201	201	201
Age Group	Pearson Correlation	.348**	1	.202**
	Sig. (2-tailed)	<.001		.004
	N	201	201	201
F1_4	Pearson Correlation	.306**	.202**	1
	Sig. (2-tailed)	<.001	.004	
	N	201	201	201
**. Correlation is significant at the 0.01 level (2-tailed).				

sometimes inappropriate content is produced and the rating certification for the audience is hardly a barrier to watching age-inappropriate content since there is no fool proof way of determining the age of the viewer once you have the membership access to the platform. Due to the inability of the viewer to distinguish between appropriate and inappropriate behaviour, which is the result of inexperience and underdeveloped moral and ethical compass due to age related factors of teenagers, it is easy to manipulate the thought process of the viewers. Often the content glorifies the 'antihero' which the teenagers relate to as being 'cool' and start to emulate such unwarranted behaviour as it seems appropriate to them. Majority of the respondents agree that OTTs often exploit controversial issues to increase the TRPs of their content and that the content is more violent in comparison to that of other countries. Often these contents do not have an objective view but rather has a skewed vision of the controversy at hand. Overall, it can be

Table 7. F1_5: Indian OTT platforms have more violent content with respect to other countries

Correlations				
		Gender	Age Group	F1_5
Gender	Pearson Correlation	1	.348**	.353**
	Sig. (2-tailed)		<.001	<.001
	N	201	201	201
Age Group	Pearson Correlation	.348**	1	.244**
	Sig. (2-tailed)	<.001		<.001
	N	201	201	201
F1_5	Pearson Correlation	.353**	.244**	1
	Sig. (2-tailed)	<.001	<.001	
	N	201	201	201
**. Correlation is significant at the 0.01 level (2-tailed).				

concluded from the responses that the majority of the respondents are in agreement that OTT contents promote violence in absence of proper regulators in India, so therefore, the corelations are significant.

Factor Two: Propagation of Cyber Bullying

Cyberbullying is increasingly becoming a social problem. With the increase is via media of social networking platforms, anonymity seems to be the new weapon in the hands of cyber delinquents. It has become easy to take 'revenge' or even inappropriately harass a schoolmate, collegemate or colleague. As the survey indicates that majority of the respondents are aware of cybercrime and its repercussions. Majority of respondents agree that OTT contents are a medium of propagation of cyberbullying. Here it is imperative to distinguish between cybercrime and cyber bullying. Cyberbullying is targeted at individu-

Table 8. F2_1 awareness about cybercrime

Correlations				
		Gender	Age Group	F2_1
Gender	Pearson Correlation	1	.348**	.378**
	Sig. (2-tailed)		<.001	<.001
	N	201	201	201
Age Group	Pearson Correlation	.348**	1	.264**
	Sig. (2-tailed)	<.001		<.001
	N	201	201	201
F2_1	Pearson Correlation	.378**	.264**	1
	Sig. (2-tailed)	<.001	<.001	
	N	201	201	201
**. Correlation is significant at the 0.01 level (2-tailed).				

Table 9. F2_2: OTT contents contribute to the rise in cyberbullying

Correlations			
		Gender	**F2_2**
Gender	Pearson Correlation	1	.276**
	Sig. (2-tailed)		<.001
	N	201	201
F2_2	Pearson Correlation	.276**	1
	Sig. (2-tailed)	<.001	
	N	201	201
**. Correlation is significant at the 0.01 level (2-tailed).			

Table 10. F2_3: OTT content promotes sexual and violent content to age-inappropriate audience

Correlations			
		Gender	**F2_3**
Gender	Pearson Correlation	1	.156*
	Sig. (2-tailed)		.027
	N	201	201
F2_3	Pearson Correlation	.156*	1
	Sig. (2-tailed)	.027	
	N	201	201
*. Correlation is significant at the 0.05 level (2-tailed).			

Table 11. F2_4: OTT content depicts actual occurrences in your immediate surroundings

Correlations			
		Gender	**F2_4**
Gender	Pearson Correlation	1	.240**
	Sig. (2-tailed)		<.001
	N	201	201
F2_4	Pearson Correlation	.240**	1
	Sig. (2-tailed)	<.001	
	N	201	201
**. Correlation is significant at the 0.01 level (2-tailed).			

als using social media primarily whereas cybercrime is a systematic network of computers committed towards criminal activities. Since, as established in the previous section, the OTT content is aiming at the reflection of the incidents in the society, highlighting them via OTT platforms ends up sometimes glamourizing such activities even though they are socially and culturally inappropriate. Majority of the respondents are in agreement that OTT content glamourises criminal behaviour. It can therefore be

Table 12. F2_5: OTT content glamourizes criminal behaviour

Correlations			
		Gender	F2_5
Gender	Pearson Correlation	1	.251**
	Sig. (2-tailed)		<.001
	N	201	201
F2_5	Pearson Correlation	.251**	1
	Sig. (2-tailed)	<.001	
	N	201	201
**. Correlation is significant at the 0.01 level (2-tailed).			

deduced that with the rise in awareness of the ways of cyberbullying due to reality-based shows on OTT the current generation of teenagers are increasing using the cyberspace to cause trouble for others. For some it may just be for fun but for others it is pure vendetta.

Table 13. F3_1: Binge watching alienates individuals from society

Correlations			
		Gender	F3_1
Gender	Pearson Correlation	1	.262**
	Sig. (2-tailed)		<.001
	N	201	201
F3_1	Pearson Correlation	.262**	1
	Sig. (2-tailed)	<.001	
	N	201	201
**. Correlation is significant at the 0.01 level (2-tailed).			

Table 14. F3_2: OTT indulgence causes youngsters to be more in virtual than in the real world

Correlations			
		Gender	F3_2
Gender	Pearson Correlation	1	.312**
	Sig. (2-tailed)		<.001
	N	201	201
F3_2	Pearson Correlation	.312**	1
	Sig. (2-tailed)	<.001	
	N	201	201
**. Correlation is significant at the 0.01 level (2-tailed).			

Table 15. F3_3: OTT content makes one fantasize about unrealistic things in life

Correlations				
		Gender	**Age Group**	**F3_3**
Gender	Pearson Correlation	1	.348**	-.002
	Sig. (2-tailed)		<.001	.978
	N	201	201	201
Age Group	Pearson Correlation	.348**	1	-.033
	Sig. (2-tailed)	<.001		.640
	N	201	201	201
F3_3	Pearson Correlation	-.002	-.033	1
	Sig. (2-tailed)	.978	.640	
	N	201	201	201
**. Correlation is significant at the 0.01 level (2-tailed).				

Table 16.+ F3_4: Affordable OTT access and on demand content has reduced family time

Correlations				
		Gender	**Age Group**	**F3_4**
Gender	Pearson Correlation	1	.348**	.297**
	Sig. (2-tailed)		<.001	<.001
	N	201	201	201
Age Group	Pearson Correlation	.348**	1	.203**
	Sig. (2-tailed)	<.001		.004
	N	201	201	201
F3_4	Pearson Correlation	.297**	.203**	1
	Sig. (2-tailed)	<.001	.004	
	N	201	201	201
**. Correlation is significant at the 0.01 level (2-tailed).				

Table 17. F3_5: OTT contents are extremely addictive

Correlations			
		Gender	**F3_5**
Gender	Pearson Correlation	1	.242**
	Sig. (2-tailed)		<.001
	N	201	201
F3_5	Pearson Correlation	.242**	1
	Sig. (2-tailed)	<.001	
	N	201	201
**. Correlation is significant at the 0.01 level (2-tailed).			

Factor Three: Social Distancing and Alienation

Today, most of us imagine the weekend as us laying down at home with some snacks and 'binge watching' shows on Netflix, Disney+Hotstar, Amazon Prime and more. It's the one day that as working professionals or students we can sit back and relax. A decade or so ago maybe, this was not the scenario. On weekends people would visit family and friends, have them over for dinner, go on short trips and hiking or adventure activities or just spend time with family. This is sadly no longer happening. Majority of the People a cooped up inside their home watching Television or OTT content and refuse to move out of their homes. The 'family time' is increasingly becoming 'me time' because of the increasing choices and options of available content. Post Covid-19 more so, people avoid going to movie theatres as they are aware that soon the movie shall be released on either one of the OTTs and can be watched in the comfort of their homes. The survey results indicate the same attitude of the respondents as discussed above. Majority of the respondents agree that the over-usage of OTT platforms creates social alienation and drive youngsters to live more and more in the virtual world, where they fantasize about unrealistic things. This also cuts the time one spends with the family, and this results in distances among family members. In future this may result in finding oneself totally alone leading to psychological reparations.

Factor Four: Psychological Impact

The last factor is the psychological impact and long-term mental repercussions that may have a detrimental effect on personality and behaviour of young people who are overly dependent on OTTs for their entertainment. The responses seem to be divided on this aspect since about only 40 percent of the respondents agree that OTT contents result in behavioural issues of viewers. Conversely about 60 percent respondents do agree that over-indulgence of OTT content hampers professional work outcome and increases use of abusive language. From the correlations provided, it's evident that there's a statistically significant relationship between gender and various aspects related to the psychological impact of Over-The-Top (OTT) content consumption among young people. The correlations showcase a connection between gender and different behavioural outcomes arising from OTT content consumption, such as defiant actions, anger/aggression, depression/anxiety, academic/professional output, and increased usage of offensive language. This division in opinion could stem from various factors, such as individual

Table 18. F4_1: OTT contents encourage defiant actions

Correlations			
		Gender	**F4_1**
Gender	Pearson Correlation	1	.255**
	Sig. (2-tailed)		<.001
	N	201	201
F4_1	Pearson Correlation	.255**	1
	Sig. (2-tailed)	<.001	
	N	201	201
**. Correlation is significant at the 0.01 level (2-tailed).			

Table 19. F4_2: OTT contents provoke youth to anger and aggression

Correlations			
		Gender	**F4_2**
Gender	Pearson Correlation	1	.365**
	Sig. (2-tailed)		<.001
	N	201	201
F4_2	Pearson Correlation	.365**	1
	Sig. (2-tailed)	<.001	
	N	201	201
**. Correlation is significant at the 0.01 level (2-tailed).			

Table 20. F4_3 OTT content induces depression and anxiety

Correlations			
		Gender	**F4_3**
Gender	Pearson Correlation	1	.527**
	Sig. (2-tailed)		<.001
	N	201	201
F4_3	Pearson Correlation	.527**	1
	Sig. (2-tailed)	<.001	
	N	201	201
**. Correlation is significant at the 0.01 level (2-tailed).			

Table 21. F4_4: Overindulgence in OTT content hampers academic/professional output

Correlations			
		Gender	**F4_4**
Gender	Pearson Correlation	1	.354**
	Sig. (2-tailed)		<.001
	N	201	201
F4_4	Pearson Correlation	.354**	1
	Sig. (2-tailed)	<.001	
	N	201	201
**. Correlation is significant at the 0.01 level (2-tailed).			

differences in susceptibility to the psychological impact of media content, diverse viewing habits, personal experiences, or cultural influences. It's important to note that while there might be disagreement among respondents, the statistical correlations between gender and these behavioural aspects indicate a consistent pattern that's worthy of attention.

Table 22. F4_5 OTT content leads to rise in the usage of offensive language among young people

Correlations			
		Gender	F4_5
Gender	Pearson Correlation	1	.416**
	Sig. (2-tailed)		<.001
	N	201	201
F4_5	Pearson Correlation	.416**	1
	Sig. (2-tailed)	<.001	
	N	201	201
**. Correlation is significant at the 0.01 level (2-tailed).			

CONCLUSION

Regulation of OTT platforms is a much-debated topic that has stirred the country at the present times. The task while challenging is necessary at the same time. The OTT platforms are newer version of providing entertainment services and the existing laws do not apply directly on to them. This while poses problem in regulating them also pressurise the government in coming up with fresh guidelines or laws that could be made applicable to these platforms. Ott platforms have been accused of showcasing content that is rich in vulgarity, obscenity and violence. As the existing laws do not directly apply to the OTT platforms censorship of the content becomes impossible often leading to the content be displayed on OTT platforms without being censored for objectionable contents. There is rising concerns about the impact of such content on viewers especially the youngsters, and it also highlights the dire need to regulate them. There have been several FIR's (Das,2023) and PILs filed against the unregulated content telecasted on OTT platforms and Courts have also emphasized the need to frame laws to regulate them. The OTT platforms are directly available through internet and are easily accessible directly to the viewer through smartphones and laptops. The content thus displayed does not pass through any censorship before reaching the viewer. Though there exists a Central Board Of Film Certification under the Cinematograph Act 1952 working under the Ministry of Information and Broadcasting of the Government of India. However, the Ministry citied incapacity in applying the Act to OTT platforms due to lack of jurisdiction over them. Owning to pressure from the Courts and the public the Government amended the Government of India (Allocation of Business) Rules, 1961. Through this amendment films and audio-visual programmes shown online were brought within the purview of Ministry of information and Broadcasting. As an effect of this amendment the OTT platforms streaming online videos have been brought under the purview of the MIB. Lack of direct regulation over OTT platforms compelled the government to directed these platforms to frame self-regulating guidelines and issued a list of don'ts for the online video streaming service providers (Government Notification 2019)

Sensing the tightening noose, the OTT platforms devised self-regulating guidelines and code of ethics for showcasing content. Guidelines provided prohibition on five parameters

a) Content banned by law or a court;
b) Content maliciously and deliberately promoting terrorism;
c) Content maliciously outraging religious sentiments;

d) Content promoting child pornography; and
e) Content maliciously and deliberately disrespecting the national emblem or the national flag.

The platforms also formulated a Universal Self-Regulation Code for Online Curated Content Providers. The platforms asserted that the code was balanced version of protection of freedom of speech and expression and compliance with the norms of the government.

The government too introduced the Information Technology (Intermediary Guidelines and Digital Media Ethics Code) Rules, 2021.

As per the new rules OTT platforms will have to self-classify the content into five age-based categories: U (Universal), U/A 7 years, U/A 13 years, U/A 16 years, and A (Adult).

The rules also lay down a soft-touch self-regulatory architecture with a Code of Ethics and three-tier grievance redressal mechanism for OTT platforms.

Every publisher should appoint a Grievance Officer based in India for receiving and redressing grievances in 15 days. The amended guidelines of 2021 were not liked by the OTT platform. They resist scrutiny by an external authority. The OTT platforms take it as excessive regulation ultimately hindering there right to freely express as guaranteed under the Indian Constitution. Ferring censorship by external authority the platforms contemplated following parameters in there self-regulation code:

a) A framework for age classification;
b) Appropriate content description;
c) Appropriate access control; and
d) A stage-based grievance redressal and escalation mechanism to be followed.

The government however rejected the proposed guidelines as formulated by the OTT platforms for it lacked third party monitoring and also the code of ethics as formulated by them did not clearly specify a prohibited content. The OTT platforms agree to two tier system of check under which they are willing to appoint a Grievance redressal officer but are not comfortable with an external authority monitoring the, the external authority as proposed by the government shall be consisting of bureaucrat and shall be headed by a judge. Both the two tier and the three-tier system as proposed to regulate the OTT platforms by the OTT platforms and the government respectively shall give rise to the problem of conflict of interest.

The debate of regulating the OTT platforms is still ongoing. Both the parties, the OTT platforms and the government are determined to find a amicable solution that balances the interest of both the parties and also does not deprive the consumers of the vast option of entertainment available to them. The government asserts that the amended IT rules provide subtle form of censorship similar to that of CBFC. But the rules are declared to be not flawless. Under the three-tier regulatory framework the third tier shall be consisting entirely of bureaucrats with no representative from the judiciary or civil society. It is thus asserted that such regulatory system shall lack independence. While it can be regulated through these guidelines that nothing illegal is shown but there are equal fears of self-censorship either voluntarily or due to external pressure. The fears though early as the guideline shave not been implemented, are not without merit.

Regulation is indeed necessary in the interest of the public for it is the duty of the governments to ensure that under the disguise of exercise of right to freedom to do something wrong is not dome to the public at large. The entertainment platforms meant to lightened the minds must not be used to fill it with lust, hatred and vengeance. In ensuring so support and cooperation of all the players involved: government, OTT platforms and the consumers shall be required.

Based on the nature, characteristics and style of functioning of OTT platforms it shall be proper to have an autonomous body to regulate the OTT platforms. This view has been supported by the Supreme Court also through PIL filed in the case of Shashank Shekhar Jha. proper way of regulating the OTT platforms shall require. (Shashank Shekhar Jha vs Union of India)

The data suggests a noteworthy relationship between gender and the perceived psychological impacts of excessive OTT content consumption. However, the divergence in respondents' opinions regarding behavioural issues versus professional outcomes and language usage emphasizes the complexity of evaluating the full scope of OTT content's effects on individuals. Further studies or qualitative research may be beneficial in understanding the nuances behind these contrasting viewpoints and exploring the broader implications of OTT content on mental health and behaviour.

REFERENCES

Aveek Sarkar v. State of West Bengal, 4 Supreme Court Cases 257 (Supreme Court of India 2014) 4 SCC 257.).

Baumol, W. J. (1990). Entrepreneurship: Productive, unproductive, and destructive. *Journal of Political Economy*, *98*(5), 893–921. doi:10.1086/261712

Cohen, R., & Blaszczynski, A. (2015). Comparative effects of Facebook and conventional media on body image dissatisfaction. *Journal of Eating Disorders*, *3*(1), 1–10. doi:10.1186/s40337-015-0061-3 PMID:26140215

Community, N. (2020). *Future of OTT in India*. Nasscom Community. https://community.nasscom.in/communities/digital-transformation/telecom-media-communities/future-of-ott-in india.html

Das, A. (2021). Supreme Courts Directs States To File Status Report On FIRs, Adjourns Hearing To August. *Tandav' Web Series Row.*

Fardouly, J., Diedrichs, P. C., Vartanian, L. R., & Halliwell, E. (2018). Social comparisons on social media: The impact of Facebook on young women's body image concerns and mood. *Body Image*, *26*, 38–45. PMID:25615425

Granovetter, M. (1985). Economic action and social structure: The problem of embeddedness. *American Journal of Sociology*, *91*(3), 481–510. doi:10.1086/228311

India, G. o. (2017). *Nationwide Registry for Organ and Tissue Donation Launched.* Press Information Bureau. http://pib.nic.in/newsite/PrintRelease.aspx?relid=131941

India, G. o. (2021). *Information Technology (Intermediary Guidelines and Digital Media Ethics Code) Rules 2021*. New Delhi: Ministry of Electronics and Information Technology https://mib.gov.in/sites/default/files/IT%28Intermediary%20Guidelines%20and%20Digital%20Media%20Ethics%20Code%29%20Rules%2C%202021%20English.pdf

Kumar, J. & George, N. (2023). *India: Government Issues Regulations For OTT Platforms And Online Content.* Mondaq. https://www.mondaq.com/india/broadcasting-film-tv--radio/1007904/government-issues-regulations-for-ott-platforms-and-online-content (last accessed on 23rd July 2023)

Kircaburun, K., & Griffiths, M. D. (2018). Instagram addiction and the Big Five of personality: The mediating role of self-liking. *Journal of Behavioral Addictions*, *7*(1), 158–170. doi:10.1556/2006.7.2018.15 PMID:29461086

Lee, S. Y., & Kim, M. S. (2018). Social capital and binge-watching on over-the-top content platforms. *Journal of Broadcasting & Electronic Media*, *62*(2), 276–294.

Lissak, G., & Mekler, E. D. (2019). Youth Online Behaviour and Social Media Use in Israel: Analysis of associations with depressive symptoms. *The Journal of Adolescent Health*, *64*(3), 334–340.

Parto, S. (2005). Economic activity and institutions: *Taking Stock. Journal of Economic Issues*, *39*(1), 21–52. doi:10.1080/00213624.2005.11506779

Ramji Lal Modi v. State of U.P., All India Reporter 620 (Supreme Court of India 1957).

Ranjit D. Udeshi v. State of Maharashtra, 1 Supreme Court Reporter 65 (Supreme Court of India 1965).

Ray, S. S. (2020). Explained: What is the measure of 'obscenity' in India. *Indian Express.* https://indianexpress.com/article/explained/explained-milind-soman-obscenity-in-india-6998750/

Rideout, V. J., Fox, S., & Roberts, D. F. (2019). Young people's news habits: Examining the role of platforms, devices, and social networks. *Journal of Computer-Mediated Communication*, *24*(5), 227–239.

https://udayindia.in/impact-of-ott-platforms-on-youth/

Shashank Shekhar Jha vs Union Of India, 15 October, 2020 https://indiankanoon.org/doc/24196538/

Stamenkovic, M. (2012). In full view: Cyber suicide, Self and Public show case of death (for real). *TC Journal, 5*(12), 73-101.

Chapter 14
The Impact of OTT Services on Television Talk Shows:
Navigating New Horizons

Elisa Paz
https://orcid.org/0000-0001-7477-0858
EU Business School, Spain

ABSTRACT

Television talk shows include several forms and styles depending on the time in which they are broadcast on linear television, including the morning magazine talk show, daytime programmes, and late-night entertaining shows. Airing timeslots help the audience manage their expectations regarding the tone and content of the programmes. With the eruption of over-the-top (OTT) services in the media landscape, this key aspect disappears in favour of on-demand consumption. This chapter delves into the transformative effects of OTT services on television talk show creation and engagement, exploring the evolving media landscape and the intricate interplay of content, technology, and audience dynamics in the current media age.

1. INTRODUCTION

The rise of over-the-top (OTT) media has brought a profound disruption in traditional television practices, not only in the way that audiences consume content but also in challenging established norms and genres of the industry. This disruption has sparked intense competition, compelling media companies to innovate in terms of narratives, perspectives, and production values in order to gain subscribers and loyal viewers, which has reshaped the present and future of media content creation and consumption.

This context presents the chance and the need to explore new dimensions of media studies in order to understand the current media environment in aspects such as cross-cultural potential and readings of media texts, audiences' engagement and media production and creation.

This new media landscape has significantly affected the essence of different genres such as fiction, due to the new possibilities related to production and new consumption patterns, whereas some other

DOI: 10.4018/979-8-3693-0116-6.ch014

macro genres such as news programmes seem more unaltered by over-the-top services and still rely on linear consumption due to its strong live component.

A specific television genre that has been greatly affected and redefined by OTT media is the television talk show. These productions are a unique form within the macro-genre of infotainment focusing on a mediated public discourse, where discussions and conversations take place in an entertaining and engaging manner (Timberg, 2002; Tolson, 2001). In conventional broadcasting, the different forms or subgenres of the television talk show had a direct connection with the airing timeslot in which they were broadcast, and three main types of talk shows could be identified: the morning magazine shows, the emotional daytime programmes, and the entertaining late-night shows (Danesi, 2016; Mittell, 2004; Timberg, 2002).

With the rise of OTT media and the on-demand nature of streaming services, the connection between talk shows and specific airing timeslots disappears, which presents as much a challenge as an exciting opportunity for media scholars and professionals. On the one hand, the detachment from specific timeslots could potentially allow producers to have greater flexibility in content creation, and experiment with different elements to build a format that is specific for on-demand services and viewers. On the other hand, audiences relied on timeslots of the talk show to anticipate the type of programme they were about to watch, which shaped their expectations and overall viewing experience.

This disruptive scenario caused by OTT platforms lead to a need for a comprehensive examination of the topic. The objective of this chapter is to explore the ways in which OTT services have disrupted the production and definition of television talk shows, emphasizing the shift from traditional scheduling to on-demand streaming and the implications for the creation and consumption of television talk shows.

The aims of this chapter include analysing the evolving landscape of television talk shows in the context of OTT services, dissecting the impact of the detachment from fixed airing timeslots on content creation, as well as discussing the implications for audience engagement from a cross-cultural perspective.

To achieve this objective, this chapter navigates the talk show from a theoretical perspective, as well as the rise of OTT services and its impact on the traditional concept of airing timeslots and audience consumption. Delving into the implications of the current scenario, the chapter will explore the effects associated with breaking free from fixed schedules, as well as analysing the type of "television" talk show genre that OTT services are implementing. Are talk shows in OTT streaming platforms more similar to morning, daytime, or late-night programmes? Is there a new genre forming in these platforms?

Addressing these questions will allow to examine the creative possibilities that OTT platforms have enabled (if any) for talk show productions, as well as analysing the implications of format adaptations and the social and cultural relevance of this disruption, addressing the diversity or lack thereof in talk show programming of OTT platforms.

2. REVIEWING THE NATURE AND SIGNIFICANCE OF THE TELEVISION TALK SHOW

2.1 Evolution Of the Television Talk Show Across Cultures and Media

The television talk show is not a simple genre to define, and, besides its hybrid and amorphous nature, it has experienced significant evolution since its conception. It is a widely influential media text that defies the established public and private realms, as well as the boundaries between the collective and the personal (Ilie, 2006).

This genre was first popularized in the United States and then exported to other countries and regions such as Europe, where it was adapted considering the sociocultural context. European broadcasters focused more on developing educative and documentary media content, and most entertainment formats were imported from the United States (Bondebjerg et al., 2008). This is why the market and context of reference for assessing the establishment and evolution of this genre is the United States, particularly since the conception and airing of NBC's shows *Today* and *Tonight*, as will be addressed in a few paragraphs.

The origins of the television talk show can be traced back to variety radio programmes and radio talk programmes in the United States, and even back to vaudeville and variety shows displayed in theatres in the 19th century. As famously put by Bob Hope, "when vaudeville died, television was the box they put it in" (Kawa, 2018, p. 28). Before television, these very popular spectacles were adapted to radio when the medium started to develop, and mainly vaudeville inspired variety shows broadcast on radio, which were more inclined towards a funny or musical tone depending on the host (Gomery, 2008). The relevance of the host within these programmes will remain throughout its years of expansion and evolution. Variety shows soon developed into different forms of talk shows with different styles, more informative or entertaining.

Productions that are popular among audiences find their way into new media and technological advances, and the talk show is no exception. Television talk shows inherited the production dynamics of their analogous radio programmes, well-known hosts and also their popularity among audiences, which increased the investment on these shows.

Television talk shows went through five cycles (Timberg, 2002): experimentation and consolidation (1948-1962), facing new challenges (1962-1974), transition and new voices (174-1980), audience participation in the post-network era (1980-1990), and rediscovery and increased social impact (1990 onwards). Although there is no established sixth cycle, one could argue that the emergence of the internet extended the popularity and segmentation of this television genre, and the appearance of OTT services could eventually result in a seventh era of television talk shows, the disruption era.

Throughout these periods, there have been several forms and structures of television talk shows, although there are several flagship programmes from the United States that have successfully adapted audience participation and infotainment to television dynamics and set the norm. Morning shows with a more informative tone and structure were modelled after *Today*, from the major network NBC while Pat Weaver was president, and influenced what we know now as breakfast television or magazine talk (Christie, 2012; I. Jones, 2004). For daytime shows, Phil Donahue initiated a formula later consolidated by Oprah and widely popular in this timeslot, later adapted by other programmes across cultures. Finally, late-night shows find their influence in the *Tonight* show, also aired and produced by NBC under Pat Weaver's presidency (Ilie, 2006; Timberg, 2002).

Although the essence of television talk shows from the United States is maintained across regions such as Europe or Asia (Bondebjerg et al., 2008; Wahab, 2011), it is noticeable that some features from the original format from the United States were adapted to specific cultural contexts and narratives. For instance, the live studio audience of French television talk shows are usually surrounding the stage, in a more active or forefront role, whereas programmes produced in the United Kingdom or Spain imitate the disposition of the audience in United States' productions, having the live studio located in front of the set, usually behind the camera in a theatre-like disposition (Vallet et al., 2012).

Another difference set by culture has to do with the dynamics of the talk itself, since it is very related to the form of communication of societies, both verbal and non-verbal, and it affects how implicit or explicit the discussion is, the use of hand gestures, the level of acceptance of interruptions, etc. For instance, whereas British speakers tend to "control the floor" without taking into consideration who is speaking next, Arab or Nigerian participants value more the fact of taking turns (Boukertouta & Chioukh, 2020; Oyeleye & Olutayo, 2012).

Throughout the years, the genre has successfully adapted not only to different cultures but also to an ever-evolving media landscape, and it is no wonder that there has been a considerable shift in the talk show arena with the rise of new media and OTT services.

The television talk show has demonstrated a great capacity to adapt to new technologies and media opportunities. For instance, one of the most relevant irruptions in the media landscape in recent years has been media content spreading through the Internet. As aforementioned, one of the characteristics of the television talk show usually common to all subgenres is their fragmented nature. This allowed for parts of the programmes to be disseminated through different platforms on the Internet, which resulted in and increased popularity of the shows (especially of those airing during late-night slots).

Besides sharing parts of the programme online as a promotional practice, television talk shows also expanded into the realm of social media creating official profiles and stimulating conversation online. This aims to spread and maintain the popularity of the programmes but also to increase audience engagement throughout the different media forms that they actively use, as they are key strategic spaces to extend their influence too.

When it comes to OTT services, we also refer to television or film content that is consumed from the internet through a network with higher standards than ordinary internet video, including live TV, time-shifted TV, and video on demand (Layton, 2015). This has shaken the media landscape from a production, distribution, promotional and, of course, consumption perspective (Matrix, 2014). This asynchronous consumption has questioned how bonding experiences through mass media productions will be affected, which is emphasized in television talk shows due to their "liveness" or at least apparent live aspects. When audiences select a programme to watch on demand, they are more aware of the lack of a synchronous experience, and it is pertinent to ask and explore how this affects the structure and discursive nature of the talk show.

Finally, retrieving a cross-cultural perspective, it is interesting to note that since talk shows are a low-cost production, they are a key format regarding original productions in OTT services, such as Netflix, in regions like Latin America (e.g.: Argentina, Mexico or Colombia) (Mastrini & Krakowiak, 2021). However, usually talk show programmes on OTT services are included under the category of "others", or along genres that have been historically a fundamental different category, such as stand-up shows (Delgado & Prado, 2010; Mastrini & Krakowiak, 2021), which may suggest that these services are overlooking a genre that has demonstrated high adaptability capabilities across the evolution of media technologies and platforms.

2.2 Social And Cultural Impact of Television Talk Shows

In all its formats, the talk show has a profound cultural impact across cultures, and they have also generated some controversy among audiences and scholars. For instance, some daytime shows are deemed as *trash talk programmes*, whereas some scholars have argued that daytime productions became a platform for voices who were traditionally excluded from the public sphere, which sparked conversations about these shows representing the democratization of television, and the corresponding criticism to this claim.

On the one hand, daytime programmes allow public participation of voices that have usually been excluded from the public debate and even topics that were associated with the private or personal realm, and they present an alternative space that challenges the traditional concept of the public sphere (Lunt & Stenner, 2005; Shattuc, 1997). On the other hand, some scholars acknowledge the power structures of media institutions, particularly in certain cultural contexts, which would limit the democratic potential of the media environment (Wahab, 2011).

Continuing with the cross-cultural discussion, while the essential elements of the talk show are recognized globally, the situational context of the programmes around the globe varies significantly, such as is the case with British, American and French talk shows, for instance (Ilie, 2006). These differences are motivated by production choices to meet audiences' cultural preferences and expectations, ultimately reflecting the different perspectives of each region.

In line with this, it is pertinent to say that talk shows exist in a context of definition, interpretation, and evaluation (Mittell, 2004), which translates into hierarchies established within talk show programmes, with social power and historical forces influencing these interpretations and the categorization of the different subgenres. For instance, daytime shows dealing with personal issues are associated with feminine content, whereas studies suggest that viewers identify late-night programmes as more sophisticated productions (Mittell, 2003; Summergrad, 2016).

The cultural significance of talk shows is further evident when considering their political influence, not only when in discussion in daytime shows (channelling the feminist motto "the personal is political") or addressing political and current issues in late-night programmes, but also by having political candidates as guests, especially in the former. In fact, popular national talk shows are part of the presidential campaign circuit in several countries. It first became popular in the genre's country of origin, the United States, and it boomed when Bill Clinton played the saxophone in the *Arsenio Hall Show* in 1992. This is still a common practice today, as seen in the 2016 election when both Donald Trump and Hillary Clinton appeared on *The Tonight Show* with Jimmy Fallon. The host was heavily criticized by audiences online after Trump's interview for "humanising a monster" (Horton, 2016), for showing an amusing attitude and having a laid-back interview considering Trump's strong political stances. The host approached the interview in a similar fashion to all presidential candidates participating in the show, but the controversy led to a significant decrease in viewership and confirmed the political influence of talk shows and the critical role they play in social and public life.

Late-night shows allow to display a more personal and laid-back side of the candidates and reach audiences that may not be particularly interested in political information (Niven et al., 2003; Peterson, 2008).

The participation of political figures on talk shows is one of those essential aspects originated in the United States and imitated by talk shows across cultures (Bennett, 2012; Ekström & Tolson, 2013; Feldman, 2020; Schultz, 2012; Tucker & Schütz, 1995; Wahab, 2011). Finally, related to the public sphere, the agenda-setting theory has also been assessed by scholars in relation to the television talk show. This theory suggests that media productions are key to shaping public opinion since they determine what issues and topics are given the most attention. Scholars have explored how programmes such as *Saturday Night Live* might influence news programmes and vice-versa, highlighting the tight relationship between current affairs and television talk shows (Abel & Barthel, 2013; Leano, 2014; Thussu, 2007).

Figure 1. Jimmy Fallon messes up Donald Trump's hair, which caused strong online backlash among audiences for handling the interview in a soft manner

Finally, when addressing the viewing experience of television talk shows, the uses and gratifications theory (UGT) exploring motivations for watching talk shows are mainly entertainment, passing time and relaxation (Cress & Rapert, 1996), although when late-night television shows are the object of discussion, being informed and keeping up with current news in a more informal manner are also important motivations and reasons to watch (Niven et al., 2003; S. Roth et al., 2014).

2.3 Defining Aspects of The Television Talk Show

The genre's interplay of entertainment and information makes the talk show a distinctive form of infotainment, blending conversations, humour, and satire to cover a wide range of topics (Timberg, 2002; Tolson, 2001). There are certain elements that talk show programmes share, particularly their category as infotainment productions and being a "host-driven medium" (Munson, 1993). The host of the television talk show is a media personality, stimulating and guiding the structure of the episode. The host works as a director and a marketing claim too. The programmes often include the name of the host in their title to capture audience's attention and turn the host into a star themselves.

Some other elements that tend to shape decisions across talk show formats, according to Ilie (2006), are audience duplicity (the host deals with a studio audience and an at-home audience), having guests (who can be experts, celebrities or regular citizens), independence of episodes (each focusing on a particular topic or guest), diverse discursive strategies (e.g.: interview, debate, game…), a usually fragmented nature (with distinguishable different sections), and the fact that they are usually inexpensive to produce.

Besides, there are two other important elements to consider when defining the television talk show. On the one hand, although the different formats have a very distinctive tone and style (informative for morning magazine productions, more inclined towards the personal in daytime shows, and a marked entertainment and satire character in late-night talk programmes), these programmes allow for blurring the strict lines between public and private, creating what scholars have coined as the "emotional public sphere" (Lunt & Stenner, 2005).

This is not only evident on daytime shows, in which intrinsic dynamics are the exact definition of that since they address personal issues (usually by marginalized voices) on a public platform such as television, but also in late-night entertainment programmes. These shows address political and current issues with a humorous and satirical tone and often have well-known guests and even politicians promoting their work or ideas, which allows for a more personal perspective of the celebrity or political candidate (Baum, 2005; Van Zoonen & Holtz-Bacha, 2000). This reinforces the idea of the emotional public sphere and the defiant nature of the talk show.

On the other hand, another common element of television talk shows is their "liveness", which means that they are either live broadcast or recorded in real-time with little editing to give the appearance of being live (Couldry, 2004; Scannel, 1991). This is a common trait among the different subgenres of the television category, and it aims to emphasize the authenticity of the viewing and the feeling of a shared experience.

However, in spite of these characteristics that seem common to the genre, defining the talk show presents quite a challenge due to its narrative overlap with other mediatized forms of talk, transcending its own discursive conventions (Ilie, 2006) and because of the different subgenres that are encompassed in this umbrella term of the talk show.

Over the years, television talk shows have adapted to suit social and cultural factors, which resulted in different forms or subgenres forming around this popular television category. These subgenres vary in tone and purpose, spanning from informative shows, to personal and issue-related, to humorous and entertaining talk shows. Hence, the traditional association of the term television talk show exclusively with daytime programmes is rather an umbrella term covering a spectrum of different formats and styles (Abel & Barthel, 2013; Marcos-García et al., 2020).

2.4 Talk Show Subgenres and Traditional Airing Timeslots

Besides these elements and considerations, there is another key factor that affects the definition, production, and consumption of television talk shows: the time in which they air. While several elements contribute to the diversity within the talk show genre, the time during which they are broadcast is a key factor that shapes the content, tone and audience engagement of these programmes. Audiences differentiate different forms within the talk show genre due to several elements such as discussion topics (news, entertainment or personal) or ethical considerations, but the classification most used by both scholars and audiences is based on broadcasting time. Considering this, there are three main talk show forms: morning, daytime, and late-night.

Each of these forms is not merely a result of scheduling practices but embodies specific characteristics that cater to the preferences and expectations of different audience segments. Morning talk shows or magazine-like programmes often focus on providing audiences with light-hearted content in an informative tone, covering a diverse range of topics from lifestyle to news updates.

Daytime television shows are the most discussed in talk show scholarship, and they are mainly regarded as a feminine genre (Cassidy, 2008). These programmes usually involve a higher audience participation discussing personal matters and delving into the emotional experience of participants (Grindstaff, 2002; Shattuc, 1997). In spite of their focus on personal or private topics, we need to remember that these programmes have also been identified as a platform for marginalised voices and although this does not automatically make them political or feminist, and there is important criticism to consider (e.g.: cultural sensitivities), it represents an opportunity to blur the distinction between private and public spheres (Cragin, 2010; Kay, 2015).

The third type of talk show form is the late-night show. Shows airing in this timeslot are bound to be entertaining, humorous, and relevant. They are perceived by audiences as a more sophisticated type of programme, and their social and cultural relevance are undeniable (Mittell, 2003; Summergrad, 2016).

These scheduling practices are, at the same time, defined by assumptions led by traditional gender roles, which expect women to be at home during the day and interested in empathetic and personal content, late-night shows are usually led by men discussing public affairs. Traditional airing timeslots, as we have seen, have an enormous influence on the definition and consumption of television talk shows, as they help audiences as a shortcut for interpretation, since genres are used as cultural categories (Mittell, 2004).

It is interesting to note, though, that the current media landscape no longer relies as heavily on traditional timeslots to manage expectations regarding media genres, since consumption is experiencing a significant shift towards asynchronous practices and on-demand consumption with OTT services.

Television talk shows have been traditionally and intrinsically defined by the time in which they air. Producers create and script shows following the formula that suits the timeslot and audiences expect to see a specific type of content depending on when they tune in. Hence, it is pertinent to ask: how have television talk shows adapted to on-demand consumption? When taking airing timeslots out of the equation, what defines talk shows?

3. METHODOLOGY: EXPLORING THE OTT TALK SHOW

Considering all the discussion around television talk shows and the current media landscape, it is pertinent to address the following research questions:

1. In the context of OTT platforms, given the absence of their traditional association with specific timeslots, what now defines and distinguishes talk shows?
2. How do audiences engage with television talk shows in the context of on-demand consumption through OTT platforms?

In order to answer the first question, a critical analysis of OTT talk shows needs to be carried out. This chapter explores the most popular OTT services globally and considers programmes that fall under the category of "Talk Shows" for analysis. If there is not a specific category for the talk show and some genres that have traditionally been classified under a different category are included (e.g.: stand-up comedy shows), only those classified as talk shows and meeting the requirements explained earlier in the chapter are included.

Addressing the second question requires discussing the observable behaviour of audiences in digital media, along with existing discussions related to on-demand consumption and new media synergies.

The limitations in this study revolve around restricted access to OTT services limited to Spanish content, which results in omitting several platforms. An important platform, Twitch, sometimes categorized as OTT, has not been included for analysis. Twitch's interactive model, hosting live discussions between streamers and audiences, is similar to YouTube, although it emphasizes livestreaming and community-building. Despite its audience participation, Twitch is excluded from analysis due to its common classification as a social media site.

On the other hand, OTT platforms often lack transparency regarding viewership metrics, hindering analysis of audience engagement. Conducting focus groups could provide deeper insights into audience behaviour, compensating for these limitations. Despite these challenges, the analysis effectively addresses fundamental questions surrounding talk show adaptation to evolving technologies and changing consumption preferences.

4. RESULTS RELATED TO THE ANALYSIS OF TALK SHOWS: ARE OTT TALK SHOWS AN UPDATED GENRE?

Finding the programmes to be analysed and form the sample is a considerable challenge. In fact, in some cases, it is not easy to find this type of programmes to begin with, and when searching for them, platforms show results of reality shows or comedy shows (stand-up specials). Finding original programmes created for OTT services is also quite challenging. Prime Video (by Amazon) includes talk shows previously aired on linear television as part of its distribution strategy, and HBO Max has its programmes on catalogue (e.g.: *Last Week Tonight with John Oliver*) to watch on demand, but this would translate into a time-shifted consumption, as the programme is not conceived as an original for OTT.

Netflix, however, seems to have a different and more specific approach than its competitors. The streaming platform is the largest SVoD in the world at the moment and has increasingly relied on original content and adapted to current conceptions of "popular television"(Wayne, 2022). Although Netflix original content started with fiction productions and is widely known for these programmes, they have extended their productions into the realm of docuseries, realities and variety and talk shows.

In fact, when searching for this category related to the streaming platform, two prominent names in the talk show and comedy world pop up: David Letterman and Chelsea Handler. Both of them seem to qualify as the type of programmes that would air on the late-night slot on conventional television, but the gender parity would already be a disruption of the late show genre, as the vast majority of these programmes have traditionally been hosted by men and even deemed as a subgenre of "male buddies"(J. P. Jones, 2009). However, and ironically enough, the programme hosted by David Letterman is the only one that still prevails, since Handler's show was cancelled after two seasons.

Although the original production of television talk shows on OTT services is not intense nor a widespread practice yet, it has proven to attract interest from audiences and recognised celebrities with well-established talent and reputation. Since Netflix is the market leader in the industry, it would not be odd for other streaming services to follow their example and bet on these programmes, but what type of programmes would this be?

OTT services present an opportunity in the sense of what the detachment from fixed schedules can represent for the genre, as it might be a sign for flexibility and format experimentation. Consistent with this idea is the fact that both programmes are significantly different from one another while, at the same time, have specific arrangements that differ from some of the protocols that audiences might be used to when it comes to talk shows. Hence, there is space to question if talk shows in OTT streaming platforms are more similar to morning, daytime, or late-night programmes, or even if there is a new genre forming in these platforms.

The number of available and original television talk shows included on OTT catalogues is not grand, and the ones that could be defined by the disengagement from airing timeslots are those in the catalogue of Netflix, since the other platforms are rather relying on time-shifted consumption from programmes that originally air or have aired on conventional television. As a consequence, it is very challenging to venture a new definition of the television talk show due to the limited sample available.

Even when analysing the productions available on Netflix, the lack of consistency between them is evident. When filtering programmes that meet the criteria explained previously and following the references of any of the talk show subgenres (morning, daytime or late-night), three programmes are found: *Chelsea,* which debuted on May 11, 2016 streaming three times a week, and was cancelled after two seasons; *The Joel McHale Show with Joel McHale*, which premiered on February 18, 2018 and was cancelled later that year; and *My Next Guest Needs No Introduction with David Letterman*, also known as *My Next Guest* and premiered on January 12, 2018, which is still being produced.

Each one has very different structures and defining factors, which makes it necessary to discuss them individually to get the full picture of the genre on this new media landscape.

4.1 *Chelsea,* Netflix First Bet Among Hosting Controversy

Chelsea Handler is a comedian, actress, writer, and producer who has a long-established reputation in the television industry of the United States and internationally. She hosted *Chelsea Lately* for seven seasons and worked with Netflix on a documentary titled *Chelsea Does* in 2016.

Due to her solid career in the comedy industry, she was one of the audience's candidates to replace David Letterman on CBS's *Late Show* when the host retired in 2015, although this role ultimately went to Stephen Colbert. This year, audience and industry agents alike pointed out to the lack of diversity in the hosting role of late-night shows in the United States. All hosts of major talk shows airing during prominent slots in the dominant major networks were white men, which sparked a conversation in the social realm as well as in the professional one, with *The Hollywood Reporter* hosting a round table in which popular female comedians participated and gave their two cents on the topic.

In this context, Netflix announced the upcoming talk show hosted by Handler, which would have new episodes three times a week on the streaming platform, each running for around 30-40 minutes. The show was cancelled after two seasons, but it managed to air 120 episodes (90 during its first season and 30 during its second).

As per the characteristics of the show, it followed an architecture similar to typical late-night shows, particularly when it came to the setting. The programme had an in-studio public, and it started with a sketch, a short introduction, and the host entering the set to a cheering audience. The episodes are composed of noticeably distinct sections, including a satirical review of different issues by the host (on her own or joined by collaborators in some cases), pre-recorded comedy sketches and interviewing A-list celebrity guests.

The main difference with a conventional late-night show is that the host performs the first section or monologue in a more distant setting (seating on the table, the cheering of the audience is shorter than it usually is on traditional late-night television talk programmes) and it may seem that audience engagement is lower.

4.2 *The Joel McHale Show with Joel McHale,* Let the Sketches Do the Talk

This programme is also included in the talk show category, but its structure, design and narrative are more similar to a sketch programme than to a talk show. The content of *The Joel McHale Show* relies on

Figure 2. Promotional poster for Netflix's talk show Chelsea, with the tagline "So easy, even a woman can open it", alluding to the host controversy addressing lack of diversity on traditional talk shows' hosts

the interchanging of satirical commenting of popular media moments and comedy sketches performed live or pre-recorded by the host and/or his collaborators.

The main shot focuses on the host on an ever-present green screen showing a somewhat neutral background and a second screen with an image of the topic that he is discussing (or joking about). Viewers assume that there is an in-studio audience presence because of the reactions to the jokes and cheering that can be heard throughout the episode, but there are no general shots for context showing the studio, which are quite common in the traditional broadcast of a talk show, which suggests an unorthodox studio or set is used.

The episodes focus mostly on the host and collaborators making jokes around different topics, which makes it seem more like an extended version of the typical opening monologue of late-night shows. Episodes last around 20 minutes and combine this monologue approach with live and pre-recorded comedy sketches.

It is also worthy of mention that celebrity guests are also invited to the show, but they appear in an acting role participating in the sketches or monologue rather than being interviewed by the host.

This formula seems to combine elements from interview late-night talk shows and the popular programme *Saturday Night Live (SNL)*, which is a live television sketch comedy and satirical show on air since 1975. *The Joel McHale Show*, unfortunately, has not been able to replicate this success, as it was cancelled by Netflix after its first season streamed.

4.3 *My Next Guest Needs No Introduction* with David Letterman, Talk Show Icon on Demand

This Netflix talk show stars David Letterman, who needs no introduction himself. He was the host of late-night television talk shows in the United States for over three decades, surpassing Johnny Carson as the longest-serving host of a late-night talk show (Rose, 2013). Recognized globally, his return to hosting a talk show on an OTT service following a notable retirement from conventional television generated a lot of interest. Viewers and industry players alike were paying attention to the premiere of this new chapter of Letterman, wanting to see how this new phase would unfold for both him and the talk show genre.

The show is still in production and currently has four seasons, having significantly evolved and adapted to various forms through its run. We will analyse the different elements that conform and have conformed the programme in chronological order.

The first episode sets the tone for the first three seasons (or two seasons and a half, at least). The idea of Letterman hosting a talk show on Netflix was more than enough to have people watching, but the first guest emphasizes the relevance and notoriety that the show aims to get.

The episode starts with an archive clip from Letterman hosting his famous late-night show interviewing Barack Obama. Letterman asks what Obama will do when he is not president, and the guest says that he was thinking that he and Letterman could play dominoes together or go to the local Starbucks, raising laughter and applause from the audience and reinforcing the idea of the emotional public sphere that characterize television talk shows, as introduced and explained earlier.

The next scene shows Letterman two years later, with a much different aspect, apparently talking to Obama on the telephone, showing a rare behind-the-scenes development. Then we see the intro to the show and the first scene of the new set, which is a theatre but much more simplified than a late-night show studio. In fact, it could be a stand-up comedy setting except for the two chairs that are in the centre of the stage.

In the first few minutes, the programme shows certain conventions form both television talk and docuseries. Letterman enters the theatre to a cheering audience, in a similar fashion to a talk show entrance, addressing the audience and acknowledging the new chapter on the new media context of SVoD

Figure 3. Promotional image of the first episode of My Next Guest

platforms. The shots that we see on screen are also different from that of a regular talk show, showing Obama's reaction off-stage, which further disrupts the feeling of liveness.

One of the most important elements that remains from talk shows is the in-studio audience, whose participation is directly requested in the first episode when Letterman asks a couple of members to guess who the interviewee will be. This participation is reduced, but the reaction of the audience to both the host and the guest adds an important dimension to the production. Obama enters the theatre and Letterman goes on interviewing him and they both discuss different topics.

The episode goes on intersecting the interview in the theatre with off-studio clips that add information to what host and guest are discussing, in a fashion similar to a docuseries. This is the structure that the rest of the five remaining episodes of the season will follow, and what set the tone for the second season too (with five episodes).

The third season run shorter than usual due to the COVID-19 pandemic, with only four episodes, and notable adaptations occurred due to the health emergency affecting the world. The first episodes were recorded before COVID-19 spread and before restrictions were put into place, and a notice clarifying this information is shown at the beginning of each episode. The fourth episode starts showing the crew preparing the interview set off-theatre and discussing the current situation and safety measures that need to be put in place. The whole episode occurs outside of a theatre, in a more private setting, and without an audience present.

The fourth season aired almost a year and a half after the release of season three, in May 2022, and it maintained the structure of the fourth episode of season three, showing the host and guest having a one-on-one conversation outside the studio. The fifth season has no official premiere date at the time of publication, so it is yet to be seen whether this direction, more similar to a documentary, will be maintained after COVID-19 restrictions have been lifted, or if the live audience will return.

The show has received mainly positive reviews and has been critically acclaimed, consistently receiving Emmy nominations in the category of "Outstanding Hosted Nonfiction Series or Special" (called "Outstanding Informational Series or Special" from 2013 until 2019) for all seasons.

This disparity shown by all three programmes, each with its own dynamics, narratives, and structures, also points to the creative possibilities enabled by OTT platforms for talk show productions, which allow for exploring format adaptation, interactive features, and audience engagement strategies.

Considering that the most successful show is the one hosted by Letterman, it could be argued that the role of the host still maintains its pivotal relevance in OTT talk shows. However, it is pertinent to note that Chelsea Handler also had a well-established reputation as a talk show host and the company did not renew her programme for as many seasons. It would be pertinent to further examine the motivations and the lack of diversity in programming, perpetrating the representation of social symbols seen on traditional television.

As per the topics discussed, the concept of the emotional public sphere is reinforced, particularly in the shows of Handler and Letterman, but there is no specific association made between particular topics and conversations in OTT talk shows and the cultural aspects they highlight, which translates into on-demand audiences receiving different messages, although all of them maintain an approach that sticks to infotainment protocols.

What seems to be clear is that out of the three forms of the television talk show, morning magazine talk shows completely disappear from the catalogue, and the late-night show formula seems to be the one that platforms are most interested in. The shows have a clear entertaining approach, and the content covers different topics discussing public and private affairs with guests, except for the case of *The Joel McHale Show*, which is more similar to a sketch programme (also more present during late-night timeslots).

As the OTT landscape continues to evolve and reshape traditional television practices, talk shows developed by these platforms will adapt to the most successful formula and continue to adapt to creative possibilities and audience demands, but it is yet to be known if this would imply replicating late-night shows dynamics or creating a new subgenre altogether.

5. RESULTS ADDRESSING AUDIENCE ENGAGEMENT WITHOUT A "LIVE" ELEMENT AND THE GLOBAL REACH OF OTT TALK SHOWS

Media disruption of OTT services affects the production and consumption of media texts, but industry players still seek out audience engagement and it is even considered a metric as important as viewership.

Audiences discuss what they are watching on television on social media platforms, voicing their impressions through what is known as a second screen, and sharing their experiences with other users without a geographical boundary, which highlights the social dimension of television. This is mostly emphasized during live events (e.g.: political debates of candidates to the presidency or sports events), but social conversations have also been identified in relation to on-demand content and even binge-watching practices (Burns & Walker, 2018; Proulx & Shepatin, 2012; Segijn et al., 2020).

The disruption of physical boundaries should also be considered in the consumption of OTT talk shows. The production country of the analysed shows is the United States, which is no surprise not only because the biggest OTT companies have their headquarters in this country, but also because it is where the talk show genre originated. However, their reach is global in this new media context, and although on-demand catalogues vary from country to country due to distribution rights agreements, platform originals are usually available in all countries in which said platform operates. This implies the potential for a more diverse viewership and cross-cultural understanding of the media texts, although it has not yet translated into a diversity in production nor in representation of cultural symbols (all three hosts are white, and two out of three are men).

When speculating on the future outlook for talk shows in the influence of OTT services, considering potential trends and innovations that may shape the genre in the coming years, global audience demands need to be considered, and particularly younger generations. These viewers are invested in on-demand content in all its form, streaming music, podcasts, and television content, which suggests that there is space and potential for the television talk show to use these platforms as an opportunity finding the right formula.

Gen Z's celebrities and referents raise to popularity in a fashion different from well-established personalities, usually from Internet platforms such as YouTube, TikTok, or (more recently) Twitch. Although television talk shows are mainly targeted at millennials, it would be wise to keep an eye on the online discussion as a resourceful tool to understand audiences and know their interests and what popular content looks like for them in the streaming era.

6. CONCLUSION

This chapter has assessed the evolution of the television talk show, addressing how the format has emerged and thrived adapting to different media technologies, traditionally tightly controlled and defined by the airing timeslots in which they were broadcast.

The television talk show genre has always found a way to engage with audiences through several eras of disruption and emergence of new technologies. From vaudeville to radio, to television, to Internet practices, talk show programmes in all its forms have reached citizens with informative, personal, and political content, and although the specific properties and structures of the formats have evolved, their popularity has prevailed throughout different subgenres and media.

The emergence of OTT services presents both a challenge and an opportunity for the genre. On the one hand, the popularity of the genre is inherited and relies to a certain extent on the familiarity that audiences have with the talk show, and expectations that have been established with it. This, at the same time, is attached to the airing timeslots in which the programmes are broadcast, which can be a challenge when considering the OTT context. In these new platforms, the content is streamed on demand, and there are no airing timeslots that audiences can rely on to manage their expectations.

On the other hand, this presents an opportunity for producers to experiment and test new forms of the talk show that resonate with current ambitious and active audiences, enhancing new ways of viewer engagement through second screens and social discussions, learning, and building novel forms of consumption and interactivity.

Considering the context of OTT platforms, when answering what defines and distinguishes talk shows without airing timeslots, research suggests that late-night show dynamics, which have demonstrated great popularity among audiences and influence in the public discourse throughout the years, are the ones that prevail the most.

Although there have not been enough productions or time to talk about an established OTT talk show subgenre, platforms seem to incline towards an entertaining style similar to that of late-night programmes, but there is a lot of space for innovation and adaptation to new formulas and audiences. The realm of OTT talk shows offers an alluring arena to comprehend media evolution and to contribute significantly to the conversation around the intersection of technology, content creation, and the evolving role of audiences in the digital age.

When addressing how do audiences engage with television talk shows in the context of on-demand consumption through OTT platforms, the role of social media cannot be ignored, both from the perspective of second-screen or social television practices, and the engagement with the official profiles of the programmes themselves. Direct interaction with audiences enhances viewer engagement and potential loyalty.

Also, considering that global audiences share key narrative readings of television talk shows, the global reach of OTT platforms offers a great opportunity for producers to address an expanded audience base with diverse cultural backgrounds.

Recommendations for OTT talk shows could involve enhancing interactive viewer engagement via social media and the show itself, fostering second-screen practices, and integrating multiple channels for a cohesive experience. Also, leveraging the data available on OTT platforms for personalized content recommendations could be important. Given the fragmented nature of talk shows and the popularity of short-form content on social media, this could help capturing audiences' attention.

In conclusion, the rise of OTT services has fundamentally altered the landscape of television talk shows, challenging both producers and audiences. However, this transformative context also catalyses creative production, multi-channel audience engagement, and global outreach, setting the stage for a demanding yet exciting environment for media professionals and scholars alike.

REFERENCES

Abel, A. D., & Barthel, M. (2013). Appropriation of Mainstream News: How Saturday Night Live Changed the Political Discussion. *Critical Studies in Media Communication*, *30*(1), 1–16. doi:10.1080/15295036.2012.701011

Baum, M. A. (2005). Talking the vote: Why presidential candidates hit the talk show circuit. *American Journal of Political Science*, *49*(2), 213–234. doi:10.1111/j.0092-5853.2005.t01-1-00119.x

Bennett, W. L. (2012). The Personalization of Politics: Political Identity, Social Media, and Changing Patterns of Participation. *The Annals of the American Academy of Political and Social Science*, *644*(1), 20–39. doi:10.1177/0002716212451428

Bondebjerg, I., Goban-Klas, T., Hilmes, M., Mustata, D., Strandgaard-Jensen, H., Veyrat-Masson, I., & Vollberg, S. (2008). American Television: Point of Reference or European Nightmare? In J. Bignell & A. Fickers (Eds.), *A European Television History* (pp. 154–183).

Boukertouta, M., & Chioukh, Z. (2020). *Cross-Cultural Turn-Taking, Yielding, and Holding Strategies Used in Talk Shows: A Case of Arabic and British Talk Shows.* University of Mohammed Seddik Ben Yahia, Jijel.

Burns, K. S., & Walker, K. K. (2018). #13ReasonsWhy Twitter Users are Tweeting about a Netflix Show about Teen Suicide. *SMSociety*, *261–265*, 261–265. Advance online publication. doi:10.1145/3217804.3217925

Cassidy, M. F. (2008). Sob Stories, Merriment, and Surprises. The 1950s audience participation show on network television and women's daytime reception. In C. Brunsdon & L. Spigel (Eds.), *Feminist Television Criticism: A Reader* (pp. 320–339). Open University Press. https://books.google.es/books?id=7Wr4AAAAQBAJ&pg=PA320&lpg=PA320&dq=sob+stories+merriment+and+surprises&source=bl&ots=_swkCAXPeV&sig=ACfU3U1aTyIrRHv56Ja50MnMX_PYEF09qA&hl=en&sa=X&ved=2ahUKEwjZkcamgI3jAhURmRoKHfJiA-sQ6AEwAXoECAkQAQ#v=onepage&q=sob storie

Christie, I. (2012). Wakening France: Observations on Télématin. *Critical Studies in Television, 7*(2). http://mendeley.csuc.cat/fitxers/f6d2dc6d3030ab4fe342f1dde4e04e73

Couldry, N. (2004). Liveness, "reality", and the mediated habitus from television to the mobile phone. *Communication Review*, *7*(4), 353–361. doi:10.1080/10714420490886952

Cragin, B. (2010). Beyond the Feminine: Intersectionality and Hybridity in Talk Shows. *Women's Studies in Communication*, *33*(2), 154–172. doi:10.1080/07491409.2010.507585

Cress, S. L., & Rapert, K. D. (1996). Talk Show Viewing Motives: Does Gender Make a Difference? *Annual Meeting of the Speech Communication Association.* ERIC. https://files.eric.ed.gov/fulltext/ED401586.pdf

Danesi, M. (2016). *Concise Dictionary of Popular Culture.* Google. https://books.google.es/books?id=61mBDQAAQBAJ&pg=PA252&dq=talk+show+cycle&hl=en&sa=X&ved=0ahUKEwiCyZjq-LfeAhULI8AKHYuYCf8Q6AEINjAC#v=onepage&q=cycle&f=false

Delgado, M., & Prado, E. (2010). La televisión generalista en la era digital. Tendencias internacionales de programación. *TELOS Cuadernos de Comunicación e Innovación*, *84*, 52–64.

Ekström, M., & Tolson, A. (2013). *Media talk and political elections in Europe and America*. Palgrave Macmillan. https://books.google.es/books?id=LtnQAQAAQBAJ&pg=PA85&dq=%22talk+show%22+europe+candidates&hl=en&sa=X&ved=0ahUKEwjo1sDy_J3jAhWtQEEAHZQuA7sQ6AEIKjAA#v=onepage&q=%22talk show%22 europe candidates&f=false

Feldman, O. (2020). The rhetoric of broadcast talk shows in Japan: The art of equivocation as a political skill. *The Rhetoric of Political Leadership: Logic and Emotion in Public Discourse*, (June), 139–155. doi:10.4337/9781789904581.00016

Gomery, D. (2008). *A history of broadcasting in the United States*. Blackwell Publishing. https://cataleg.uab.cat/iii/encore/record/C__Rb1798501?lang=cat

Grindstaff, L. (2002). *The money shot : trash, class, and the making of TV talk shows*. University of Chicago Press. doi:10.7208/chicago/9780226309088.001.0001

Ilie, C. (2006). Talk Shows. In K. Brown (Ed.), *Encyclopedia of Language & Linguistics* (2nd ed., pp. 489–494). Elsevier. doi:10.1016/B0-08-044854-2/00357-6

Jones, I. (2004). *Morning glory: A history of British breakfast television*. Kelly. https://books.google.es/books?id=WpQ_esoMKLMC&printsec=frontcover&source=gbs_ge_summary_r&cad=0#v=onepage&q&f=true

Jones, J. P. (2009). I Want My Talk TV: Network Talk Shows in a Digital Universe. In A. D. Lotz (Ed.), *Beyond Prime Time: Television Programming in the Post-Network Era* (pp. 14–35).

Kawa, K. (2018). *Television: The Small Box That Changed The World*. Lucent Press. https://books.google.es/books?id=F9doDwAAQBAJ&pg=PA28&dq=when+vaudeville+died+television+was+the+box+they+put+it+in&hl=en&sa=X&ved=0ahUKEwjkwovM9bfeAhWUfMAKHc5RCm8Q6AEIMDAB#v=onepage&q=vaudeville&f=false

Kay, J. (2015). *Gender, Feminism and Talk on British Television, 1970-1990*. De Monfort University.

Layton, R. (2015). Netflix Comes to the Nordics: Lessons in OTT Video. *Journal of NBICT*, *1*(1), 109–138. doi:10.13052/NBICT.2015.005

Leano, J. (2014). The Agenda-Setting Power of Saturday Night Live. *The Elon Journal of Undergraduate Research in Communications*, *5*(1), 81–89. http://www.elon.edu/docs/e-web/academics/communications/research/vol5no1/09leanoejspring14.pdf

Lunt, P., & Stenner, P. (2005). The Jerry Springer Show as an emotional public sphere. *Media Culture & Society*, *27*(1), 163–4437. doi:10.1177/0163443705049058

Marcos-García, S., Alonso-Muñoz, L., & López-Meri, A. (2020). Extending influence on social media: The behaviour of political talk-show opinion leaders on twitter. *Communicatio Socialis*, *33*(2), 277–293. doi:10.15581/003.33.2.277-293

Mastrini, G., & Krakowiak, F. (2021). Netflix en Argentina: Expansión acelerada y producción local escasa. *Comunicación y Sociedad*, *7915*(1), 1–23. doi:10.32870/cys.v2021.7915

Matrix, S. (2014). The Netflix Effect: Teens, Binge Watching, and On-Demand Digital Media Trends. *Jeunesse: Young People, Texts. Cultures*, *6*(1), 119–138. doi:10.1353/jeu.2014.0002

Mittell, J. (2003). Audiences Talking Genre: Television Talk Shows and Cultural Hierarchies. *The Journal of Popular Film and Television*, *31*(1), 36–46. doi:10.1080/01956050309602867

Mittell, J. (2004). *Genre and television: From Cop Shows To Cartoons in American Culture*. Routledge. https://cataleg.uab.cat/iii/encore/record/C__Rb1622959__Sgenre and television__Orightresult__U__X7?lang=cat

Munson, W. (1993). *All Talk: the talkshow in media culture*. Temple University Press. http://cataleg.uab.cat/record=b1315794~S1*cat

Niven, D., Lichter, S. R., & Amundson, D. (2003). The Political Content of Late Night Comedy. *The Harvard International Journal of Press/Politics*, *8*(3), 118–133. doi:10.1177/1081180X03008003007

Oyeleye, A. L., & Olutayo, O. G. (2012). Interaction Management in Nigerian Television Talk Shows. *International Journal of English Linguistics*, *2*(1), 149–161. doi:10.5539/ijel.v2n1p149

Peterson, R. L. (2008). Strange Bedfellows: The Politics of Late-Night Television Comedy. *Poroi*, *5*(1), 61–83. doi:10.13008/2151-2957.1020

Proulx, M., & Shepatin, S. (2012). *Social TV : how marketers can reach and engage audiences by connecting television to the web, social media, and mobile*. John Wiley & Sons.

Rose, L. (2013, November 4). *CBS Extends David Letterman Contract Through 2015*. The Hollywood Reporter. https://www.hollywoodreporter.com/tv/tv-news/cbs-extends-david-letterman-contract-643439/

Roth, S., Weinmann, C., Schneider, F. M., Hopp, F. R., & Vorderer, P. (2014). Seriously Entertained: Antecedents and Consequences of Hedonic and Eudaimon.... *Mass Communication & Society*, *17*(3), 379–399. doi:10.1080/15205436.2014.891135

Scannel, P. (1991). *Broadcast Talk* (P. Scannel, Ed.). Sage Publications., https://cataleg.uab.cat/iii/encore/record/C__Rb1060460?lang=cat

Schultz, D. (2012). *Politainment: The Ten Rules of Contemporary Politics: A Citizens' Guide to Understanding Campaigns and Elections*. Google. https://books.google.es/books?id=-w-ftgAACAAJ

Segijn, C. M., Maslowska, E., Araujo, T., & Viswanathan, V. (2020). Engaging with TV events on Twitter: The interrelations between TV consumption, engagement actors, and engagement content. *Internet Research*, *30*(2), 381–401. doi:10.1108/INTR-08-2018-0389

Shattuc, J. (1997). *The Talking Cure: TV Talk Shows and Women*. Routledge. http://cataleg.uab.cat/record=b1394015~S1*cat

Summergrad, S. (2016). *Can We Talk? A Discussion on Gender Politics in the Late-Night Comedy Career of Joan Rivers*. Scribd. https://es.scribd.com/document/319661192/Summergrad-bu-0017N-12201-pdf?secret_password=HWQUYCrkHYCsCnPfG2Tn#download&from_embed

Thussu, D. K. (2007). *News As Entertainment: The Rise of Global Infotainment*. Sage. https://cataleg.uab.cat/iii/encore/record/C__Rb1735030__Snews as entertainment__Orightresult__U__X7?lang=cat

Timberg, B. (2002). *Television Talk: A History of the TV Talk Show*. University of Texas Press.

Tolson, A. (2001). *Television talk shows : discourse, performance, spectacle*. Lawrence Erlbaum., https://cataleg.uab.cat/iii/encore/record/C__Rb1492862?lang=cat doi:10.4324/9781410600950

Tucker, D. C., & Schütz, A. (1995). Entertainers, experts, or public servants? Politicians' self-presentation on television talk shows. In Political Communication (Vol. 12, Issue 2). doi:10.1080/10584609.1995.9963066

Vallet, F., Essid, S., Carrive, J., & Richard, G. (2012). High-Level TV Talk Show Structuring Centered On Speakers' Interventions. In Y. Kompatsiaris, B. Merialdo, & S. Lian (Eds.), *TV Content Analysis: Techniques and Applications* (p. 245).

Van Zoonen, L., & Holtz-Bacha, C. (2000). Personalisation in Dutch and German politics: The case of talk show. *Javnost (Ljubljana)*, *7*(2), 45–56. doi:10.1080/13183222.2000.11008743

Wahab, J. A. (2011). Television Talk Shows and The Public Sphere. *Malaysian Journal of Communication*, *27*(2), 29–45.

Wayne, M. L. (2022). Netflix audience data, streaming industry discourse, and the emerging realities of "popular" television. *Media Culture & Society*, *44*(2), 193–209. doi:10.1177/01634437211022723

ADDITIONAL READING

Gilles, F., & Grece, C. (2017). *Trends in the EU SVOD market*. Research Gate.

Lunt, P., & Stenner, P. (2005). The Jerry Springer Show as an emotional public sphere. *Media Culture & Society*, *27*(1), 163–4437. doi:10.1177/0163443705049058

Tang, W., & Wei, M. (2023). Streaming media business strategies and audience-centered practices: A comparative study of Netflix and Tencent Video. *Online Media and Global Communication*, *2*(1), 3–24. doi:10.1515/omgc-2022-0061

Timberg, B. (2002). *Television Talk: A History of the TV Talk Show*. University of Texas Press.

KEY TERMS AND DEFINITIONS

Binge-Watching: To watch several episodes of the same show in a row without a break.

Daytime: Airing timeslot, approximately from 10 am to 4 pm, in which emotional television talk shows are broadcast.

Late-Night Shows: Entertaining and satirical programmes addressing current issues and interviewing well-known public figures.

Morning Magazine Shows: Television programmes with an informative yet laid-back tone part of the talk show genre.

Social Television: Audience practice in which audiences share their impressions and the experience of watching television content through social media (mainly Twitter) with other viewers.

SVoD: Subscription Video on Demand, a specific and popular form of over-the-top service.

Television Talk Show: Infotainment programmes that encompass morning, daytime and late-night programmes.

Compilation of References

Aaker, D. A. (2012). *Building Strong Brands*. Simon & Schuster.

Abel, A. D., & Barthel, M. (2013). Appropriation of Mainstream News: How Saturday Night Live Changed the Political Discussion. *Critical Studies in Media Communication, 30*(1), 1–16. doi:10.1080/15295036.2012.701011

Abi-Jaoude, E., Naylor, K. T., & Pignatiello, A. (2020, February 9). Smartphones, social media use and youth mental health. *Canadian Medical Association Journal, 192*(6), E136–E141. doi:10.1503/cmaj.190434 PMID:32041697

Adjust. (2023). *What is over-the-top (OTT)?* Adjust. https://www.adjust.com/glossary/ott-over-the-top/: https://www.adjust.com

Adomavicius, G., Bauman, K., Tuzhilin, A., & Unger, M. (2022). Context-aware recommender systems. In F. Ricci, L. Rokach, & B. Shapira (Eds.), *Recommender systems handbook* (pp. 211–250). Springer. doi:10.1007/978-1-0716-2197-4_6

Adulla, S. (n.d.). *The Rise of Binge-Watching and its Impact on Television Consumption*. Revidd .https://www.revidd.com/blogs/the-rise-of-bi-nge-watc-hing-and-its-im-pact-on-televisionconsumption

Afsar, M. M., Crump, T., & Far, B. (2021). Reinforcement learning based recommender systems: A survey. *Information Retrieval*. doi:https://doi.org//arXiv.2101.06286 doi:10.48550

Agarwal, M. (2018). *Prime Added Maximum Users In India In Its First Year In Amazon's History: Jeff Bezos*. Inc42 Media. https://inc42.com/buzz/prime-added-maximum-users-in-india-in-its-first-year-in-amazons-history-jeff-bezos/

Ahlawat, R., & Ahlawat, P. (2023). AN ANALYSIS OF THE ROLE OF OVER-THE-TOP (OTT) PLATFORMS IN THE CHANGING FACE OF INDIA'S FILM AND TELEVISION INDUSTRY. [IJMR]. *EPRA International Journal of Multidisciplinary Research, 9*(11), 378–386.

Ahmed, M. A. & Abdel, A. (2017). *New Era of TV Watching Behavior Binge Watching and its Psychological Effects.*

Ahmed, O., Nayeem Siddiqua, S. J., Alam, N., & Griffiths, M. D. (2021, February). The mediating role of problematic social media use in the relationship between social avoidance/distress and self-esteem. *Technology in Society, 64*, 101485. doi:10.1016/j.techsoc.2020.101485

Akter, S., Dwivedi, Y. K., Sajib, S., Biswas, K., Bandara, R. J., & Michael, K. (2022, May). Algorithmic bias in machine learning-based marketing models. *Journal of Business Research, 144*, 201–216. doi:10.1016/j.jbusres.2022.01.083

Alam, I., & Khusro, S. (2020). *Tailoring Recommendations to Groups ofViewers on Smart TV: A Real-Time ProfileGeneration Approach*. IEEE. doi:10.1109/ACCESS.2020.2980206

Albarrati, A., Zafar, H., Alghadir, A. H., & Anwer, S. (2018). Effect of Upright and Slouched Sitting Postures on the Respiratory Muscle Strength in Healthy Young Males. *BioMed Research International, 2018*, 1–5. doi:10.1155/2018/3058970 PMID:29682532

Algolia. (2022). *What is content discovery, and how can you make it easier for your users to find what they want?* Algolia. https://www.algolia.com/blog/ux/what-is-content-discovery-and-how-can-you-make-it-easier-for-your-users-to-find-what-they-want/

Allam, J., & Thrideep, N. (2023). *Why Video Streaming Platforms Should Embrace AI and Analytics*. Themathcompany. https://themathcompany.com/blog/why-video-streaming-platforms-should-embrace-ai-and-analytics

Alsharif, A. H., Md Salleh, N. Z., & Baharun, R. (2021). Neuromarketing: Marketing research in the new millennium. *Neuroscience Research Notes*, *4*(3), 27–35. doi:10.31117/neuroscirn.v4i3.79

Altexsoft. (2021). *Recommender Systems: Behind the Scenes of Machine Learning-Based Personalization*. Retrieved from https://www.altexsoft.com: https://www.altexsoft.com/blog/recommender-system-personalization/

Angel One. (2023). *India's media and entertainment industry: A sector on the rise*. Retrieved Nov 02, 2023, from https://www.angelone.in: https://www.angelone.in/blog/india-media-entertainment-industry-a-sector-on-the-rise

Ano, E. C., & Morisio, M. (2017, November). Hybrid Recommender Systems: A Systematic Literature Review. *Intelligent Data Analysis*, *21*(06), 1487–1524. doi:10.3233/IDA-163209

Appel, H., Gerlach, A. L., & Crusius, J. (2016, June). The interplay between Facebook use, social comparison, envy, and depression. *Current Opinion in Psychology*, *9*, 44–49. doi:10.1016/j.copsyc.2015.10.006

Arnold, R., Bott, J., & Hildebrandt, H. (2018). *Die Nutzung von Daten durch OTT-Dienste zur Abschöpfung von Aufmerksamkeit und Zahlungsbereitschaft: Implikationen für Daten- und Verbraucherschutz*. WIK: Diskussionsbeitrag, Nr.431.

Arthofer, F., Kon, M., Lee, E., Rose, J., & Hardarson, Á. (2016). *The Future of Television: The Impact of OTT on Video Production Around the World*. Retrieved Jul 15, 2023, from bcg.com: https://www.bcg.com/publications/2016/media-entertainment-technology-digital-future-television-impact-ott-video-production

Arti. (2021). *Netflix or Amazon Prime: Who Uses AI and Machine Learning Better?* Retrieved Jul 12, 2023, from https://www.analyticsinsight.net: https://www.analyticsinsight.net/netflix-or-amazon-prime-who-uses-ai-and-machine-learning-better/

Aveek Sarkar v. State of West Bengal, 4 Supreme Court Cases 257 (Supreme Court of India 2014) 4 SCC 257.).

Axinom. (2021). *Metadata: Key to Value Generation in OTT*. Retrieved from axinom.com: https://www.axinom.com/article/metadata-in-ott

Ayten, A., Bulat, S., & İnceismail, E. (2019). A Study of Generation Z Viewing Habits in Context of Uses and Gratification Theory: The Protector Netflix Series Case. *Communication and Technology Congress – CTC 2019*.

Bakke, A. (2020). Everyday googling: Results of an observational study and applications for teaching algorithmic literacy. *Computers and Composition*, *57*, 1–16. doi:10.1016/j.compcom.2020.102577

Balki, B. (2021). *OTT Personalization- An AI/ML Game-Changer*. Retrieved Jul 14, 2023, from www.globalligic.com: https://www.globallogic.com/wp-content/uploads/2021/02/OTT-Personalization.pdf

Bambha, M. (2023). *My own personal space: AB testing OTT experiences for user engagement, inclusion and growth*. Retrieved Jul 24, 2023, from timesofindia.com: https://timesofindia.indiatimes.com/blogs/voices/my-own-personal-space-ab-testing-ott-experiences-for-user-engagement-inclusion-and-growth/?source=app&frmapp=yes

Bandura, A. (1986). *Social foundations of thought and action: A social cognitive theory*. Prentice-Hall.

Banerjee, D. (2022). *OTT Platforms – Trends to Look Out for in the Next Five Years*. Retrieved from https://www.muvi.com/: https://www.muvi.com/blogs/ott-platforms-trends-to-look-out-for-in-the-next-five-years

Barraclough, L. (2016). Amazon prime video now available in more than 200 countries. *Variety*. https://vari-ety.com/2016/digital/glo-bal/amazon-prime-video-now-available-in-more-than-200-countries-1201941818/

Barry, C. T., & Wong, M. Y. (2020, August 7). Fear of missing out (FoMO): A generational phenomenon or an individual difference? *Journal of Social and Personal Relationships*, *37*(12), 2952–2966. doi:10.1177/0265407520945394

Barth, S., & de Jong, T. D. M. (2017). The privacy paradox – Investigating discrepancies between expressed privacy concerns and actual online behavior – A systematic literature review. *Telematics and Informatics*, *34*(7), 1038–1058. doi:10.1016/j.tele.2017.04.013

Baum, M. A. (2005). Talking the vote: Why presidential candidates hit the talk show circuit. *American Journal of Political Science*, *49*(2), 213–234. doi:10.1111/j.0092-5853.2005.t01-1-00119.x

Baumol, W. J. (1990). Entrepreneurship: Productive, unproductive, and destructive. *Journal of Political Economy*, *98*(5), 893–921. doi:10.1086/261712

Beer, D. (2009). Power through the algorithm? Participatory web cultures and the technological unconscious. *New Media & Society*, *11*(6), 985–1002. doi:10.1177/1461444809336551

Beer, D. (2017). The social power of algorithms. *Information Communication and Society*, *20*(1), 1–13. doi:10.1080/1369118X.2016.1216147

Beer, D. (2019). The data gaze: Capitalism, power and perception: Society and space series. *Sage (Atlanta, Ga.)*.

Belenguer, L. (2022). AI bias: Exploring discriminatory algorithmic decision-making models and the application of possible machine-centric solutions adapted from the pharmaceutical industry. *AI and Ethics*, *2*(4), 771–787. Retrieved October 28, 2023, from https://link.springer.com/article/10.1007/s43681-022-00138-8. doi:10.1007/s43681-022-00138-8 PMID:35194591

Ben Lutkevich. (2022). *digital asset management (DAM)*. Retrieved from TechTarget.com: https://www.techtarget.com/searchcontentmanagement/definition/What-is-digital-asset-management

Benjamin Habegger, O. H. (2014). *Personalization vs. Privacy in Big Data Analysis*. Retrieved from https://www.researchgate.net/publication/295121842_Personalization_vs_Privacy_in_Big_Data_Analysis

Bennett, W. L. (2012). The Personalization of Politics: Political Identity, Social Media, and Changing Patterns of Participation. *The Annals of the American Academy of Political and Social Science*, *644*(1), 20–39. doi:10.1177/0002716212451428

Beyens, I., Frison, E., & Eggermont, S. (2016, November). "I don't want to miss a thing": Adolescents' fear of missing out and its relationship to adolescents' social needs, Facebook use, and Facebook related stress. *Computers in Human Behavior*, *64*, 1–8. doi:10.1016/j.chb.2016.05.083

Bharat, D. & Pawan, S. M. (2021). Psychosocial impact of web series and streaming content: A study on Indian youth. *Global Media Journal*. https://www.global mediajournal.com/open-access/psychosocial-impact-of-web-series-and-streaming-content-a-study-on-indian-youth.php?aid=90530#6

Bhaskar, M. (2016, September 30). In the age of the algorithm, the human gatekeeper is back. *The Guardian*. https://www.theguardian.com/technology/2016/sep/30/age-of-algorithm-human-gatekeeper

Bhattacharyya, D. R., Kohli, D. S., & More, D. R. (2020). Change In Consumption Habits Of Entertainment During Lockdown And The Role Of OTT Platforms. *Ilkogretim Online - Elementary Education*, *19*(4), 4686-4695. doi:10.17051/ilkonline.2020.04.764875

Bhattacharyya, R., Kohli, S., & Rupali, M. (2020). Change In Consumption Habits Of Entertainment During Lockdown And The Role Of OTT Platforms. *Ilkogr. Online-Elem. Educ. Online*, *19*(4), 4686–4695.

Bhullar, A., & Chandigarh, R. (2020). Key Factors Influencing Users ' Adoption Towards OTT Media Platform : An Empirical Analysis. *International Journal of Advanced Science and Technology*, *29*(11), 942–956.

Bihade, V., & Kumar, M. (2023). Customer Preference towards OTT Platform in India. *Global Media Journal*, *21*(61), 355.

Binge Watching TV Linked to Higher Rates Of Depression And Anxiety. (2015). *Medical Daily*. https://www.medicaldaily.com/binge-watching-tv-linked-higher-rates-depression-and-anxiety-360776

Blazques, D., & Domenech, J. (2018). Big data souces and methods for social and economic analyses. *Technological Forecasting and Social Change*, *130*(C), 99–113. doi:10.1016/j.techfore.2017.07.027

Bondebjerg, I., Goban-Klas, T., Hilmes, M., Mustata, D., Strandgaard-Jensen, H., Veyrat-Masson, I., & Vollberg, S. (2008). American Television: Point of Reference or European Nightmare? In J. Bignell & A. Fickers (Eds.), *A European Television History* (pp. 154–183).

Bong-Goon, S., & Park, D. H. (2021). Effective Strategies for Contents Recommendation Based on Psychological Ownership of over the Top Services in Cyberspace. *Journal of Theoretical and Applied Electronic Commerce Research*, *16*(4), 976–991. doi:10.3390/jtaer16040055

Boni, M., Jambavalika, A., Roy, S., Naggar, J., & Shah, S. (2017). *The End of TV*. American Marketing Association.

Booth, J. (2020). *Visions for 2020: Key trends shaping the digital marketing landscape*. Retrieved Jun 30, 2023, from https://blogs.oracle.com/: https://blogs.oracle.com/advertising/post/visions-for-2020-key-trends-shaping-the-digital-marketing-landscape

Boukertouta, M., & Chioukh, Z. (2020). *Cross-Cultural Turn-Taking, Yielding, and Holding Strategies Used in Talk Shows: A Case of Arabic and British Talk Shows*. University of Mohammed Seddik Ben Yahia, Jijel.

BrandEquity. (2021). *How the pandemic emerged as a blessing for India's OTT industry*. Retrieved Jul 10, 2023, from brandequity.com: https://brandequity.economictimes.indiatimes.com/news/digital/how-the-pandemic-emerged-as-a-blessing-for-indias-ott-industry/84056159

Breese, J. S., Heckerman, D., & Kadie, C. (1998). Empirical analysis of predictive algorithms for collaborative filtering. *In Proceedings of the Fourteenth Conference on Uncertainty in Artificial Intelligence,* (pp. 43-52). Publication History.

Brown, A. (2019). Changing the channel: How OTT is reshaping the media landscape. *Forbes*.

Brown, A. (2019). The role of Instagram in OTT video marketing: A Netflix case study. *Journal of Media Business Studies*, *16*(1), 42–54.

Brown, K. (2019). Leveraging Instagram for OTT media promotion: A new strategy. *Journal of Digital Media Management*, *7*(3), 275–289.

Brown, K. (2019). *On-demand: Exploring the impacts of OTT on traditional television*. MediaShift. [Link]

BründlS.MattC.HessT. (2015). Wertschöpfung in Datenmärkten. Eine explorative Untersuchung am Beispiel des deutschen Marktes für persönliche Daten. *Forum Privatheit*. doi:10.7892/boris.105186

Bucher, T. (2017). The algorithmic imaginary: Exploring the ordinary affects of Facebook algorithms. *Information Communication and Society*, *20*(1), 30–44. doi:10.1080/1369118X.2016.1154086

Bucher, T. (2018). *If...Then: Algorithmic power and politics.* Oxford University Press. doi:10.1093/oso/9780190493028.001.0001

Buchholz, K. (2020). *International Brands Rise to the Top of Indian Streaming Market.* Retrieved Nov 01, 2023, from https://www.statista.com: https://www.statista.com/chart/23009/market-share-streaming--ott--platforms-in-india/

Buchholz, K. (2020). *International Brands Rise to the Top of Indian Streaming Market.* Retrieved Nov 01, 2023, from Statista: https://www.statista.com/chart/23009/market-share-streaming--ott--platforms-in-india/

Bugeja, S. M. (2020). *The influence of web personalisation on the consumer's decision-making process* [Unpublished doctoral dissertation, L-Università ta' Malta, Malta].

Buglass, S. L., Binder, J. F., Betts, L. R., & Underwood, J. D. (2017, January). Motivators of online vulnerability: The impact of social network site use and FOMO. *Computers in Human Behavior, 66*, 248–255. doi:10.1016/j.chb.2016.09.055

Bundhun, R. (2023). How Netflix can capitalise on Indian Oscar wins to boost its subscriber base. *The National.* https://www.thenationalnews.com/business/2023/03/20/how-netflix-can-capitalise-on-indian-oscar-wins-to-boost-its-subscriber-base/#:~:text=Netflix%20subscriber%20numbers%20in%20India,firm%20Arthur%20D%20Little%20shows

Burke, R., O'Mahony, M. P., & Hurley, N. J. (2015). Robust Collaborative Recommendation. In L. R. Francesco Ricci, *Recommender Systems Handbook* (pp. 961-995). Springer. Retrieved Jul 12, 2023, from https://link.springer.com/book/10.1007/978-1-4899-7637-6

Burke, R. (2002). Hybrid recommender systems: Survey and experiments. *User Modeling and User-Adapted Interaction, 12*(4), 331–370. doi:10.1023/A:1021240730564

Burnell, K., George, M. J., Vollet, J. W., Ehrenreich, S. E., & Underwood, M. K. (2019, July 12). Passive social networking site use and well-being: The mediating roles of social comparison and the fear of missing out. *Cyberpsychology (Brno), 13*(3). Advance online publication. doi:10.5817/CP2019-3-5

Burns, K. S., & Walker, K. K. (2018). #13ReasonsWhy Twitter Users are Tweeting about a Netflix Show about Teen Suicide. *SMSociety, 261–265*, 261–265. Advance online publication. doi:10.1145/3217804.3217925

Burroughs, B. (2019). House of Netflix: Streaming media and digital lore. *Popular Communication, 17*(1), 1–17. doi:10.1080/15405702.2017.1343948

Busch, O. (2016). The Programmatic Advertising Principle. In O. Bush (Ed.), *Programmatic Advertising The Successful Transformation to Automated, Data-Driven Marketing in RealTime* (pp. 3–16). Springer. doi:10.1007/978-3-319-25023-6_1

BVDW. (2015). *Zielgruppengenaues Targeting unter Nutzung von Online- und Offline-Daten.* BVDW. https://www.bvdw.org/presseserver/LeitfadenTargeting/leitfaden_targeting_zielgruppengenaues-targeting-unter-nutzung-von-online-und-offline-daten_2015.pdf

Canet, L. (2022). *Churn It Down: How Media Companies Can Use AI To Keep And Win Subscribers.* Retrieved Jul 12, 2023, from www.forbes.com: https://www.forbes.com/sites/googlecloud/2022/06/13/churn-it-down-how-media-companies-can-use-ai-to-keep-and-win-subscribers/?sh=26c37c733744

Caruana, S. (2021). An overview of audiovisual input as a means for foreign language acquisition in different contexts. *Language and Speech, 64*(4), 1018–1036. doi:10.1177/0023830920985897 PMID:33435785

Cassidy, M. F. (2008). Sob Stories, Merriment, and Surprises. The 1950s audience participation show on network television and women's daytime reception. In C. Brunsdon & L. Spigel (Eds.), *Feminist Television Criticism: A Reader* (pp. 320–339). Open University Press. https://books.google.es/books?id=7Wr4AAAAQBAJ&pg=PA320&lpg=PA320&dq=sob+stories+merriment+and+surprises&source=bl&ots=_swkCAXPeV&sig=ACfU3U1aTyIrRHv56Ja50MnMX_PYEF09qA&hl=en&sa=X&ved=2ahUKEwjZkcamgI3jAhURmRoKHfJiA-sQ6AEwAXoECAkQAQ#v=onepage&q=sob storie

Cast, A. D., & Burke, P. J. (2002, March 1). A Theory of Self-Esteem. *Social Forces*, *80*(3), 1041–1068. doi:10.1353/sof.2002.0003

Chakraborty, D., Siddiqui, M., Siddiqui, A., Paul, J., Dash, G., & Dal Mas, F. (2023). Watching is valuable: Consumer views -Content consumption on OTT platforms. *Journal of Retailing and Consumer Services*, *70*, 1031–1048. doi:10.1016/j.jretconser.2022.103148

Chandra, S., Verma, S., Lim, W. M., Kumar, S., & Donthu, N. (2022). Personalization in personalized marketing: Trends and ways forward. *Psychology and Marketing*, *39*(8), 1529–1562. doi:10.1002/mar.21670

Chang, P.-C., & Chang, H.-Y. (2020). Exploring the Factors Influencing Continuance Usage of Over- the-Top Services : The Interactivity, Consumption Value. *International Journal of Technology and Human Interaction*, *16*(4), 118–138. doi:10.4018/IJTHI.2020100108

Chan-Olmsted, S. M. (2019). A review of artificial intelligence adoptions in the media industry. *International Journal on Media Management, 21*(3-4), 193-215.

Charts, M. (2020). *Consumers Are Streaming More Since the COVID-19 Outbreak – but What About Pay-TV On-Demand?* Marketing Charts. https://www.marketingcharts.com/television/tv-audiences-and-consumption-113253

Chase, C. W. Jr. (2013). Using big data to enhance demand-driven forecasting and planning. *The Journal of Business Forecasting: Methods & Systems*, *32*(2), 27–34.

Chatterjee, A. N. (2012). Inequalities in the public sphere: Emergence of community television in India. *Asian Ethnicity*, *13*(3), 229–250. doi:10.1080/14631369.2012.638803

Cheney-Lippold, J. (2011). A New Algorithmic Identity. *Theory, Culture & Society*, *28*(6), 164–181. doi:10.1177/0263276411424420

ChenG.ChanT. Y. (2023). The Effects of Diversity in Algorithmic Recommendations on Digital Content Consumption: A Field Experiment. SSRN. https://papers.ssrn.com/sol3/papers.cfm?abstract_id=4365121 doi:10.2139/ssrn.4365121

Chen, Y. K. (2019). Competitions between OTT TV platforms and traditional television in Taiwan : A Niche analysis. *Telecommunications Policy*, *43*(9), 101793. doi:10.1016/j.telpol.2018.10.006

Chiang, J. (2021). 7 Types of Hybrid Recommendation System. *Medium.* https://medium.com/analytics-vidhya/7-types-of-hybrid-recommendation-system-3e4f78266ad8

Choi, J., & Kim, Y. (2020). Time-Aware Learning Framework for Over-The-Top Consumer Classification Based on Machine- and Deep-Learning Capabilities. *Applied Sciences, 10*(23), 8476, 1-17. doi:10.3390/app10238476

Choi, C. H., & You, Y. Y. (2017). The study on the comparative analysis of EFA and CFA. *Journal of Digital Convergence*, *15*(10), 103–111.

Chong, D. (2020). *Deep Dive into Netflix's Recommender System.* Towards Data Science. https://towardsdatascience.com: https://towardsdatascience.com/deep-dive-into-netflixs-recommender-system-341806ae3b48

Chorianopoulos, K. (2008). Personalized and mobile digital TV applications. *Multimedia Tools and Applications*, *36*(1-2), 1–10. doi:10.1007/s11042-006-0081-8

Christie, I. (2012). Wakening France: Observations on Télématin. *Critical Studies in Television, 7*(2). http://mendeley.csuc.cat/fitxers/f6d2dc6d3030ab4fe342f1dde4e04e73

Chukwuemeka, E. S. (2023, April 7). Countries with the highest young/youth population 2023. *Top (Madrid), 11*. https://bscholarly.com/countries-with-the-highest-youth-young-population-2022-top-9/

Cialdini, R. B. (2001). *Influence: Science and practice* (4th ed.). Allyn & Bacon.

Cobbe, J., & Singh, J. (2019). Regulating recommending: Motivations, considerations, and principles. *SSRN*, *10*(3), 1–49. doi:10.2139/ssrn.3371830

Cohen, R., & Blaszczynski, A. (2015). Comparative effects of Facebook and conventional media on body image dissatisfaction. *Journal of Eating Disorders*, *3*(1), 1–10. doi:10.1186/s40337-015-0061-3 PMID:26140215

Colombo-Mendoza, L. O., Valencia-García, R., Rodríguez-González, A., Alor-Hernández, G., & Samper-Zapater, J. J. (2015). RecomMetz: A context-aware knowledge-based mobile recommender system for movie showtimes. *Expert Systems with Applications*, *42*(3), 1202–1222. doi:10.1016/j.eswa.2014.09.016

Community, N. (2020). *Future of OTT in India*. Nasscom Community. https://community.nasscom.in/communities/digital-transformation/telecom-media-communities/future-of-ott-in india.html

Conlin, L., Billings, A. C., & Averset, L. (2016). Time-shifting vs. appointment viewing: The role of fear of missing out within TV consumption behaviours. *Communicatio Socialis*, *29*, 151–164.

Conviva. (2021). *Why Content Discovery in OTT Matters*. Conviva. https://www.conviva.com/why-content-discovery-in-ott-matters/

Cooltrack. (2021). *What is Cognitive Personalization?* Cooltrack. https://www.clootrack.com: https://www.clootrack.com/knowledge_base/cognitive-personalization

Couldry, N. (2004). Liveness, "reality", and the mediated habitus from television to the mobile phone. *Communication Review*, *7*(4), 353–361. doi:10.1080/10714420490886952

Cragin, B. (2010). Beyond the Feminine: Intersectionality and Hybridity in Talk Shows. *Women's Studies in Communication, 33*(2), 154–172. doi:10.1080/07491409.2010.507585

Cress, S. L., & Rapert, K. D. (1996). Talk Show Viewing Motives: Does Gender Make a Difference? *Annual Meeting of the Speech Communication Association*. ERIC. https://files.eric.ed.gov/fulltext/ED401586.pdf

Creswell, J. W., & Creswell, J. D. (2018, January 6). *Research Design: Qualitative, Quantitative, and Mixed Methods Approaches*.

Crowly. (2023). *Decoding Mobile Ad Networks: Your Key to Successful App Marketing*. App Samurai. https://appsamurai.com: https://appsamurai.com/blog/decoding-mobile-ad-networks-your-key-to-successful-app-marketing/

Damani, V. (2022) 5 Key Challenges for Netflix in India. *TechApp*. https://techpp.com/2016/01/07/netflixindia-challenges/

Danesi, M. (2016). *Concise Dictionary of Popular Culture*. Google. https://books.google.es/books?id=61mBDQAAQBAJ&pg=PA252&dq=talk+show+cycle&hl=en&sa=X&ved=0ahUKEwiCyZjq-LfeAhULI8AKHYuYCf8Q6AEINjAC#v=onepage&q=cycle&f=false

Dang, V. T., Nguyen, N., & Pervan, S. (2020). Retailer corporate social responsibility and consumer citizenship behavior: the mediating roles of perceived consumer effectiveness and consumer trust. *Journal of Retailing and Consumer Services, 55*(1), 102082, 1-10. https://doi.org/ doi:10.1016/j.jretconser.2020.102082

Dangwal, S. (2017, April 27). Reliance Entertainment launches BIGFLIX, India's first global multi-language HD movie platform. *India.com.* https://www.india.com/business/reliance-entertainment-launches-bigflix-indias-first-global-multi-language-hd-movie-platform-2074662/

Das, A. (2021). Supreme Courts Directs States To File Status Report On FIRs, Adjourns Hearing To August. *Tandav' Web Series Row.*

Dasgupta, S., & Grover, P.DASGUPTA. (2019). Understanding Adoption Factors of Over-the-Top Video Services Among Millennial Consumers. *International Journal of Computer Engineering & Technology, 10*(1), 61–71. doi:10.34218/IJCET.10.1.2019.008

Datareportal (2023, April). *digital 2023 April global statshot report.* https://datareportal.com/reports/digital-2023-april-global-statshot

Davenport, T. H., & Beck, J. C. (2001). *The Attention Economy: Understanding the New Currency of Business.* Harvard Business Press.

David, A. S. & Moe, W. (2016). Binge Watching and Advertising. *Sage Journals.* https://journals.sagepub.com/doi/10.1509/jm.15.0258

Davis, F. D. (1989). Perceived usefulness, perceived ease of use, and user acceptance of information technology. *Management Information Systems Quarterly, 13*(3), 319–340. doi:10.2307/249008

De Cicco, T., Cangiano, F., & De Felice, M. (2019). Using hashtags for a purpose: The case of Instagram. *New Media & Society, 21*(1), 1–20.

Deci, E. L., & Ryan, R. M. (1985). *Intrinsic motivation and self-determination in human behaviour.* Springer. doi:10.1007/978-1-4899-2271-7

Deldjoo, Y., Jannach, D., Bellogin, A., Difonzo, A., & Zanzonelli, D. (2023). Fairness in recommender systems: Research landscape and future directions. *User Modeling and User-Adapted Interaction.* doi:10.1007/s11257-023-09364-z

Delgado, M., & Prado, E. (2010). La televisión generalista en la era digital. Tendencias internacionales de programación. *TELOS Cuadernos de Comunicación e Innovación, 84,* 52–64.

Desai, D. (2017). *A study of design aspects of web personalization for online users in India.* (Corpus ID: 64977506) [Doctoral dissertation, Gujarat Technological University Ahmedabad]. Semantic Scholar.

Dhanuka, A., & Bohra, A. (2019) *Binge-Watching: Web-Series Addiction amongst Youth.* RSET. https://www.rset.edu.in/download/dsims/2_Binge_Watching_Web_Series_Addiction_am ongst_Youth.pdf

DhimanB. (2023). A Paradigm Shift in the Entertainment Industry in the Digital Age: A Critical Review. Preprints. doi:10.20944/preprints202306.1115.v1

DhimanD. B. (2023). A Critical Analysis of Vulgar Language on OTT Platforms: A Systematic Review. *Available at* SSRN 4404547. doi:10.2139/ssrn.4404547

Diakopoulos, N. (2015). Algorithmic accountability. *Digital Journalism (Abingdon, England), 3*(3), 398–415. doi:10.1080/21670811.2014.976411

Dijck, J. V. (2013). *The culture of connectivity: A critical history of social media.* Oxford University Press. doi:10.1093/acprof:oso/9780199970773.001.0001

Dourish, P. (2016). Algorithms and their others: Algorithmic culture in context. *Big Data & Society, 3*(2), 1–11. doi:10.1177/2053951716665128

Eg, R., Tønnesen, Ö. D., & Tennfjord, M. K. (2023). A scoping review of personalized user experiences on social media: The interplay between algorithms and human factors. *Computers in Human Behavior Reports, 9*, 100253. doi:10.1016/j.chbr.2022.100253

Eitan, T., & Gazit, T. (2023, January). No social media for six hours? The emotional experience of Meta's global outage according to FoMO, JoMO and internet intensity. *Computers in Human Behavior, 138*, 107474. doi:10.1016/j.chb.2022.107474

Eklund, O. (2022). Custom thumbnails: The changing face of personalisation strategies on Netflix. *Convergence (London), 28*(03), 737–760. doi:10.1177/13548565211064520

Ekström, M., & Tolson, A. (2013). *Media talk and political elections in Europe and America.* Palgrave Macmillan. https://books.google.es/books?id=LtnQAQAAQBAJ&pg=PA85&dq=%22talk+show%22+europe+candidates&hl=en&sa=X&ved=0ahUKEwjo1sDy_J3jAhWtQEEAHZQuA7sQ6AEIKjAA#v=onepage&q=%22talk show%22 europe candidates&f=false

Elhai, J. D., Levine, J. C., Dvorak, R. D., & Hall, B. J. (2016, October). Fear of missing out, need for touch, anxiety and depression are related to problematic smartphone use. *Computers in Human Behavior, 63*, 509–516. doi:10.1016/j.chb.2016.05.079

Endavo. (2023). *What is OTT?* Endavo. https://www.endavomedia.com: https://www.endavomedia.com/what-is-ott/

Erman, J., Gerber, A., Ramadrishnan, K. K., Sen, S., & Spatscheck, O. (2011). Over-the-Top Video: The Gorilla in Cellular Networks. In J. Erman, A. Gerber, K. K. Ramadrishnan, S. Sen, & O. Spatscheck (Eds.), *Proceedings of the 2011 ACM SIGCOMM Conference on Internet Measurement Conference* (pp. 127-136). Association for Computing Machinery. 10.1145/2068816.2068829

ET. T. E. (2023). India's entertainment & media industry revenues to reach $73.6 bn by 2027: Report. *The Economic Times*. https://economictimes.indiatimes.com/industry/media/entertainment/media/indias-entertainment-media-industry-revenues-to-reach-73-6-bn-by-2027-report/articleshow/101863251.cms

ETCFO. (2019). How OTT Platforms, 5G Technology will impact Entertainment Industry. *Economic Times.* https://cfo.economictimes.indiatimes.com/news/media-advertising-entertainment-industry-the-moment-of-becoming-and-the-future/71805710

ETtimes. (2021). OTT platforms – the challenges of balancing creativity with customer centricity. *ET Times.* https://brandequity.economictimes.indiatimes.com/news/digital/ott-platforms-the-challenges-of-balancing-creativity-with-customer-centricity/86111079

Faminiano, M. T., & Yango, A. R. (2023, June 9). Netflix viewing habit, grammatical competence, and academic self-efficacy of Selected Senior High School Students In Tagaytay City, Cavite. *Technium Social Sciences Journal, 44*, 316–331. doi:10.47577/tssj.v44i1.8947

Fardouly, J., Diedrichs, P. C., Vartanian, L. R., & Halliwell, E. (2018). Social comparisons on social media: The impact of Facebook on young women's body image concerns and mood. *Body Image, 26*, 38–45. PMID:25615425

Farooqui, J. (2021, May 7). Disney+ Hotstar has 41% share of Indian online video subscription market: Omdia. *Exchange4Media.* https://www.exchange4media.com/digital-news/disney-hotstar-has-41-share-of-indian-online-video-subscription-market-omdia-112817.html

Farooqui, M. (2022). *ZEE5 to increase originals by 2X, investment in content to be up by 50% in 2022.* Moneycontrol. https://www.moneycontrol.com/news/trends/entertainment/zee5-to-increase-originals-by-2x-investment-in-content-to-be-up-by-50-in-2022-8081711.html

Fatemi, F. (2021, February 1). How The Pandemic Has Changed Video Content And Consumption. *Forbes.* https://www.forbes.com/sites/falonfatemi/2021/02/01/how-the-pandemic-has-changed-video-content-and-consumption/?sh=3ea570f36ec0

Fdokumen. (2022). *OTT Personalization - GlobalLogic.* Fdokumen. www.fdocumen.id: https://fdokumen.id/dokumen/9562f_ott-personalization-globallogic.html

Federation of Indian Chambers of Commerce and Industry. (2019, March 12). *Press Release.* FICCI. https://www.ficci.in/pressrelease-page.asp?nid=3374

Feldman, O. (2020). The rhetoric of broadcast talk shows in Japan: The art of equivocation as a political skill. *The Rhetoric of Political Leadership: Logic and Emotion in Public Discourse*, (June), 139–155. doi:10.4337/9781789904581.00016

Festinger, L. (1954, May). A Theory of Social Comparison Processes. *Human Relations*, *7*(2), 117–140. doi:10.1177/001872675400700202

FICCI. (2019). *Indian Media and Entertainment industry clocks 13% growth to reach INR 1.67 trillion in 2018: FICCI-EY report.* FICCI. https://beta.ficci.in/pressrelease-page.asp?nid=3374

Fitzgerald, S. (2019). Over-the-Top Video Services in India: Media Imperialism after Globalization. *Media Industries*, *6*(2).

FMI. (2020). *OTT Content Market.* Future Marketimng Insights. https://www.futuremarketinsights.com/reports/over-the-top-ott-content-market

Foucault, M. (2019). *Özne ve İktidar* (I. Ergüden & O. Akınhay, Trans.). Ayrıntı.

Fouquaert, T. (2019). *The Algorithm Paradox: knowledge of versus attitudes towards curation algorithms,* [Unpublished master dissertation, Ghent University, Belgium].

Fouquaert, T., & Mechant, P. (2021). Making curation algorithms apparent: A case study of "Instawareness" as a means to heighten awareness and understanding of Instagram's algorithm. *Information Communication and Society*, *25*(12), 1–21.

Franssen, C. L. (2017). The Netflix Addiction: Why Our Brains Keep Telling Us to Press Play. *HuffPost.* https://www.huffpost.com/entry/the-netflix-addiction_b_8473094

Friederich, F., Palau-Saumell, R., Matute, J., & Meyer, J.-H. (2023). Digital natives and streaming TV platforms: An integrated perspective to explain continuance usage of over-the-top services. *Online Information Review.* doi:10.1108/OIR-03-2022-0133

Fu, X., Chen, N., Gao, P., & Li, Y. (2023). Privacy-Preserving Personalized Recommender Systems. *SRN.* https://papers.ssrn.com/sol3/papers.cfm?abstract_id=4202576

Furey, M. (2023). *How Reelgood is Putting an End to Decision Fatigue.* Reel Good. https://data.reelgood.com/how-reelgood-is-putting-an-end-to-decision-fatigue/

Gallier, E. (2021). *SVOD vs TVOD vs AVOD: What's the Best Content Delivery System?* Harmonic Inc. https://www.harmonicinc.com/insights/blog/svod-vs-tvod-vs-avod-whats-the-best-content-delivery-system/

Gambarato, R., & Heuman, J. (2022). Beyond fact and fiction: Cultural memory and transmedia ethics in Netflix's The Crown. *European Journal of Cultural Studies*, *0*(0). Advance online publication. doi:10.1177/13675494221128332

Gemmis, M. d., Lops, P., Musto, C., Narducci, F., & Semeraro, G. (2015). Semantics-Aware Content-Based Recommender Systems. In L. R. Francesco Ricci, *Recommender Systems Handbook* (pp. 119-159). Springer. https://link.springer.com/book/10.1007/978-1-4899-7637-6

Ghalawat, S., Yadav, E., Kumar, M., Kumari, N., Goyal, M., Girdhar, A., & Agarwal, S. (2021). Factors Influencing Consumer's Choice of Streaming Over the top (OTT) Platforms. *Indian Journal of Extension Education*, *57*(03), 99–101. doi:10.48165/IJEE.2021.57323

Ghosh, A. (16 Aug 2023). Preserving Films means Preserving History, Culture and Memories. *Times of India*. https://timesofindia.indiatimes.com/india/preserving-films-means-preserving-history-culture-and-memories/articleshow/102755505.cms?from=mdr. Accessed on 31/08/23

Gillespie, T. (2014). The relevance of algorithms. media technologies: Essays on communication. In T. Gillespie, P. J. Boczkowski, & K. A. Foot (Eds.), *Materiality and society* (pp. 167–193). MIT Press.

Globallogic. (2021). *How to Elevate Your OTTThrough Predictive Personalization*. Globalogic.

Gokul, M. (2022). *Personalization In The OTT Space For Better Recommendations And Smarter Video Analytics*. Argoid. https://www.argoid.ai/blog/personalization-in-the-ott-space-for-better-recommendation-and-smarter-video-analytics

Gomery, D. (2008). *A history of broadcasting in the United States*. Blackwell Publishing. https://cataleg.uab.cat/iii/encore/record/C__Rb1798501?lang=cat

Gomez-Uribe, A. C., & Hunt, N. (2015). The Netflix recommender system: Algorithms, Business Value, and Innovation. *ACM Transactions on Management Information Systems*, *6*(4), 1–19. doi:10.1145/2843948

Gonçalves, V. G., Evens, T., Alves, A. P., & Ballon, P. (2014). Power and Control Strategies in Online Video Services. At *the 25th European Regional Conference of the International Telecommunications Society (ITS)*. ACM.

Granovetter, M. (1985). Economic action and social structure: The problem of embeddedness. *American Journal of Sociology*, *91*(3), 481–510. doi:10.1086/228311

Grindstaff, L. (2002). *The money shot : trash, class, and the making of TV talk shows*. University of Chicago Press. doi:10.7208/chicago/9780226309088.001.0001

Grover, S. (2023). *OTT vs CTV: Differences Explained for Publishers*. Adpushup https://www.adpushup.com/blog/ott-vs-ctv/

Guest, G., Bunce, A., & Johnson, L. (2006, February). How Many Interviews Are Enough? *Field Methods*, *18*(1), 59–82. doi:10.1177/1525822X05279903

Gupta, G., & Singharia, K. (2021). Consumption of OTT media streaming in COVID-19 lockdown: Insights from PLS analysis. *Vision (Basel)*, *25*(1), 36–46. doi:10.1177/0972262921989118

Gupta, P. (2021). The factors effecting shift of Indian customers from TV series to web series-the future of OTT services in India. [IJMR]. *EPRA International Journal of Multidisciplinary Research*, *7*(2), 143–150.

Habib, S., Hamadneh, N., & Hassan, A. (2022). The Relationship between Digital Marketing, Customer Engagement, and Purchase Intention via OTT Platforms. *Journal of Mathematics, 22. Journal of Mathematics, 5327626*, 1–12. doi:10.1155/2022/5327626

Haleem, A., Javaid, M., Asim Qadri, M., Pratap Singh, R., & Suman, R. (2022). Artificial intelligence (AI) applications for marketing: A literature-based study. *International Journal of Intelligent Networks, 3*(1), 119–132. doi:10.1016/j.ijin.2022.08.005

Hallur, G., Aslekar, A., & Prabhu, S. (2023). Digital Solution for Entertainment: An Overview of Over the Top (OTT) and Digital Media. *Digital Entertainment as Next Evolution in Service Sector: Emerging Digital Solutions in Reshaping Different Industries,* 35-53. Research Gate.

Hamilton, A. J. S. (1988). Evidence for biasing in the CfA survey. *Astrophysical Journal, 331.*

Han, B. C. (2019). *Psikopolitika: Neoliberalizm ve yeni iktidar teknikleri* (H. Barışçan, Trans.). Metis.

Harsoor, S. (2023). Recommendation Systems: An Overview. *Medium.* https://medium.com/@sharanharsoor/recommendation-systems-an-overview-a9ff7d32b043

Hayran, C., & Anik, L. (2021, February 18). Well-Being and Fear of Missing Out (FOMO) on Digital Content in the Time of COVID-19: A Correlational Analysis among University Students. *International Journal of Environmental Research and Public Health, 18*(4), 1974. doi:10.3390/ijerph18041974 PMID:33670639

Hennig-Thurau, T., Gwinner, K. P., Walsh, G., & Gremler, D. D. (2004). Electronic word-of-mouth via consumer-opinion platforms: What motivates consumers to articulate themselves online? *Journal of Interactive Marketing, 18*(1), 38–52. doi:10.1002/dir.10073

Henten, A., & Tadayoni, R. (2020). *Fading public control of audiovisual media. International Telecommunications Society.* ITS.

Herlocker, L. J., Konstan, A. J., & Riedl, J. (2000). Explaining Collaborative Filtering Recommendations. *CSCW '00: Proceedings of the 2000 ACM conference on Computer supported cooperative work.* ACM. 10.1145/358916.358995

Hickman, M. (2023). *The Power of Personalized Marketing: AI, Customer Behaviour, and Recommender Systems.* LinkedIn. https://www.linkedin.com: https://www.linkedin.com/pulse/power-personalized-marketing-ai-customer-behaviour-systems-hickman/

Hill, C. (2020). Streaming Services Now Have Nearly 1 Billion Subscribers Globally. *Forbes.*

Hollebeek, L. D., & Macky, K. (2019). Digital content marketing's role in fostering consumer engagement, trust, and value: Framework, fundamental propositions, and implications. *Journal of Interactive Marketing, 45,* 27–41. doi:10.1016/j.intmar.2018.07.003

Hsu, C. L., & Wang, E. T. (2018). Understanding the psychological process underlying audience engagement with OTT content. *Internet Research, 28*(5), 1209–1228.

https://udayindia.in/impact-of-ott-platforms-on-youth/

Huang, Y., Cui, B., Zhang, W., Jiang, J., & Xu, Y. (2015). TencentRec: Real-time stream recommendation in practice. *In Proceedings of the 2015 ACM SIGMOD International Conference on Management of Data- SIGMOD'15.* Association for Computing Machinery.

Hussein, W., Ismail, R. M., Gharib, T. F., & Mostafa, M. G. M. (2013). A personalized recommender system based on a hybrid model. *JUCS -. Journal of Universal Computer Science, 19*(15), 2224–2240. doi:10.3217/jucs-019-15-2224

Hyken, S. (2017, October 29). Personalized customer experience increases revenue and loyalty. *Forbes.* https://www.forbes.com/sites/shephyken/2017/10/29/personalized-customer-experience-increases-revenue-and-loyalty/#3852914d4bd6

IBEF. (2021). *OTT Video - Small Screen, Big Play.* IBEF. https://www.ibef.org/research/india-study/ott-video-small-screen-big-play

IBEF. (2022). *Media and Entertainment Industry Report.* IBEF. https://www.ibef.org/industry/entertainment-presentation

IBM. (2021). *How AI is changing advertising?* IBM. https://www.ibm.com: https://www.ibm.com/watson-advertising/thought-leadership/how-ai-is-changing-advertising

Ilie, C. (2006). Talk Shows. In K. Brown (Ed.), *Encyclopedia of Language & Linguistics* (2nd ed., pp. 489–494). Elsevier. doi:10.1016/B0-08-044854-2/00357-6

India Times. (2020). Always connected: Indians consume over 11GB data daily, spend 70 mins a day on OTT platforms. *The Economic Times.* https://economicti-mes.india-times.com/magazines/panache/always-con-nected-indians-con-sume-over-11gb-data-daily-spend-70-m-ins-a-day-on-ott-platfo-rms/articlesh-ow/74333875.cms

India, G. o. (2017). *Nationwide Registry for Organ and Tissue Donation Launched.* Press Information Bureau. http://pib.nic.in/newsite/PrintRelease.aspx?relid=131941

India, G. o. (2021). *Information Technology (Intermediary Guidelines and Digital Media Ethics Code) Rules 2021.* New Delhi: Ministry of Electronics and Information Technology https://mib.gov.in/sites/default/files/IT%28Intermediary%20Guidelines%20and%20Digital%20Media%20Ethics%20Code%29%20Rules%2C%202021%20English.pdf

Indian Retailer. (2022). *How Data Analytics is Driving Personalization?* Indian Retailer. https://www.indianretailer.com/article/technology-e-commerce/digital-trends/how-data-analytics-driving-personalization

Indian Retailer. (2022). *How Digital Marketing Can Help in Increasing Consumer Engagement.* Indian Retailer. https://www.indianretailer.com/article/technology-e-commerce/digital-trends/how-digital-marketing-can-help-increasing-consumer

IndianExpress. (2018). Original content to drive growth for Rs 3,300cr investment in OTT services: Report. *India Express.* https://indianexpress.com: https://indianexpress.com/article/technology/tech-news-technology/original-content-to-drive-growth-for-rs-3300cr-investment-in-ott-report-5029883/

Iqbal, J., Asghar, M. Z., Ashraf, M. A., & Rafiq, M. (2022, July). Social Media Networking Sites Usage and Depression Among University Students During the COVID-19 Pandemic: The Mediating Roles of Social Anxiety and Loneliness. *Social Media + Society, 8*(3), 205630512211076. doi:10.1177/20563051221107633

ITConvergence. (2023). *The Role of Machine Learning in Recommendation Systems.* IT Convergence. https://www.itconvergence.com/blog/the-role-of-machine-learning-in-recommendation-systems/

Jackson, D. (2017). The Netflix Prize: How a $1 Million Contest Changed Binge-Watching Forever. *ThrillList.* https://www.thrillist.com: https://www.thrillist.com/entertainment/nation/the-netflix-prize

Jackson, M. (2020). Building anticipation: How Netflix utilised Instagram Stories to promote "Stranger Things.". *Media and Communication, 8*(2), 329–337.

Jackson, S. (2020). The influence of Instagram on OTT media marketing: A case study of Netflix's "Stranger Things.". *Journal of New Media Marketing, 19*(2), 76–88.

Jain, K. (2021). The Rise of Ott Platform: Changing Consumer Preferences [IJMR]. *EPRA International Journal of Multidisciplinary Research, 7*(6), 257–261. doi:10.36713/epra2013

Jang, W. E., Bucy, E. P., & Cho, J. (2018, August). Self-esteem moderates the influence of self-presentation style on Facebook users' sense of subjective well-being. *Computers in Human Behavior, 85*, 190–199. doi:10.1016/j.chb.2018.03.044

Javed, U., Shaukat, K., Hameed, A., Iqbal, I., Mahboob, F., Alam, T., & Luo, S. (2021). A Review of Content-Based and Context-Based Recommendation Systems. [iJET]. *International Journal of Emerging Technologies in Learning*, *16*(03), 274–306. doi:10.3991/ijet.v16i03.18851

Jeckmans, A., Beye, M., Erkin, Z., Hartel, P. H., Lagendijk, R. L., & Tang, Q. (2013). Privacy in Recommender Systems. *Chapter in Book/Report/Conference proceeding*. London: Springer. 10.1007/978-1-4471-4555-4_12

Jenkins, H. (2006). *Convergence culture: Where old and new media collide*. NYU Press.

Johnson, L. (2019). *How to use Instagram's new algorithm to boost your reach*. Social Media Today. [Link]

Johnson, M. (2019). The Impact of Instagram on Modern Media Consumption. *Journal of New Media Studies*, *3*(2), 45–59.

Johnson, M. A., & White, B. R. (2018). The Psychological Impact of Binge-Watching: Exploring Escapism and Emotional Attachment. *Journal of Media Psychology*, *23*(3), 141–152.

Johnson, S. K., Tullis, T. S., & Shaw, H. (2017). Browsing behaviours, information seeking, and cognitive load during learning from the Web. *Memory & Cognition*, *45*(3), 422–436.

Jones, I. (2004). *Morning glory: A history of British breakfast television*. Kelly. https://books.google.es/books?id=WpQ_esoMKLMC&printsec=frontcover&source=gbs_ge_summary_r&cad=0#v=onepage&q&f=true

Jones, J. P. (2009). I Want My Talk TV: Network Talk Shows in a Digital Universe. In A. D. Lotz (Ed.), *Beyond Prime Time: Television Programming in the Post-Network Era* (pp. 14–35).

Jones, P. C. (2017). The Impact of Netflix on Binge-Watching Habits: A Case Study. *International Journal of Communication*, *11*, 2785–2803.

Jones, R. (2020). *Streaming Wars: Who will win the battle for your eyeballs?* BBC.

Jones, R. (2020). The Streaming Revolution: A Comparative Analysis of OTT Platforms. *Journal of Media Trends*, *17*(3), 120–137.

Jose, R. J. (2020). Factors influencing the shift from traditional TV to OTT platforms in India. *International Journal of Advanced Science and Technology*, *29*(7), 4044–4051.

Juetten, M. (2021). Content Curated With A Human Touch: Bookshlf. *Forbes*. https://www.forbes.com/sites/maryjuetten/2021/09/07/content-curated-with-a-human-touch-bookshlf/?sh=2eabbc6f435b

Kaatib, A. (2022). *How Too Much Binge-Watching Is Damaging Your Health*. MUO. https://www.makeuseof.com/tag/binge-watching-damaging-health/

Kakkar, A., & Nayak, K. (2019). Analysis of Product Placement in Web Series and its Influence on Consumer Buying Behavior. *Journal of Business*. https://journalofbusiness.org/index.php/GJMBR/article/download/2755/2656/

Kala, D., & Chaubey, D. S. (2018). The effect of eWOM communication on brand image and purchase intention towards lifestyle products in India. *International Journal of Services Economics and Management*, *9*(2), 143–157. doi:10.1504/IJSEM.2018.096077

Kala, G. (2022). The Growing Popularity of OTT platform and its impact on the younger generation. *Mahratta*, *1*(2), 1–7.

Kalorth, N. (2018). *Social Media Experiences and Narratives Formation of Opinions in the Age of Post–Truth*. Research Gate.

Kanstrén, T. (2020). *A Look at Precision, Recall, and F1-Score*. Towards Data Science. https://towardsdatascience.com/a-look-at-precision-recall-and-f1-score-36b5fd0dd3ec

Kaplan, A. M., & Haenlein, M. (2010). Users of the world, unite! The challenges and opportunities of Social Media. *Business Horizons*, *53*(1), 59–68. doi:10.1016/j.bushor.2009.09.003

Kapoor, S. (2023). OTT 2.0 — India is ready. *Times of India.* https://timesofindia.indiatimes.com: https://timesofindia.indiatimes.com/blogs/voices/ott-2-0-india-is-ready/

Kara, B. B., & McAleese, S. (2021). *Algorithmic awareness: conversations with young canadians about artificial intelligence and privacy.* MediaSmarts. https://mediasmarts.ca/sites/default/files/publication-report/full/report_algorithmic_awareness.pdfBlinded for Review.

Karmakar, D. (2015). Binge Watching TV Linked To Higher Rates Of Depression And Anxiety. *Medical Daily.* https://www.medicaldaily.com/binge-watching-tv-linked-higher-rates-depression-and-anxiety-360776

Kasula, C. P. (2020). *Netflix Recommender System — A Big Data Case Study.* Towards Data Science. https://towardsdatascience.com/netflix-recommender-system-a-big-data-case-study-19cfa6d56ff5

Kasula, C. P. (2020). *Netflix Recommender System — A Big Data Case Study.* Towards Science Data. https://towardsdatascience.com/: https://towardsdatascience.com/netflix-recommender-system-a-big-data-case-study-19cfa6d56ff5

Kawa, K. (2018). *Television: The Small Box That Changed The World.* Lucent Press. https://books.google.es/books?id=-F9doDwAAQBAJ&pg=PA28&dq=when+vaudeville+died+television+was+the+box+they+put+it+in&hl=en&sa=X&ved=0ahUKEwjkwovM9bfeAhWUfMAKHc5RCm8Q6AEIMDAB#v=onepage&q=vaudeville&f=false

Kay, J. (2015). *Gender, Feminism and Talk on British Television, 1970-1990.* De Monfort University.

Keles, B., McCrae, N., & Grealish, A. (2019, March 21). A systematic review: The influence of social media on depression, anxiety and psychological distress in adolescents. *International Journal of Adolescence and Youth*, *25*(1), 79–93. doi:10.1080/02673843.2019.1590851

Keller, K. L. (2017). Managing the growth tradeoff: challenges and opportunities in luxury branding. Advances in Luxury Brand Management. Springer.

Kharwal, A. (2023). *Content Based Filtering and Collaborative Filtering: Difference.* The Clever Programmer. https://thecleverprogrammer.com/2023/04/20/content-based-filtering-and-collaborative-filtering-difference/: https://thecleverprogrammer.com/2023/04/20/content-based-filtering-and-collaborative-filtering-difference/

Khurana, D., Koli, A., Khatter, K., & Singh, S. (2022). Diksha Khurana, Aditya Koli, Kiran Khatter & Sukhdev Singh. *Multimedia Tools and Applications*, *82*, 3713–3744. doi:10.1007/s11042-022-13428-4 PMID:35855771

Kim, J., Kim, S., & Nam, C. (2015). Telematics and Informatics Competitive dynamics in the Korean video platform market : Traditional pay TV platforms vs. OTT platforms. *Telematics and Informatics.* Advance online publication. doi:10.1016/j.tele.2015.06.014

Kim, M. S., Kim, E., Hwang, S., Kim, J., & Kim, S. (2017). Willingness to pay for over-the-top services in China and Korea. *Telecommunications Policy*, *41*(3), 197–207. doi:10.1016/j.telpol.2016.12.011

Kim, S., & Bae, J. (2016). Cross-cultural differences in concrete and abstract corporate social responsibility (CSR) campaigns: Perceived message clarity and perceived CSR as mediators. *International Journal of Corporate Social Responsibility*, *1*(6), 1–14. doi:10.1186/s40991-016-0009-1

Kircaburun, K., & Griffiths, M. D. (2018). Instagram addiction and the Big Five of personality: The mediating role of self-liking. *Journal of Behavioral Addictions*, *7*(1), 158–170. doi:10.1556/2006.7.2018.15 PMID:29461086

Kitchens, B., Johnson, S. L., & Gray, P. (2020). UNDERSTANDING ECHO CHAMBERS AND FILTER BUBBLES: THE IMPACT OF SOCIAL MEDIA ON DIVERSIFICATION AND PARTISAN SHIFTS IN NEWS CONSUMPTION. *Management Information Systems Quarterly*, *44*(4), 1619–1649. doi:10.25300/MISQ/2020/16371

Knobloch-Westerwick, S. (2014, July 14). *Choice and Preference in Media Use: Advances in Selective Exposure Theory and Research*. https://doi.org/ doi:10.1604/9780805855159

Koka, V. (2023). The shift towards digital: A thriving OTT market. *Times of India*. https://timesofindia.indiatimes.com/blogs/voices/the-shift-towards-digital-a-thriving-ott-market/

Kollmann, P., Hill, M. E., Allen, R. C., McNutt, R. L. Jr, Brown, L. E., Barnes, N. P., Delamere, P., Clark, G., Andrews, G. B., Salazar, N., Westlake, J., Romeo, G., Vandegriff, J., Kusterer, M., Smith, D., Nelson, K., Jaskulek, S., Decker, R. B., Cheng, A. F., & Stern, S. A. (2019). Pluto's Interaction With Energetic Heliospheric Ions. *Journal of Geophysical Research. Space Physics*, *124*(9), 7413–7424. doi:10.1029/2019JA026830 PMID:35860291

Konstantoulaki, K., Rizomyliotis, I., & Papangelopoulou, A. (2019). Personalised content in mobile applications and purchase intentions: An exploratory study. *Business and Management Studies*, *5*(4), 13–23. doi:10.11114/bms.v5i4.4571

Koo, H. (2018). Factors affecting streamers' loyalty to live streaming platforms. *22nd Biennial Conference of the International Telecommunications Society (ITS): "Beyond the Boundaries: Challenges for Business, Policy and Society.*

Koravi, V. S. (2019). Analysis of various effects of web series streaming online on Internet on Indian youth. *IJRULA*, *2*(1), 28–42.

Koren, Y., & Bell, R. (2015). Advances in Collaborative Filtering. In L. R. Francesco Ricci, *Recommender Systems Handbook* (pp. 77-118). Springer. https://link.springer.com/book/10.1007/978-1-4899-7637-6

Koren, Y., Rendle, S., & Bell, R. (2022). Advances in collaborative filtering. In F. Ricci, L. Rokach, & B. Shapira (Eds.), *Recommender systems handbook* (pp. 91–142). Springer. doi:10.1007/978-1-0716-2197-4_3

Kotler, P., Kartajaya, H., & Setiawan, I. (2021). *Pazarlama 5.0 insan için teknoloji* (T. Gezer, Trans.). Nişantaşı Üniversitesi Yayınları.

Kour, G., & Chhabria, B. (2022). Understanding platform strategies for consumer stickiness on OTT platforms. *Journal of Indian Business Research*, *14*(4), 540–555. doi:10.1108/JIBR-04-2021-0122

Krieger, M., & Systrom, K. (2012). *Instagram: From Zero to a Billion*. Stanford Business.

Krings, E. (2023). *VOD Streaming – What It Is and How It Works with OTT*. DAcast. https://www.dacast.com/blog/vod-streaming/

Krishna, G., & Sen, A. (2022). The Global Entertainment Major Has Completed Five Interesting Years in India, Focussed on Its Premium Positioning. What Lies Ahead? *Business Today*. https://www.businesstoday.in/interactive/immersive/netflix-india-popular-ott-platform-in-india/

Kumar, J. & George, N. (2023). *India: Government Issues Regulations For OTT Platforms And Online Content*. Mondaq. https://www.mondaq.com/india/broadcasting-film-tv--radio/1007904/government-issues-regulations-for-ott-platforms-and-online-content (last accessed on 23rd July 2023)

Kumari, S. (2022). *Indian OTT platforms rely heavily on marketing, or do they?* Best Media Info. https://bestmediainfo.com/2022/06/indian-ott-platforms-rely-heavily-on-marketing-or-do-they

Kumari, T. (2020). A Study on Growth of Over the Top (OTT) Video Services in India. *International Journal of Latest Research in Humanities and Social Science*, *03*(09), 68–73.

Kumar, J., Gupta, A., & Dixit, S. (2020). Netflix: SVoD entertainment of next gen. *Emerald Emerging Markets Case Studies*, *10*(3), 1–36. doi:10.1108/EEMCS-04-2020-0108

Kumar, M. K., & Gangwar, R. (2022). Necessity of OTT Regulation in Indian Context. *Bayan College International Journal of Multidisciplinary Research*, *2*(2), 78–90.

Kwon, Y., Park, J., & Son, J. (2020). *Accurately or accidentally ? Recommendation agent and search experience in over-the-top (OTT) services*. Emerald. doi:10.1108/INTR-03-2020-0127

Lakens, D. (2022). Sample Size Justification. *Collabra. Psychology*, *8*(1), 33267. Advance online publication. doi:10.1525/collabra.33267

Layton, R. (2015). Netflix Comes to the Nordics: Lessons in OTT Video. *Journal of NBICT*, *1*(1), 109–138. doi:10.13052/NBICT.2015.005

Leano, J. (2014). The Agenda-Setting Power of Saturday Night Live. *The Elon Journal of Undergraduate Research in Communications*, *5*(1), 81–89. http://www.elon.edu/docs/e-web/academics/communications/research/vol5no1/09leanoejspring14.pdf

Lee, C. C., Nagpal, P., Ruane, S. G., & Lim Hyoun Sook. (2018). Communications of the IIMA Factors Affecting Online Streaming Subscriptions SUBSCRIPTIONS. *Communications of the IIMA*, *16*(1).

Lee, C. C., Nagpal, P., Ruane, S. G., & Lim, H. S. (2018). Factors affecting online streaming subscriptions. *Communications of the IIMA*, *16*(1). doi:10.58729/1941-6687.1394

Lee, S. Y., & Kim, M. S. (2018). Social capital and binge-watching on over-the-top content platforms. *Journal of Broadcasting & Electronic Media*, *62*(2), 276–294.

Liang, T.-P., Lai, H.-J., & Ku, Y.-C. (2007). Personalized Content Recommendation and User Satisfaction: Theoretical Synthesis and Empirical Findings. *Journal of Management Information Systems*, *23*(3), 45–70. doi:10.2753/MIS0742-1222230303

Lidhoo, P. (2022). Was Bollywood saved by OTT during the pandemic? For many producers, the answer is a big Yes. *Business Today*. https://www.businesstoday.in: https://www.businesstoday.in/trending/entertainment/story/was-bollywood-saved-by-ott-during-the-pandemic-for-many-producers-the-answer-is-a-big-yes-348410-2022-09-28

Lindecrantz, E. (2020). *Personalizing the customer experience: Driving differentiation in retail*. McKinsey and Company. https://www.mckinsey.com/industries/retail/our-insights/personalizing-the-customer-experience-driving-differentiation-in-retail

Lin, J. S., & Lu, H. P. (2011). Why people use social networking sites: An empirical study integrating network externalities and motivation theory. *Computers in Human Behavior*, *27*(3), 1152–1161. doi:10.1016/j.chb.2010.12.009

Lin, L. Y., Sidani, J. E., Shensa, A., Radovic, A., Miller, E., Colditz, J. B., Hoffman, B. L., Giles, L. M., & Primack, B. A. (2016, January 19). ASSOCIATION BETWEEN SOCIAL MEDIA USE AND DEPRESSION AMONG U.S. YOUNG ADULTS. *Depression and Anxiety*, *33*(4), 323–331. doi:10.1002/da.22466 PMID:26783723

Lissak, G., & Mekler, E. D. (2019). Youth online behavior and social media use in Israel: Analysis of associations with depressive symptoms. *The Journal of Adolescent Health*, *64*(3), 334–340.

Lissak, G., & Mekler, E. D. (2019). Youth Online Behaviour and Social Media Use in Israel: Analysis of associations with depressive symptoms. *The Journal of Adolescent Health*, *64*(3), 334–340.

Løkke, E. (2020). *Mahremiyet Dijital Toplumda Özel Hayat. (D. Başak, Çev.)*. Koç Üniversitesi Yayınları.

Luca, M. (2015). User-generated content and social media. In *Handbook of media Economics* (Vol. 1, pp. 563–592). North-Holland.

Lunt, P., & Stenner, P. (2005). The Jerry Springer Show as an emotional public sphere. *Media Culture & Society*, *27*(1), 163–4437. doi:10.1177/0163443705049058

M&M. (2022). *Over the Top Market by Type (Game Streaming, Audio Streaming, Video Streaming, and Communication), Monetization Model (Subscription-based, Advertising-based, and Transaction-based), Streaming Device, Vertical and Region - Global Forecast to 2027*. M&M. https://www.marketsandmarkets.com/Market-Reports/over-the-top-ott-market-41276741.html

Madhani, R., & Nakhate, V. (2020). Comparative Study Of Viewers ' Behaviour Over Traditional Television Channels And Over Ott Video Platforms In Maharashtra. *International Journal of Advanced Science and Technology*, *29*(12), 1046–1057.

Madnani, D., Fernandes, S., & Madnani, N. (2020). Analysing the impact of COVID-19 on over-the-top media platforms in India. *International Journal of Pervasive Computing and Communications*, *16*(5), 457–475. doi:10.1108/IJPCC-07-2020-0083

Magan, S. (25 Jan 2023). Percentage of citizens likely to visit cinemas increased by 150%: Local Circles Survey. *Business Insider*. https://www.businessinsider.in/entertainment/news/percentage-of-citizens-likely-to-visit-cinemas-increased-by-150-as-perreport/articleshow/97281514.cms. .

Malhotra, S. (2020). *Recommendation Engines for OTT Platforms To Personalize Streaming*. Artificial Intelligence. https://artificialintelligence.oodles.io: https://artificialintelligence.oodles.io/blogs/recommendation-engines-for-ott-platforms/

Marcos-García, S., Alonso-Muñoz, L., & López-Meri, A. (2020). Extending influence on social media: The behaviour of political talk-show opinion leaders on twitter. *Communicatio Socialis*, *33*(2), 277–293. doi:10.15581/003.33.2.277-293

Marcus, C. (2023). *OTT Advertising: How to Advertise on Streaming Service*. Color Matics. https://www.colormatics.com/article/ott-advertising-how-to-advertise-on-streaming-service/

Markham, A., Stavrova, S., & Schlüter, M. (2018). Netflix, imagined affordances, and the illusion of control. In T. Plothe & A. M. Buck (Eds.), *Netflix at the nexus: Content, practice and production in the age of streaming television* (pp. 29–46). Peter Lang.

Marsh, H. W., Muthén, B., Asparouhov, T., Lüdtke, O., Robitzsch, A., Morin, A. J., & Trautwein, U. (2009). Exploratory structural equation modeling, integrating CFA and EFA: Application to students' evaluations of university teaching. *Structural Equation Modeling*, *16*(3), 439–476. doi:10.1080/10705510903008220

Martinez, B. B., & Costa-Montenegro, E. (2010). A hybrid content-based and item-based collaborative filtering approach to recommend TV programs enhanced with singular value decomposition. *Information Sciences*, *180*(22), 4290–4311. doi:10.1016/j.ins.2010.07.024

Marx, G. T. (2004). What's new about the "new surveillance"?: Classifying for change and continuity. *Surveillance & Society*, *1*(1), 9–29. doi:10.24908/ss.v1i1.3391

Masciantonio, A., Résibois, M., Bouchat, P., & Bourguignon, D. (2023). Social Network Sites and Well-Being: Is it Only a Matter of Content? *Revue Internationale de Psychologie Sociale*, *36*(1), 6. doi:10.5334/irsp.736

Mastrini, G., & Krakowiak, F. (2021). Netflix en Argentina: Expansión acelerada y producción local escasa. *Comunicación y Sociedad*, *7915*(1), 1–23. doi:10.32870/cys.v2021.7915

Matrix, S. (2014, June). The Netflix Effect: Teens, Binge Watching, and On-Demand Digital Media Trends. *Jeunesse: Young People, Texts. Cultures*, *6*(1), 119–138. doi:10.3138/jeunesse.6.1.119

McKinnon, I. (2022). *Consumer Insights And The Evolution of Personalized Website Recommendation Systems*. Rosetta. https://rosetta.ai: https://rosetta.ai/blog/consumer-insights-and-the-evolution-of-personalized-website-recommendation-systems

Mehta, B. (2022). Why do millennials prefer OTT platforms over traditional Theaters? *Agency Reporter.* https://www.agencyreporter.com/why-do-millennials-prefer-ott-platforms-over-traditional-theaters/

Menon, D. (2020). *Reduced Attention Spans In The Digital Age*. LinkedIn. https://www.linkedin.com/pulse/reduced-attention-spans-digital-age-deepak-menon/

Miguel Alves Gomes, T. M. (2023). A review on customer segmentation methods for personalized customer targeting in e-commerce use cases. *Information Systems and e-Business Management*, *21*(3), 527–570. doi:10.1007/s10257-023-00640-4

Minzheong, S. (2021). A Comparative Study on Over-The-Tops, Netflix & Amazon Prime Video:Based on the Success Factors of Innovation. *International Journal of Advanced Smart Convergence*, *10*(01), 62–74. doi:10.7236/IJASC.2021.10.1.62

Mittell, J. (2004). *Genre and television: From Cop Shows To Cartoons in American Culture*. Routledge. https://cataleg.uab.cat/iii/encore/record/C__Rb1622959__Sgenre and television__Orightresult__U__X7?lang=cat

Mittell, J. (2003). Audiences Talking Genre: Television Talk Shows and Cultural Hierarchies. *The Journal of Popular Film and Television*, *31*(1), 36–46. doi:10.1080/01956050309602867

Mitter, S. (2019). After two unsuccessful attempts at video streaming, here's how ZEE cracked the OTT puzzle with ZEE5. *YourStory.com*. https://yourstory.com/2019/06/ott-zee5-original-content-partnerships-startups

Moats, D., & Seaver, N. (2019). "You social scientists love mind games": Experimenting in the "divide" between data science and critical algorithm studies. *Big Data & Society*, *6*(1), 1–11. doi:10.1177/2053951719833404

Mobasher, B. (2007). Data Mining for Web Personalization. Brusilovsky, P., Kobsa, A., Nejdl, W. (eds) The Adaptive Web Methods and Strategies of Web Personalisation. Lecture Notes in Computer Science içinde (s.90-136). Springer. doi:10.1007/978-3-540-72079-9_3

Mohan, M., & Jadhav, A. (2022). Predicting Customer Churn on OTT Platforms: Customers with Subscription of Multiple Service Providers. *Journal of Information and Organizational Sciences*, *46*(2), 433–451.

Moneycontrol.com. (2023). Disney+ Hotstar faces outage amid the India-Australia test match. *Moneycontrol*. https://www.moneycontrol.com/news/business/disney-hotstar-faces-outage-amid-the-india-australia-test-match-10109821.html

Moochhala, Q. (2018). *The Future of Online OTT Entertainment Services in India*. Lexipedia.

Moore, A. (2023). *Increase Your Website's Ad Revenue with Ad Exchanges: A Step-by-Step Guide*. EZAOIC.

Mordor Intelligence. (2021). *Marché Mondıal Over The Top (Ott) - Croıssance, Tendances, Impact du Covıd-19 et Prévısıons. (2023-2028)*. Mordor Intelligence. https://www.mordorintelligence.com/fr/industry-reports/over-the-top-market

Mulla, T. (2022, April). Assessing the factors influencing the adoption of over-the-top streaming platforms: A literature review from 2007 to 2021. *Telematics and Informatics*, *69*, 101797. doi:10.1016/j.tele.2022.101797

Mundel, J., Wan, A., & Yang, J. (2023, February 24). Processes underlying social comparison with influencers and subsequent impulsive buying: The roles of social anxiety and social media addiction. *Journal of Marketing Communications*, 1–18. doi:10.1080/13527266.2023.2183426

Munson, W. (1993). *All Talk: the talkshow in media culture.* Temple University Press. http://cataleg.uab.cat/record=b1315794~S1*cat

Mu, R. (2018). *A survey of recommender systems based on deep learning.* Digital Object Identifer., doi:10.1109/ACCESS.2018.2880197

Muralidharan, G. (2020). *Personalization in the OTT Space for Better Recommendation and Smarter Video Analytics.* LinkedIn. https://www.linkedin.com: https://www.linkedin.com/pulse/personalization-ott-space-better-recommendation-video-muralidharan/

MyStory. (2023). *EVERYTHING YOU NEED TO KNOW ABOUT OTT TECHNOLOGY.* Mystory. https://yourstory.com/mystory/everything-you-need-to-know-about-ott-technology

Nafees, L., Mehdi, M., Gupta, R., Kalia, S., Banerjee, S., & Kapoor, S. (2021). Netflix in India: Expanding to success. *Emerald Emerging Markets Case Studies, 11*(2), 1–31. doi:10.1108/EEMCS-10-2019-0285

Nagaraj, S., Singh, S., & Yasa, V.R. (2021). Factors affecting consumers' willingness to subscribe to over-the-top (OTT) video streaming services in India. *Technology in* Society, *65*(C), 1-7. doi:10.1016/j.techsoc.2021.101534

Nagy, P., & Neff, G. (2015). Imagined affordance: Reconstructing a keyword for communication theory. *Social Media + Society, 1*(2), 1–9. doi:10.1177/2056305115603385

Naresh, S. (2021). Smart Recommendation System For OTT platforms. *Medium.* https://medium.com/mobiotics/smart-recommendation-system-for-ott-platforms-f0e79b8e520

Necula, S.-C., & Păvăloaia, V.-D. (2023). AI-Driven Recommendations: A Systematic Review of the State of the Art in E-Commerce. *Applied Sciences (Basel, Switzerland), 13*(9), 5531. doi:10.3390/app13095531

Netflix, Inc. (2018). Netflix Declares Binge Watching is the New Normal. *PR News Wire.* https://www.prnewswire.com/news-releases/netflix-declares-binge-watching-is-the-new-normal-235713431.html

Netflix. (2019). *How Netflix's Recommendations System Works?* Netflix https://help.netflix.com/en/node/100639

Nijhawan, G. S., & Dahiya, S. (2020). ROLE OF COVID AS A CATALYST IN INCREASING ADOPTION OF OTTS IN INDIA : A STUDY OF EVOLVING CONSUMER CONSUMPTION PATTERNS. *Journal of Content. Community & Communication, 12*, 298–311. doi:10.31620/JCCC.12.20/28

Niven, D., Lichter, S. R., & Amundson, D. (2003). The Political Content of Late Night Comedy. *The Harvard International Journal of Press/Politics, 8*(3), 118–133. doi:10.1177/1081180X03008003007

Nvidia. (2022). *Recommendation System.* Nvidia. https://www.nvidia.com: https://www.nvidia.com/en-us/glossary/data-science/recommendation-system/

O'Neil, C. (2017, November 14). The ivory tower can't keep ignoring tech. *The New York Times.* www.nytimes.com/2017/11/14/opinion/academia-tech-algorithms.html

Okumuş, M. S. (2023). The Audience Struggle between Television, Cinema, and OTT Platforms: The Case of Netflix and Disney+ In Turkey. *Turkish Online Journal Of Design Art And Communication, 13*(1), 108–123. doi:10.7456//11301100/008

Oliveira, T., Fiorese, A., & Sargento, S. (2018). *Forecasting Over-the-Top Bandwidth Consumption Applied to Network Operators.* In *Proceedings of the 2018 IEEE Symposium on Computers and Communications (ISCC),* Natal, Brazil. 10.1109/ISCC.2018.8538539

Omukić, S., Činjarević, M., & Peštek, A. (2022). How “Netflix Effect'' is (Re)shaping the Media Consumption Patterns of Y-ers and Z-ers? Information Systems and Technologies. WorldCIST 2022. Springer, Cham. doi:10.1007/978-3-031-04819-7_54

Ong, J. W. (2012). *Sözlü ve yazılı kültür: Sözün teknolojileşmesi* (S. Postacıoğlu Banon, Trans.). Metis.

Osgood, C. E., & Tannenbaum, P. H. (1955). The Principle of Congruity in the Prediction of Attitude Change. *Psychological Review, 62*(1), 42–55. doi:10.1037/h0048153 PMID:14357526

Ota, R., Ray, S. S., & Chandra, A. (2020). *An analysis of customer preference towards OTT Platform during a pandemic : A special reference to Jamshedpur Market. IX*(Viii), 192–202.

Ott, B. L., & Mack, R. L. (2020). *Critical media studies: An introduction.* John Wiley & Sons.

Oyeleye, A. L., & Olutayo, O. G. (2012). Interaction Management in Nigerian Television Talk Shows. *International Journal of English Linguistics, 2*(1), 149–161. doi:10.5539/ijel.v2n1p149

Özel, S. & Özay, D. (2021). Yeni medya ortamlarında izleyici seçimi ve öneri algoritmaları. *İlef Dergisi, 8*(2), 297-324.

Özel, S. (2020). Talebe bağlı video servisleri çağında Netflix etkisi. *İnsan& İnsan. 7*(26), 115-138.

Paivio, A. (1986). *Mental representations: A dual coding approach.* Oxford University Press.

Pajkovic, N. (2022). Algorithms and taste-making: Exposing the Netflix Recommender System's operational logics. *Convergence (London), 28*(1), 214–235. doi:10.1177/13548565211014464

Palomba., A (2022). Building OTT brand loyalty and brand equity: impact of original series on OTT services. *Telematics and Informatics, 66*(3), 101733, 1-14. doi:10.1016/j.tele.2021.101733

Panda, S., & Pandey, S. C. (2017). Binge watching and college students: Motivations and outcomes. *Young Consumers, 18*(4), 425–438. doi:10.1108/YC-07-2017-00707

Pandey, R. (2023). *The Future is Now: How AI and Machine Learning are Revolutionizing the Software Industry.* LinkedIn. https://www.linkedin.com: https://www.linkedin.com/pulse/future-now-how-ai-machine-learning-revolutionizing-software-pandey-/

Papagelis, M., & Plexousakis, D. (2005). Qualitative analysis of user-based and item-based prediction algorithms for recommendation agents. *Engineering Applications of Artificial Intelligence, 18*(7), 781–789. doi:10.1016/j.engappai.2005.06.010

Parihar, S., & Kant, D. K. (2021). Impact of Marketing Mix on Consumers Satisfaction-A Study of Consumers of OTT Platforms in India. *IJRAR, 8*(3), 260–272.

Park, A. (2015). This Is What Binge-Watching TV Does to Your Health. *Time.* https://time.com/3767458/tv-binge-watching-health/

Parto, S. (2005). Economic activity and institutions: *Taking Stock. Journal of Economic Issues, 39*(1), 21–52. doi:10.1080/00213624.2005.11506779

Pasquale, F. (2015). *The black box society: The secret algorithms that control money and information.* Harvard University Press. doi:10.4159/harvard.9780674736061

Patel, M. K., Khadia, R., & Awasya, G. (2020). A Study : OTT Viewership in “ Lockdown ” and Viewer ' s Dynamic Watching Experience. *International Journal on Transformations of Media. Journalism & Mass Communication, 5*(2), 10–22.

Pathak, P. (2019). JioCinema app: How to use, features and everything related to know. *India Today*. https://www.indiatoday.in/technology/features/story/jiocinema-app-how-to-use-features-and-everything-related-to-know-1423371-2019-01-04

Pazzani, M. J., & Billsus, D. (2007). Content-Based Recommendation Systems. Brusilovsky, P., Kobsa, A., Nejdl, W. (eds) The Adaptive Web Methods and Strategies of Web Personalisation. Lecture Notes in Computer Science içinde (s.325-341). Springer. doi:10.1007/978-3-540-72079-9_10

Periaiya, S., & Nandukrishna, A. T. (2023). What drives user stickiness and satisfaction in OTT video streaming platforms? A mixed-method exploration. *International Journal of Human-Computer Interaction*, 1–17. doi:10.1080/10447318.2022.2160224

Peterson, R. L. (2008). Strange Bedfellows: The Politics of Late-Night Television Comedy. *Poroi*, *5*(1), 61–83. doi:10.13008/2151-2957.1020

Petty, R. E., & Cacioppo, J. T. (1986). *Communication and Persuasion: Central and Peripheral Routes to Attitude Change*. Springer. doi:10.1007/978-1-4612-4964-1

Pirolli, P., & Card, S. (1999). Information foraging. *Psychological Review*, *106*(4), 643–675. doi:10.1037/0033-295X.106.4.643

Pittman, M., & Sheehan, K. (2015). Sprinting a media marathon: Uses and gratifications of binge-watching television through Netflix. *First Monday*, *20*(10). doi:10.5210/fm.v20i10.6138

Polaris, M. R. (2023). *Global Over the Top (OTT) Market Projected to Grow USD 2,228.36 Billion By 2032, at 27.0% CAGR: Polaris Market Research*. Global News Wire. https://www.globenewswire.com/en/news-release/2023/04/11/2644610/0/en/Global-Over-the-Top-OTT-Market-Projected-to-Grow-USD-2-228-36-Billion-By-2032-at-27-0-CAGR-Polaris-Market-Research.html

Popat, A., & Tarrant, C. (2022, June 7). Exploring adolescents' perspectives on social media and mental health and well-being – A qualitative literature review. *Clinical Child Psychology and Psychiatry*, *28*(1), 323–337. doi:10.1177/13591045221092884 PMID:35670473

Pradhan, B., Kishore, K., & Gokhale, N. (2023, February 8). Social media influencers and consumer engagement: A review and future research agenda. *International Journal of Consumer Studies*, *47*(6), 2106–2130. doi:10.1111/ijcs.12901

Prasad, S. S. (2022). Impact of OTT media on the society: Insights from path analysis. *Asia-Pacific Journal of Business Administration*, *14*(2), 185–198. doi:10.1108/APJBA-06-2021-0261

Press Trust of India. (2020, February 27). Always connected: Indians consume over 11GB data daily, spend 70 mins a day on OTT platforms. *The Economic Times*. https://economictimes.indiatimes.com/magazines/panache/always-connected-indians-con-sume-over-11gb-data-daily-spend-70-mins-a-day-on-ott-platforms/articleshow/74333875.cms

Primack, B. A., Shensa, A., Sidani, J. E., Whaite, E. O., Lin, L. Y., Rosen, D., Colditz, J. B., Radovic, A., & Miller, E. (2017, July). Social Media Use and Perceived Social Isolation Among Young Adults in the U.S. *American Journal of Preventive Medicine*, *53*(1), 1–8. doi:10.1016/j.amepre.2017.01.010 PMID:28279545

Proulx, M., & Shepatin, S. (2012). *Social TV : how marketers can reach and engage audiences by connecting television to the web, social media, and mobile*. John Wiley & Sons.

Przybylski, A. K., Murayama, K., DeHaan, C. R., & Gladwell, V. (2013, July). Motivational, emotional, and behavioral correlates of fear of missing out. *Computers in Human Behavior*, *29*(4), 1841–1848. doi:10.1016/j.chb.2013.02.014

Przybylski, A. K., & Weinstein, N. (2017, January 13). A Large-Scale Test of the Goldilocks Hypothesis. *Psychological Science*, *28*(2), 204–215. doi:10.1177/0956797616678438 PMID:28085574

Radia, N. (2016). The Arrival Of Netflix In India: All That You Need To Know. *Inc42 Media*. https://inc42.com/resources/the-arrival-of-netflix-in-india/

Rajpal, A. (2020). Web Series: A Look into an Emerging Industry. *Youth Inc. Magazine*. https://youthincmag.com/web-series-an-emerging-industry

Rakshit, P., Saha, S., Chatterjee, A., Mistri, S., Das, S., & Dhar, G. (2022). A Popularity-Based Recommendation System Using Machine Learning. In H. K. Deva Sarma, V. Piuri, & A. K. Pujari (Eds.), *Machine Learning in Information and Communication Technology. Lecture Notes in Networks and Systems* (Vol. 498). Springer.

Ramesh, M. (2023). Indian OTT market set to reach ₹30,000 crore by 2030. *The Hindu- Business Line*. https://www.thehindubusinessline.com/news/indian-ott-market-set-to-reach-30000-crore-by-2030/article66760012.ece

Ramesh, A., & Jaggi, R. K. (2022). The contemporary film public relations' ecosystem in India – from stars to stories. *International Journal of Indian Culture and Business Management*, *25*(1), 17–37. doi:10.1504/IJICBM.2022.120922

Ramji Lal Modi v. State of U.P., All India Reporter 620 (Supreme Court of India 1957).

Ranjit D. Udeshi v. State of Maharashtra, 1 Supreme Court Reporter 65 (Supreme Court of India 1965).

Ray, S. S. (2020). Explained: What is the measure of 'obscenity' in India. *Indian Express*. https://indianexpress.com/article/explained/explained-milind-soman-obscenity-in-india-6998750/

ResearchAndMarkets. (2023). *OTT Streaming Global Market Report 2023: Major Players Include Facebook, Netflix, Amazon, Microsoft, Google, Apple, Hulu, Tencent, Rakuten and YouTube*. Globenewswire. https://www.globenewswire.com/en/news-release/2023/04/07/2643207/28124/en/OTT-Streaming-Global-Market-Report-2023-Major-Players-Include-Facebook-Netflix-Amazon-Microsoft-Google-Apple-Hulu-Tencent-Rakuten-and-YouTube.html

Researchwire. (2022). Trends in OTT technology — How AI and ML are transforming content production and delivery. *Research Wire*. https://www.researchwire.in/resources/trends-in-ott-technology-how-ai-and-ml-are-transforming-content-production-and-delivery/

Reshma, & Chaithra. (2020). Proliferation of OTT apps in India: an empirical study of OTT apps and its impact on college students. *International Journal of Research and Analytical Reviews (IJRAR)*, *7*(1), 427–435.

Rideout, V. J., Fox, S., & Roberts, D. F. (2019). Young people's news habits: Examining the role of platforms, devices, and social networks. *Journal of Computer-Mediated Communication*, *24*(5), 227–239.

Robert Amor, J. D. (2021). The promise of automated compliance checking. *Developments in the Built Environment*, *5*(1), 100039. doi:10.1016/j.dibe.2020.100039

Robert, M. P. W., & Raj, J. J., & JOSEPH, D. T. (2022). THE FUTURE OF MOVIES: WILL OTT TAKE OVER THEATRES? *Journal of Positive School Psychology*, *6*(3), 7614–7620.

Roberts, K. (2020). Instagram: A powerful platform for visual storytelling. *Journal of Contemporary Rhetoric*, *10*, 89–97.

Roberts, H. (2017). *How Instagram is revolutionising audience engagement for creators*. Tubular Insights. [Link]

Roberts, H. (2020). Instagram as a storytelling platform: Leveraging visual content for brand narratives. *Journal of Social Media Strategy*, *6*(1), 45–57.

Roberts, S. (2017). From Follower to Fan: Investigating User Engagement in OTT Media through Instagram. *Media Studies Journal*, *25*(4), 78–92.

Robosoft. (2022). *Building cross-platform OTT apps: best practices in design & development.* Robosoft. https://www.robosoftin.com/blog/cross-platform-ott-apps-design-development

Rogers, E. M. (1962). *Diffusion of Innovations.* Free Press.

Romans, C. (2022). *Try Out These 9 Apps to Help Alleviate Loneliness.* MUO. https://www.makeuseof.com/apps-alleviate-loneliness/

Rose, L. (2013, November 4). *CBS Extends David Letterman Contract Through 2015.* The Hollywood Reporter. https://www.hollywoodreporter.com/tv/tv-news/cbs-extends-david-letterman-contract-643439/

Roth, S., Weinmann, C., Schneider, F. M., Hopp, F. R., & Vorderer, P. (2014). Seriously Entertained: Antecedents and Consequences of Hedonic and Eudaimon.... *Mass Communication & Society, 17*(3), 379–399. doi:10.1080/15205436.2014.891135

Roy, A. (2020). *Introduction To Recommender Systems- 1: Content-Based Filtering And Collaborative Filtering.* Towards Data Science. https://towardsdatascience.com: https://towardsdatascience.com/introduction-to-recommender-systems-1-971bd274f421

Rudra, N. R. (2023, April 19). *Disney+ Hotstar gets a new look; See what's changed.* Smartprix. https://www.smar-tprix.com/by-tes/disney-hot-star-ge-ts-a-new-lo-ok-see-whats-changed/

Sadagheyani, H. E., & Tatari, F. (2020, October 16). Investigating the role of social media on mental health. *Mental Health and Social Inclusion, 25*(1), 41–51. doi:10.1108/MHSI-06-2020-0039

Sadana, M., & Sharma, D. (2021). How over-the-top (OTT) platforms engage young consumers over traditional pay television service? An analysis of changing consumer preferences and gamification. *Young Consumers, 22*(3), 348–367. doi:10.1108/YC-10-2020-1231

Salman, H. (2023). Unraveling the Power of Recommendation Systems: Personalization in the Digital Age. *Medium.* https://medium.com: https://medium.com/@hanifesalman0/unraveling-the-power-of-recommendation-systems-personalization-in-the-digital-age-a85623f111a9

SamritiD.SharmaP. (2020). OTT-existing censorship laws and recommendations. SSRN 3735027.

Sarkar, G. (2020). Indian OTT platforms dish out special fare for kids. *Indian Television.* https://www.indiantelevision.com/iworld/over-the-top-services/indian-ott-services-targetkids-with-special-fare-200601

Sarker, I. H. (2021). Deep Learning: A Comprehensive Overview on Techniques, Taxonomy, Applications and Research Directions. *SN Computer Science, 2*(420), 420. doi:10.1007/s42979-021-00815-1 PMID:34426802

Saurwein, F., & Spencer-Smith, C. (2021). Automated trouble: The role of algorithmic selection in harms on social media platforms. *Media and Communication, 9*(4), 222–233. doi:10.17645/mac.v9i4.4062

Saxena, P. (2023). *Driving Engagement and Loyalty: The Impact of Social Media Marketing.* AdLift. https://www.adlift.com/in/blog/driving-engagement-and-loyalty-the-impact-of-social-media-marketing/

Scannel, P. (1991). *Broadcast Talk* (P. Scannel, Ed.). Sage Publications., https://cataleg.uab.cat/iii/encore/record/C__Rb1060460?lang=cat

Schafer, J. B., Konstan, J., & Riedl, J. (1999). Recommender systems in e-commerce. *In Proceedings of the 1st ACM Conference on Electronic Commerce,* (pp. 158-166). Association for Computing Machinery Schulz, C. (2022). A new algorithmic imaginary. *Media Culture & Society, 45*(3), 451–681.

Schmuck, D. (2021, September 1). Following Social Media Influencers in Early Adolescence: Fear of Missing Out, Social Well-Being and Supportive Communication with Parents. *Journal of Computer-Mediated Communication, 26*(5), 245–264. doi:10.1093/jcmc/zmab008

Schultz, D. (2012). *Politainment: The Ten Rules of Contemporary Politics: A Citizens' Guide to Understanding Campaigns and Elections.* Google. https://books.google.es/books?id=-w-ftgAACAAJ

Schweidel, D. A., Bart, Y., Inman, J. J., Stephen, A. T., Libai, B., Andrews, M., Rosario, A. B., Chae, I., Chen, Z., Kupor, D., Longoni, C., & Thomaz, F. (2022). How consumer digital signals are reshaping the customer journey. *Journal of the Academy of Marketing Science, 50*(6), 1257–1276. doi:10.1007/s11747-022-00839-w PMID:35221393

Seaver, N. (2017). Algorithms as culture: Some tactics for the ethnography of algorithmic systems. *Big Data & Society, 4*(2). doi:10.1177/2053951717738104

Segijn, C. M., Maslowska, E., Araujo, T., & Viswanathan, V. (2020). Engaging with TV events on Twitter: The interrelations between TV consumption, engagement actors, and engagement content. *Internet Research, 30*(2), 381–401. doi:10.1108/INTR-08-2018-0389

Sekścińska, K., & Jaworska, D. (2022, April). Who felt blue when Facebook went down? - The role of self-esteem and FoMO in explaining people's mood in reaction to social media outage. *Personality and Individual Differences, 188*, 111460. doi:10.1016/j.paid.2021.111460

Sell, A., Mezei, J., & Walden, P. (2014). Walden, P. An attitude-based latent class segmentation analysis of mobile phone users. *Telematics and Informatics, 31*(2), 209–219. doi:10.1016/j.tele.2013.08.004

Senal Group. (2022, May 19). Amazon Prime Video ramps up local originals in India. *Senal News.* https://senalnews.com/en/research/amazon-prime-video-ramps-up-local-originals-in-india

Seonmi, L. (2021). *Examining factors influencing early paid over-the-top video streaming market growth: A cross-country empirical study.* MDPI.

Shah, A. (2016). Belly up to the TV: Binge watching could lead to more stomach fat. *The Seattle Times.* https://www.seattletimes.com/life/wellness/belly-up-to-the-tv-binge-watching-could-lead-to-more-stomach-fat/

Shah, S., & Mehta, N. (2022). Over-the-Top (OTT) Streaming Services: Studying Users' Behaviour Through the UTAUT Model. *Management and Labour Studies, 0*(0). doi:10.1177/0258042X221137438

Sharma, A. (2023). *OTT VS Traditional TV: The Battle for Viewership.* Next Gen IOTs. https://nexgeniots.com/ott-vs-traditional-tv-the-battle-of-viewership/

Sharma, N. (2021). *OTT Channels and their marketing strategies* [Doctoral dissertation, School of Petroleum Management].

Sharma, A., Sreen, N., & Baishya, K. (2023). Identifying gratification behind the consumption of the OTT platforms in an emerging market: A means-end theory approach. *Marketing Intelligence & Planning, 41*(5), 593–612. https://www.emerald.com/insight/content/doi/10.1108/MIP-12-2022-0558/full/html?skipTracking=true. doi:10.1108/MIP-12-2022-0558

Sharma, K., & Lulandala, E. E. (2023). OTT platforms resilience to COVID-19 – a study of business strategies and consumer media consumption in India. *The International Journal of Organizational Analysis, 31*(1), 63–90. doi:10.1108/IJOA-06-2021-2816

Sharpe, I. (2020). *OTT 2.0: understanding the importance of interactivity and engagement.* TVB Europe. https://www.tvbeurope.com/media-delivery: https://www.tvbeurope.com/media-delivery/ott-2-0-understanding-the-importance-of-interactivity-and-engagement

Shashank Shekhar Jha vs Union Of India, 15 October, 2020 https://indiankanoon.org/doc/24196538/

Shattuc, J. (1997). *The Talking Cure: TV Talk Shows and Women*. Routledge. http://cataleg.uab.cat/record=b1394015~S1*cat

Shaw, K. (2021). *Netflix India Launches The Red Notice Shop Turnıng Fans Into Shoplifters Via 22feet Trıbal Worldwıde Indıa*. Campaign Brief. https://campaignbriefasia.com/2021/11/29/netflix-india-launches-the-red-notice-shop-turning-fans-into-shoplifters-via-22feet-tribal-worldwide-india/

Shim, D., Lee, C., & Oh, I. (2022). Analysis of OTT Users' Watching Behavior for Identifying a Profitable Niche: Latent Class Regression Approach. *Journal of Theoretical and Applied Electronic Commerce Research*, *17*(4), 1564–1580. doi:10.3390/jtaer17040079

Shim, H., & Kim, K. J. (2018). An exploration of the motivations for binge-watching and the role of individual differences. *Computers in Human Behavior*, *82*, 94–100. doi:10.1016/j.chb.2017.12.032

Shin, D. D. (2023). *Algorithms, Human and Interactions: How Do Algorithms Interact with People? Designing Meaningful AI Experiences*. Routledge.

Shin, D., Hameleers, M., Park, Y. J., Kim, J. N., Trielli, D., Diakopoulos, N., Helberger, N., Lewis, S. C., Westlund, O., & Baumann, S. (2022). Countering algorithmic bias and disinformation and effectively harnessing the power of AI in media. *Journalism & Mass Communication Quarterly*, *99*(4), 887–907. doi:10.1177/10776990221129245

Shin, D., Lim, J. S., Ahmad, N., & Ibahrine, M. (2022). Understanding user sensemaking in fairness and transparency in algorithms: Algorithmic sensemaking in over-the-top platform. *AI & Society*, 1–14. doi:10.1007/s00146-022-01525-9

Shin, D., Rasul, A., & Fotiadis, A. (2022). Why am I seeing this? Deconstructing algorithm literacy through the lens of users. *Internet Research*, *32*(4), 1214–1234. doi:10.1108/INTR-02-2021-0087

Shinde, K. S., & Kulkarni, U. (2012). Hybrid personalized recommender system using centering-bunching based clustering algorithm. *Expert Systems with Applications*, *39*(1), 1381–1387. doi:10.1016/j.eswa.2011.08.020

Shon, M., Shin, J., Hwang, J., & Lee, D. (2021). Free contents vs. inconvenience costs: Two faces of online video advertising. *Telematics and Informatics*, *56*, 101476. doi:10.1016/j.tele.2020.101476

Silvia, S. (2019). The importance of social media and digital marketing to attract millennials' behavior as a consumer. *Journal of International Business Research and Marketing*, *4*(2), 7–10. doi:10.18775/jibrm.1849-8558.2015.42.3001

Simons, H. (2021). *Amazon Prime Video's biggest problem isn't content, it's everything else*. Android Authority. https://www.androidauthority.com/amazon-prime-video-problems-1228014/

Sindhu, M., & Vani, C. (2021). *The OTT (Over the Top)*. Platforms and Movie Watching Experience of the Audience.

Singh, D. (2020). 8 shows that give us a peek into the gen-Z life, on Netflix and Disney+ Hotstar. Vo*uge India*. https://www.vogue.in/culture-and-living/content/8-shows-that-give-us-a-peek-into-the-gen-z-life-on-netflix-and-disney-hotstar

Singh, M. (2023, May 10). *Disney's Hotstar loses 8.4 million subscribers as Ambani's JioCinema ascends*. TechCrunch+. https://techcrunch.com/2023/05/10/disney-hotstar-loses-8-4-million-subscribers-as-ambani-jiocinema-takes-off/?guccounter=1

Singh, S. (2018). *A study on factors leading to the adoption of OTT services among millennial consumers in India*.

Singh, K. K., Makhania, J., & Mahapatra, M. (2023). Impact of ratings of content on OTT platforms and prediction of its success rate. *Multimedia Tools and Applications*, 1–18.

Singh, N., Arora, S., & Kapur, B. (2022). Trends in over the top (OTT) research: A bibliometric analysis. *VINE Journal of Information and Knowledge Management Systems*, *52*(3), 411–425. doi:10.1108/VJIKMS-12-2021-0316

Singh, P. (2019). New Media as a Change Agent of Indian Television and Cinema: A study of over the top Platforms. *Journal of Content. Community and Communication*, *9*(1), 131–137.

Singh, S., Singh, N., Kalinić, Z., & Liébana-cabanillas, F. J. (2020). Assessing determinants influencing continued use of live streaming services: An extended perceived value theory of streaming addiction. *Expert Systems with Applications*, *114241*. doi:10.1016/j.eswa.2020.114241

Skyquestt. (2022). *Global OTT market insights*. Skyquestt. www.skyquestt.com: https://www.skyquestt.com/report/over-the-top-ott-market

Smith, J. (2018). Understanding Over-the-Top (OTT) Services: A Comprehensive Analysis. *Media Studies Journal*, *35*(2), 215–230.

Smith, J. (2020). *Visual storytelling on social media: The case of Disney*. Social Media Today.

Smith, T. (2018). Influencer Culture: The Changing Dynamics of Media Promotion. *Communication Review*, *41*(2), 215–230.

Smith, T. (2018). Instagram's influence on visual storytelling. *Journal of Visual Communication*, *17*(3), 297–315.

Smith, T. (2018). *OTT platforms and the power of visual storytelling*. The Drum.

Smith, T. (2020). Crafting visual narratives on Instagram: Disney+ case study. *Visual Media Journal*, *23*(4), 489–505.

Sontakke, K. S. (2021). Trends in OTT Platforms Usage During COVID-19 Lockdown in India. *Journal of Scientific Research*, *65*(8), 23. doi:10.37398/JSR.2021.650823

Spacek, D. (2018). *Personalisierte Medien und Unterhaltung*. Walderwyss. https://www.walderwyss.com/user_assets/publications/2359.pdf

Srinivasan, A. (2023). *Covid-19 fuels AI platforms causing cloud providers to invest*. LinkedIn. https://www.linkedin.com/pulse/covid-19-fuels-ai-platforms-causing-cloud-providers-aarthi-srinivasan/

Srnicek, N. (2017). *Platform capitalism*. Polity Press.

Stamenkovic, M. (2012). In full view: Cyber suicide, Self and Public show case of death (for real). *TC Journal*, *5*(12), 73-101.

Stanimirovic, U. (2023). *What Is OTT: A Definitive Guide to Over-the-Top Streaming*. Target. https://target-video.com/what-is-ott/#8-how-is-ott-content-delivered

Starosta, J., Izydorczyk, B., & Lizińczyk, S. (2019). Characteristics of people's binge-watching behaviour in the "entering into early adulthood" period of life. *Health Psychology*, *7*, 149–164.

StartIO. (2023). *Maximizing Revenue in 2023: Proven Strategies for App Monetization – Statistics, Models and Best Practices*. StartIO. https://www.start.io/blog/maximizing-revenue-proven-strategies-for-app-monetization-statistics-models-and-best-practices/

Statista (2023). *Video streaming worldwide - statistics & facts*. Statista. https://www.statista.com/topics/7527/video-streaming-worldwide/#topicOverview

Statista. (2021). *Number of monthly active Instagram users from January 2013 to June 2021*. Statista.

Statista. (2022). *OTT Video - Worldwide.* Statista. https://www.statista.com/outlook/amo/media/tv-video/ott-video/worldwide

Statista. (2023). *OTT Video - Worldwide.* Statista. https://www.statista.com: https://www.statista.com/outlook/amo/media/tv-video/ott-video/worldwide

Steiner, E., & Xu, K. (2020). Binge-watching motivates change: Uses and gratifications of streaming video viewers challenge traditional TV research. *Convergence (London)*, *26*(1), 82–101. doi:10.1177/1354856517750365

Storyly. (2023). *What is content personalization?* Storyly. https://www.storyly.io/glossary/content-personalization

Strategus. (2021). *12 New Developments In Ott Platforms For 2022.* Strategus. https://www.strategus.com/blog/new-developments-ott

Sujata, J., Sohag, S., Tanu, D., Chintan, D., Shubham, P., & Sumit, G. (2015). Impact of Over the Top (OTT) Services on Telecom Service Providers. *Indian Journal of Science and Technology*, *8*(February), 145–160. doi:10.17485/ijst/2015/v8iS4/62238

Sujith, T. S., & Sumathy, M. (2021). Anticidence of Buying Behaviour of Parents Towards Educational Mobile Applications. *SJCC Management Research Review*, 1-12.

Sujith, T. S., & Jisha, M. K. (2017). Tourism in India: Opportunities and Challenges. *Imperial Journal of Interdisciplinary Research*, *3*(10), 201–204.

Sujith, T. S., & Julie, C. D. (2018). Environmental accounting: A conceptual study. *IJAR*, *4*(12), 147–149.

Sumathy, M., & TS, S. (2018). A Comparative Study on Perception of Customers towards Service Quality of Canara and ICICI Bank. *RESEARCH REVIEW International Journal of Multidisciplinary, Special Issue*, 187-190.

Sumathy, M., & Sujith, T. S. (2018). Effect of Brand on Customer Loyalty among SBI Banking Customers. *International Journal of Scientific and Engineering Research*, *6*(9), 2015–2018.

Sumeet, S. (2023). *Stay One Step Ahead: AI-Driven Tactics for OTT Customer Retention.* LinkedIn. https://www.linkedin.com/pulse/stay-one-step-ahead-ai-driven-tactics-ott-customer-retention-shah/

Summergrad, S. (2016). *Can We Talk? A Discussion on Gender Politics in the Late-Night Comedy Career of Joan Rivers.* Scribd. https://es.scribd.com/document/319661192/Summergrad-bu-0017N-12201-pdf?secret_password=HWQUYCrkHYCsCnPfG2Tn#download&from_embed

Sundaravel, E., & Elangovan, N. (2020). *Emergence and future of Over-the-top (OTT) video services in India : an analytical research. 08*(02), 489–499.

Suriati, S., Dwiastuti, M., & Tulus, T. (2017). Weighted hybrid technique for recommender system. *International Conference on Information and Communication Technology (IconICT)* (pp. 1-8). IOP. https://iopscience.iop.org/article/10.1088/1742-6596/930/1/012050

Tandon, A., Dhir, A., Islam, N., Talwar, S., & Mäntymäki, M. (2021, November). Psychological and behavioral outcomes of social media-induced fear of missing out at the workplace. *Journal of Business Research*, *136*, 186–197. doi:10.1016/j.jbusres.2021.07.036

Tarus, K. J., Niu, Z., & Mustafa, G. (2018). Knowledge-based recommendation: A review of ontology-based recommender systems for e-learning. *Artificial Intelligence Review*, *50*(21), 21–48. doi:10.1007/s10462-017-9539-5

Taylor, K. (2022). *What is Cross-Channel Personalization?* Hitechnectar. https://www.hitechnectar.com/blogs/cross-channel-personalization/

Team YourDost. (n.d.). 26-Year-Old Gurgaon Professional Diagnosed With 'Binge Watching Addiction.' *YourDost.* https://your-dost.com/blog/2017/08/binge-watc-hing-addi-ction.html?q=/blog/2017/08/binge-watching-addic-tion.html

Tefertiller, A. (2020). Cable cord-cutting and streaming adoption: Advertising avoidance and technology acceptance in television innovation. *Telematics and Informatics, 51,* 1-9. doi:10.1016/j.tele.2020.101416

Tefertiller, A. C., & Maxwell, L. C. (2018, October 3). Depression, emotional states, and the experience of binge-watching narrative television. *Atlantic Journal of Communication, 26*(5), 278–290. doi:10.1080/15456870.2018.1517765

Telecom Regulatory Authority of India. (2020, January 8). Indian Telecom Services Performance Indicator Report. *TRAI.* https://trai.gov.in/sites/default/files/PR_No.04of2020.pdf

Theodore, P. (2016). to binge or not to binge: A qualitative analysis of college students' binge-watching habits. *Fla Commun J, 44,* 77–88.

Thomas, F. (2023). *Plateformes OTT: quel intérêt pour les créateurs de contenu?* JND. https://www.journaldunet.com/media/publishers/1520017-plateformes-ott-quel-interet-pour-les-createurs-de-contenu/

Thomas, M. (2022). A clinic in India's Silicon Valley is treating its first case of Netflix addiction. *Quartz.* https://qz.com/india/1416875/bengalurus-nimhans-is-now-treating-netflix-addiction

Thorat, B. P., Goudar, M. R., & Barve, S. (2015). Survey on collaborative filtering, content-based filtering and hybrid recommendation system. *International Journal of Computer Applications, 110*(4), 31–36. doi:10.5120/19308-0760

Thussu, D. K. (2007). *News As Entertainment: The Rise of Global Infotainment.* Sage. https://cataleg.uab.cat/iii/encore/record/C__Rb1735030__Snews as entertainment__Orightresult__U__X7?lang=cat

Timberg, B. (2002). *Television Talk: A History of the TV Talk Show.* University of Texas Press.

Times, E. (18 July 2023). Don't demean Indian society, culture in the name of creative freedom. *Times of India.* https://timesofindia.indiatimes.com/articleshow/101881313.cms?from=mdr&utm_source=contentofinterest&utm_medium=text&utm_campaign=cppst. Accessed on 31/08/23.

Tiwari, V. (2019.). OTT Platforms: Their Revenue Model and Rise. *Insider.* https://insider.finology.in/investing/ott-platform-revenue-model

Tolson, A. (2001). *Television talk shows : discourse, performance, spectacle.* Lawrence Erlbaum., https://cataleg.uab.cat/iii/encore/record/C__Rb1492862?lang=cat doi:10.4324/9781410600950

Tran, T., Tran, Q., & Le, H. (2020). An Empirical Study on Continuance Using Intention of OTT Apps with Young Generation. *Springer Nature Singapore Pte Ltd., 3,* 219–229. doi:10.1007/978-981-32-9244-4_31

TS, S., & Sumathy, M. (2021). Millennial Satisfaction on Amazon Prime Video Platform with Special Reference to Thrissur District. *Vidyabharati International Interdisciplinary Research Journal,* 3153-3157.

TS, S., & Sumathy, M. (2021). User Perception Towards OTT Video Streaming Platforms in Kerala (With Special Reference to Thrissur). *Analytical Commerce and Economics, 2*(4), 27–32.

TS, S., & Sumathy, M. (2022). Application of Technology Acceptance Model (TAM) on Adoption of Food Delivering Applications (Apps.) among University students in Tamil Nadu. *RVIM Journal of Management Research, 22.*

TS, S., & Sumathy, M. P, S., & K, MN. (2022). Sustainability of over the top (OTT) video platforms in india: Examining the TAM model on the adoption of OTT video streaming platform among millennial consumers. *International Journal of Biology, Pharmacy and Allied Sciences, 11*(1), 628–640.

Tucker, D. C., & Schütz, A. (1995). Entertainers, experts, or public servants? Politicians' self-presentation on television talk shows. In Political Communication (Vol. 12, Issue 2). doi:10.1080/10584609.1995.9963066

Turner, G. (2019). Approaching the cultures of use: Netflix, disruption and the audience. *Critical Studies in Television, 14*(2), 222–232. doi:10.1177/1749602019834554

Udoakpan, N., & Tengeh, R. K. (2020). The Impact of Over-the-Top Television Services on Pay-Television Subscription Services in South Africa. *Journal of Open Innovation, 6*(4), 139. doi:10.3390/joitmc6040139

Ulvi, O., Karamehic-Muratovic, A., Baghbanzadeh, M., Bashir, A., Smith, J., & Haque, U. (2022, January 11). Social Media Use and Mental Health: A Global Analysis. *Epidemiologia, 3*(1), 11–25. doi:10.3390/epidemiologia3010002 PMID:36417264

Uram, P., & Skalski, S. (2020, December 10). Still Logged in? The Link Between Facebook Addiction, FoMO, Self-Esteem, Life Satisfaction and Loneliness in Social Media Users. *Psychological Reports, 125*(1), 218–231. doi:10.1177/0033294120980970 PMID:33302798

Valkenburg, P. M., van Driel, I. I., & Beyens, I. (2021, December 31). The associations of active and passive social media use with well-being: A critical scoping review. *New Media & Society, 24*(2), 530–549. doi:10.1177/14614448211065425

Vallet, F., Essid, S., Carrive, J., & Richard, G. (2012). High-Level TV Talk Show Structuring Centered On Speakers' Interventions. In Y. Kompatsiaris, B. Merialdo, & S. Lian (Eds.), *TV Content Analysis: Techniques and Applications* (p. 245).

Van Dijck, J. (2014). Datafication, dataism and dataveillance: Big data between scientific paradigm and ideology. *Surveillance & Society, 12*(2), 197–208. doi:10.24908/ss.v12i2.4776

Van Dijck, J. (2017). Foreword. In T. M. Schäfer & K. van Es (Eds.), *The datafied society studying culture through data* (pp. 12–13). Amsterdam University Press. doi:10.1515/9789048531011-002

Van Zoonen, L., & Holtz-Bacha, C. (2000). Personalisation in Dutch and German politics: The case of talk show. *Javnost (Ljubljana), 7*(2), 45–56. doi:10.1080/13183222.2000.11008743

Vatsal. (2021). *Recommendation Systems Explained.* Towards Data Science. https://towardsdatascience.com: https://towardsdatascience.com/recommendation-systems-explained-a42fc60591ed

Verduyn, P., Ybarra, O., Résibois, M., Jonides, J., & Kross, E. (2017, January). Do Social Network Sites Enhance or Undermine Subjective Well-Being? A Critical Review. *Social Issues and Policy Review, 11*(1), 274–302. doi:10.1111/sipr.12033

Verma, M., & Kalorth, N. (Eds.). (2017). *Essays on Contemporary Media Theory and Practices: With an Introductory Article by Prof.* Denis McQuail on the Future of the Field of Communication. Amity University Rajasthan.

Vesanen, J. (2007). What is personalization? A conceptual framework. *European Journal of Marketing, 41*(5/6), 409–418. doi:10.1108/03090560710737534

Vesanen, J., & Raulas, M. (2006). Building bridges for personalization – a process model for marketing. *Journal of Interactive Marketing, 20*(1), 1–16. doi:10.1002/dir.20052

Vijayanagar, K. R. (2021). *How do Content Recommendation Engines Work?* OTT Verse. https://ottverse.com/what-is-content-video-recommendation-engines-ott-vod/

Viswanathan, V., Hollebeek, L. D., Malthouse, E. C., Maslowska, E., Jung Kim, S., & Xie, W. (2017). The dynamics of consumer Engagement with mobile technologies. *Service Science, 9*(1), 36–49. doi:10.1287/serv.2016.0161

Vivek, S. D., Beatty, S. E., & Morgan, R. M. (2012). Customer engagement: Exploring customer relationships beyond purchase. *Journal of Marketing Theory and Practice*, *20*(2), 122–146. doi:10.2753/MTP1069-6679200201

Wahab, J. A. (2011). Television Talk Shows and The Public Sphere. *Malaysian Journal of Communication*, *27*(2), 29–45.

Wang, C.-D. (2018). Serendipitous Recommendation in E-commerce using Innovator-Based Collaborative Filtering. *IEEE Explore*, (pp. 2168-2275). IEEE. doi:10.1109/TCYB.2018.2841924

Wayne, M. L. (2022). Netflix audience data, streaming industry discourse, and the emerging realities of "popular" television. *Media Culture & Society*, *44*(2), 193–209. doi:10.1177/01634437211022723

WE Forum. (2018). *How to Prevent Discriminatory Outcomes in Machine Learning*. WeForum. https://www3.weforum.org: https://www3.weforum.org/docs/WEF_40065_White_Paper_How_to_Prevent_Discriminatory_Outcomes_in_Machine_Learning.pdf

Welle, D. (2021). How India's Covid Crisis Has Changed Bollywood? *Outlook India.* https://www.outlookindia.com/website/story/entertainment-news-how-indias-covid-crisis-has-changed-bollywood/390387

Werd, S. (2021). *Personalization as a tool to retain users of your OTT service*. Jump Data Driven. https://www.jump-datadriven.com/personalization-as-a-tool-to-retain-users-of-your-ott-service/

Wheeler, K. (2015). *The Relationships Between Television Viewing Behaviors, Attachment, Loneliness, Depression, and Psychological Well-Being*. [Honors College Theses, Georgia Southern]. https://digitalcommons.georgiasouthern.edu/honors-theses/98

White, G. R. T., Samuel., A., Thomas R., & Jones P. (2021). Programmatic advertising: An exegesis of consumer concerns. *Computers in Human Behavior, 116*(1), 106657, 1-9. doi:10.1016/j.chb.2020.106657

Wilbert, M. (2023, June 15). *The 10 Best OTT Platforms + OTT Services in 2023.* Dacast https://www.dacast.com/blog/5-business-ott-platforms-for-over-the-top-video-content/

Williams, C. (2022). *The influencer economy: Understanding its impact on modern marketing*. Marketing Profs.

Williams, J. (2022). The Instagram Phenomenon: Exploring Visual Culture in the Digital Age. *International Journal of Visual Culture*, *14*(1), 102–120.

Williams, S. E. (2019). Challenges and Opportunities for Traditional TV Networks in the Era of OTT Dominance. *Journal of Broadcasting & Electronic Media*, *63*(2), 301–318.

Wind, J., & Rangaswamy, A. (2001). Customerization: The next revolution in mass customization. *Journal of Interactive Marketing*, *15*(1), 13–33. doi:10.1002/1520-6653(200124)15:1<13::AID-DIR1001>3.0.CO;2-#

Wong, S. (2021). *Over The Top TV (OTT), Big Data and The Future Of Predictive Buyer Analytics.* Research Gate.

Wordstream. (2022). *Click-Through Rate (CTR): Understanding Click-Through Rate for PPC.* Wordtream. https://www.wordstream.com/click-through-rate

World Health Organization [WHO] (2022, August). *WHO Coronavirus (COVID-19) Dashboard: Bangladesh.* WHO Health Emergency Dashboard.

Yakimova, N. (2016). *The Experience of Binge-watching Television Serials: A Phenomenological Description.* University Of Groningen.

Yeole, D. S., Saha, D. L., & Bhaisare, P. C. (2022). A study on User Perspective on OTT platform in India. *Journal of Positive School Psychology*, *6*(3), 7351–7366.

Yesilada, M., & Lewandowsky, S. (2022). Systematic review: YouTube recommendations and problematic content. *Internet Policy Review, 11*(1), 1–22. doi:10.14763/2022.1.1652 PMID:36466439

Yoon, H. S. (2018). *Motivations for binge-watching measure*. PsycTESTS Dataset.

Yousaf, A. (2021). A cross-country analysis of the determinants of customer recommendation intentions for over-the-top (OTT) platforms. *Information & Management, 58*(8), 103543.

Yue, Z., Zhang, R., & Xiao, J. (2022, February). Passive social media use and psychological well-being during the COVID-19 pandemic: The role of social comparison and emotion regulation. *Computers in Human Behavior, 127*, 107050. doi:10.1016/j.chb.2021.107050 PMID:34646057

Zajonc, R. B. (1968). Attitudinal effects of mere exposure. *Journal of Personality and Social Psychology, 9*(2), 1–27. doi:10.1037/h0025848

Zangerle, E., & Bauer, C. (2022). Evaluating Recommender Systems: Survey and Framework. *ACM Computing Surveys, 55*(08), 1–38. doi:10.1145/3556536

Zeigarnik, B. (1927). Das Behalten erledigter und unerledigter Handlungen. *Psychologische Forschung, 9*(1), 1–85.

Zengin, F. (2020). Akıllı makine çağı sinemasına giriş: Sinema sanatında yapay zekâ teknolojilerinin kullanımı. *İletişim Çalışmaları Dergisi, 6*(2), 151- 177.

Zhang, Q., Lu, J., & Jin, Y. (2020). Artificial intelligence in recommender systems. *Complex & Intelligent Systems, 7*(1), 439–457. https://link.springer.com/article/10.1007/s40747-020-00212-w. doi:10.1007/s40747-020-00212-w

Zhang, Yu. (2023). Research on media communication methods in the context of intelligent algorithms. *International Conference on Mathematics, Modeling, and Computer Science (MMCS2022)*. SPIE. 10.1117/12.2670491

Zhang, Z., Jiménez, F. R., & Cicala, J. E. (2020, September 13). Fear Of Missing Out Scale: A self-concept perspective. *Psychology and Marketing, 37*(11), 1619–1634. doi:10.1002/mar.21406

Zheng, Y. (2022, January 17). Context-Aware Collaborative Filtering Using Context Similarity: An Empirical Comparison. *Information (Basel), 13*(1), 42. doi:10.3390/info13010042

Zuboff, S. (2019). *The Age of Surveillance Capitalism: The Fight for a Human Future at the New Frontier of Power*. Public Affairs.

About the Contributors

Nithin Kalorth is a UGC NET qualified educator, filmmaker, and researcher at the forefront of media studies and digital storytelling. With over 12 years of experience in academia and a passion for exploring the intersections of media, culture, and technology, he is currently working as an Associate Professor at the School of Media, Mahindra University in Hyderabad. Dr. Kalorth holds a PhD in Film Studies and Mass Communication from Mahatma Gandhi University, Kottayam, which was pursued with a Junior Research Scholarship from the UGC. His commitment to academic excellence was further acknowledged when he completed his Masters in Electronic Media with a Gold Medal from the University of Madras. His foundational education includes a Bachelor's degree in Visual Communication from the University of Madras. He holds two additional postgraduate degrees – one in Mass Communication and Journalism from Madurai Kamraj University, and another in Sociology from Indira Gandhi Open University. His academic prowess is not only confined to formal education; he has also obtained numerous certifications from prestigious universities around the globe through MOOC platforms. Dr. Kalorth is an accomplished photographer and documentary filmmaker, currently embarking on his latest film "Bottleneck." His research prowess lies in the domain of Film Studies, Visual Culture, and Digital Media, and his intellectual curiosity has yielded numerous research papers, articles, and conference presentations. An ardent advocate for innovative learning, Dr. Kalorth has conducted transformative mobile and digital storytelling workshops for diverse audiences, including WHO, the Foreign Correspondence Club in New Delhi, and esteemed universities like IIT Goa and BITS Pilani Goa. He is the visionary behind "Stories - The Mobile Way," a platform that empowers storytelling through technology, and the co-founder of "Cinema Peedia," a hub fostering growth among filmmakers and educators. His dedication to media education is further evidenced by his co-founding of "In-Depth Communication," a groundbreaking initiative that promotes media research and education. He also serves as the editor of the esteemed journal "Photosensor: A Journal of Visual Communication".

Harry B. is a Research Scholar in the Department of English, School of Social Sciences and Languages, Vellore Institute of Technology, Vellore. He is pursuing his research in gender studies. His research interests include linguistics, Indian Writing in English, Post-colonial Studies, Diaspora Studies, African American Literature and Canadian Literature. ORCID: 0000-0003-4538-977X.

Nitesh Behare is an accomplished author with a wealth of knowledge and 15 years of experience in the academic field. He currently holds the esteemed position of Associate Professor at the Balaji Institute of International Business (BIIB), Sri Balaji University Pune (SBUP). Throughout his career, Dr. Behare has made significant contributions to the academic world through the publication of numerous research papers and book chapters, establishing himself as a recognized authority in his field. His dedication to scholarship and commitment to the advancement of knowledge make him a valuable asset.

Malobika Bose is an education professional with academics and corporate exposure, proactive planner with abilities in executing strategies for augmenting progress, identifying needs, cementing healthy relationships. She is currently associated with Amity University Uttar Pradesh Lucknow as Assistant Professor Grade II. Ms. Bose has a research oriented teaching methodology and provide guidance for research work to students. She has published papers on relevant and contemporary issues and has a expertise in designing systems & procedures and contributing towards improved performance, heightened productivity and enhanced internal controls. With total experience of more than 15 years, Ms. Bose is an innovative professional, adept at creating and formulating strategies for accelerated growth, focused and hard working with unsurpassed communication, organized presentation, and interpersonal skills.

Kemal Deniz was born in 1983 in Istanbul, Turkey. He worked as a Research Assistant between 2014 to 2019 at Istanbul University, Faculty of Communication, where he completed his Ph.D. in 2019. He has been working at Munzur University, Faculty of Communication, as a faculty member since 2019. His academic research interests are Communication Studies, Television Studies, Visual Culture, Visual Narrative, New Communication Technologies, and Film Studies.

Sridevi Gopakumar is currently a full time PhD Scholar at Loyola Institute of Business Administration, Chennai. After earning an MBA in Marketing and Human Resources from SRM University, she began a prosperous corporate job, but her desire to learn ànd explore new territory prompted her to pursue research. Presently, she is pursuing her research in the field of sustainability marketing.

Ushmita Gupta is a dedicated and seasoned professional having more than 15 years of experience in research & teaching subjects like Managerial Economics, Marketing of Financial Services, Foreign Exchange Management & Regulation, Currency, Banking & Exchange to name a few.

C.A. Vishwanathan Iyer is associated with academics for 29 years. He specialises in Financial Accounting and Financial management. To gain better insights about the world of finance, he qualified as a Chartered Accountant in 2005. To explore academics, he pursued for a doctorate and qualified as a Ph.D. holder in June 2021. During this period, his inclination towards Research increased to a great extent. He has 14 Research papers to his credit, which were presented and published at various National and International conferences. His paper is published in UGC care journal as well. His paper with a student, Mr Gangesh Dubey, was declared as the Best Paper at National Conference conducted by Vedanta College, Ulhasnagar in April 2023. He believes Research holds great significance in the academic field and hopes to publish papers and submit chapters in Scopus Indexed publications and ABDC Journals at the earliest.

Daman Jeet joined IBS Hyderabad, The ICFAI Foundation for Higher Education as Assistant Professor in the department of Finance and Accounting in August, 2023. Prior to this she has been teaching at CBIT Hyderabad, National Institute of Technology (NITJ), Balaji University and visiting Pune University and other premier institutes. She also has experience of working with Finance Team in MNC. She is a Gold Medallist in Finance, University Topper and Scholarship holder throughout. Her PhD is from a premier university and holds research interests in studying different ownership patterns of Indian Firms and the determinants impacting. Her research contributions are in ABDC, Scopus and UGC Care Journals.

Elif Karakoç Keskin graduated from Istanbul University Journalism Department and Communication Sociology master's programme. She completed her PhD at the same university in the Department of Radio, Television and Cinema within the scope of the Higher Education Council of Türkiye Doctoral Scholarship. She continues her research in the fields of communication studies, digital technologies and new media.

Sheeba Khalid is doctorate (PhD) in Sociology from Jadavpur University, Kolkata, West Bengal India, presently serving as Assistant professor of Sociology in Amity University Lucknow at School of Law her present research interest includes Ageing, Gender and Family, Migration, Women Problems, Religion and Society, Social equality. Dr. Khalid has served as Assistant Professor (Sociology) in different universities and colleges; she has more than 14 years' experience in academics. Working as an Honorary Editorial Support Service at Netaji Nagar Day College Computer Centre, Kolkata, she is a Member of Indian Muslims for Progress and Reforms (IMPAR), Selected Working Group to join: Women Empowerment Group.

İbrahim Kırçova is a faculty member in the Department of Business Administration at Yıldız Technical University and is the Head of the Department of Business Administration. He works in the field of Production Management and Marketing Research.

Vijayakumar M. is an Associate Professor in the Department of English, School of Social Sciences and Languages, Vellore Institute of Technology, Vellore. He has presented numerous research papers at National and International conferences. His research interests include Indian Writing in English, Post-colonial Studies, Diaspora Studies, African-American Literature and Canadian Literature. He has authored a few books and several book chapters. ORCID: 0000-0002-1079-5383.

Rashmi Mahajan, Professor, is a triple post graduate and is a Masters of Computer Management, Post Graduate Diploma in Business Management [Marketing] & Masters of Business Studies [Marketing]. She has completed her PhD in Marketing Management and a Diploma in Training & Development from Indian Society for Training & Development, Pune Chapter. She has around 19+ years of experience teaching undergraduate as well as post graduate students and has 3 PhD scholars pursuing their PhD under her. She has published various papers in National as well as International journals and has 2 patents and 1 copyright credited to her name. She alswo has 1 Chapter Published. She is a Professor, Head of Department of International Business & Dy. Director of BIIB in Sri Balaji University Pune (SBUP).

Tabrej Mulla is an Assistant Professor in the Department of MBA in Arihant Institute of Busines Management , Pune. She is a passionate academician, perfect blend of science and management. She has vast experience of teaching and administration in the field of academics. She pursued MBA from SPPU specialized in Information technology in the year 2016, MSc from SPPU specialized in Electronic science. Her primary area of interest is in Digital Business, Digital Marketing, Information Technology Management and CSR amongst others. She has a teaching experiencc from 2008. She has more than

15+ years of experience in the academics. She has published multiple scholarly research paper in various peer reviewed national and international journals. He has coordinated and handled various academic and administrative responsibilities like Marketing, International Conference, Bi-annual Journal, Examination and Admissions, to mention a few. She has also worked with the College of Computer Sciences, Pune for 9+ years. She has also served on the Editorial Board of INNOVATION Biannual Journal In CCS She has attended a number of National and International Conferences where she has presented research papers in her area of specialization. Keen on learning, she constantly upgrades herself through workshops, Refreshers course & faculty development initiatives. She has a flair for teaching subjects like Management Control System, Digital business, Corporate social Responsibility, Computer Fundamental, Start-up and New Venture Management, Mobile Computing, Digital Signal Processing, Embedded System, Microcontroller, Semiconductor, Computer Networks, Digital Electronics and analog Electronics etc. Apart from being a passionate educator, She has coordinated various curricular, extra-curricular and outbound activities.

Ruth Neyah is an internal full-time Ph.D. scholar at Vellore Institute of Technology, Vellore. She is pursuing her research in African American Diaspora literature.

Adya Pandey is Assistant Professor at Amity Law School, Lucknow. She has teaching experience of working as Assistant Lecturer at Hidayatullah National Law University, Raipur. She has a teaching experience of about 7 years. She did her Bachelors in Law from Lucknow University and completed her post graduation from National Law University, Jodhpur. Her area of interest is corporate laws and has experience of teaching subjects like mergers and acquisitions, insurance and corporate governance. She has published various papers in national and international journals and attended national and international conferences.

Madhava Priya Dananjayan is Assistant Dean – Academics, Assistant Professor of Finance and Chair – International Relations, teaching Finance Courses at LIBA. She was awarded the Research scholarship by WFI- Ingolstadt and AUDI, Germany. She has over 5 years of corporate expe- rience in capital markets in various roles and 11 years of experience in teaching. Her research interests include Capital Market, Behavioural Finance and Financial Mod- elling. She has presented more than 50 research papers in various conference and has published papers in Interna- tional and National peer reviewed journals. She has also conducted several conference and FDP. She is a registered research guide with the University of Madras.

Vinayak Shitole is a seasoned professional with a combined experience of 5 years in the corporate sector and 2 years in academia. He has demonstrated expertise in International Finance and Expenses and is currently affiliated with Assistant Professor, where he plays a pivotal role in the field. Academic Experience: Prof. Shitole has been imparting his knowledge to the academic community. He has served as an Assistant Professor at RIIM-Arihant Group of Institutes since June 2023, teaching subjects like Financial Derivatives and Risk Management, International Business Environment, Marketing of Financial Services, and Corporate Financial Restructuring. His academic responsibilities also include supervisory roles, program coordination, and mentoring of MBA students. During his tenure at BVDU-IMRDA, Sangli, from June 2021 to June 2023, Prof. Shitole educated students on subjects such as International Financial Management, Corporate Finance, Financial Management, Enterprise Business Applications, and Investment Analysis & Portfolio Management. He actively contributed to university examination paper setting, acted as a paper checker, and assisted with NAAC Assessment criteria related to teaching and learning. Corporate Experience: Prior to his academic career, Prof. Shitole worked as an IT Expense Specialist at Optimas OE Solutions, Pune, from August 2019 to May 2023. His role involved managing IT procurement processes for North America and Asia Pacific, tracking purchase expenses, and closely collaborating with the global finance team. Prof. Shitole also worked as an Outbound and RMA Executive at DHL Supply Chain - Dell Logistics, Pune, for a brief period, where he was responsible for processing orders, maintaining order records, and coordinating with customers. Before his academic journey, he served as a Purchasing Executive at New Bharat Diesels, Sangli, from May 2017 to May 2018. His responsibilities included negotiating prices with suppliers, maintaining records of goods ordered, and ensuring timely fulfillment of orders. Education: Prof. Shitole is currently pursuing a Ph.D. in Management Studies from BVDU-IMRDA, Sangli, with an expected completion date in June 2024. His research focuses on "A Study of Marketing Strategies for the Revival of the Wine Industry in Western Maharashtra, with Special Reference to Sangli District." His research contributions span areas such as economic growth, cultural heritage preservation, enhancing consumer satisfaction, ensuring regulatory compliance, fostering competitiveness, promoting sustainability, respecting regional nuances, and encouraging stakeholder collaboration. His research guide is Dr. Pratap Desai, Deputy Director, BVDU-IMRDA, Sangli. In addition to his Ph.D., Prof. Shitole holds a Diploma in Taxation Law from BVDU-IMRDA, Sangli, and an MBA in Finance and Production Management from the same institution. He also gained recognition for his internship project at RICO AUTO Industries Ltd., Gurugram, Delhi. His educational journey began with a Bachelor of Engineering in Mechanical Engineering from PVPIT, Budhgaon, Sangli, and a Diploma in Mechanical Engineering from MSBTE-Shantiniketan Polytechnic, Sangli. Personal Interests: Prof. Vinayak is a dedicated and passionate educator with a commitment to contributing to the academic and corporate domains. He brings his unique blend of experience and expertise to the subject matter of the book chapter, ensuring that it provides valuable insights and perspectives.

Meenakshi Singh is an accomplished academician with over 11 years of experience in the field of education. Her journey in education has been characterized by an unwavering commitment to teaching and mentoring students from diverse social and cultural backgrounds. Meenakshi's expertise extends across various disciplines related to management and economics, where she excels due to her exceptional administrative, verbal communication, and written skills. Meenakshi is not only an educator but also an accomplished author with several books and case studies to her name. Her publications encompass books on international business, economics, and strategic human resource management, as well as case studies that enrich the academic world.

Pritesh Pradeep Somani, an Academician with over 11 years of teaching experience with a keen interest across research. With a keen interest towards S.P.S.S. and data crunching, open to collaboration across Qualitative and Quantitative Research.

Suraj Ashok Sonawane BE, MBA (Marketing & Operations) Sinhgad Institute Of Management Biography: Suraj Ashok Sonawane is an Assistant Professor at Sinhgad Institute Of Management With a background in Marketing and Operations . Education: BE SPPU 2017 MBA SPPU 2019 Professional Experience: Asst.Professor, Sinhgad Institute Of Management, 2 years Research Interests: Marketing, Business Management

Shrikant Waghulkar has 9 years of teaching experience in the field of management education. He has been awarded with Doctorate degree in management faculty by Savitribai Phule Pune University, Pune. His academic interest includes subjects like Research methodology, Personal Management, Rural Marketing, and Digital Marketing. He is passionate social worker and leading the charitable trust aiming to the social elevation of farmer's children by helping them to receive better education.

Aradhana Yadav is a faculty of law at Amity University, Uttar Pradesh. Previously she has practiced in the Supreme Court of India, High Court of Delhi & various courts across New Delhi and District Court of Lucknow, India. Her area of practice has been in the area of Criminal Laws, including White Collar Crimes and Family Laws. Aradhana Yadav completed her graduation from Government Law College, Mumbai and went on to do her Post Graduation, with specialization in Constitutional Law, from Amity Law School, Amity University, Lucknow Campus.

Index

P

R

S

T

U

V

W

Z

Ensure Quality Research is Introduced to the Academic Community

Become an Evaluator for IGI Global Authored Book Projects

The overall success of an authored book project is dependent on quality and timely manuscript evaluations.

Applications and Inquiries may be sent to:
development@igi-global.com

Applicants must have a doctorate (or equivalent degree) as well as publishing, research, and reviewing experience. Authored Book Evaluators are appointed for one-year terms and are expected to complete at least three evaluations per term. Upon successful completion of this term, evaluators can be considered for an additional term.

If you have a colleague that may be interested in this opportunity, we encourage you to share this information with them.

www.ingramcontent.com/pod-product-compliance
Lightning Source LLC
LaVergne TN
LVHW062145300926
849161LV00010B/2636

* 9 7 9 8 3 6 9 3 0 1 1 6 6 *